KF 8725 .B47 1990
Berk-Seligso[illegible]s

The Bilingual Courtroom

NEW ENGLAND INSTITUTE
OF TECHNOLOGY
LEARNING RESOURCES CENTER

Language and Legal Discourse
A series edited by William M. O'Barr and John M. Conley

The Bilingual Courtroom
Court Interpreters in the Judicial Process
by Susan Berk-Seligson

Rules and Relationships
The Ethnography of Legal Discourse
by John M. Conley and William M. O'Barr

Getting Justice and Getting Even:
Legal Consciousness among Working-Class Americans
by Sally Engle Merry

The Bilingual Courtroom

Court Interpreters in the Judicial Process

Susan Berk-Seligson

The University of Chicago Press/Chicago and London

NEW ENGLAND INSTITUTE
OF TECHNOLOGY
LEARNING RESOURCES CENTER

#20453959

5-92

Susan Berk-Seligson is associate professor of Spanish at the University of Pittsburgh.

The University of Chicago Press, Chicago 60637
The University of Chicago Press, Ltd., London

© 1990 by the University of Chicago
All rights reserved. Published 1990
Printed in the United States of America

99 98 97 96 95 94 93 92 91 90   5 4 3 2 1

Library of Congress Cataloging in Publication Data

Berk-Seligson, Susan.
The bilingual courtroom : court interpreters in the judicial process / Susan Berk-Seligson.
p. cm.—(Language and legal discourse)
Includes bibliographical references.
ISBN 0-226-04371-1 (alk. paper).—ISBN 0-226-04373-8 (pbk. : alk. paper)
1. Courts—United States—Translating services. I. Title. II. Series.
KF8725.B47 1990
347.73'5'014—dc20
[347.3075014]   89-27792
CIP

⊗ The paper used in this publication meets the minimum requirements of the American National Standard for Information Sciences—Permanence of Paper for Printed Library Materials, ANSI Z39.48-1984.

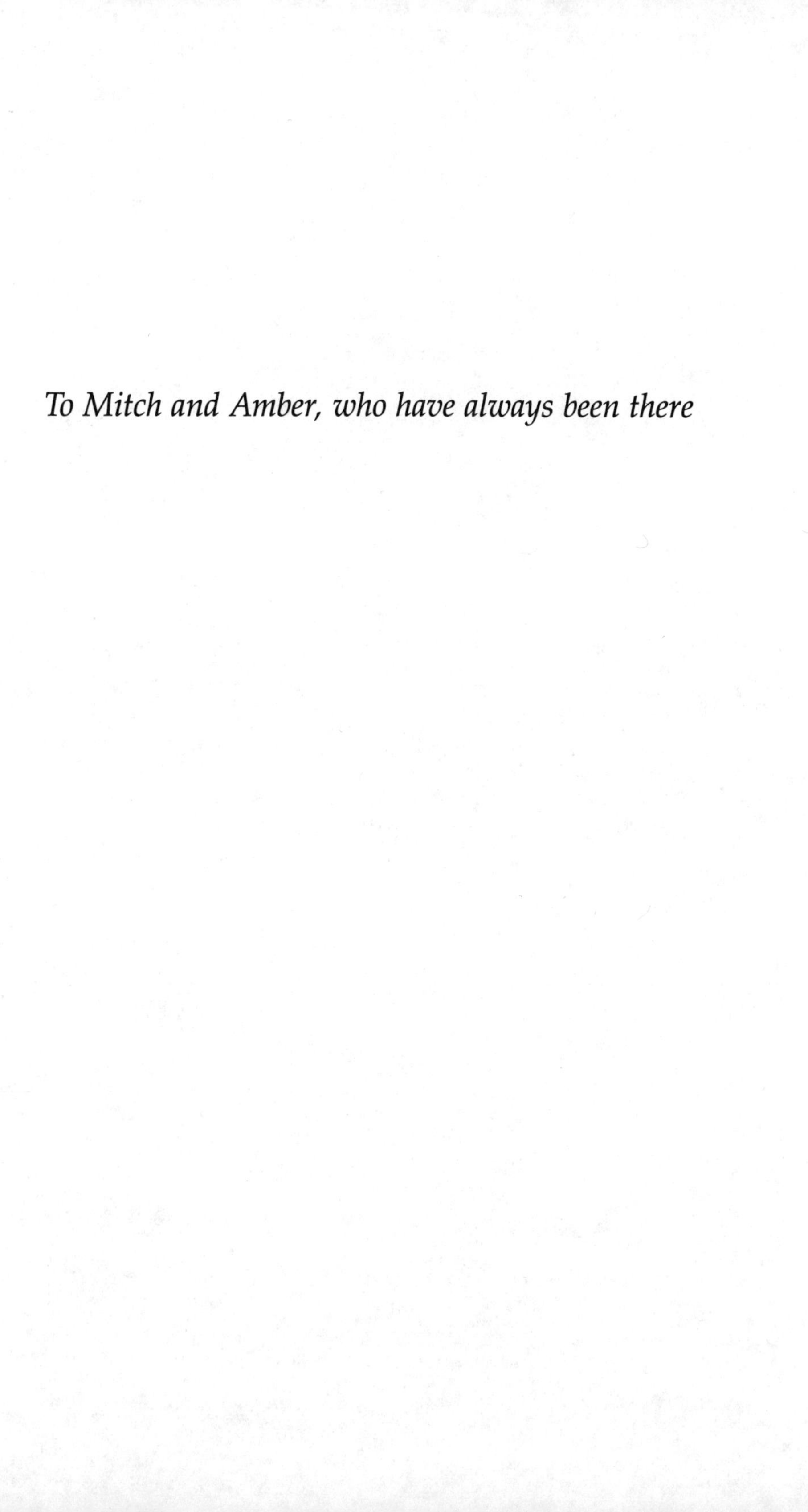

To Mitch and Amber, who have always been there

Contents

Tables and Figures

Tables

Figures

Acknowledgments

This book would not have been possible without the continued support of the U.S. National Science Foundation (grants SES 8114617, SES 834 1766, and RII-8516746). I also would like to thank the Department of Linguistics of Northwestern University for inviting me to be a visiting professor there, and the students in my course on language and the law for their helpful insights on some of the ideas presented in this book. I am also grateful to the graduate students who helped me in the data-gathering phase of the project: Marisa Alicea, Parek McGreal, and Vanessa McGreal. Special thanks go to the court interpreters, attorneys, defendants, and judges who so graciously cooperated with me in the ethnographic phase of the research. I am equally grateful to the numerous people at the Centro Latino (Universidad Popular), Lakeview Learning Center, Templo Calvario of Elgin, North Park College, the Elgin Centro de Información, University of Illinois at Chicago, Network for Youth Services, Elgin Community College, ASPIRA, St. Augustine Junior College, Humboldt Park G.E.D. program, and McCormick College.

In addition to the debt of gratitude that I owe to the National Science Foundation for funding the research, I also wish to thank Purdue University for an XL grant, and the University of Pittsburgh Central Research Development Fund for grant support. The responsibility for this book, however, is entirely my own.

Three of the chapters drew heavily on articles of mine that have been published elsewhere. Chapter 5, "The Ethnography of the Bilingual Courtroom," is essentially a reprint of "Bilingual Court Proceedings: The Role of the Court Interpreter," to appear in a collection edited by Judith N. Levi and Ann Graffam Walker, *Language in the Judicial Process,* Plenum Press. Chapter 7, "The Intersection of Testimony Styles in Interpreted Judicial Proceedings: Pragmatics and the Lengthening of Testimony," is a revised form of my article, "The Intersection of Testimony Styles in Interpreted Judicial Proceedings:

Pragmatic Alterations in Spanish Testimony," which appeared in the journal *Linguistics* (volume 25) in 1987. Chapter 8, "The Impact of the Interpreter on Mock Juror Evaluations of Witnesses," draws heavily on three articles of mine: "The Impact of Politeness in Witness Testimony: The Influence of the Court Interpreter," which appeared in *Multilingua* (volume 7, number 4) in 1988; "The Importance of Linguistics in Court Interpreting" which was published in Fall 1988 in *La Raza Law Journal* (volume 2, number 1); and "The Role of Register in the Bilingual Courtroom: Evaluative Reactions to Interpreted Testimony: The Influence of the Court Interpreter," which appeared in *Multilingua* (volume 7, number 4) in 1988; "The Importance of Linguistics in Court Interpreting," which was published in Fall 1988 in *La Raza Law Journal* (volume 2, number 1); and "The Role of Register in the Bilingual Courtroom: Evaluative Reactions to Interpreted Testimony," which was published in a special issue of the *International Journal of the Sociology of Language* (volume 79, 1989), edited by Irene Wherritt and Ofelia García, and entitled *U.S. Spanish: The Language of Latinos.* However, chapters 1, 2, 3, 4, 6, 9, and the second half of chapter 8 are original, and appear in this book for the first time.

I would like to emphasize that throughout the book, whenever textual material is presented from actual court cases, the names of interpreters, defendants, witnesses, attorneys, judges, and any other parties referred to in these cases have deliberately been changed, in order to preserve the anonymity of the persons truly involved. This was done to fulfill the promise that I had made to all the persons who had been involved in the ethnographic phase of the research project, a condition that they made upon granting me permission to tape-record them in court. Similarly, for the purpose of keeping anonymous the identity of these individuals, I changed all the place names that had been referred to in the original judicial proceedings. Thus, there is no correspondence between persons and places named in the texts and the true names of these persons and places. Whereas they might have been referred to with expressions such as "Mr. X" and "City Y," for the sake of easier readability I have chosen to use fictitious names instead.

1
Introduction

The Bilingual Courtroom

Since the late 1960s, with America's awakening sensitivity to the social needs and rights of linguistic minorities, there has been a veritable explosion in the use of foreign language interpreting in American courtrooms. The climate engendered by the civil rights movement of the 1960s certainly laid the foundation for the growing sensitivity to linguistic minorities. But one seminal event can be seen as the driving force behind the current growing trend toward greater use of court interpreting in American courtrooms: the enactment in 1978 of Public Law No. 95–539, the federal Court Interpreters Act. Although it is restricted to the jurisdiction of federal courts, it has served to stimulate parallel measures in state and municipal courts. Thus, through the precedent of federal legislation, courts of lower level jurisdiction are increasingly assigning foreign-language interpreters to non-English-speaking defendants, litigants, and witnesses. This change in judicial policy comes as a result of a now well-established recognition by the courts that to deny the non-English speaking and the hearing-impaired the services of a court-appointed interpreter is to deny them their constitutionally guaranteed right to a fair trial.

For judges, attorneys, defendants, litigants, and witnesses alike, the presence of a foreign language interpreter transforms normal courtroom proceedings into bilingual events. This book will show how the courtroom is transformed in the presence of the court interpreter, and how these transformations have an impact on judicial proceedings. The study will present findings based on seven months of ethnographic observation and tape-recording of interpreted judicial proceedings in three tiers of court: federal, state, and municipal. Drawing on 114 hours of taped recordings, this book will show that in a number of ways—some subtle, others quite dramatic and obvious—the nature of judicial proceedings is altered when these proceedings are mediated through the mechanism of a foreign language interpreter. Specifically, it will be shown that interpreting is a highly complicated process, and that the role of the interpreter within the social structure of the courtroom poses its own problematic. Whereas court personnel assume that the interpreter is nothing short of a machine that converts the English speech of attorneys, judges, and English-speaking witnesses into the mother tongue of the non-English-speaking defendant or witness, and the foreign language testimony of non-English speaking witnesses into English for the benefit of the court, the output of that machine is by no means perfect, nor can it ever be, because of the problems inherent in the interpreting process. At best, it can be excellent; at worst, a gross distortion of what has been said.

The problematical role of the court interpreter is not limited to the difficulties inherent in the interpreting process, but rests on the more fundamental contradiction between how the interpreter defines her[1] role and how other court personnel and court clients perceive it. Her very social status in the courtroom is perceived differently by different elements in the social structure of the courthouse. It will be shown that many of the problems regularly encountered by the court interpreter are a result of a misunderstanding of her role not only by clients (defendants, litigants, and witnesses), but also by lawyers and judges.

While one major source of problems commonly found in interpreted judicial proceedings stems from contradictory perceptions of the interpreter's role, another important source of difficulty is the general lack of awareness on the part of most interpreters of a field of linguistics called "pragmatics."[2] Professional interpreters overwhelmingly view vocabulary as their number one linguistic problem. Problems of syntax and pragmatic scope are given slight attention, if any at all. Yet observation of interpreters at work reveals that inattention to pragmatic aspects of language results in a skewing of a speaker's intended meaning: an interpreter can make the tone of a witness's testimony or an attorney's questions more harsh and antagonistic than it was when it was originally uttered, or, conversely, she can make its effect softer, more cooperative, and less challenging than the original. For the most part, these changes are made unconsciously. On the whole, when interpreters make such fine alterations in the conversion of one language to another they seem completely unaware of the important impact that these alterations can have on judges and jurors. On the other hand, an interpreter who has either unconscious or conscious biases can take full advantage of such linguistic mechanisms to suit her own purposes, and where there is a conflict of interest but it is not perceived as such by court personnel, the interpreter's interpretations can and do serve to slant what a speaker is trying to say. Thus, it will be shown in chapter 6 that an interpreter has the power to make a witness's testimony cast more (or less) blame than it did in the source language—that is, the language in which it was originally uttered, and, alternatively, she can remove from the testimony any blame-laying strategies it may have contained. Moreover, an interpreter can make an attorney look more polite and less aggressive to a witness, and a witness more, or alternatively, less cooperative to an attorney. Finally, it will be shown that interpreters often introduce an element of coercion into the examination process when they interpret for witnesses and defendants.

Spanish in the Courtroom

Court interpreting is currently being conducted in federal, state, and municipal courts in a variety of languages (see Tables 1.1 and 1.2). As the interpreter logbooks of federal courthouses and state courthouses show, the need for interpreting arises in a multitude of languages. These range from what are historically the more commonplace American immigrant mother tongues, such as Spanish, Italian, German, and Polish (i.e., languages brought to the United States by immigrants from Europe and Latin America), to what interpreters' organizations call "exotic languages"—that is, the languages of Asia, Africa, the Middle East, and the languages spoken by Amerindian groups.[3] In addition, a great deal of court interpreting is carried out in various sign language systems for the benefit of hearing-impaired defendants and witnesses. Whereas the preponderance of such interpreting is done in American Sign Language, often the need arises for foreign sign language systems.[4]

Table 1.1, which is drawn from the logbooks of two southwestern courthouses, a northeastern metropolitan courthouse, and a midwestern metropolitan courthouse,[5] and Table 1.2, a summary of data derived from all federal U.S. district courts, both point clearly to the same conclusion: Spanish is the language of most frequent use in American court-interpreted proceedings. This is not unexpected if one considers the fact that Spanish is the most commonly spoken non-English mother tongue used in the United States.

The importance of Spanish in the American courtroom becomes obvious if one looks at the log of one U.S. district court (i.e., a federal

Table 1.1. Court Interpreter Appearances for Spanish versus All Other Languages

	Southwestern Federal Court (1982)		Northeastern Federal Court (1987)		Southwestern State Court (1982)		Midwestern State Court (Jan.–June, 1985)	
	Number	%	Number	%	Number	%	Number	%
Appearances for Spanish	1,298	96.6	2,636	81.3	3,331	96.3	8,574	92.0
Appearances for all other languages	45[a]	3.4	607[b]	18.7	129[c]	3.7	741[d]	8.0
Total court appearances	1,343	100.0	3,243	100.0	3,460	100.0	9,315;	100.0

Note: Whereas one of the courthouses reports three times as many interpreter appearances in its first six months as do two of the other courts in a twelve-month period, the wide disparity may be due to differences in the way that interpreter appearances are reported in different courthouses. The figures appearing in this table were provided by the chief interpreter in each of the respective courthouses, and are based upon logs that that they are required to keep on a daily basis. The annual statistics are broken down more finely, reporting the number of appearances for each "exotic" language. For the purposes of this table, however, what is important is not the raw number of interpreter appearances per language, but rather the percentage use of Spanish versus that of all the other languages. [a]The category of "other languages," usually designated as "exotic languages," in this court comprised only four: Hindi, Punjabi, Mandarin Chinese, and Apache.

[b]The category of "other languages" included the following 26 languages: Arabic, Armenian, Bulgarian, Chinese (designated as "Cantonese', 'Fukinese', 'Mandarin', Taiwanese), Creole (i.e., Haitian Creole), Dutch, Farsi, French, German, Gujarati, Hakka, Hebrew, Hindi, Ibo, Italian, Korean, Polish, Portuguese, Punjabi, Pushtu, Russian, Serbo-Croatian, Urdu, Vietnamese, and Yoruba.

[c]In this court, the category of "other languages" comprised the following 23 languages: American Sign Language, Arabic, Cambodian, Cantonese, Farsi, French, Greek, Japanese, Italian, Korean, Laotian, Mandarin, Navajo, Papago, Pima, Polish, Portuguese, Punjabi, Russian, Serbo-Croatian, Thai, Vietnamese, and Urdu.

[d]The category of "other languages" included the following 20 languages: Albanian, Armenian, Bulgarian, Cambodian, Chinese, Greek, Korean, Lithuanian, Pakistani, Philipino, Polish, Rumanian, Russian, Serbo-Croatian, Sign Language, Thai, Turkish, Ukranian, Vietnamese, and Yugoslavian.

court) located in a northeastern metropolis. As Table 1.2 shows, during the course of 1987 there were 2,636 court appearances of interpreters for Spanish interpreting alone. That figure should be compared with the total of 607 court appearances for *all* the other twenty-six languages that required interpreting.[6] In other words, there were nearly 4.5 times as many Spanish interpreted proceedings as there were interpreted proceedings for all other foreign languages combined. The particular courthouse from which these data are derived is located in a city that has a highly varied non-English-speaking pop-

Table 1.2. Court Interpreting Services, United States Federal District Courts (Fiscal Year 1986)

Language	Number of Times Used	Language	Number of Times Used
Spanish	43,166	Romanian	19
Haitian Creole	381	French Creole	17
Arabic	354	Indonesian	15
French	196	Bengali	13
Italian	187	Dutch	12
Portuguese	177	Edo	11
Russian	175	Gujarati	11
Mandarin	165	Ibo	10
Korean	156	Serbo Croatian	10
Turkish	150	Albanian	9
Chinese	99	Hausa	7
Thai	98	Hmong	7
Farsi	94	Bulgarian	5
Sicilian	88	Laotian	4
Armenian	86	Afrikaans	3
Yoruba	82	Singhalese	3
Urdu	65	Swedish	3
Tagalog	62	Tamil	3
Navaho	61	Zuni	3
Japanese	50	Twi	2
Cantonese	47	Yiddish	2
Greek	43	Ceylonese	1
Filipino	41	Samoan	1
Hindi	34	Yavapi	1
Polish	34		
Hebrew	31		
German	29		
Punjabi	29		
Vietnamese	28	Bankruptcy Courts	
Sign (For Deaf)	27	Spanish	19
Apache	24	Sign	3
Napolese	24	Chinese	1
Czech	22	Navaho	1

Source: Administrative Office of the United States Courts.

It should be noted that the data in this table are derived from the records of court interpreting offices and reflect a failure to collapse language categories that in fact represent different varieties of the same language (e.g., Italian listed in three ways, as Italian, Napolese, and Sicilian). But even if these variants were combined, the table would demonstrate an overwhelming preponderance of Spanish interpreting in United States federal district courts.

ulation. One would expect the typical southwestern large city to have a much higher proportionate use of Spanish. In fact, judging by the logbook of interpreting services in the federal court of one such city (see Table 1.1), Spanish constitutes 96.8 per cent of all foreign language interpreting in the courthouse. Even in the midwestern metropolitan courthouse Spanish comprises 92 per cent of all court interpreting.

Spanish is the foreign language of most widespread use in the United States today, and can be expected to remain in this position of dominance for the foreseeable future (Bills 1987; Fishman 1966).[7] Coupled with the evidence found in Tables 1.1 and 1.2, this indicates that if any interpreting situation needs to be studied in the American courtroom, it is the one involving Spanish. For this reason, this study bases its analysis exclusively on observations of Spanish/English interpreted judicial proceedings. This is not to say that it is not just as important to study what goes on in court interpreting situations involving other languages: court interpreting for the hearing-impaired and for speakers of other foreign languages is also worthy of study. However, studies of Spanish interpreting clearly cannot be postponed, for tens of thousands of appearances of Spanish language interpreters are being made annually in American courtrooms, while virtually nothing is known about what actually goes on when judicial proceedings are conducted with the aid of an interpreter.[8]

Duties of the Court Interpreter

The Court Interpreters Act does not prescribe specific judicial proceedings at which interpreters must be present, yet a look at the annual interpreter log of two federal district courts reveals a virtually identical concordance of tasks performed (see Table 1.3). More striking still is the fact that state courts make use of their interpreters in much the same way, despite the fact that they are not subject to the jurisdiction of the federal act.

A look at the interpreter's log of a federal district court located in an eastern metropolis, a federal district court located in a southwestern medium-sized city, and a superior court (i.e., criminal trial court) of a large southwestern city, reveals that in all three courts interpreters are on duty for basically the same range of procedures: initial appearances,[9] hearings related to the setting of bail bond, preliminary hearings, pretrial and in-trial motions, pleas and changes of plea, sentencings, trials, and probation department recommendations. Where federal district courts differ from one another and from superior courts is in the use of court-appointed interpreters for attorney/client conferences. As can be seen in Table 1.3, below, one federal district court uses its interpreters extensively for attorney/client conferences, whereas the other federal district court does so on rare occasions. This may simply be a function of the high availability of bilingual Spanish-speaking attorneys in the jurisdiction of the latter court: every case requiring a Spanish interpreter that was observed in this particular court utilized a Spanish-speaking defense attorney. Thus, for interviews or conferences with defendants, such attorneys would not have needed the services of an interpreter. In the other federal district court, however, not a single case observed during the fieldwork involved a Spanish-speaking defense attorney. In the case of the superior court, a clear, written policy stipulates that court-appointed interpreters are made available to all court-appointed defense attorneys, prosecutors, probation officers, court-appointed psychiatrists and investigators for interviews with a defendant in preparation for trial or sentencing, but that privately retained attorneys in both civil and criminal matters must contract with a private interpreter for attorney/client interviews. This explicit, official policy of the courthouse may account for the high number (557) of interpreter-assisted attorney/client interviews.

An additional difference in interpreter task-load between one court and another has to do with the structure and legal purview of federal courts versus those of state courts. For one thing, superior courts can subsume under their jurisdiction juvenile courts. Thus, in some state court systems, court-appointed interpreters working in superior courts are responsible for juvenile cases. The log of the superior court in question shows that during a one-month period court interpreters were present at advisory hearings, adjudication hearings, disposition hearings, and dependency review hearings in juvenile court. Furthermore, because of the role of justice of the peace (JP) courts in carrying out preliminary hearings on persons who have been arraigned in superior court, superior courts send their interpreters to JP courts for such hearings. The superior court log in question shows that court interpreters are sent to JP court not only for preliminary hearings, but also for pretrial disposition hearings, arraignments, and trials, including civil trials.

Finally, superior court interpreters do a great deal more interpreting in civil matters than do federal court interpreters, as Table 1.3 demonstrates. Superior court interpreters appear not only in cases involving litigation, but also in matters associated with domestic relations: default dissolutions, orders to show cause, conciliation court sessions, and arbitration hearings. Orders to show cause why family support is not being met is one of the more common types of domestic relations proceedings at which superior court interpreters will appear.

Whereas some state courts make specific provision for the assignment of court-appointed interpreters to civil cases, as does the southwestern superior court referred to in Table 1.3, other states are more restrictive in their policies in this regard. New Jersey, for example, provides free interpreting services to defendants in criminal cases, but does not guarantee it to parties involved in civil cases.[10] This is particularly troublesome given the finding of one legal scholar (Hippchen 1977:269), that "bilingual interpreter services are needed in a much greater number of civil cases compared with criminal cases" in New Jersey county and municipal courts.[11] Municipal courts in general, insofar as they deal with traffic cases and infractions of municipal ordinances, are heavily oriented toward civil cases, and so in areas of high concentrations of non-English-speaking populations, they would be in greater need of court interpreters for civil than for criminal cases. The reason why the need for interpreters is particularly acute in municipal court is that much of what goes on there involves persons telling their version of an incident directly to a judge, without the benefit of a defense attorney to speak for them. Perhaps for this reason, in large cities in the southwest some municipal courts routinely assign staff interpreters even to civil cases.

Like many state courts and most municipal courts, federal courts tend to restrict the use of court-appointed interpreters largely to criminal cases and to only narrowly defined civil cases. The federal Court Interpreters Act, as will be shown in chapter 3, permits the use of court-appointed interpreters in civil cases only when it is the United States government that initiates an action against some party. If non-English-speaking litigants were to sue the federal government, under the terms of the law, they would not be entitled to free interpreting services provided by the court. As a response to this federal restriction on the use of court-appointed interpreters in federal court, some lawyers have entered into contractual agreements with federally certified interpreters, guaranteeing to pay their fees in civil cases that are not covered under the terms of the federal law. These lawyers guarantee to pay the interpreters, whether or not their client wins the lawsuit. In this way, even a poor litigant who initiates a suit against the federal government can benefit from the services of a highly qualified interpreter. Such informal arrangements between lawyers and interpreters, however, are not the norm. Consequently, non-English-speaking persons who are poor are not likely to sue the federal government. Even in a federal courthouse where lawyers have an informal private arrangement with interpreters, such as the eastern courthouse referred to in Table 1.3, the instances of civil cases employing interpreters are very infrequent, compared to criminal cases.

What the preceding discussion demonstrates, then, is that for the most part non-English-speaking persons involved in civil actions do not receive the benefit of free court-interpreting services. The consequence of this reality is that such individuals must provide their own interpreter in civil court. Because the vast majority of the non-English-speaking fall into socio-economically disadvantaged groups, this means in effect that the American judicial system places the non-English-speaking at a distinct disadvantage in civil court. The disadvantage lies in the inevitable consequence of such judicial policy: parties to a civil action tend to bring bilingual relatives or friends to serve as their interpreter, and as the present study and one other major study has found (New Jersey Supreme Court Task Force, 1986), the quality of interpreting rendered by such nonprofessional interpreters is quite poor indeed.

One final finding that emerges from a comparison of federal and state log records is that a state court can do a great deal more interpreting per year than a federal court. This is probably a function of the fact that a state court covers the needs of other courts related to it (i.e., J.P. court, primarily through preliminary hearings, and juvenile court). In addition, state courts cover certain noncriminal areas of law (e.g., conciliation court, domestic relations) that do not fall under the purview of federal courts.

This examination of the duties of court interpreters demonstrates that in federal and state courts alike, court interpreters are assigned to the non-English-speaking and hearing-impaired at all the various judicial proceedings at which a given defendant is required to be present. While the task of interpreting is a constant, the contexts in which interpreters must perform their job are highly varied.

Overview of this Book

The purpose of this introduction has been to bring to the reader an awareness of the extent to which foreign language court interpreters, especially Spanish/English interpreters, are utilized in contemporary

Table 1.3. Official Appearances of Spanish Interpreters, 1982

	Federal U.S. District Court (East Coast)	Federal U.S. District Court (Southwest)	State "Superior" Court (Southwest)[a]
Trial	72	49	132
Initial Appearance	42	243[b]	297
Arraignment	82	108	138
Plea and Change of Plea[c]	37	157	54
Motion	15	112	36
Bail Hearing	7	85	—
Preliminary Hearing	94	4	246
Sentencing	84	143	228
Assorted Hearings (Probation Status, etc.)	117	55	450
Attorney/Client Conference	60	13	557
Conciliation Court	—	—	27
Domestic Relations	—	—	182
Civil	—	—	94
Juvenile	—	—	321
J. P. Court	—	—	695[d]
Deposition	—	35	—
Waiver	—	206	—
Petty Offenses	—	101	—
Appointments of Attorneys and Defendants' Requests for Attorneys	—	36	—
TOTAL:	610	1,347	3,460

[a]Since the statistics provided by the chief interpreter of the southwestern superior court were not broken down by *type* of judicial procedure for the year—such records were kept only on a monthly basis—and because only two months of such itemized logged appearances were available, data for the superior court are projected from the months of January and February 1983, and are used in conjunction with the more global figure from 1982. Note that the "total" figure in the table (3,460) is not a projected figure, but an actual one for 1982. The total number of appearances calculated by adding the projected figures comes to 3,457, revealing a high congruence with the actual total.

[b]This figure includes the initial appearance of material witnesses.

[c]The category "plea and change of plea" includes only those appearances that were listed by chief interpreters in such a separately labeled category. It does not include those pleas that were counted by interpreters as part of the arraignment.

[d]The figure of 695 does not include the JP-court-held preliminary hearing proceeding. The 246 preliminary hearings, all of which took place in JP court, were listed separately.

American courtrooms. Chapter 2 explains why and how language is a crucial dimension in court proceedings, concentrating particularly on spoken legal language and the issue of control of witness testimony. Chapter 3 lays out the legal raison d'être behind the growing trend among courts to provide linguistic minorities with court interpreting services. It explains why the federal government has passed a Court Interpreters Act, and how that piece of legislation is implemented in terms of interpreter certification. Insights into court interpreter training programs are presented, based upon the author's experience as a participant in one such training program. Chapter 4 describes the fieldwork procedures that were used to come to the ethnographic conclusions that are presented in chapter 5. Chapter 5 analyzes the verbal and nonverbal interaction between interpreters and other participants in the courtroom, showing how all parties involved in some way misconstrue the interpreter's role. Chapters 6 and 7 demonstrate the various ways in which interpreters alter pragmatic elements of attorneys' questions and witnesses' answers, changing passive voice to active voice and vice versa, and inserting a number of different pragmatic elements that have been found to characterize what has been termed "powerless testimony style" (O'Barr 1982).

Chapters 8 and 9 demonstrate that the linguistic alterations made by interpreters are not inconsequential. Rather, they have an impact on mock jurors, leaving them with a significantly different social-psychological evaluation of a witness's trustworthiness, convincingness, intelligence, and competence. In addition, as chapter 9 shows, there is a growing awareness on the part of defense attorneys that the quality of interpreting services provided by the courts for their clients is deficient. With this awareness comes a dramatic increase in appeals based upon the claim of poor interpreting quality. In other cases, appeals have been based upon the failure of the courts to provide an interpreter altogether. In short, actors in the legal process are increasingly becoming aware of the importance of foreign language interpreting, and are beginning to pay closer attention to the issue surrounding it as a basis for appeal.

2

Law and Language

Out of the field of inquiry known as socio-linguistics, which studies the nexus between language and society, has come the general conclusion that the way in which a person will speak at a given moment in time is determined by a host of factors. Some of these factors have to do with the speaker's social characteristics: his or her age, sex, level of education, occupation, and income, for example. Other factors are elements present in the setting in which the person is speaking: the level of formality of the setting (e.g., a university lecture hall versus a schoolyard), the specialization of the setting (e.g., a doctor's office or a court of law, versus a grocery store or cafeteria). Further factors that can affect the style in which a person speaks have to do with the relationship of the speaker to the person being addressed: the degree of intimacy between them (e.g., husband/wife or brother/sister versus salesperson/client, attorney/defendant), the relative social distance between them and the role relationship in which they find themselves (e.g., employer/employee, parent/child, judge/defendant). The interplay between such factors produces a rich variety of speech styles commanded by one and the same person. Thus, a judge will speak in a highly ritualized, formal style when giving a jury instructions on to how to arrive at a verdict, and perhaps will speak in an equally formal style when deciding on a motion in open court. He will, however, use a less ritualized style when he questions a witness or potential juror during the voir dire,[1] and yet a lower register[2] when he talks privately to his secretary in his chambers. His speech style is likely to be more casual still when he talks to his wife and children at the breakfast table.

Thus far references to "language" have been restricted to the oral/aural medium. Language can be conveyed, however, through the written medium as well, and choice of medium adds another dimensional layer that conditions the style in which an utterance is expressed. Language set in written form is generally more formal than language that is spoken. Thus, the style in which statutes, briefs, and appellate opinions are written is generally highly formal, as is the style used in such documents as insurance policies, contracts, leases, and wills. So rigidly constrained, in fact, is the style of the latter that it can be considered to be reflective of what one linguist (Joos 1967) has called "frozen" style. In effect, it means that documents written in this style admit virtually no leeway in the range of their expression, no deviation from preset norms.

Joos has observed that English uses five basic styles, ranging in formality from intimate to frozen. According to his conceptualization, the particular nature of a person's speech or writing is conditioned both by the style he/she chooses and by the mode in which it is expressed. Mode, in turn, is subdivided into written on the one hand, and spoken on the other. The spoken mode can be further divided into composed and spontaneous speech. Thus, the Miranda rights warning, witnesses' oaths, and jury verdicts use frozen language (the patterns of lexical choice and grammatical usage are completely predictable and standardized), whereas attorneys' opening statements and closing arguments alternate between formal and consultative style. When an attorney's speech is unplanned—that is, he has no notes or other composed format from which to speak, such as is the case when he talks privately to his client—his speech style will shift downward, accordingly, varying between "consultative" and "casual" style. The examination of a witness by a lawyer is generally conducted in consultative style.

Joos has defined his five English styles in the following way. "Frozen" style is a "style for print and for declamation. The reader or hearer is not allowed to cross-question the writer or speaker" (1967:39). As the most highly formal of the styles, it employs the most complex grammatical sentence structure and the most formal vocabulary. It uses formulaic, ritualized expressions that allow listeners or readers to recognize the larger speech event in which it is embedded (e.g., the marriage vow, a judicial sentencing).

The defining features of "formal" style are detachment and cohesion. This style requires advanced planning and is intended for a captive audience. The speaker or writer "is under obligation to provide a plan for the whole sentence before he begins uttering it, and a delimitation of field for his whole discourse before he embarks on it" (1967:37). One of the defining characteristics of formal speech is the absence of participation of the interlocutor. Its pronunciation is explicit, it does not allow ellipsis (i.e., omissions), and keeps the structure of sentences elaborate (e.g., uses complex sentences to provide background information). Formal style is intended to inform.

"Consultative" style is the normal style for speaking to strangers—

that is, for persons who are neither acquaintances, nor friends, or relatives of the speaker. The two defining features of consultative style are: (1) "the speaker supplies background information—he does not assume that he will be understood without it . . . , and (2) the addressee participates continuously" (Joos 1967:23). It is unplanned speech. It is clear from Joos's description of it that it is the "unmarked," or baseline type of speech in American English among persons who do not know each other. The other styles are defined in relation to it, from the point of view of how they are distinct from it. Joos best describes it by reproducing the transcription of a business conversation that had taken place via telephone. The conversation is filled with contractions (e.g., "we're," for "we are," and "that's" for "that is"), fillers and hedges (e.g., "oh," "I see," "ah," and "well").

"Casual" style is for friends and acquaintances. It makes no use of background information, and does not rely on the listener's participation. Its two defining devices are ellipsis and slang, both of which signal to the addressee that he is socially an insider in relation to the speaker or writer. Ellipsis comes in the form of omission of either phonological, grammatical, or lexical units. Thus, instead of saying, "I believe that I can find one," a clerk might say to a customer, "I believe I can find one" (omitting "that"), or "Believe I c'n find one" (omitting the subject pronoun "I" and the full vowel *a* of "can").

"Intimate" style is far more elliptical than even casual style speech. If the sentence "Coffee's cold" is an example of casual speech style, then "Cold" would be the equivalent sentence in intimate style. So, too, would utterances such as, "Huh?" used as a full question, or "Uh-uh" as a negative reply to a question. Intimate style is not often heard in court proceedings, although the affirmative answer "Uh-huh" is sometimes used by witnesses. Intimate style may well be used among jurors during their deliberations, after they have come to interact in an intense fashion.

Legalese, or Legal English

Whereas Joos, a linguist, was properly able to distinguish between spoken language and written language, scholars analyzing legal language have largely ignored this distinction. Perhaps the first to both theoretically distinguish between *spoken* legal language and *written* legal language, and to empirically investigate the spoken, are O'Barr (1982) and his associates (O'Barr et al. 1976). Other scholars have used the term "legalese," or "legal English" to mean that register of English that is used by lawyers and judges specifically for legal proceedings and usually is too complicated for the lay person to comprehend. This is a blanket notion, however, one that implies that legalese is a homogeneous register used for written and spoken purposes alike. In actuality, past descriptions of legalese have been studies of *written* legal language (Melinkoff 1963; Crystal and Davy 1969; Hager 1959; Charrow and Crandall 1978; Shuy and Larkin 1978), and even in those areas where the linguistic medium was purportedly oral, as in the case of jury instructions (Charrow and Charrow 1979a, 1979b; Sales et al. 1977), it can be argued that the particular linguistic vehicle chosen for analysis ultimately is not oral, for the instructions are composed in written form, and then read aloud to the jury. Furthermore, some judges regularly give a written copy of their instructions to the jury, leaving jury members with continuous access to that document throughout their deliberations.

There is no question that what has been termed legalese is an integral part of the American legal system, and because of its importance it will be described below. Yet it must be cautioned that what follows is a description drawn almost exclusively from analyses of written legal language (i.e., documents such as contracts, insurance policies, wills, statutes, briefs, and so on). For a defendant going through the stages of criminal pretrial and trial process, and for jurors following a criminal trial, the type of legalese whose description follows is *not* the preponderance of language that he/she will hear. Rather, this type of legal language will form only a small subset of language samples that he/she is exposed to. This should be kept in mind in the light of the primary role of the court interpreter, to be discussed in the following chapters.

Danet (1980a), in her review of the literature on language in the legal process, provides an excellent synthesis of the linguistic features that have been found by other scholars to be characteristic of Legal English. Her treatment, based on a sentence taken from a Citibank loan form analyzed previously by Charrow and Crandall (1978), essentially is restricted to a description of written legal language, if one considers jury instructions not truly to be spoken language, and uses the authoritative work of Melinkoff (1963) for its main framework of analysis. Danet (474–81) finds that there are essentially three categories of features that typify legal English. They deal with lexicon, syntax, and discourse.

Nine lexical features are characteristic of legal English: (1) technical terms ("distraint," "default"); (2) common terms with an uncommon meaning ("assignment" meaning "the transference of a right, interest or title," rather than its general meaning, "something assigned, a task or duty"); (3) words whose origin is Latin ("insolvent"), French ("property"), or Old English ("hereafter"); (4) polysyllabic words ("collateral"); (5) unusual prepositional phrases ("in the event of default," meaning "if"); (6) doublets—that is, combinations of a word of Anglo-Saxon origin with a word derived from either French or Latin ("will and testament"); (7) formality (the use of "shall" in place of "will"); (8) vagueness (lack of specificity, such as the phrase "all the rights and remedies available"); (9) overprecision (the use of absolute terms such as "all" and "none").

Legal English is characterized by eleven syntactic features—that is, features relating to the permissible ways in which words are joined to form sentences: (1) nominalizations, or the formation of nouns or noun phrases from verbs ("make assignment" in place of "assign"); (2) passive constructions ("may *be provided* by law"); (3) conditionals ("in the event of default"); (4) unusual anaphora, specifically, referring back to previously mentioned nouns by use of the same noun rather than a pronoun (the repetition of "borrower" in two consecutive phrases of a sentence: "any obligation or any collateral on the borrower's part to be performed or observed; or the undersigned borrower shall die"—in standard written English the subject of the second phrase would be "he" or "she"); (5) *whiz* deletion: the deletion of a relative pronoun, such as "who," "which," or "that," and a form of the verb *be* in a relative clause ("all the rights and remedies [which are] available to a secured party"); (6) high frequency of prepositional phrases and their unusual placement between the subject and predicate of a sentence (the prepositional phrase "without demand or notice" in the following excerpt: "a right . . . (at its option) without demand or notice of any kind, to declare . . ."; normally the phrase would go in a position following the verb, as in "a right to declare without demand or notice (at its option . . .)"; (7) lengthy sentences (the Citibank loan form sentence analyzed by Danet [1980] contains 242 words, and is punctuated by five semicolons—this in contrast to the twenty-five-word mean length of sentences in government documents and business publications); (8) unique determiners: the use of "such" and "said" preceding nouns in phrases where normally other determiners ("this," "that") are used ("in any such event," rather than "in this event"); (9) impersonality: a preference for the third person over the first or second person (references to "the party," "the borrower," and "the lessee," as opposed to "I" or "you"); (10) a wide variety of semantically negative words, beyond the grammatical negative "not" ("never," "unless," "except," and words containing the prefix "un-"); (11) parallel structure in the linking of words and phrases by means of the conjunctions "or" and "and" ("now or hereafter," "to be immediately due and payable").

At the level of discourse, legal language is characterized by two general features. First, legal English has a lack of cohesion. Because of the limited use of anaphora, it is characterized by what would seem to be lists of sentences strung together, similar to the style of writing found in reading primers. Second, legal English is overly compact. Each sentence contains a great deal of information, and this information is not restated afterward in a different manner to help the reader absorb it. This is in marked contrast to ordinary written English, which strives to aid reader comprehension through rephrasing.

Comprehensibility of Legal Language

The overall impact of the conglomeration of features noted by Danet produces in readers a diminished comprehension of legal documents. Consequently, the main thrust of complaints against written legal language is that it is incomprehensible to the lay person, or nonlawyer. Studies of some of these individual features have shown that their presence adversely affects comprehension.

The comprehensibility of legalese has been shown to be affected both by the lexical nature of a text—that is, characteristics of the words that are used—and by syntactic features. When a legal document contains a relatively high percentage of uncommon words, the level of comprehension is lower than when it uses more common, or high frequency words, in their place. Charrow and Charrow's (1979) experimental study of jury instructions has demonstrated this fact. The studies of jury instructions by Sales et al. (1977) and Elwork et al. (1977) have found a similar relationship between lexical difficulty and comprehensibility of legal language.

Lexicon is not the sole linguistic factor that determines the comprehensibility of a legal text. The syntactic properties of a text will affect the degree to which persons can understand it. Charrow and Charrow (1979) have found that among the syntactic features that characterize legalese, certain ones lower comprehensibility: nominalizations, *whiz*-deletion, embedded clauses, phrases placed in unusual syntactic locations, and multiple negatives. While the evidence presented here is restricted to linguistic features that have been found to affect the comprehensibility of legal language alone, the research of the three major teams that have worked in this area of law and language—namely, Charrow and Charrow (1979), Sales, et al. (1977), and Elwork et al. (1977)—relies heavily on the findings of prior psycho-linguistic research on comprehensibility, which they cite. Thus, their findings in regard to legalese are supported by the outcome of prior research on nonlegal language, which gives their own conclusions greater weight.

The net result of the growing awareness of legalese as a separate variety of English[3] is the defense of it by those in the legal profession (e.g., Aiken 1960; Melinkoff 1963) who see the necessity of maintaining often archaic vocabulary and unusual syntactic structure, arguing that the need for precision and lack of ambiguity require such linguistic mechanisms. For such persons, legal language is intended for practitioners of the law and not for the lay public subject to it. Others (Hager 1959; Semegan 1980), however, adherants of the "plain English" movement, have actively voiced the need to reform legalese, so that legal documents may become more intelligible and hence more accessible to the public at large. While the plain English movement has had some degree of success thus far, particularly in regard to the enactment of state legislation prescribing standards of readability for consumer contracts, such as insurance policies (Pressman 1979; Semegan 1980) and action on the part of the federal government regarding the readability of warranties on consumer goods and of Federal Reserve Board loan forms (Lown 1979), the extent to which the movement to reform plain English can or will be effectuated remains an open question. How beneficial such reforms have been for the consumer is yet another, debatable question, as some analysts have observed (Charrow 1977; Siegel 1981).

Spoken Legal Language in the Courtroom

Attention thus far has been devoted to written legalese. Until recently, relatively little systematic research has been done on spoken legal language, particularly in terms of describing how language is used in a courtroom setting. Most of the pioneering work in this area has been done by O'Barr and his associates (O'Barr 1981, 1982; O'Barr and Conley 1976; O'Barr and Lind 1981; Conley, O'Barr, and Lind 1978; Lind and O'Barr 1979), Atkinson and Drew (1979), and Danet and her associates (Danet 1976, 1980b; Danet and Bogoch 1980; Danet, Hoffman, and Kermish 1980; Danet et al. 1980; Danet and Kermish 1978).

O'Barr (1982) is very much aware of the inappropriate use of the terms "legalese" and "legal English" as cover words for both written and spoken varieties of this register, when in actuality what these words have described is essentially a written speech variety. To repair this overgeneralization, O'Barr has formulated his own descriptive schema, based upon ethnographic observation in a North Carolina courthouse. He has found (O'Barr 1982:25) four varieties of spoken legal language, which he describes as follows:

> FORMAL LEGAL LANGUAGE: The variety of spoken language used in the courtroom that most closely parallels written legal language; used by the judge in instructing the jury, passing judgment, and "speaking to the record"; used by lawyers when addressing the court, making motions and requests, etc.; linguistically characterized by lengthy sentences containing much professional jargon and employing a complex syntax.
>
> STANDARD ENGLISH: The variety of spoken language typically used in the courtroom by lawyers and most witnesses; generally labeled CORRECT English and closely paralleling that taught as the standard in American classrooms; characterized by a somewhat more formal lexicon than that used in everyday speech.
>
> COLLOQUIAL ENGLISH: a variety of language spoken by some witnesses and a few lawyers in lieu of standard English; closer to everyday, ordinary English in lexicon and syntax; tends to lack many attributes of formality that characterize standard English; used by a few lawyers as their particular style or brand of courtroom demeanor.
>
> SUBCULTURAL VARIETIES: Varieties of language spoken by segments of the society who differ in speech style and mannerisms from the larger community; in the case of the particular courts studied in North Carolina, these varieties include Black English and the dialect of English spoken by poorly educated whites.

Each of the four varieties of spoken language is considered to be a separate register of court talk, and whereas a given speaker may not use all four registers in the courtroom, within the range of his or her own repertoire a speaker will shift depending upon situational factors. Thus, while lawyers are presumed to speak consistently in formal legal language, in actuality they may shift to colloquial English. O'Barr (1982:25–26) notes that:

> Lawyers are likely to address prospective jurors during *voir dire* colloquially, as though seeking solidarity with them. They may joke frequently during this aspect of a trial and

> emulate the speech styles of "ordinary folks." When questioning witnesses, they are likely to remove themselves from hostile witnesses either by attempting to make the colloquial or subcultural varieties of language appear "stupid" and unlike their own speech, or by attempting to suggest that expert witnesses for the opposition are using "big words to obscure relatively simple matters."

Consistent with the findings of O'Barr that speakers who command several spoken legal registers shift between them is the finding of Philips (1984) that judges' speech style varies, depending upon the formality of the speech situation, initial appearances in court being a relatively more informal situation, and changes of plea being a more formal one.

Spoken Legal Language and Social Control

The preceding discussion has shown that the language spoken during judicial proceedings can be viewed as a series of registers, or styles. With this repertoire of speech styles speakers can manipulate the impressions that others in the courtroom have of them and of their interlocutors. This is to say that through a conscious or unconscious strategy, participants in courtroom proceedings try to phrase their questions and answers in such a way as to make themselves look better, and the opposing side worse. Thus, through a variety of verbal tactics, lawyers try to make their own witnesses look credible, sincere, and competent, while they attempt to make witnesses for the opposing side appear dishonest, unreliable, and, in general, incompetent. Witnesses and defendants, in contrast, try to use verbal strategies to enhance their image before the judge or jury, and in a variety of subtle linguistic ways try to ward off the verbal demeaning of the opposition in an effort to preserve a positive image.

Looking at witness testimony, O'Barr and his colleagues (O'Barr and Conley 1976; Erickson et al. 1978; Conley et al. 1978; Lind and O'Barr 1979) have found that a constellation of speech traits previously thought to be characteristic of women's style alone (Lakoff 1975) could be found in the speech of male and female witnesses alike, and that when this series of traits was present, the witness gave the impression of being less convincing, less truthful, less competent, less intelligent, and less trustworthy than when his speech was lacking in these traits. The particular set of speech traits that comprise this composite style, which O'Barr and his colleagues have called "powerless" style, includes (1) hedges (noncommittal, cautious, or ambiguous expressions, such as "sort of," "kind of," "I guess," "it seems like"); (2) superpolite forms ("I'd really appreciate it if . . . ," "Would you please open the door, if you don't mind?"); (3) tag questions (questions that suggest the answer, such as "It's hot in here, isn't it?" and "You were there that night, weren't you?"); (4) speaking in italics (extra word stress to convey emphasis, parallel to the use of underlining in writing, as in "It was *so* good of you to come," "That was *very* nice of you"); empty adjectives (adjectives that convey no substantive information but serve mainly to express the speaker's feelings about the noun referred to, such as "divine," "charming," "cute," "sweet," "adorable," and "lovely"); (6) hypercorrect grammar and pronunciation (bookish grammar and very careful enunciation); (7) lack of sense of humor (the inability to tell a joke well, and a tendency to miss the point in jokes told by others); (8) direct quotations (quoting directly rather than paraphrasing); (9) special lexicon (highly specialized vocabulary in certain lexical domains, for example, color terms such as "magenta," "chartreuse," and "cerise"); (10) question intonation in declarative contexts (answering a question with a questionlike response, such as answering the question "When will dinner be ready?" with the reply, "Around six o'clock?" indicating that the response calls for approval by the questioner).

An additional discourse variable present in the speech of witnesses or defendants who are testifying is narrative versus fragmented testimony style. Persons testifying in narrative style will answer a question with a relatively long answer, whereas persons using fragmented style will answer in brief, nonelaborated responses, as in the examples below given by O'Barr (1982:76):

NARRATIVE STYLE

Q. Now, calling your attention to the twenty-first day of November, a Saturday, what were your working hours that day?
A. Well, I was working from, uh, 7 A.M. to 3 P.M. I arrived at the store at 6:30 and opened the store at 7.

FRAGMENTED STYLE

Q. Now, calling your attention to the twenty-first day of November, a Saturday, what were your working hours that day?
A. Well, I was working from 7 to 3.
Q. Was that 7 A.M.?
A. Yes.
Q. And what time that day did you arrive at the store?
A. 6:30.
Q. 6:30. And did, uh, you open the store at 7 o'clock?
A. Yes, it has to be opened by then.

Whether a witness will answer a question in fragmented or narrative style is largely controlled by the interrogating attorney.[4] Lawyers usually allow their own witnesses to answer in narrative style, but restrict witnesses for the opposition from doing so. This practice is based on the implicit assumption of lawyers that jurors have a higher regard for witnesses answering in narrative style and have a poorer opinion of witnesses who testify in fragmented style. Using this as the hypothesis of an experimental study, O'Barr (1982) found that the hypothesis does in fact bear out: witnesses testifying in narrative style were rated as being more competent and socially dynamic than were witnesses who testified in fragmented style. Furthermore, the interrogating attorney was believed to hold a similar estimation of the witnesses in question.

Another stylistic variant in witness testimony is "hypercorrect" speech. In O'Barr's (1982) experimental studies, hypercorrect style is defined in terms of frequent errors in grammar and vocabulary made by the witness in an attempt to speak formally. This style, when contrasted with a formal testimony style devoid of such errors, was associated with mock juror negative perceptions of the witness's convincingness, competence, intelligence, and appearance of being qualified.

Witnesses testifying on the stand have at their disposal a variety of linguistic techniques for mitigating, or softening, the illocutionary force of damaging assertions. That is, witnesses can talk about an adversative situation and make it seem less negative in a number of ways. They can opt for one lexical item over another, such as "baby" versus "fetus," as Danet (1980) found in an abortion trial. Grammatically, they can use passive constructions rather than active ones, and nominalizations rather than verbs, both of which serve to keep the identity of the agent inexplicit.

Questions and Control

Whereas witnesses have some degree of control over how they present testimony, clearly linguistic power in the courtroom lies primarily with attorneys and judges. Perhaps the most crucial way in which attorneys and judges hold linguistic control over witnesses and defendants is through the interrogation process. Analyses of question/answer sequences have shown that questions are used as weapons for the purpose of testing or challenging claims, and as mechanisms for making accusations (Atkinson and Drew 1979; Churchill 1978; Danet and Bogoch 1980). In most contexts questions have the force of a summons (Schegloff 1972; Goody 1978). However, as Walker (1987:59–60) notes, "in a legal adversary interview a question becomes more than that: it becomes an *order* that the respondent's *knowledge* be displayed in an appropriate form."

Questions in a courtroom vary according to the degree to which they coerce or constrain an answer, Danet and her colleagues have discovered (Danet and Kermish 1978; Danet et al., 1980b). In order of coerciveness, they have found, declaratives are the most coercive, since rather than to ask a question, they make a statement (e.g., "You did it . . ."). The next most coercive types of questions are interrogative yes/no questions (e.g., "Did you do it?") and choice questions (e.g., "Did you leave at nine or at ten o'clock?"). Third in order of coerciveness are open-ended *wh-* questions—that is, questions that use interrogative words such as *who, what, where, when, why, how,* and so on (e.g., "What did you do that night?"). The least coercive, and simultaneously most polite and indirect, are what Danet and her colleagues call "requestions," questions that on the face of it seem to ask the witness whether or not he/she is able to answer a question, but actually ask for information, although in an indirect manner (e.g., "Can you tell us what happened?"). The findings of Danet and Bogoch (1980), Bresnahan (1979), and Woodbury (1984) indicate that coercive questions are used heavily in cross-examination, but in relatively low proportions during direct examination. Furthermore, Danet and Bogoch (1980) find that the frequency with which coercive questions are used is directly related to the seriousness of the offense in question: the more serious the offense, the higher the proportion of coercive questions asked by prosecutors on cross-examination. In addition, coercive questions have been found to produce shorter answers (Danet et al. 1980b; Bresnahan 1979). Shorter answers, it should be recalled, are associated with a more negative estimation by jurors.

Although question type can often be seen to be correlated with degree of coerciveness, the relationship is not a constant one, for, as Danet (1980:522) herself acknowledges, "The form of a question alone does not necessarily determine how coercive it is. A noncontroversial assertion cast in the declarative is less coercive in context than a supposedly open-ended *wh-* question."[5] For example, one important element that enters into the perception of a question as being coercive is the status of the person who has asked it. Questions coming from judges may be considered coercive in and of themselves because of the superior status of the judge in the courtroom (Philips

1979). This is consonant with the conclusions of Walker (1987:78), who finds that in interrogations that take place in legal settings, "Power is viewed by all parties as being role connected, and vested in the examiner, who has the right to compel responsive answers from the witness."

An important category of questions that plays a significant role in courtroom interaction is the category of leading question. Leading questions are important because they allow lawyers to predetermine the substance of an impending answer, and thereby to tightly control what a witness is going to say. Leading questions thus enable lawyers to establish their own interpretation of the facts and events that are the subject of discussion. The use of leading questions is constrained by rules of courtroom procedure: leading questions generally may not be asked on direct examination, but may be asked during cross-examination. The exception to the rule against leading questions on direct is the case of witnesses who for a number of specific reasons may have difficulty in understanding the questions (e.g., the linguistically impaired, including the non-English-speaking and the hard-of-hearing, very old or very young persons, and mentally handicapped persons).

When a lawyer asks a leading question at a time when he is not supposed to, the opposing attorney has the right to object. Beyond the fact that improperly conducted leading questions result in sustainable objections, leading questions carry with them other behavioral side effects: in simulated trials they result in a higher incidence of guilty verdicts than do more neutral questions (Kaspryzk et al. 1975), and they can increase the possibility of a witness making a mistaken identification.

Other Linguistic Devices for Controlling Witness Testimony

Besides question format, lawyers and judges have at their disposal several other means of controlling what and how much a witness or defendant will say while under oath. One technique available to the examiner is interrupting the witness. Surprisingly, whereas interrupting a witness or defendant clearly is a way to gain control of what is being said, subjects acting as jurors in an experiment (O'Barr 1982) concluded that when a lawyer interrupts a person who is testifying, the lawyer is perceived as having less control over the testimony. The same study also demonstrated that mock jurors consider a lawyer to have lost some control over a person's testimony at any point when the witness or defendant speaks simultaneously with the lawyer—that is, whenever their speech overlaps. This was found to be equally as true of situations where it was the witness who interrupted the lawyer. In other words, whenever verbal clashes arose, no matter who initiated the aggressive verbal behavior, the lawyer was perceived as having lost some control over the person testifying.

What a witness or defendant will say can to a large extent be manipulated linguistically by the examiner. Experimental studies of eyewitness testimony have shown that eyewitnesses can be led to recall things they had never seen at the scene of the event they had witnessed when a definite article ("the") is used in place of an indefinite article ("a"). Loftus and Zanni (1975) found that subjects who after watching an experimentally filmed automobile accident were asked, "Did you see the broken headlight?" were much more likely to report that they had seen it than were those who had been asked, "Did you see a broken headlight?" when in fact there had been no broken headlight in the film. The definite article "the" presupposes the existence of the noun to which it refers, while the indefinite "a" does not. Such an existential presupposition apparently can affect the memory and, consequently, the testimony of eyewitnesses.

Another linguistic resource available to lawyers that can affect a witness's recall and, hence, testimony, is the manipulation of lexical presupposition. In another experiment (Loftus and Palmer 1974) involving a film of an automobile accident, it was found that subjects who were asked the question, "About how fast were the cars going when they smashed into each other?" reported a significantly higher speed than did those who were asked, "About how fast were the cars going when they hit each other?" Thus, the fact that the lexical presupposition of the verb "smash"—namely, violent collision—is much more weakly conveyed by the verb "hit," affected eyewitnesses' testimony regarding the speed of the cars that they had observed.

The Impact of the Interpreter on Court Talk

It will be demonstrated throughout this book that the court interpreter affects the verbal outcome of attorneys' and judges' questions, and witnesses' or defendants' answers. In a variety of ways the interpreter will be seen to interact with the key verbal participants in the courtroom, and often through no fault of her own, interferes with the attempts of examiners to get out their questions in the way that they want to, and the efforts of testifying witnesses or defendants to formulate their replies as they would wish to. It will be seen that the role of the interpreter, as performed currently in American courthouses at every judicial level, often serves to alter the pragmatic intent of speakers in the course of on-the-record judicial proceedings.

3

The Bilingual American Courtroom: A Legal Raison d'Etre

The bilingual American courtroom is not perceived as such by court personnel. For all intents and purposes the proceedings go on as usual, with the exception that an interpreter is present and doing her job. Ultimately, what is said aloud for the court record is in English, and since the record is what ultimately "counts" in terms of admissible evidence and material utilizable in future appeals, what is said in the foreign language is perceived as "not counting." Officially that is in fact the case.

In courts located in linguistically homogeneous areas of the United States, such as small midwestern towns, the use of court interpreters often is unheard of. When the need for an interpreter arises, as might occur when the non-English-speaking spouse of a foreign university student appears in court, judges make use of any bilingual speaker available. Usually this will be a bilingual relative or friend of the defendant or litigant, or a university professor who speaks the foreign language. Areas of linguistic diversity, however, which either tend to attract large numbers of immigrants (cities such as New York, Chicago, and Los Angeles), or regions of stable bilingualism,[1] such as the southwest, have long had institutional mechanisms for dealing with the problems of the non-English-speaking person called to appear in court. Consequently, it is no coincidence that the states that have some formal mechanism for appointing interpreters to non-English-speaking persons in court are precisely those states that have concentrations of non-English-speaking populations.

State Provisions for Court-Appointed Interpreters[2]

Two states have gone the furthest legislatively in establishing the availability of court appointed interpreters: New Mexico and California. These states have made provisions for court interpreter services in their constitutions. Thus, New Mexico's constitution (Art. 2, §14) guarantees that a defendant in a criminal case has the right "to have charge and testimony interpreted to him in a language he understands." California's state constitution (Art. 1, §14) guarantees that, "a person unable to understand English who is charged with a crime has a right to an interpreter throughout the proceedings."

Whereas the constitutional guarantee to a court interpreter is the strongest level of commitment a state can make in this regard, short of that, statutory provision is the next most powerful form of legislation. As Pousada (1979:193) points out, of the twenty-four states that in some way provide for court interpreters, the majority do so by way of administrative or judicial regulations, not by statute. Among the states that do provide the statutory right to a court interpreter are Arizona, California, Colorado, Illinois, Massachusetts, Minnesota, New Mexico, New York, and Texas.

Where statutory provision is made, it is sometimes broad and vague, and its effectuation generally controlled by the presiding judge in the case. Thus, both the New York Code of Criminal Procedure (§308) and the Illinois Annotated Statutes (ch. 51, §47) are vaguely written when they deal with the right to a court interpreter, the Illinois statute providing that "interpreters may be sworn in when necessary." An instance of a more explicit statute is that of the Michigan Statutes Annotated (§28, 1256, [1]) and the Michigan Compiled Laws Annotated (§775.192, Art. 2), which guarantee the following:

> If any person is accused of any crime or misdemeanor and is about to be examined or tried before any justice of the peace, magistrate or judge of a court of record, and it appears to the . . . judge that such a person is incapable of adequately understanding the charge or presenting his defense thereto because of lack of ability to understand or speak the English language . . . the . . . judge shall appoint a qualified person to act as an interpreter.

Below the level of statutory provisions is the level of administrative or judicial regulations. A good example of such regulations is the California Evidence Code (section 752 [a]), which provides that "when a witness is incapable of hearing or understanding the English language or is incapable of expressing himself in the English language so as to be understood directly by counsel, court and jury, an interpreter whom he can understand and who can understand him shall be sworn to interpret for him."

Of all the states, California probably has been the most progressive in making legislative advances that provide high quality court interpreting services for the non-English-speaking.[3] A case in point is law A.B. 2400, enacted in 1978, which establishes a program for training and testing court interpreters. The program was established to provide interpreters with areas of expertise seen as necessary for doing a competent job in the courts—namely, an understanding of courtroom procedures and legal terminology. Specifically, the act makes the following provisions: (1) the collection of reliable data on the use of court interpreters, so that such data may be used to upgrade the quality of court interpreting services; (2) assigning to the State Personnel Board the role of developing court interpreter examinations; (3) publishing a list of qualified court interpreters in each county on whom courts may draw when interpreters are needed; (4) the annual testing and certification of court interpreters by the State Personnel Board; and (5) empowering the Judicial Council with the task of collecting, analyzing, and publishing pertinent interpreter utilization statistics, with commentary, as part of the "Annual Report of the Administrative Office of the California Courts." The goal of this last provision is to establish standards of court interpreting and to determine exactly the need for interpreters in specified languages and in particular courts.

Case Law

Case law originating in state and federal courts alike has served to establish the right of the non-English-speaking to court-appointed interpreters. Frankenthaler and McCarter (1978:144–48) have reviewed the case law of California courts relating to issues revolving around the right to an interpreter, and have found that the issues have emerged in both criminal and civil cases. In citing the cases mentioned below, Frankenthaler and McCarter (1978:144) conclude that California case law reflects "the degree to which the issues have crystallized in the California courts, while at the same time pointing out the limitations of judicial response."

By 1967, with the case of People v. Annett (1967:251 Cal. App. 2d 858, 59 Cal. Rep. 888), the right of a non-English-speaking defendant to have an interpreter in a criminal case was established. The ruling of the court in People v. Annett was as follows:

> Failure of a trial court to appoint an interpreter for a defendant who has requested one, or whose conduct has made it obvious to the court that he is unable because of linguistic difficulties knowingly to participate in waiving his rights, is "fundamentally unfair" and requires reversal of a conviction.

In this particular case no interpreter was provided for the defendant, for the judge had determined that the defendant did not really need one. In California, as in other states, the decision as to whether a given defendant or litigant is linguistically in sufficient need of an interpreter is entirely up to the discretion of the presiding judge.

Thus, the judge is tacitly assumed to have the linguistic capability of assessing the level of a defendant's or litigant's comprehension of English.[4]

Two cases dealing with the right of a litigant in a civil matter to a court-appointed interpreter resulted in opposite rulings. The case of Gardiana v. Small Claims Court In and For San Leandro-Haya (1976:59 Cal. App. 3d 412, 130 Cal. Rptr. 675) dealt with two defendants in a small claims suit, both of whom were indigent and could neither speak nor understand English. The defendants requested that the court appoint an interpreter, at no cost to them. The request was denied, the argument being that the court did not hold any inherent or statutory power to appoint an interpreter at the county's expense, nor could it do so at the expense of any other public body. The decision was appealed, and in the appeal the ruling was reversed. The judge ruled that the court did in fact have the inherent power to appoint an interpreter at public expense in those cases where the litigant was non-English-speaking and indigent, and, in addition, upheld the provisions of section 752(a) of the California Evidence code for appointing an interpreter to a *witness* who either could not communicate in or understand English.

In a subsequent case, however, Jara v. Municipal Court (1978:21 Cal. 3d 181, 578 P.2d 94, 145 Cal. Rptr. 847), the supreme court of California decided that there was nothing in the state constitution that required the courts to appoint, at public expense, interpreters to indigent non-English-speaking defendants when such defendants were represented by counsel. The California supreme court was thus distinguishing between small claims cases, which generally are carried out without the use of attorneys or rules of evidence, and cases held in municipal courts, where litigants do have recourse to representation by counsel. It was this distinction that the court used to justify an apparent reversal of the decision held in the case of Gardiana. Frankenthaler and McCarter (1978:147) note:

> In contrast to *Gardiana*, the *Jara* court found no statutory basis for appointment of an interpreter at public expense since it stated that section 752 of the California Evidence code refers to interpreters for witnesses only, not litigants. The *Jara* court went on to distinguish between witness interpreters and party interpreters and characterized the role of the witness interpreter as a "different and much less burdensome function" than that of a party interpreter. Notwithstanding that statement, the court then said the witness interpreter is always essential to the proceeding and the party interpreter is not when counsel is present.

The California supreme court suggested, furthermore, that in place of court-appointed interpreters, litigants in municipal courts make use of family, friends, neighbors, and private organizations to provide them with interpreting services.

The dissenting voice of one of the judges in the Jara case, Justice Tobriner, is worth quoting, for it expresses the sentiment and reasoning behind the movement that culminated in the enactment of the Federal Court Interpreters Act. Justice Tobriner concluded (1978:21 Cal. 3d 181, 578 P.2d 94, 145 Cal Rptr. 850–51) that the majority opinion of the justices in the Jara decision would result in a proceeding which for the litigant would be "an empty and meaningless ritual," and consequently he dissented, stating:

> I cannot agree with the majority's assessment of the confusion, the despair, and cynicism suffered by those who in intellectual isolation must stand by as their possessions and dignity are stripped from them by a Kafka-esque ritual deemed by the majority to constitute, nonetheless, a fair trial.

Interpreter for the Witness versus Interpreter for the Party

The issue of whether an interpreter should be appointed by the court only for witnesses rather than for witnesses and parties alike, has been one of the most disputed points of contention in interpreter-related case law. In the case of U.S. v. Desist (384 F.2d 888, 891–92, 2d Cir. [1967]) the court ruled that an interpreter was indeed necessary to enable the defendant to testify and have his thoughts adequately conveyed to the jury, but that the defendant had no right to a personal interpreter who would simultaneously interpret for him everything that was said in the courtroom.

In other cases interpreters have in fact been provided for defendants seated at the defense table, yet they have not interpreted all the ongoing testimony during the trial. In two such cases, Tapia-Corona v. U.S. (369 F.2d 366, 9th Cir. [1966]) and Markiewicz v. State (109 Neb. 514, 191 N.W.648, 650 [1922]), the courts found that so long as an interpreter was seated at the defense counsel table and was available for consultation, it was not necessary that she interpret all the testimony for the defendant.

Frankenthaler (1980:52) has correctly identified a "double standard" at work underlying decisions such as the ones held in U.S. v. Desist, Tapia-Corona v. U.S., and Markiewicz v. State. At the heart of this double standard, she finds, are the needs of the court for a "smooth and orderly sequence of trial," which would entail making foreign language testimony comprehensible to the court and to the jury, and fulfilling the personal needs of the non-English-speaking party to understand English language testimony being leveled against him. Frankenthaler (1980:52) crystalizes this duality very aptly:

> Since a witness interpreter is appointed so that witnesses can communicate with the court in a manner which as closely as possible approximates the communication of English-speaking witnesses, one might assume that this type of logic is also carried over to the appointment of party interpreters, i.e., so that the non-English speaking defendant can understand all testimony and communicate with his attorney in a manner which as closely as possible puts him in the same position as an English-speaking defendant. However, if we bear in mind that *the benefit of the party interpreter is primarily personal to the party, while the benefit of the witness interpreter is primarily for the court as a whole* [emphasis added], we may find it more comprehensible to deal with the "double standard," whereby the same party may have better interpreter services as a witness than when exercising his right of confrontation as a party.

Federal legislation, however, as will be shown below, has elected to abolish this double standard, at least insofar as federal district courts are concerned. Thus, for many involved in improving court interpreter services, the right of confrontation of the non-English-speaking party has been seen as being equally as important a consideration as the need of the court for smoothly carried out judicial process.

When one speaks of the "needs of the party" and the "needs of the court," a critical point should be kept in mind: anything said in a foreign language in an American courtroom does not "count" as far as official judicial procedure is concerned. It does not count because it is not entered into the record. Only English-language testimony, attorney or judges' questioning, motions, and so on, can be recorded during a judicial procedure. Court reporters do not record anything said in a language other than English. This has important ramifications for appellate cases based on the issue of inaccurate interpreting, as will be shown in chapter 9.

Waiving One's Right to an Interpreter

An important issue concerning the right to a court-appointed interpreter, one that has emerged out of case law, is the question of what constitutes a party's waiver of his right to an interpreter. Essentially the issue has been that of interpreting a party's failure to request the services of an interpreter as an unspoken waiver of his right to them. In effect, then, a party's silence in this regard has been considered by the courts to signify a waiver. Two important cases that involved this issue are *People v. Ramos* (26 N.Y. 2d 272, 258 N.E.2d 906 [1970]) and *U.S. ex rel Negrón v. N.Y.* (310 F. Supp. [E.D.N.Y. 1970], aff'd 434 F.2d 386 [2d Cir. 1970]).

In the Ramos case, ten years after being convicted for a narcotics offense, the defendant appealed the conviction on the grounds that he had not been given a fair trial because he had not been appointed an interpreter. Ramos lost in the appeal, the court ruling that because he had not made an affirmative assertion regarding his inability to understand, Ramos had thereby waived his right to an interpreter. The court argued that to grant Ramos a new trial would be tantamount to allowing a defendant to remain silent throughout the course of a trial, and then to grant him a retrial if the outcome was adverse, all on the grounds that he had not been provided an interpreter.

The case of U.S. ex rel Negrón v. N.Y. demonstrates a ruling that came to the opposite conclusion over the question as to whether a failure to request an interpreter could be considered a waiver of a party's right to an interpreter. The Negrón case involved a Spanish-speaking migrant worker who had been convicted of second-degree murder and had been given a twenty-year prison sentence. During the trial an interpreter was called to interpret Negrón's Spanish testimony as well as that of two other Spanish-speaking witnesses. No interpreter, however, was provided to interpret into Spanish the English testimony of the twelve other witnesses who testified against him, probably because Negrón and his attorney had not requested one. Again, this is a case in point of the distinction that courts have made between interpreting for a witness and interpreting for a party.

After filing a series of appeals that subsequently were denied, Negrón was granted a writ of habeas corpus by the federal district court on the grounds that he had been denied his constitutional rights, specifically, the right to due process. The court's opinion (U.S. ex rel Negrón v. N.Y. 310 F. Supp. [E.D.N.Y. 1970], aff'd 434 F.2d [2d Cir. 1970] at 1309) in the case of Negrón was a significant one, for it rejected the concept of silence as constituting a waiver of a party's right to an interpreter:

> Considering Negrón's background and his total ignorance of and unfamiliarity with our legal system or the rights accorded him thereunder, his failure [to request an interpreter] is clearly understandable. Similarly, it would be manifestly unjust to charge Negrón's attorney with waiving this right since the courts have as of today not clearly defined this right. The flaw in the waiver argument in the present case is that the right was unknown and accordingly there could be no intention to waive it. Therefore, the court finds that neither Negrón nor his attorney may be charged with a waiver.

Federal Measures

Before the enactment of the Federal Court Interpreters Act,[5] only two federal judicial regulations had directly provided for interpreters in the federal courts, according to Pousada (1979:192): rule 28(b) of the Federal Rules of Criminal Procedure and rule 43(f) of the Federal Rules of Civil Procedure. While rule 289(b) is very brief and unspecific, stating simply that "the court may appoint an interpreter of its own selection," the Advisory Committee on Rules added some specificity to it in 1966, noting that it applied to interpreting for the deaf, and in 1969, that it applied to interpreting the testimony of non-English-speaking witnesses or helping non-English-speaking defendants understand the proceedings or communicate with their attorney. Rule 43(f) of the Federal Rules of Civil Procedure specifies that the court has the right to select an interpreter, and decide upon a reasonable compensation for her services. According to this rule, the compensation, which is provided by the Criminal Justice Act of 1964 (18 U.S.C. 3006A 9e), "shall be paid out of funds provided by law or by one or more of the parties as the court may direct and may be taxed ultimately as costs in the discretion of the court" (Pousada 1979:192).

Justification of the right to an interpreter in federal courts can be made both on constitutional grounds and on the basis of existing federal legislation. Arguments based on the United States Constitution have been made in reference to sixth, fifth, and fourteenth amendments.

The sixth amendment guarantees a criminal defendant's right to confront witnesses who testify against him. It also gives the defendant the right to the effective assistance of legal counsel. It has been argued (Morris 1967) that a non-English-speaking person who is not given the services of an interpreter may be *physically* present at his trial, but he is not *linguistically* present, which means that he is unable to confront witnesses during cross-examination, and he is rendered unable to communicate with his attorney, which therefore prevents him from aiding his attorney in the defense on his behalf. The fifth and fourteenth amendments guarantee due process—that is, the right not to be deprived of life, liberty, or property without due process of law. If due process is to be guaranteed the non-English-speaking defendant, he must be provided an interpreter, so that he may be accorded the same "fundamental fairness" as an English-speaking defendant (U.S. ex rel. Negrón v. N.Y., 434 F.2d 386, 389 [2d Cir. 1970]).

Grounds for appointing interpreters to non-English-speaking persons in civil cases where they are not defendants have been argued by Frankenthaler and McCarter (1978). They find the current applicability of the Federal Court Interpreters Act far too limited in the context of civil cases, as is discussed below, and see in equal protection clauses of federal legislation the constitutional basis for extending the right to an interpreter to a broader civil context. Frankenthaler and McCarter (1978:129–31) propose that section 2000d of the Civil Rights Act of 1964 be used as the grounds on which to extend the presently limited scope of the Federal Court Interpreters Act, citing the statement of the Department of Justice as to the purpose of Title VI of the Civil Rights Act (28 C.F.R. §42.101 [1978]):

> . . . that no person in the United States shall, on the ground of race, color, or national origin, be excluded from participation in, be denied the benefits of, or otherwise be subjected to discrimination under any program or activity receiving federal financial assistance from the Department of Justice.

The Court Interpreters Act

The Court Interpreters Act, signed into law in 1978, represents a milestone in federal legislation aimed at extending justice to the linguistically disadvantaged. It is the first federal statute that grants the right to a court interpreter.

The act is intended to provide interpreters for defendants and witnesses in both civil and criminal cases in federal district courts. Persons deemed to be in need of interpreters are those who either do not speak or understand English, or who have a hearing or speech impairment. The act also allows a limited use of Spanish in the district court of Puerto Rico, whenever the presiding judge considers it to be in the interest of justice. The actual wording of the terms of the act is as follows (Court Interpreters Act, Pub. L. no. 95–539, §2[a], 92 Stat. 2040[1978]), guaranteeing a court-appointed interpreter:

> In any criminal or civil action initiated by the United States in a United States district court (Including a petition for a writ of habeas corpus initiated in the name of the United States by a relator), if the presiding judicial officer determines on such officer's own motion or on the motion of a party that such party (including a defendant in a criminal case), or a witness who may present testimony in such action—
> (1) speaks only or primarily a language other than the English language; or
> (2) suffers from a hearing impairment (whether or not suffering also from a speech impairment)
> so as to inhibit such party's comprehension of the proceedings or communication with counsel or the presiding judicial officer, or so as to inhibit such witness' comprehension of questions and the presentation of such testimony.

It is important to note that the determination as to whether a given defendant or witness is in need of an interpreter is in the hands of the presiding judge. The determination of lack of proficiency in English is clear-cut in some cases: some parties or witnesses know no English whatsoever. Where the difficulties arise are in cases of persons who know English to a certain extent. It is here that the judge must use his discretion in arriving at a linguistic evaluation that probably only a trained linguist could properly make.

Furthermore, the act is rather limited in the sphere of civil actions. As Frankenthaler and McCarter (1978:128) point out:

> We are faced with the anomalous situation where a non-English speaking plaintiff suing the United States on a legitimate claim would not be entitled to a court interpreter under this Act while a defendant in a civil suit would be. In addition, substantial rights are not limited to litigation where the United States is a party. In civil actions between private parties, access to the courts may be effectively foreclosed to any non-English speaking litigant who cannot afford to pay for the services of an interpreter, since the Act is silent in this area.

In dealing with the matter of waiving one's right to a court-appointed interpreter, the act reflects an implicit cognizance of case law dealing with the issue of what constitutes a waiver. It mandates that the right to an interpreter may be waived by a party, not by a witness, and only when such a waiver has been expressly requested by the party after consulting with his attorney, and after the judge has explained to the party, through an interpreter, what he is doing by waiving his right. Finally, the judge must approve the waiver, before it can go into effect. Once the waiver is approved, the party may select his own interpreter, one not approved by the court, although here, too, the judge can exercise his discretion and block the use of an interpreter whom he considers to be either unreliable or insincere in her interpreting function.

The Training and Certification of Federal Court Interpreters

When a judge determines in a given case that the party or witness is rightfully in need of an interpreter, under the provisions of the act he should give preference to the most readily available interpreter who has federal certification. Federal certification, in turn, is given to those interpreters who have passed the Federal Court Interpreters Examination, a test constructed for and administered by the director of the Administrative Office of the U.S. Courts, who is also directly responsible for the implementation of the act as such. Besides being responsible for a certification program for interpreters, the director sees to it that every district court maintains a list of certified interpreters in its district, and determines the fee rate for interpreting services, for both court-appointed and not court-appointed interpreters alike.[6] In criminal actions interpreters receive their payment from the director of the Administrative Office, the funds for which are provided by the federal judiciary. In civil actions it is up to the discretion of the presiding judge to decide whether the interpreter's fees will be paid by the court, divided between parties, or taxed as costs.

The Federal Court Interpreters Examination. The director of the Administrative Office delegates the task of constructing a court interpreters examination to a team of persons comprising court interpreters, international conference interpreters, bilingual federal court judges, language specialists, and specialists in test construction. At present, the exam is administered in two parts: written and oral. Only those persons who have passed the written component may go on to take the oral section, which is administered on a separate occasion. By May 1984, 220 interpreters had been federally certified. The first exam was administered in 1980, and by its third administration, 4,600 persons had taken the written portion, but only 1,500 of them qualified to take the oral portion (Leeth 1986). As of February 1986, only 4 percent of those who had initially taken the exam passed it in its entirety (292 out of 7,000 persons), and many of those who ultimately passed the exam had had to take a portion of it repeatedly before being able to pass the entire exam (Leeth 1986). Clearly the test is a rigorous one, and aims at sorting out the most highly qualified interpreters from among the applicants.

The written component of the exam is a two-and-a-half hour multiple-choice test, comprising two comparable tests, one in English and one in Spanish. A candidate must pass *both* the English and the Spanish segments of the written test with a total correct score of 76–78 percent.[7] Of the 100 test items constructed for each language, most (60%) comprise vocabulary: knowledge of synonyms, antonyms, word-meaning as reflected in fill-in-the-blank sentence completions. In the English section of the exam these are geared toward fourteenth to eighteenth grade level (the type found in Graduate Record Examinations). In the Spanish portion, however, the vocabulary tested is of a lower level of difficulty (e.g., ordinary occupational terms such as *albañil,* "stonecutter, mason," words dealing with cooking, such as *espumador,* "skimmer," in short, words known to a native Spanish speaker who has not had any higher education).[8] Reading comprehension, as tested by questions based on four passages of about 400 words each, constitutes 20 percent of the exam. The remaining 20 percent of the exam is devoted to "usage," a section divided between the testing of grammar and the testing of idiomatic expressions. The grammar items test knowledge of the most highly formal written style of English (e.g., "None of them *was* present at the hearing" versus spoken style "None of them *were* present at the hearing," or "It's she" versus "It's her"), and similarly, the most formal written style of Spanish (e.g., the use of the conditional tense in the resultant clause of a contrary-to-fact assertion, such as, *Si yo lo hubiera sabido no lo habría hecho,* "If I had known it, I would not have done it," as opposed to the spoken, and in most dialects standardly accepted, *Si yo lo hubiera sabido, no lo hubiera hecho.*[9] Finally, the written exam tests knowledge of idioms and sayings (e.g., "He *hit the roof* when he heard what she had done," "She went *from the frying pan into the fire*"; *Cocinaba con ojo de buen cubero,* "she cooked with a sure eye").

The written exam specifically avoids the testing of legal vocabulary. It is intended basically to sort out those candidates who have, in both English and Spanish, a college-level vocabulary, college-level reading ability, a knowledge of formal written grammatical style, and a knowledge of idioms and sayings. The oral test, in contrast, is specifically geared toward legal terminology and interpreting skills. Furthermore, whereas the written test is a test of passive knowledge—that is, it tests the ability to recognize a correct answer from among several choices—the oral test is a test of production, intended to reveal what the interpreter will actually say in simulated courtroom proceedings.

There are three basic modes of interpreting: simultaneous, consecutive, and summary. While court interpreters are expected to be able to perform all three, the report of the Senate Committee of the Judiciary, which accompanies the Court Interpreters Act, recommends that the consecutive mode be used in general. Consecutive interpreting involves a speaker's pausing at regular intervals to allow the interpreter to render his or her speech into the target language, aloud for everyone in the courtroom to hear. Thus, the speaker and the interpreter take turns, and no overlapping speech should be heard. This mode of interpreting is typically used for foreign language witness testimony, the interpreter rendering the testimony in English for the court, and then interpreting the attorney's and judge's questions into the foreign language for the benefit of the witness. Everything rendered in English by the interpreter is recorded for the court, whereas none of the foreign language testimony or questions rendered by the interpreter in the foreign language is recorded by the court reporter.

The Court Interpreter Examination tests this mode of interpreting in a fifteen-minute simulated examination of both a Spanish-speaking witness and an English-speaking witness, one speaking in the highly technical style of an expert witness, and the other representing the speech of a low socio-economic status person. A panel of certified interpreters evaluates the interpretation, listening for specific items they will score. Of particular interest to them are specialized vocabulary: slang, vocabulary related to narcotics, weapons, medical vocabulary of the type typically used by medical expert witnesses, and so on.

The second mode of interpreting, simultaneous, is given lower preference in the Senate Committee of the Judiciary report. Simultaneous interpreting in the courtroom involves the interpreter's rendering into the foreign language whatever is being said in English, involving no pauses on the part of the English speaker. This is the mode used at the counsel table, whereby the interpreter interprets for the defendant or litigant what the attorneys, judge, and English-speaking witnesses are saying. The product of simultaneous interpreting, since it is in a foreign language, is not recorded by the court. Perhaps most importantly, it is not even heard by anyone in the courtroom other than the defendant or litigant. Simultaneous interpreting is supposed to be done in such a low voice that only the interested party can hear the interpretation, or else it is done via special equipment that allows a spatial distance between interpreter and party, and still ensures that the court does not hear the interpreter's foreign language interpretation. The Senate Committee of the Judiciary report discourages the use of simultaneous interpretation because of the greatly increased interpreting costs that it entails. On the oral portion of the Court Interpreter Examination simultaneous interpreting is tested in an approximately ten-minute segment.[10] Typically the simultaneous interpreting segment of the exam consists of jury instructions, an opening statement of an attorney, or a closing argument.

The third mode of interpreting, summary interpreting, involves distilling or condensing what has been said in the source language into the target language. This mode of interpreting is to be kept to a minimum in court interpreting, and is restricted to interpreting highly technical legal language, language that would be difficult to follow even for a native speaker of English. An example of material that is considered to be justifiably suitable for summary interpretation is a composed, written motion that is read aloud by an attorney and is intended exclusively for the ears of the judge.

One of the tasks of a court interpreter is to translate foreign language documents into English for both attorneys and the court. These are done during the interpreter's working hours, when she is not making an appearance in the courtroom. A related task of the interpreter, one that is carried out in the course of formal judicial procedure and is recorded by the court reporter, is "sight translating." Sight translating involves skimming over a piece of text silently and subsequently—within a few minutes of having skimmed it—translating it aloud, either for the benefit of the court or for the benefit of the party. Typical of the types of texts that require sight translation in court are police reports or the reports of other expert witnesses (e.g., physicians, psychologists, and so on), formal documents such as birth certificates, wills, and contracts, and transcriptions of oral statements, such as depositions.

Because sight translating involves the translating of English and foreign language documents, the Court Interpreters Examination involves the testing of both types of tasks, giving about three and a half minutes for each. Altogether, the oral component of the exam takes forty-five minutes, during which time a specific number of items are scored.[11] Between forty-five to fifty errors are permitted, allowing the interpreter an approximately 20 percent error leeway. In addition to grading the scorable points, the testing team gives a subjective evaluation of the smoothness of the overall performance.

One of the foremost considerations in evaluating the quality of an interpreter's oral examination is her ability to maintain the tone and style of the original speech. Thus, if a witness is testifying in a *barrio* (street talk) type of Spanish slang, the interpreter is expected to render her translation into the nearest equivalent English slang. Similarly, if an expert witness is testifying in a highly specialized type of vocabulary embedded in a formal English speaking style, the interpreter is expected to render her interpretation into an equivalently technical, formal Spanish style. The preservation of the original style is considered to be a crucial aspect of court interpreting.

Significantly, however, the notions of tone and style have been conceptualized very narrowly, the focus having been lexical equivalence. Even the issue of what to interpret comes under the purview of maintaining the tone and style of the speaker. A case in point is what to do with epithets and expletives. The feeling within the court interpreting professional associations and the judiciary is unequivocal: "vulgar" language used in court must be interpreted.

The broader conception behind the Court Interpreters Examination is expressed by Jon Leeth (n.d.:2), who has worked in the Administrative Office of the U.S. Courts setting up the certification program, who for years served as director of the Office of Court Reporting and Interpreting Services:

> The Court Interpreter's Act is not designed as an intercultural tool to integrate people into American society. It is an Act designed to bring justice to those individuals just as if they were English speaking. It's not designed to give them an advantage in the American judicial system. It is designed only to prevent miscarriages of justice. They have the same responsibilities as anybody else coming into a federal court to say, "I don't know what you are talking about. Could you make that clear?" So, it's on that premise and on that very firm foundation that we developed our certification test.

Interpreter Training Programs

Partly in response to the federal certification program, and partly in response to state certification programs that are either already in existence (e.g., the California program) or are being debated in state legislatures (Florida, Illinois, Iowa, Minnesota, New Jersey, and Utah [Farmer 1983:14]), several programs geared specifically to court interpreting have sprung up. In 1984 alone the Monterrey Institute of International Studies held two summer sessions in court interpreting, the University of Arizona held a four-week intensive Summer Institute for Court Interpretation, Florida International University conducted its ongoing year-round program in general translation and legal interpreting, and San Diego State University had its year-round certification program in translation and court interpreting. One of the most comprehensive new programs is the New Jersey Project on Legal Interpretation, led by the Center for Legal Studies of Montclair State College under the auspices of the New Jersey Consortium of Educators in Legal Interpretation and Translation. In 1987, the first year of its existence, the New Jersey project held an Educators' Pedagogical Institute on Legal Interpretation. It now has underway plans for "courses to upgrade the educational level of currently practicing court interpreters, continuing education courses for practicing interpreters, undergraduate preparatory programs and, ultimately, one or more graduate-level professional programs in legal interpretation, either as certificate or degree-granting programs," within its consortium of six New Jersey colleges (New Jersey Consortium, Curricular Guidelines 1988:iii).

Aside from summer courses and year-round accredited academic courses in court interpreting, there are workshops held by various court interpreter associations, the most active of which by far is the California Court Interpreters Association (C.C.I.A.). The C.C.I.A. holds an annual two-day convention, at which experienced, usually federally certified interpreters share their expertise with other members. The six-hundred member strong association also conducts regional workshops throughout the year, and keeps its members informed of news helpful to professional and would-be interpreters through its newsletter, *The Polyglot*. Other active court interpreter associations are the Court Interpreters and Translators Association (C.I.T.A.), recently renamed N.A.J.I.T. (National Association of Judiciary Interpreters and Translators), a New York–based association that draws its members primarily from the East Coast, the Judiciary Interpreters Association of Texas, and the Arizona Court Interpreters Association.

The premise behind the activities and functions of these various court interpreter training programs is that the court interpreter is a professional, one who has developed a highly specialized set of skills, along with a wide range of specialized vocabularies that regularly emerge in the courtroom. In a reprinted letter to the editor of the *Los Angeles Times,* the chairman of the Greater Los Angeles Chapter of the C.C.I.A. (Lopez 1984:3) firmly insists on the distinction between bilingual persons who seek free-lance work as court interpreters but have had no training in such work, and professional court interpreters:

> First of all, Court Interpreting is a profession which requires not just an acquaintance with courtroom procedures, but rather a comprehensive knowledge of them. Beyond that, specialized studies in the field are very often necessary, either through courses offered at colleges and universities that have recognized the need, or via participation in . . . workshops and seminars. . . . What all this means, is that Court Interpreting is a profession that requires highly specialized training. It means that one does not find a court interpreter in a beauty salon, in a store, or even in one's parents.

In essence, then, to be a well-qualified court interpreter one must indeed by bilingual. However, being bilingual is merely a necessary, but not a sufficient, condition for interpreting: technical interpreting skills combined with a wide range of vocabulary domains are necessary as well.

In the following chapter the methodology that was used to study Spanish/English interpreted proceedings will be explained, followed by an examination of the actual ongoing everyday tasks that the court interpreter's role subsumes. It will be seen that much of what occurs during the course of interpreted judicial proceedings not only contradicts the norms that professional interpreter associations have established, but undermines the intent of the judicial system, which has authorized such proceedings to go on in the first place.

4
Fieldwork Procedures

Ethnography

The basic methodology for gaining an understanding of Spanish/English interpreted judicial proceedings was that of ethnography—that is, an anthropological approach to the description of cultural groups. Whereas ethnographers in the past had restricted themselves to studying the cultures of non-Western peoples, today they include Western, urban groups as legitimate objects of anthropological study as well. Furthermore, the notion that was crystalized by Hymes (1962) as the "ethnography of speaking" has legitimized for ethnographers the possibility of studying the "ways of speaking" of any social or cultural group, be it the speech of an African tribe, a Polynesian island society, a U.S. inner-city youth group, or persons regularly engaged in courtroom interaction.

With the ethnography-of-speaking concept firmly in mind, over a period of seven months during the fall of 1982 and spring of 1983, I made nearly daily visits to courthouses to which I had been granted permission to carry out my research. At the end of the seven-month period a total of 114 hours of judicial proceedings had been tape-recorded. The tapes include the entire gamut of courtroom procedures in which interpreters regularly make their official appearances: initial appearances, preliminary hearings, arraignments, pleas, pretrial motions, trials themselves, and sentencings. Off-the-record events in which court interpreters are generally present, such as plea-bargaining sessions and attorney-client conferences, were treated as confidential, and thus fell outside the domain of this study. In essence, only those appearances by the interpreter that are considered to be accessible to the public were observed and tape-recorded.

Throughout the period of ethnographic observation tape-recording was accompanied by detailed note-taking and extensive interviewing of court interpreters and attorneys who regularly handle cases involving the use of Spanish interpreters. Thus, interviews with a number of public defenders and prosecutors became an important source of information on how the use of an interpreter alters the attorney's normal method of functioning in the courtroom. Since the overwhelming majority of appearances by court-appointed interpreters involve criminal actions (see Table 1.3), and since the modus operandi of this study was basically that of following court interpreters around during the course of their work day, nearly all the cases observed were criminal actions. The only exceptions to this pattern were cases involving nonpayment of family support fees, a civil suit, and traffic court proceedings.

Fieldwork was conducted in three tiers of court: federal district U.S. courts, state courts (to be referred to in this study as "superior courts"), and municipal courts. Whenever a case in superior court required that the court interpreter appear in a J.P. court, as was the case in preliminary hearings, such interpreted proceedings were included in the study as well. Altogether, fieldwork was conducted in nine courthouses: two federal district, three superior, two municipal, and two justice of the peace. These courthouses were located in one eastern metropolis, one large southwestern city, one middle-sized southwestern city, and one southwestern small town.

A total of eighteen interpreters were observed and tape-recorded. Of the eighteen, twelve were women and six were men. Six of the eighteen were federally certified, and six of the eighteen worked full-time in their courthouses solely in the capacity of official court interpreters. Another six worked officially in some other capacity in their courthouse, but were regularly called in by judges to perform as interpreters. A third category comprised those interpreters who were hired on a free-lance basis, and called in at a moment's notice; six fell into this category.

One cannot presuppose in a blanket fashion that a given free-lance interpreter will be called in to interpret more or less often than will a person who is employed in a courthouse in a capacity other than interpreter, but is often called on to serve as an interpreter. In a metropolis, where generally there are more federally certified interpreters available, such interpreters are usually given top priority in federal district courts.[1] Lower level courts, however, not bound by the provisions of the Court Interpreters Act and often unwilling to pay the higher fees that federally certified interpreters are entitled to, may prefer to hire free-lance noncertified interpreters. Thus, for a given interpreter to hold federal certification is by no means a guarantee of work in state or municipal courts.

In small towns, where interpreting/translating agencies and free-lance interpreters are relatively scarce and the volume of cases requiring interpreting services too low to warrant a full-time court-employed interpreter, the most common solution of the court is to make use of bilingual court employees as court interpreters when the situation demands interpreting services. Thus, in the small-town superior courthouse and municipal courthouse that I observed, the regular court interpreters were a bilingual bailiff and a bilingual court clerk, respectively.

Even in the superior court of a medium-sized city, where two full-time interpreters are employed, occasions arise when both are scheduled simultaneously for court appearances, and a third case requires an interpreter at the same moment. In such a case, rather than pay for the services of a free-lance interpreter, the court usually prefers to make use of a bilingual clerk or bailiff. A similar situation regularly arises in courthouses that have no full-time court-employed interpreter, but have contracts with interpreting agencies. In one such case the contract allows for the agency interpreters to be present in the courthouse and available for appearances for certain high-volume hours of the day (9:00 to 12:00 and 1:30 to 3:30). During low-volume hours on the court docket the need for interpreters is met through the use of bilingual bailiffs and clerks. Thus, depending upon the size of the court and the number of persons per day who will require the services of an interpreter, a court accordingly will either hire outside interpreters or make use of bilingual staff who normally work for the court in a different capacity.

The net result of this interplay of court size and hiring policy is that a bailiff/interpreter in a small town courthouse will be the sole interpreter, and may function as an interpreter several times per day, whereas a bailiff or clerk in a large city courthouse may be called in only occasionally (one or two times per week), while such court personnel in a metropolitan courthouse would rarely if ever be called in for interpreter duty. Clearly, the two factors most responsible in determining the use of outside interpreting services are (1) the budget of the court, and (2) the local availability of free-lance interpreters.

Challenges in the Fieldwork

Timing of Proceedings

One of the major difficulties encountered in this project was the unpredictability and ultimate indeterminacy of the occurrence of scheduled interpreted proceedings. Interpreted proceedings typically make up a small proportion of the daily events on a court calendar: a random sample of the initial appearances in a southwestern superior court shows that the percentage of persons needing an interpreter fluctuates between 4 and 8 percent, in a city with a population that is 40 percent Hispanic. Unless there is a trial going on for a non-English-speaking defendant, the total amount of time during which Spanish interpreting is going on in a superior court of a middle-sized city can range from zero hours to a total of four hours.

Most problematical for a single field-worker is the fact that courthouses tend to schedule short procedures (e.g., arraignments, pleas, pretrial motions) in the same given time slot, so that two or three cases needing interpreting services will be scheduled for the same time slot in different courtrooms. This occurs because judges tend to schedule the short procedures as the first event of the day, leaving the rest of the day open to trials in progress. When two interpreters are sitting in different courtrooms during the same time slot, it is impossible for a single field-worker to "catch" the appearances of both interpreters. One will have to be foregone. Furthermore, in the lower level courts observed, the listing of the various cases for a given time slot of a particular judge has no relation to reality: in some courthouses judges do not call the parties in the order in which their names appear on the court calendar. Thus, there may be six defendants listed for the 8:30–10:00 A.M. slot, but they will not at all necessarily be called in the order in which their names appear. Thus, the possibility of running from one courtroom to another in order to catch defendant Rodríguez who is listed first on Judge Jones' calendar, and then to observe the case of defendant Hernández, who is sixth on Judge Brown's calendar, will not work at all. It should be noted, however, that federal district courts function in a much more orderly, predictable way, so that when defendant Gómez is scheduled to appear for his arraignment at 9:30, his arraignment can be expected to begin at 9:30.

Another element of indeterminacy is whether a scheduled judicial procedure will occur at all. A superior court interpreter, not knowing if defendant Alvarez will actually have his change of plea at 8:45 A.M., as listed on the daily calendar, may discover at 10:00 A.M. that the change of plea will not occur at all because the defendant has changed his mind. Thus, for the interpreter, the need for patience and a sense of uncertainty are part of the normal everyday routine. For the ethnolinguist, they present a tremendous stumbling block and a constant source of frustration in gathering data.

Typically, scheduled judicial procedures do not happen in the courtroom because one of the attorneys, more often than not the defense attorney, requests a "continuation," or postponement, of the procedure. This is often a request for additional time to prepare the case adequately, and in the case of public defenders, who are usually the ones assigned to the non-English-speaking, typically indigent defendant, enormous case loads do indeed justify the requests for continuation.

Most frustrating of all for the ethnolinguist is the last-minute plea bargaining before the onset of a trial. Since most courtroom procedures are relatively brief, only trials can provide hours and hours of linguistic material. More than once during the course of the fieldwork, trials that had been scheduled to begin on a specific date were called off altogether on account of a plea bargain that had been reached—an hour before the scheduled beginning of the trial.

Tape-Recording in the Courtroom

Tape-recording in the courtroom involved two principal problems: obtaining the permission to tape and devising a feasible method of overcoming the logistical difficulties of taping. Overwhelmingly, the chief judges who were asked to cooperate in the project did so willingly and were supportive of my efforts. They facilitated the project by passing on memos to the other judges, asking them to cooperate with me. Nevertheless, before tape-recording in any given judge's courtroom, I made sure to contact the individual judge through his/her clerk, to obtain further permission and to inform him/her that I would be present and taping that morning.

The right to tape-record was often justified by court administrative rules. In one state where fieldwork was carried out, for example, a one-year experimental ruling had just been put into effect allowing the mass media to bring television and other kinds of electronic equipment into the courtrooms of state courts. In this particular courthouse I had the right to tape-record under this new ruling and under an additional rule that permitted persons to bring in electronic equipment by right of "educational exemption" from the general rule prohibiting the use of such equipment.

In addition to asking the permission of every individual judge, permission to tape-record was asked of every defendant and of his attorney before an impending judicial procedure. Only in one instance was permission denied by an attorney. This was a drug case in a federal district court involving a very large sum of narcotics money. The defense attorney, a highly paid lawyer who had been brought in from another part of the country to defend this particular client, was very suspicious of persons affiliated with the court, so much so that he refused the services of the federally certified court interpreter and hired his own private interpreter instead. The court, fearing a potential mistrial over the quality of the ensuing interpreting, assigned its own interpreter to be present throughout the trial, as a check on the defense's interpreter. The defense attorney did not want my recording equipment present at the defense table, fearing that I would be privy to confidential attorney/client conferences. For this reason, he denied me permission to record his interpreter.

A further problem in gaining the court's permission to tape-record came from an interpreter. The person in question headed a translating/interpreting agency that held the annual contract to provide all interpreting services to a municipal courthouse. This interpreter, herself federally certified, was ever-suspicious of persons who might become competitive with her agency. Always guarding her expertise, she feared that my tape-recording her would ultimately divulge the secrets of her trade to others who might wish to enter into the interpreting profession. This was no small hurdle to overcome, for the presiding judge in the courthouse was equally as mistrustful of the motives behind the request to tape-record, and it took a great deal of persuasion to convince him before he ultimately gave his consent.

Difficulties in taping sometimes came from entirely unexpected sources. One such case was that of a court reporter. On the whole, court reporters were somewhat suspicious of someone taping court proceedings, inasmuch as they earn their livelihood by transcribing their notations and selling their transcriptions to interested parties. However, when I explained to them that it was absolutely necessary for me to tape the proceedings because they were not reporting any of the Spanish speech, their fears were assuaged. Nevertheless, in one instance an older reporter who had a reputation for being cantankerous, literally exploded in anger upon seeing my recording equipment. It was only after my personal appeal to the judge in his chambers and the judge's subsequent mollification of the reporter that I was allowed to proceed with my taping.

Above and beyond the question of obtaining permission to tape, there was the technical problem of simultaneously taping several speakers: the interpreter, the examining attorney, the witness, and the judge. The tape-recording facilities available in many courtrooms proved to be ineffectual in recording both interpreters and other parties at the same time. For one thing, even when the court's recording equipment was turned on (and in courts where reporters were present this was rarely the case), no microphone could have picked up the hushed tones of an interpreter doing simultaneous interpreting. In some courts (e.g., municipal and justice of the peace courts), where no court reporter was present and all proceedings were regularly taped for the purpose of future transcription in the event of an affirmative arraignment to superior court, or in the case of an appeal in city court, making use of the court's recording equipment would have been only moderately effective. It would have provided a good recording of consecutive interpreting, either at the witness stand, or before the judge, in instances where the judge examines a defendant. It still would have omitted all the simultaneous interpreting that goes on at the defense counsel table, and, as will be discussed in chapter 5, this constitutes the bulk of an interpreter's job in the courtroom.

Once the possibility of using the court's recording facilities was dismissed, a personal recording setup had to be devised. It required a two-track, or stereo, input, so that for the purposes of transcription the tracks could later be separated. In addition, it required inconspicuousness. Thus, the notion of placing individual recorders on the tables of each of the attorneys, on the judge's bench, and on the witness stand was dismissed. Furthermore, because lawyers move around from counsel table to the witness stand, to the judge's bench, and to the clerk's desk, placing a fixed recorder on the counsel table would have been entirely ineffectual. The recording system, therefore, had to be in my possession, to be controlled by me as speakers moved about.

To capture the speech of the attorneys, judge, and witnesses, therefore, a sensitive "zoom" type of condenser microphone was chosen (Sony ECM Z300). This is similar to the type of microphone used in presidential news conferences. Its utility lies in the fact that it picks up sounds over long distances and magnifies them. In addition, the microphone is directional, so that it can control the radius of sounds that it will pick up. Thus, whoever is holding the microphone can either expand the range from which sounds will be received, or can narrow the range, to the voice of a single speaker, for instance. In other words, it is superior to a regular condenser microphone, which picks up all sounds evenly, giving a cough from behind the same volume as a voice from in front. Furthermore, the zoom microphone has the added advantage that its directionality is totally controlled by the hand. Thus, it allows the recording operator to sit perfectly still, the only visible movement being a rotation of the wrist as the microphone is pointed alternately at the examining attorney, witness, and judge. The ability to be physically still and to make only the most imperceptible movements is crucial in a trial, where unobtrusiveness on the part of outside observers is mandatory. The zoom microphone thus turned out to be an ideal solution to the problem of taping mobile participants in the courtroom.

The problem of taping the interpreter was the greatest challenge of all, since she too is physically mobile—moving from defense table to witness stand during trials, and from defense table to judge's bench during arraignments, changes of plea, and sentencings. Furthermore, the problem of recording the simultaneous interpreting that is done in a near-whisper had to be overcome. A microphone was needed that was sufficiently sensitive to pick up such a low volume. The answer to the problem of speaker mobility and low volume of speech was a clip-on condenser microphone (Realistic 33–1056A), the type used by television newscasters and talk-show hosts. This microphone was clipped onto the interpreter's blouse or dress, and the other end plugged into a Sony TCS 300 stereo cassette recorder, usually with an extension cord between.

Thus, plugged into the cassette recorder were both the zoom microphone, pointed at the English speakers, and the clip-on microphone that was connected to the interpreter. The entire recording kit, along with several extra extension cords, a battery pack, and a supply of cassette tapes, fit comfortably into an attaché case, which made transportation within the courthouse easy, and appearances in the courtroom unobtrusive. In keeping with courtroom decorum and protocol, and in an effort to look as inconspicuous as possible, I dressed in formal attorney-style clothing, and in fact was often mistaken for an attorney by other attorneys. Other court personnel eventually began to associate me with the court interpreters' offices, and gradually accepted my presence without undue attention and commentary.

Transcribing the Tapes

The transcription process was begun shortly after the taping process was initiated. It was expected that transcribing the tapes would consume many hours of research assistant time, and in fact it did. To fully transcribe a 90-minute cassette of interpreted proceedings took an average of 40 hours: about 20 hours to transcribe the Spanish and 20 hours to transcribe the English. Given that 76 90-minute cassettes were recorded, or 114 hours of recorded material, it is estimated that 4,500 hours of labor went into transcribing the tapes. To make sure the transcriptions were accurate, a separate set of transcribers were hired to listen to the recordings and to correct any errors or fill in gaps that were present in the original transcriptions. An additional 2,000 hours went into this checking procedure.

To ensure the highest possible quality of the transcriptions, and to prevent the possible contaminating effect of the English recorded speech on the transcription of the Spanish, and vice versa, I decided to use two separate sets of transcribers. One group consisted of monolingual English speakers who were assigned the task of transcribing the English speech. While it had been assumed at the outset that the large pool of Mexican-American students studying at my home university would be the logical source of my Spanish transcribers, this turned out not to be the case, for after administering to a number of such students a brief transcribing test, I discovered that very few had a sufficient command of spoken Spanish to do the task, and that their ability to write Spanish was even more limited. Hence, the other group consisted of students of Latin American origin, most of whom had completed high school in their respective Spanish-speaking country of origin, but all of whom had gone as far as junior high school in a Spanish-speaking educational system. This ensured a group that was not only in command of spoken Spanish, but had a command of written Spanish as well. Some had been schooled in Mexican border cities. Others had been educated in Puerto Rico, and were in mainland U.S.A. to obtain their higher education.

In sum, while the transcribing of the cassette tapes was an enormous task, the final product is of high quality, both on account of the checking procedure, and because of the availability of literate native English speakers and native Spanish speakers who were equally as literate in their mother tongue.

Participant Observation in Court Interpreter Training Programs

To discover what professional court interpreters consider to be the major problems of court interpreting, and to find out what they perceive to be the important issues to keep in mind in the course of interpreting and in their capacity as court personnel, I participated in a four-week intensive institute in court interpreting, the statewide conferences of two court interpreters associations, and a conference on interpreting/translating held by an association dedicated to the academic study of that field.

In the summer of 1983, having completed the fieldwork in the courtroom and having had a large number of the tapes transcribed, I became one of sixty students to enroll in the experimental Summer Institute for Court Interpretation held at the University of Arizona. This was an intensive (140-hour) institute that taught the techniques of simultaneous and consecutive interpreting, sight translating, selected features of nonstandard Spanish and English, American criminal procedure and terminology related to it, a number of aspects related to the duties of the court interpreter, including ethical considerations associated with the job, and, finally, a familiarization with domains of vocabulary that frequently emerge in the courtroom.

The institute was staffed by four main instructors, three of whom were federally certified court interpreters, and were among the consultants who gave input into each newly created federal court interpreters examination. Sofia Zahler, director of court interpreting services in the federal Central District of California, had been a professor of law in Chile before immigrating to the United States. Her expert knowledge of the differences between the American legal system and Latin American systems of justice is widely renowned, and she has taught courses in "Spanish for lawyers" at some of the University of California campuses. Ely Weinstein, a former president of the California Court Interpreters Association, had worked for years in Los Angeles as a full-time municipal and then superior court interpreter until her untimely death. Frank Almeida, the third court interpreter trainer, is a high school Spanish instructor who works part-time as a court interpreter. Zahler and Almeida are co-authors of two manuals for court interpreters (Almeida and Zahler 1977; Almeida, Rainoff, and Zahler 1979), both of which contain extensive glossaries of terms considered to be among the most frequently needed by court interpreters. The fourth instructor at the institute was Theodore Fagan, who for many years had served as chief interpreter at the United Nations.

In addition to learning the techniques of court interpreting from experts in the field, I attended the annual conference of the C.C.I.A., which is a three-day series of workshops for actual and prospective interpreters. In addition, I attended a meeting of the Arizona Court Interpreters Association, and a series of locally held workshops organized by professional court interpreters, intended to expand the knowledge of persons working in the profession. Finally, I attended the meeting of the Translators and Interpreters Educational Society (T.I.E.S.), an association interested in translating and interpreting in general, from an academic standpoint (i.e., teaching and conducting research on the subject).

It is worth noting that participant observation at the various court interpreter training programs became a highly valuable complement to the seven months of participant observation and tape-recording in the various courthouses that I had visited. The training programs revealed the "ideal type" of court interpreter: they explained how an interpreter *ought to* behave in the courtroom, they laid out the dos and don'ts of court interpreting. They gave me a guidepost by which to measure the behavior that I had observed in the real-life courtroom situations. At the same time, they revealed those aspects of court interpreting that interpreters and judicial officers consider to be the important ones, and, conversely, in their lack of attention to entire realms of linguistic behavior, revealed that these realms were not given consideration at all. As will be shown in the next chapters, interpreters and interpreter trainers are overwhelmingly concerned with vocabulary, very little concerned with grammar, and almost completely unaware of pragmatic aspects of speech. Finally, whereas interpreters are to an extent aware of the problematical situations in which attorneys and judges often place them, they are only dimly aware of their coercive influence on persons testifying on the witness stand.

5

The Ethnography of the Bilingual Courtroom

Ethnographers interested in linguistic behavior have long looked at the speaker's role as a key variable in determining what a person will say in a given situation and how he or she will say it (Hymes 1962; 1972). Participants in a particular linguistic setting have various sorts of expectations regarding the verbal behavior of other participants. This chapter explores the verbal behavior of a relatively new participant in what is typically a highly ritualized linguistic setting: the courtroom. It demonstrates that what is expected in terms of verbal behavior on the part of an official verbal participant in the courtroom is far from fulfilled. Specifically, this chapter analyzes the behavior of the foreign language court interpreter and tries to show what it is that the social setting would require of her, and why it is that these expectations in reality are not fulfilled.

It is the thesis of this book that in an ideal world, the American legal system would choose to have the court interpreter physically invisible and vocally silent, if that were at all possible. That is to say, ideally she should not exist as a distinct verbal participant in her own right during the course of a judicial proceeding. In effect, she is meant to speak solely in place of the other participants in the courtroom, those considered to legitimately hold the right to speak: the attorneys, witnesses, plaintiffs, defendants, and the judge. The interpreter must perform this function whenever English speech needs to be interpreted into a foreign language for the benefit of a non-English-speaking witness or defendant, and whenever foreign language testimony must be interpreted into English for the benefit of the judge, attorneys, and jury.

It will be shown in this chapter why the wishes of the judicial system are far from realized, and that in fact, the court interpreter plays a far more active verbal role than the system actually realizes. Finally, it will be shown that the interpreter's verbal role is very much tied to the linguistic control of "legitimate" participants in judicial proceedings, a degree of control that often is tantamount to linguistic coercion.

How Attention is Shifted to the Interpreter by Court Proceedings and by Other Parties

Consciousness of the Presence of the Court Interpreter

When an interpreter is at work during a judicial proceeding, she is not simply "part of the furniture" of the courtroom. She does not simply melt into the woodwork, even though judges would prefer that she do so. Rather, attention is constantly drawn to her for a number of reasons. As the following sections demonstrate, some of these reasons have to do with the actions of the judge and the attorneys, while others have to do with the behavior of the interpreter herself.

How Judges and Attorneys Draw Attention to the Interpreter. From the moment an interpreter begins functioning as an interpreter at a judicial proceeding, attention is directed toward her. Before she is permitted to begin her work in any given courtroom at any stage of a case pending before the court, the interpreter must be sworn in. Interpreters are required to swear an oath to the effect that they will interpret to the best of their ability, as accurately as possible, the proceeding at hand. This sworn statement must be made in each courtroom in which the interpreter is scheduled to interpret. It means being sworn in several times a day, and raises the very possibility that her interpretation might not always be accurate. Thus, the requirement of the court that the interpreter must take an oath in open court calls attention to the interpreter from the outset of a proceeding.

The issue of interpreter accuracy, which is raised by the swearing-in process, becomes salient when interpretations given by court interpreters are challenged in the course of the proceeding. The challenge is usually made by bilingual attorneys. When such cases arise the interpreter is put on the stand as a witness, and must testify to the accuracy of her choice of words. If the routine, daily swearing-in process itself calls attention to the interpreter, then the challenging of an interpreter's interpretations throws an even brighter spotlight on her. It certainly acts to make other persons in the courtroom aware that the interpreter is not a computerlike translating machine, one that needs only to be plugged in at will. It calls attention to the fact that the interpreter is a person who has developed a set of skills to a greater or lesser degree, and, additionally, that she is a person whose integrity cannot automatically be taken for granted. She is held accountable for the accuracy of her interpreting.

Interpreters are asked to testify not only to the accuracy of their own interpretations, but to that of other interpreters as well, when disputes arise. A common situation in which interpreters are made to give expert testimony is in cases in which the translation of documents and formulaic statements is called into question. One federal court interpreter (personal communication) has had to testify to the accuracy of the Spanish translation of a "consent to search" form used by the Federal Drug Enforcement Administration. This form allows federal drug enforcement officials to search a person and his premises without a regular search warrant. The person who is to be searched must sign that he has been "requested" to consent to a search of his person and premises. One Spanish translation of this form used the word *requerir,* "require," rather than an equivalent of the verb "request," such as *pedir.* The result of this poor translation was an attempt on the part of the defense attorney to have the case against his client dismissed on the grounds that the client had not been given a valid "consent to search" form to sign.

In another case (Reese and Reese 1984), the improper translation of the Miranda rights was at issue. In People v. Diaz (1983) [140 Cal. App. 3d 812], report Reese and Reese (1984), the court ruled that the defendant had not been effectively advised of his rights, because of an inadequate translation of the fourth branch of the Miranda rights. In English that right reads as follows: "If you cannot afford to hire a lawyer, one will be appointed to represent you before any questioning, if you wish one." The California Highway Patrol Miranda card had the following translation printed on it: *Si no puede conseguir un abogado, se le puede nombrar uno antes de que le hagan preguntas.* Two certified court interpreters testified that the translation was inaccurate, for it did not imply that if a person could not *afford* a lawyer, one would be appointed to represent him. The Court agreed with the interpreters, acknowledging that the Spanish word *conseguir,* "obtain," did not convey the idea intended by the Miranda rights—namely, that indigent defendants have a right to be represented by an attorney *at no cost to them,* if they cannot pay for one. The Court, relying on the expert testimony of the two interpreters, came to the following conclusion (Reese and Reese 1984:5):

> If the phrase "sin pagar" (meaning "without pay" or "without paying") had been used in the advisement in question, appellant would certainly have been adequately advised that indigent status would entitle him to appointed counsel. In so stating, we recognize that frequently there is no single word in a foreign language which carries the identical meaning of a single word in the English language. In this regard, we examined four different Spanish translations (including the California Highway Patrol card used in this case) of the Mi-

randa advisement at issue. We discovered that none of the translations were identical. However, unlike the California Highway Patrol's translation, those translations which used the word "conseguir" also contained additional qualifying phrases such as "sin pagar."

Apparently, at the heart of this questioning of the accuracy of the Miranda rights translation is the translator's rendition of the word "afford." Whereas dictionaries do list near-equivalents, such as *costearse*, apparently the translator of the document in question had not been familiar with this lexical item or with some other satisfactory gloss. Critical to this case is the difference in meaning between the words "afford" and "obtain" (the English equivalent of the Spanish word used in the translation, *conseguir*): "afford" implies "capable of paying," whereas "obtain" carries no such implication. One rendition found to be satisfactory by the judge quoted above is to add to the verb *conseguir* the additional phrase *sin pagar.*

The Voir Dire. Even when interpreters are not in the limelight of the witness stand, but are merely sitting unobtrusively at the defense counsel table doing simultaneous interpreting, judges bring the interpreter to the attention of others in the courtroom. Nowhere is this more explicitly done than during jury selection. References to the presence of the court interpreter and questions regarding the attitudes of prospective jurors toward the use of an interpreter during bilingual trials are a regular feature of the voir dire—that is, the questioning of prospective jurors for purposes of selection to the jury panel. Judges generally begin questioning the pool of juror candidates in this regard by formally introducing the interpreter to them. This is usually done at the time when the attorneys are introduced by name to the prospective jurors. Just as the attorneys must be identified to jurors, so too must the interpreter, whose presence at the defense table must somehow be accounted for. Otherwise the jury might conclude that she is an attorney herself, a member of the defense team. The following text comes from the voir dire of a federal narcotics trial:[1]

5.1 JUDGE: All right. Now the defendant before you is Mr. Juan Carlos Ortega. Would you mind standing up? [pause] And also face these folks back here. All right, any of you know Mr. Ortega? All right, thank you. Uh, the, uh, defendant is represented by Mr. John Turner, T-U-R-N-E-R. Any of you know Mr. Turner? And now, sitting with, uh the defendant, Mr. Ortega, Mrs. Alicia Calderón, who's the interpreter, . . . Spanish interpreter. All right, now the government is represented by Mr. William M. Donelly, and he's an assistant United States Attorney here in the First district of El Paso. Sitting with him is a drug enforcement agent, Miss Kelly Porter. Uh, any of you know either of them?

The judge might then briefly explain the role of the interpreter, and go on to ask if any of the prospective jurors have any objection to the use of an interpreter during the trial, or would feel uncomfortable about her carrying out this task. The following text is typical of the voir dire questions that were asked at trials observed by this investigator:

5.2 JUDGE: Now you'll notice the defendant is having this translated for him into Spanish. Would the fact that uh, he, he, uh speaks Spanish, and not English, would that affect your ability to be absolutely, to be absolutely fair? And to the uh, government?

In one federal trial that was observed, the judge did not include in the voir dire any questions regarding the use of an interpreter, yet a prospective juror raised the issue as one that was problematical for her. The following interchange took place between judge and prospective juror:

5.3 JUDGE [addressing panel of jurors]: Very often in questioning a jury I miss the most important question, as to whether or not you can sit as a completely fair and impartial juror. It would be nice if we had a little crystal ball we could look into and know, uh what you are thinking right now. Maybe I wouldn't wanna know. [Laughter from jurors]. But, it might be helpful to us, uh, in determining whether you can sit as a completely fair and impartial juror. So whether I refer to it in any way whatsoever, let me ask you if you can think of any reason why you could not sit and be a completely fair and impartial juror. And maybe you might think, "Well, this might sound silly and I really don't want to, uh, state it," but if you think of anything, tell us about it. Thank you. Yes?
PROSPECTIVE JUROR: Your honor, I work with deaf people as an interpreter, a volunteer interpreter, and I know the problems that are involved in, lacking verbal communication, and it really bothers me

that they, the defendants do not speak English and have to,—no reflection on the interpreter—but it depends solely on the interpreter, for their understanding.

JUDGE: Of what is going on here?

PROSPECTIVE JUROR: Yes, ma'am, and what is happening.

JUDGE: It used t'be in the, in the, just about five or six years ago we didn't even have an interpreter in the courtroom.

PROSPECTIVE JUROR: I know [laughing].

JUDGE: It is, it is difficult, uh, of course, it's acceptable and it's legal the way it's done and, uh, I think we have one of the best interpreters, uh,

PROSPECTIVE JUROR: Yes, ma'am.

JUDGE: You agree with that, too?

PROSPECTIVE JUROR: I agree, but I also deal with deaf people and I know that many times they tell you they understand and they don't.

JUDGE: Well are you, uh [pause], are you uh telling me that you, you're not sure you can be fair and impartial or uh . . .

PROSPECTIVE JUROR: I'm telling you I don't,—I think it would influence me greatly, yes, ma'am.

JUDGE: Uh, of course, what is going to be testified to has already occurred. All of what is going on here is just an interpretation of what the witnesses say. Uh, it doesn't affect the act itself or the alleged act itself or anything of that nature, which to me is a little different than, uh, if we were just starting with the, all the acts now. I'm not trying t'influence you, but I am not sure that that would affect you, uh, in deciding the case. Yes?

DEFENSE ATTORNEY: Can I say something your honor?

JUDGE: Sure.

DEFENSE ATTORNEY: They both speak English, but they're more comfortable with their entire language in Spanish, too, in the courtroom.

JUDGE: Does that affect you in any way?

PROSPECTIVE JUROR: No, that satisfies me.

JUDGE: Thank you, and I really appreciate your speaking out.

What the voir dire sequence in text 5.3 shows is that a jury candidate has called extra attention to the interpretation process, attention of an unflattering kind. She has implied that interpreting is not always as effective as persons are led to believe. Her comments raise the whole issue of whether interpreting should be carried out in the first place, and casts doubt on the validity of the interpretation that is to follow. Interestingly, because of the objection raised by the prospective juror, one piece of information regarding the co-defendants emerges: they understand and speak English, but feel more comfortable hearing Spanish in addition to English.

This type of situation, where the defendant is bilingual but asks to have an interpreter by his side throughout the trial, occurs frequently. Judges approve such requests sometimes in order to avoid the risk of a future appeal should the trial end in a conviction, since failure to be provided with an interpreter is a frequently used ground for appeals (e.g., State v. Vasquez, 1942). The fact that the defendants in this particular case understand English well emerged publicly only because of the hesitancy expressed by the prospective juror. The whole issue of whether the interpreter should be there at all was thus inadvertently raised by the jury candidate and became even more subject to question as a result of the attorney's efforts to allay the woman's qualms. In effect, the comments of the prospective juror inadvertently opened up a can of worms regarding the use of a court interpreter in that trial.

Addressing the Interpreter rather than the Witness or Defendant. Judges and attorneys alike inadvertently draw attention to the interpreter by departing from one of the standard rules for addressing interpreter-assisted witnesses or defendants. That rule, as formulated by the Texas Judiciary Interpreters Association, for example, states (Texas Judiciary[2]):

> The interpretation shall be conducted in the first and second person, as if the interpreter did not exist. The non-English speaking client should be informed of this, so as to avoid confusion. For instance, the question should be "What is your name?" NOT "Ask him what his name is." Likewise, the interpreter shall respond for the client "My name is . . ." NOT "He says his name is . . ."

Similarly, the guidelines proposed by the California Judicial Council (Standards of Judicial Administration, sec. 18.1, 1981) instruct interpreters in the following way: "All statements made in the first person should be interpreted in the first person. For example, a statement or question should not be introduced with the words, 'He says. . . .'" Furthermore, in the instructions to counsel, the guidelines state that, "All questions by counsel examining a non-English speaking witness should be directed to the witness and not the interpreter. For example, do not say, 'Ask him if. . . .' "

Many lawyers, particularly those who have never examined a witness through an interpreter, are clearly not aware of this basic approach to asking questions of a non-English-speaking witness. However, even attorneys and judges who have worked frequently with interpreters will sometimes lapse into addressing the interpreter rather than the witness or defendant. This usually comes about during moments of confusion and frustration, when the examiner has asked the same question more than once, but is not getting an appropriate reply to the question. Typically, this occurs during arraignments and changes of plea, when the judge explains to the defendant the alternative pleas that are available to him and the consequences of choosing one versus another.

The following text, taken from a change of plea proceeding illustrates a typical situation in which the interpreter is suddenly addressed directly by the judge or attorney, and is requested to ask the defendant a particular question. Here, rather than lapsing unconsciously into directly addressing the interpreter, the attorney deliberately asks permission of the judge to speak directly to the interpreter:

5.4 JUDGE: All right, what is your plea to count two, "guilty" or "not guilty"?

INTERPRETER: *Bien, ¿cómo se declara Ud. del cargo número dos, "culpable" o "no culpable"?*

DEFENDANT: *¿De la, que la traía? Sí.*

INTERPRETER: Of having brought it? Yes.

JUDGE: Now, now what you're charged with in count two is having the cocaine, having possession of it with intent to distribute it, that is, to give it to somebody else, or to sell it or, . . .

INTERPRETER: *De lo que la acusan en el cargo número dos, es de haber tenido en su poder la cocaína, de haber tenido posesión con intención de distribuirla, o sea dársela a alguna otra persona.*

DEFENDANT: *De distribuirla, no.*

INTERPRETER: Not to distribute it.

JUDGE: Mrs. García, tell me, were you going, what were you gonna do with that cocaine you had?

INTERPRETER: *Bueno, señora García, dígame una cosa, ¿y qué iba Ud. a hacer con esa cocaína que traía?*

DEFENDANT: *La iba a dar. En el aeropuerto.*

INTERPRETER: I was going to give it at the airport.

JUDGE: All right now, so what do you plead, "guilty" or "not guilty" to that charge two?

INTERPRETER: *Bien, ahora, entonces, ¿cómo se declara Ud., "culpable" o "no culpable" de ese cargo número dos?*

DEFENDANT: *¿De posesión?*

INTERPRETER: Of the possession?

JUDGE: Yes, what are you, guilty or not guilty?

DEFENDANT: *Sí, porque lo traía.*

INTERPRETER: *¿Culpable o no culpable, señora?*

DEFENDANT: *¿Cómo?*

INTERPRETER: What?

JUDGE: *Culpable* [said in Spanish], excuse me, guilty or not guilty?

INTERPRETER: [slowly and distinctly] *¿Culpable o no culpable?*

DEFENDANT: *Sí, porque yo lo traía.*

INTERPRETER: Yes, because I had it.

JUDGE: See, you must either tell me you are guilty or not guilty. Do you plead guilty?

INTERPRETER: *No, tiene Ud. que decirme o que es culpable, o que no es culpable.*

DEFENDANT: *Sí, porque lo tenía.*

INTERPRETER: Yes, because I had it.

DEFENSE ATTORNEY: Judge, can I me-, merely tell her, she doesn't seem to explain it to her, she must say it out loud to the judge that she is guilty or not guilty?

INTERPRETER: *¿Podría yo decirle?* [addressing defendant] *Parece, tiene Ud. que decirle al juez que es Ud. culpable o que no es culpable.* (It seems that you have to tell the judge either that you're guilty or that you're not guilty.)

DEFENDANT: *Sí.*

INTERPRETER: Yes.

DEFENSE ATTORNEY [addressing interpreter]: So she's gotta say it, tell her to say it.

INTERPRETER: *O sea que tiene Ud. que decirlo. ¡Dígalo! ¿Qué es?* (That is, you have to say it. Say it! What are you?)[3]

DEFENSE ATTORNEY: Say it!

INTERPRETER: *¡Dígalo!*

JUDGE: Can you say the word *"culpable"*?[4]
INTERPRETER: *¿Puede Ud. decir la palabra "culpable"?*
DEFENDANT: *Culpable, ¡ah, sí!*
INTERPRETER: Guilty, oh yes!
JUDGE: Is that what you are? Are you guilty?
INTERPRETER: *¿Eso es lo que es, es Ud. realmente culpable?*
DEFENDANT: *Sí, culpable.*
INTERPRETER: Yes, guilty.
JUDGE: Now, you're making this plea of guilty voluntarily and of your own free will?
INTERPRETER: *Ahora, se está Ud. declarando culpable voluntariamente de su propia voluntad?*
DEFENDANT: *Sí.*
INTERPRETER: Yes.

It should be stressed that the situation presented above is characterized by increasing frustration and irritation on the part of the judge, and a mounting tension in the defense attorney, who is trying to effectuate the change of plea as smoothly as possible. The failure on the part of the defendant to produce the word "guilty" eventually leads the judge to prompt the defendant, and to go so far as to use the Spanish equivalent of the word "guilty" ("Can you say the word *culpable?*"). This particular type of confusion, where a defendant or a witness answers yes/no to a *wh-* type of question (i.e., a type of question requiring more substantive information for an answer), is very common in proceedings involving the non-English-speaking. It is particularly problematical during the plea and change of plea, where the Court insists upon the defendant's stating the words "guilty" or "not guilty."

As can be seen in the instance cited above, when communications break down between the examiner and the defendant, the examiner will temporarily dispense with the norm of speaking directly to the defendant through the interpreter, and instead will talk to the interpreter, instructing her to convey the question to the party undergoing examination ("So she's gotta say it, tell her to say it"). Thus, the examiner will violate the basic rules for questioning a defendant or witness through an interpreter. This, in turn, forces the interpreter into the position of giving instructions to the witness or defendant, which fundamentally alters the nature of her prescribed role in court. Instead of merely rendering speech from the source language into the target language, she becomes an active verbal participant in the interaction, one who, from an observer's vantage point, appears to be initiating dialogue with the person under oath.

In lower-level courts, particularly municipal courts, the active participation of the interpreter is even greater. There attorneys, and judges as well, will concede to the interpreter a degree of authority that officially is restricted to attorneys. This transfer of attorneylike functions to the interpreter is a result of the absence of defense attorneys at various sorts of municipal proceedings. For instance, during the course of traffic arraignments, a proceeding that sometimes is combined with sentencings, judges rely heavily on interpreters to process the cases. In text 5.5, cited below, the judge asks the interpreter her opinion as to whether the defendant has understood the charges against her:

5.5 JUDGE: All right, uhm, I'm gonna find you guilty because I believe that,—when you crossed over,—the two cars had to,—stop or slow down,—and they had the right of way to go through without stopping,—that when you crossed over,—you violated their right of way to keep going without interruption.

INTERPRETER: *Entonces la voy a encontrar culpable porque creo que Ud. cuando cruzó la carretera había dos carros que tuvieron que detenerse o detener su velocidad y estos dos carros tenían el derecho de paso de, de, sin tener que detenerse. Cuando Ud. cruzó Ud. violó su derecho de paso de poder continuar sin tener que, sin tener interrupción de* [

DEFENDANT: [*Yo tenía buen rato en la "middle line" esperando. Yo tenía buen rato esperando en el "middle line" cuando el oficial*

INTERPRETER: I'd been, uh, I'd been waiting at the, uh middle lane for a while when the officer

JUDGE [addressing interpreter]: Do you feel that she understands the charge or not?

INTERPRETER [addressing judge]: Yes, your honor.

DEFENDANT: Yes, I understand.

In this case, the defendant is bilingual, although a dominant Spanish speaker. The violation of the norm that interpreters should speak only on behalf of another speaker seems to lead the defendant to break the rule that defendants and witnesses are supposed to follow—namely, speak only when you have been addressed directly. Thus, the defendant answers the judge, even though she has not been spoken to during the interchange. At a moment such as this, then, once one rule of procedure has been broken, other rules of verbal interaction fall by the wayside as well, and so the entire routine of question/answer sequences has been temporarily halted. There has been, in effect, a temporary reinterpretation of the arraignment format, and this is a direct consequence of the judge's abandoning the court's own norms regarding the role of the interpreter. According to those norms, the judge should not have asked the interpreter whether she believed that the defendant had understood the charges. Rather, he should have addressed his question to the defendant directly, using the interpreter as an interpreter, and not as an active third party to the interaction.

The Interpreter's Own Attention-Drawing Behavior

Interpreters try their best to be as inconspicuous as possible during courtroom proceedings. They are fully aware that they are not supposed to make their presence felt, and that everyone's attention ought to be riveted on the speakers for whom they are interpreting. Nevertheless, circumstances arise in which the interpreter feels she must intrude upon the proceeding, and this usually occurs when she recognizes a problem of interpreting.

It must be emphasized that professional court interpreters are expected to interpret verbatim what a speaker has said.[5] This means that if an attorney or judge has made any linguistic errors in the formulation of a question or statement, theoretically it is the interpreter's duty to interpret the erroneously worded English utterance into as close an equivalent as possible in the target language, in this case Spanish. Similarly, if a witness or defendant in reply to a question answers improperly (e.g., tangentially, off-target), the interpreter's obligation is to interpret that response in the nearest English equivalent, even though the outcome potentially may sound evasive or even nonsensical to those in the courtroom. Clearly, accurately interpreting a witness's off-target reply will put the interpreter into a certain jeopardy: she runs the risk of looking incompetent herself. In other words, if an interpreter correctly interprets a poorly worded answer, it is very possible that the monolingual judge or attorney might assume that a faulty interpretation has been made.

Furthermore, if the interpreter is highly professional, she will not succumb to the temptation of switching from the first-person pronoun to a third-person reference to the witness (i.e., she will refrain from prefacing her interpretation with the phrase, "He says that . . ."). Consequently, when a good interpreter is interpreting for a noncomprehending witness or defendant, she must bear the burden of possibly sounding stupid, inept, and incompetent. Often this impression accompanies a reply of *No comprendo,* or, "I don't understand." Attorneys and judges at times are not certain if the interpreter is speaking for herself, or interpreting for the witness or defendant. Jurors, who have far less experience in observing interpreters at work, may even more easily jump to the conclusion that the English statement "I don't understand" is a statement originating with the interpreter rather than with the Spanish speaker.

Interpreter Attempts to Clarify Witnesses' or Defendants' Answers and Attorneys' Questions. When a witness or defendant clearly is confused and keeps responding to a question in a meaningless fashion, even highly professional interpreters may interject themselves into the court record. This is usually done by asking the judge for permission to speak in order to explain to the attorney and to the judge the source of the witness's/defendant's conclusion. In effect, the interpreter tries to clarify the witness's/defendant's answer.

Probably the most common context in which Spanish speakers answer a question in a nonmeaningful manner is during the plea and change of plea. Very often, as in text 5.4 above, a defendant will respond *Sí* to the judge's question,"How do you plead, 'guilty' or 'not guilty' "? Sometimes, as in 5.4, it is the lawyer or judge who tells the interpreter to clarify the confusion of the defendant or witness. At other times, however, the interpreter herself takes the initiative to talk to the person undergoing examination. According to accepted practice, this should be done only after the interpreter has obtained permission from the judge to do so. Most interpreters are aware of court protocol, however, and know that before they attempt conversation with a testifying witness or defendant, they must first be granted permission from the judge.

Clarifying the Attorney's Questions. Interpreters frequently address themselves to the examining attorney for clarification of a question that has just been asked. Often the interpreter's need for clarification is simply a matter of not having heard the question clearly, or else one of not having noted down a sufficient portion of the question to be able to render a complete interpretation of it.[6] The following texts reflect the attorney-directed request for clarification.

5.6 Prosecuting attorney: And did the pilot ask you to pay him any money in Caño Seco?

INTERPRETER: *Y el piloto le pidió a Ud. que le pagara algo de dinero en Caño Seco, en Caño Seco?*
WITNESS: *Sí, todos le pagamos.*
INTERPRETER: Yes, all of us paid him.
PROSECUTING ATTORNEY: How much did you pay in?
INTERPRETER: *¿Cuánto le pagó cada uno de Uds.?*
WITNESS: *Ochocientos.*
INTERPRETER: Eight-hundred each of us.
PROSECUTING ATTORNEY: Did you protest this payment?
INTERPRETER [addressing attorney]: Did you "protest," sir, "protest"?
PROSECUTING ATTORNEY [addressing interpreter]: Yes.
INTERPRETER: *¿Protestaron Uds. de este pago, seño-, señorita?*
WITNESS: *No.*
INTERPRETER: No.

5.7 DEFENSE ATTORNEY: Did you tell the border patrol agents that Mr. Durán first approached you while you were staying at the hotel?
INTERPRETER [addressing attorney]: Well, you were "standing" or "staying," sir?
DEFENSE ATTORNEY [addressing interpreter]: Staying.

5.8 PROSECUTING ATTORNEY: After you were arrested by the police, were you interviewed by anybody?
INTERPRETER [addressing attorney]: How's that, sir?
PROSECUTING ATTORNEY [addressing interpreter]: "Interview."
INTERPRETER: *Después de que Ud. fue arrestado por la policía ¿le hizo a Ud. alguien una entrevista? ¿Le hizo una?*
INTERPRETER [addressing attorney]: I don't think he understood the word "interview," sir.
PROSECUTING ATTORNEY [addressing interpreter]: Okay. Ah, discussions.
INTERPRETER: *Después de que lo arrestaron a Ud. ¿tuvo Ud. alguna plática con alguna persona, es decir de la policía que los arrestó?*

5.9 DEFENSE ATTORNEY: So if you told Manuel Antonio Gutiérrez that you only remained overnight in Juárez, that would be incorrect?
INTERPRETER [addressing defense attorney]: "That you remained only" what, sir?

DEFENSE ATTORNEY [addressing interpreter]: Overnight in Juárez. That would be incorrect?
DEFENSE ATTORNEY: And the first time you met him was in the desert on October fourteenth?
INTERPRETER [addressing attorney]: Was there another word after "desert," Mrs. Zolin? I did not translate anything after "desert."
DEFENSE ATTORNEY [addressing interpreter]: No.
INTERPRETER [addressing attorney]: "The first time you saw him was in the desert."
DEFENSE ATTORNEY [addressing interpreter]: In the desert.
INTERPRETER: *Y la primera vez que Ud. lo conoció fue en el desierto.*
WITNESS: *Sí.*
INTERPRETER [addressing attorney]: And he answered "yes."

Whereas many of these clarification procedures are relatively brief, as are the texts 5.7 and 5.8, some involve more extensive verbal participation on the part of the interpreter, as can be seen in texts 5.6 and 5.9. In text 5.8 the interpreter initiates two kinds of clarification routines, one in which she is not sure of the word that had been uttered by the attorney, and the other whereby she informs the attorney that the witness may not have understood that particular word ("interview"). The two types of clarification procedures do not come together by chance. What appears to be happening in effect, is that the interpreter is indirectly criticizing the attorney for choosing a word whose Spanish equivalent is unfamiliar to the witness. The interpreter, probably having had previous experiences of witnesses being unable to understand the word *entrevista,* "interview," is subtly influencing the attorney to change his choice of words. She does so via a two-step clarification procedure.

In text 5.9, in contrast to 5.8, the interpreter is genuinely trying to obtain a complete, accurate version of the attorney's question. This interpreter does all her consecutive interpreting by noting down questions in shorthand, a rare skill among interpreters. Most interpreters use a variety of note-taking methods that incorporate only the key concepts of a speaker's utterance, and rely on memory to provide the rest of the utterance. Because this interpreter takes notes in shorthand, she is able to read back a question or an answer in the source language in its entirety. This makes for potentially remarkable accuracy in interpreting, and in fact this particular interpreter is exceptionally skilled at rendering accurate interpretations. She does so, however, at a cost to the proceeding. As can be seen in 5.9, she first makes a statement to the examining attorney about the way she interpreted the question, she then reads aloud the attorney's question as she has taken it down in shorthand, and finally for the clarity of the court record, she refers to the witness in the third person ("And he answered 'yes' "), something that violates the guidelines of court interpreting.[7] At this point in the text, however, the interpreter is correct in assessing the need for third-person reference, for if she had simply said, "yes," the attorney might well have repeated the question, in order to make sure that the "yes" response was in fact a reply to his last question. In reality, what has happened during this segment of witness examination is a separation of attorney question from witness answer over time, and the additional element of lapsed time is due to the clarification attempts by the interpreter.

A situation that commonly results in an interpreter's request for the attorney to repeat a question is that following a ruling on an objection. Because of the time lag between the uttering of an attorney's question and the ultimate ruling by the judge after an objection has been raised, interpreters relying on memory for consecutive interpretation will have to ask that the question be repeated. This can be done either by having the court reporter read back the question, or by asking the attorney to repeat it himself. In the text below the interpreter chooses the latter tactic. What is interesting in her request for a repetition is the metacommentary on interpreting as a skill ("Would you repeat the question, sir, so I can do it justice please?"):

5.10 DEFENSE ATTORNEY: You don't believe things will be better for you if you cooperate with the officials?

INTERPRETER: *¿Pero está Ud. atestiguando, señor, porque Ud. cree que las cosas le van a salir mejor si Ud. atestigua?*

WITNESS: *No no, yo no sé, yo, yo no más estoy diciendo lo que sé.* (Oh no, I don't know, I'm only saying what I know.)

PROSECUTING ATTORNEY: Pardon me, your honor; objection. Hasn't answered.

INTERPRETER [addressing witness]: *Está, este, está objetando el Señor Licenciado a la pregunta.* (The attorney is, uh, is objecting to the question.)

JUDGE: Well, I, I'll overrule the objection, but I, I think the witness is having some difficulty in understanding what you're getting at, Mr. McGee.

Defense attorney: I'll try to take a different tactic, sir.
Judge: Well, uh.
Interpreter [addressing attorney]: Would you repeat the question, sir, so I can do it justice please?
Defense attorney: Do you believe that things might go better for you if you cooperate with the officials?

A second way in which the interpreter enters into dialogue with the attorney is by informing him of the interpretation that she has just made. This appears to be a tacit way of asking the attorney for approval of an interpretation that the interpreter senses may be somewhat off the mark in its wording. The following texts typify this type of interpreter attempt at clarification.

5.11 Prosecuting attorney: Do you feel that you could follow the path if you would go through it during the day? Is that the problem, that it was dark and you could not pick out landmarks?
Interpreter [addressing attorney]: Sir, the way I put the question is, "It is your answer, then, that if it were during the day you could follow that road. But it was because it was at night that you cannot follow that road." And his answer was, "Yes."

5.12 Prosecuting attorney: When you got to the motel did you get a room?
Interpreter: *Cuando Uds. llegaron al, al motel, ah, ¿se registraron Uds. para que les dieran un cuarto?*
Witness: *No, no fui yo, no hablo inglés.*
Interpreter [addressing attorney]: I, I asked the question "Did you register so that a room would be given to you?" and he said, "It wasn't I; I don't speak English."

5.13 Prosecuting attorney: Had you expected that you would have to pay another eight hundred dollars?
Interpreter: *¿Esperaba Ud. tener que pagar ochocientos dólares adicionales, señora?*
Witness: *¿Adicionales, cómo?*
Interpreter: Uh, I said, "Were you ups—, were you, uh, did you expect to pay, uh, eight hundred additional dollars?" and she doesn't understand the word "additional" in Spanish that I used.

PROSECUTING ATTORNEY: Eight hundred more dollars?
INTERPRETER: *Ah, ¿esperaba Ud. tener que pagar ochocientos dólares más, además de lo que ya había pagado?*

In text 5.13 above, rather than interpreting for the attorney the witness's answer, an answer that reveals the witness's failure to comprehend the question, the interpreter gives an accounting of her interpretation of the question and reports to the attorney what she perceives to be the difficulty that the witness is experiencing. In this case, then, a report on her interpretation is intended to speed up the question/answer sequence at a point where there is a comprehension gap on the part of the witness. If the interpreter had followed the guidelines of court interpreting, at such a problematical point she would have interpreted the witness's query, *¿Adicionales, cómo?* ("Additional ones? How's that?"). An interpretation of the witness's response would have entailed the attorney's rephrasing of the question and the subsequent interpretation of that question into Spanish. By not following the guidelines, the interpreter has cut short the length of the interchange, thereby making the examination process more efficient. She has also, however, taken on a role not intended by the courts.

Some of the dialogues initiated by interpreters for the purpose of clarifying attorney questions become quite lengthy. In text 5.14 below, the interpreter addresses the attorney three times, once to inform him of the interpretation she has just completed, once to clarify what he meant by his question, and once to inform him about the revised interpretation she is about to make. Thus, the interpreter becomes much more prominent than is customary in the examination process:

5.14 DEFENSE ATTORNEY: What about the man that you've, that you describe or that you know by the name "Calvo"? Was he in the truck or did he get out of the truck?
INTERPRETER: *Eh, y si nos referimos al hombre que Ud. describe al cual se refiere Ud. como "el calvo," ¿dijo él algo? La persona que Ud. identificó al que Ud. se refiere como "el calvo," ¿se quedó él adentro del troque o se bajó del troque?* (Uh, and if we refer to the man that you describe, the one you refer to as "Calvo," did he say something? The person that you've identified, the one you refer to as "Calvo," did he stay inside the truck or did he get out of the truck?)
WITNESS: *Se quedó en él.* (He stayed in it.)

INTERPRETER [addressing attorney]: Excuse me. I thought I made the sentence, sir, in the sense that—did he say anything—because I thought that you were continuing the other question.
DEFENSE ATTORNEY [addressing interpreter]: Okay, yes.
INTERPRETER [addressing attorney]: What you mean is, "Did Calvo stay in the truck or did he get out of the truck?" Is that the question?
DEFENSE ATTORNEY [addressing interpreter]: Yes.
INTERPRETER [addressing attorney]: Excuse me, I'm gonna make it now, then, "He remained in the truck."

Experienced court interpreters are aware of the court record, and are conscious of the fact that their interpretations are being reported as they speak. The prefatory phrase of the interpreter in text 5.14 ("I'm gonna make it now . . .") reflects the fact that she is very much addressing the court record, more so perhaps than she is addressing the attorney. Sometimes, fidelity to the record leads interpreters to challenge or correct an attorney during his examining routine. Texts 5.15 and 5.16 exemplify the ways in which interpreters can challenge an attorney, and demonstrate the ways in which attorneys react to the challenge:

5.15 DEFENSE ATTORNEY: What was his destination?
INTERPRETER [addressing attorney]: I translated that, sir.
DEFENSE ATTORNEY [addressing interpreter]: Try again.

5.16 DEFENSE ATTORNEY: All right. When he came back with the other man.
INTERPRETER [addressing attorney]: Uh . . . Excuse me, sir. Excuse me, he said, "With a friend."
DEFENSE ATTORNEY [addressing interpreter]: Okay, okay. When he came back with the other person, did you go any place with the person you've identified in the court and that other person?

In both 5.15 and 5.16 above, the attorney is irritated by the interpreter's attempt to correct him. In text 5.15 his reply is a verbal "put-down" of the interpreter: he sticks to his guns. In text 5.16 the attorney accedes to the interpreter's indirect request for a correction, but does so through a compromise term. Thus, while the interpreter reminds him that the witness had used the word "friend," and the attorney is referring to "the other man," the attorney comes up with the neutral noun "person." This is a concession to the interpreter, but not a complete buckling to her will. His tone of annoyance is reflected in the prefatory, "Okay, okay."

Sometimes an interpreter will try to correct, or alter, the phrasing of an attorney's question on some syntactic basis. An interpreter's explicit attempt to achieve such an alteration produced the following dialogue:

5.17 DEFENSE ATTORNEY: So, are you saying that you wouldn't have told the border patrol officer

INTERPRETER: Excuse me, sir. I have to tell you that you're using the negative all the time and his answer really doesn't mean much when you're using the negative form of questioning because when he answers "no" it actually comes out "yes". If you say, "Wouldn't do this," or "Wouldn't do that, yes I wouldn't." You see what I mean? You're using the negative and it's confusing him tremendously.

What the interpreter is trying to explain to the attorney is a difference between the linguistic habits of English speakers and Spanish speakers. When an English speaker answers "no" to a negatively worded question, as in 5.18 below, the speaker is responding in the negative. A Spanish speaker, however, can answer either *Sí* or *No* to the same question, and still be answering the question negatively, as 5.18 demonstrates.

5.18 A: So she wasn't at the bar that night?
B [American]: No (= no, she wasn't).
C [Latin American]: Yes (= yes, you're right: she wasn't there).
No (= no, she wasn't).

The interpreter in text 5.18, a hypothetical situation, is trying to explain this point to the attorney, but fails to do so adequately.

In other instances, when something in the wording of a question seems ambiguous to the interpreter, or a case of polysemy[8] occurs, she will realize that by choosing one sense of a word rather than the other she runs the risk of incorrectly interpreting the question. At such a moment, a well-trained interpreter is supposed to request a clarification from the attorney. In the case of text 5.19 below, however, the interpreter's feeling that the phrase "hit with a gun" is ambiguous would seem to be off the mark. Thus, while it is the intention of the interpreter to clarify what she perceived to be an ambiguity, the net result is a clarification procedure that need not have occurred, had the interpreter had a native speaker's command of English:

5.19 PROSECUTING ATTORNEY: Okay, now after he tried to hit you with a gun, what happened after that?
INTERPRETER [addressing attorney]: Excuse me, I have to clarify something. When you say "hit with a gun," do you mean "shoot with a gun," or actually "hit him with a gun"?
PROSECUTING ATTORNEY [addressing interpreter]: No, I mean, strike with a gun, not shoot.
INTERPRETER [addressing attorney]: Okay, I'm sorry, I, that wasn't clear.
PROSECUTING ATTORNEY [addressing interpreter]: Okay.

The interpreter is wrong in intuiting an ambiguity in the phrase, "hit with a gun." Whereas an expression such as, "He was hit," is in fact ambiguous in the sense of being shot, on the one hand, and of being given a blow, on the other, "hit you with a gun" is much more likely—given the context—to have only the latter meaning. It is probably the nonnative intuition of the Spanish-dominant interpreter that finds ambiguity in the phrase. Furthermore, if one notices that the interpreter's second example ("actually, 'hit him with a gun'") is virtually a repetition of the original phrase with the addition of the pronoun "him" and a shift from a definite article ("the") to an indefinite ("a"), it becomes apparent that the interpreter's attempts to verbalize a clarification were defective, because of her inability to elucidate the matter adequately on the spur of the moment. Similarly, the interpreter's attempt to explain via illustration the problematical aspects of interpreting negatively worded questions also failed, as she was unable to state her case with sufficient clarity. The net result is further confusion for the examining attorney, and resentment on the interpreter's part. In some small way such clarification attempts must make the attorney feel that his questioning procedure is being challenged, and by someone whom he considers not to be professionally his equal.[9]

Clarifying the Witness's Answer. Interpreters often halt the examination process because of a problem related to the witness's answer.

This may concern the linguistic problems posed in translating a specific word (see texts 5.20–5.24 below), a grammatical construction that differs from language to language (see 5.25–5.26), the apparent inadequacy of the witness's response (texts 5.27–5.28), the failure of the answer to be heard or to be produced (texts 5.29–5.32), or the tendency of witnesses to make comments to the interpreter on the side (see 5.33–5.36). Each of these categories is considered in the discussion below.

One very common type of problem that leads interpreters to clarify a witness's answer is difficulty of translating words that vary dialectally in the Spanish-speaking world. Text 5.20 typifies the interpreter's attempts to clarify the meaning of a Spanish word that has different referents in different countries. The fact that the interpreter is aware of the variance in meaning speaks well of her, and her need to stop the examination process is motivated by her keen desire for accuracy:

5.20 INTERPRETER [addressing attorney]: Excuse me, he used a term that's, *buso*, that I'm not familiar with, sir. May I clarify if he means a sweater or a shirt?
INTERPRETER: *¿Qué quiere decir 'buso' señor?* [What does *buso* mean, sir?]
WITNESS: *Es una especie de chaqueta saco.* [It's a kind of jacket.]
INTERPRETER [addressing attorney]: Oh, it's something like a jacket, he says.

In the examination of a witness that is cited below, the issue revolves around the multiple meanings of the verb *cancelar.* It should be noted that the attorney is irritated by the interpreter's interruption, considering her commentary to be something to which the jury should not have access:

5.21 PROSECUTING ATTORNEY: All right, what else was said, if anything?
INTERPRETER: *¿Qué más se* [*ha* . . . (What else was . . .)
WITNESS: [*No es no más, o sea que era la segunda parte que le daba, era la parte del trato.*
INTERPRETER: That is, that this was the second portion, uhm, of the money, and the last installment. And this would cancel the deal . . . would *complete* the deal.

INTERPRETER [addressing attorney]: Excuse me, sir, the South Americans, I believe, and . . . and I would like to pursue this, but I . . . In my past experience they use the verb *cancelar,* "cancel," as "to complete." May I pursue if this is what he means?
PROSECUTING ATTORNEY: Your honor, can, can we discuss this, uh, off the record? I . . . I don't think it's proper for the jury [to
JUDGE: [Very well.

Sometimes the interpreter halts the examination process because she has heard a Spanish word that she is totally unfamiliar with. Most codes of ethics for court interpreters specify that whenever such a linguistic problem arises, it is the interpreter's duty to inquire as to the meaning of the word, so that she may interpret it correctly. It is usually only the most competent interpreters who do so, however, since it requires a great deal of self-confidence to admit to a lack of knowledge in public, and on the record. In the following text, the word that the interpreter must inquire about, *pani,* turns out to be a Spanish-speaker's mispronunciation of the English word "Spanish":

5.22 WITNESS: *Donde llegamos, llegamos a al Hotel Pani nada más, pero no sé cómo ha, ha llegado todo esto.* (Where we arrived, we arrived at the Hotel Pani, that's all, but I don't know how, how all this happened.)
INTERPRETER: Well, we arrived to where the *pani* is.
INTERPRETER [addressing the judge]: He uses a term I'm not acquainted with. May I pursue what he means by *pani,* sir?
JUDGE: Yes.
INTERPRETER: *¿Qué quiere decir "pani" señor?* (What does *pani* mean, sir?)
WITNESS: *Es el Hotel Spanish.* (It's the Spanish Hotel.)

Some lawyers, understandably, lack an interest in what seem to them to be overly fine semantic distinctions. Rather than cooperate with the interpreter's attempt to clarify the meaning of a word uttered by the witness, they will override the interpreter's request, and use a different lexical item instead. In the example below, the interpreter tries to point out that the word *troque* could possibly mean "station wagon" or "truck." Skirting the issue of how to refer to it in English, in his next question the attorney avoids both choices and uses a third, more general term, "vehicle." By doing so, however, he is minimizing the significance of the possibility that the noun *troque* may have two meanings. Thus, the efforts of the interpreter to achieve semantic precision are often construed by attorneys as hairsplitting or nit-picking.

5.23 PROSECUTING ATTORNEY: Where was Mr. Sandoval at that time?
INTERPRETER: *¿Dónde estaba el señor Sandoval en ese tiempo?*
WITNESS: *Fue por el troque.*
INTERPRETER: He had gone to get the, uh, truck.
PROSECUTING ATTORNEY: Did he say [that
INTERPRETER [addressing attorney]: [It could also, excuse me, it could also mean "station wagon," because *camioneta* means both things.
PROSECUTING ATTORNEY: Before he left, did he tell you he was going to get the vehicle?

An interesting case involving polysemy is 5.24 below, in which what is at issue for the interpreter is her inability to recall how she interpreted a polysemous word the previous day during the examination of a witness. The word in question is *moreno,* which can mean either "dark" or "black," and the same witness is testifying for the second day. It is clear from observing these interpreters that once an interpreter has decided on a particular target language equivalent for a given word in the source language, she will try to stick to that lexical item each time it occurs. Thus, in 5.24, the interpreter would like to continue using the English equivalent of *moreno,* but cannot remember which meaning she had been using the day before:

5.24 INTERPRETER [addressing judge]: Um, your honor, I have, uh, uh, a little uh, worry of when she said, "a fat, a fat black man" or "a fat dark man." I'm not sure if I translated it "dark" or, or "black" and I would like to determine if this—Oh, that was objected to. Excuse me. All right, thank you. All right, okay.

Problems of grammar seem to involve the lengthiest type of interpreter-initiated interruptions. In text 5.25 the judge is clearly annoyed by the interchange between interpreter and attorney. Interestingly, the interpreter reaches a compromise solution to the problem of choosing between the pronouns "I" and "he": she uses the impersonal term "somebody." The irritation of the judge is expressed in his reaction, "All right, all right. All right, let's just,—."

5.25 DEFENSE ATTORNEY: Would you relate that conversation?
INTERPRETER: *¿Puede Ud. relatarnos esa conversación?*
WITNESS: *No, si podía acompañarlo a los Esta, a Estados Unidos. Si yo no conozco, y no hablo inglés.* (Well, whether I [or, he] could accompany him to the Uni-, to the United States, since I'm not familiar with—, and I don't speak English.)
INTERPRETER: Uh, could I accompany him.
INTERPRETER [addressing attorney]: I really don't know because he's using a pronoun that could—can be "I asked if he could, uh, or, if I could accompany him." It could apply to both, so it's a very ambiguous answer. Somebody asked if he could accompany him to the United States. It could be "he." It could be "I."
DEFENSE ATTORNEY: Your honor, I don't think that's the entire answer. I think the answer was, "I asked to accompany him to the U-United States because I don't speak English."
INTERPRETER [addressing attorney]: Well, I was going to translate the other part, "I don't speak English," but the thing is that he didn't use a pronoun, sir.
JUDGE: All right, all right. All right, let's just,—we understand that. You state the, the complete answer then.
INTERPRETER [addressing judge]: Yes.
INTERPRETER [addressing the record]: Somebody accompanied him to the United States. Uh, I don't speak English.

The interpreter is quite correct in noting the ambiguity of the verb *podía*. All verbs of the *-ir* infinitive class in Spanish are semantically ambiguous among the first, second, and third person singular (i.e., *podía* could mean either "I could," or "you could," or "he/she could"). What is interesting in this case is that the defense attorney is bilingual, and thus feels competent to dispute the interpreter's interpretation. The pairing of Spanish-speaking attorneys with Spanish-speaking defendants is quite common in courthouses located in the southwest. Both prosecutors' offices and public defenders' offices make a conscious effort to assign Spanish-speaking lawyers to Spanish-speaking clients. Thus there often are occasions when bilingual attorneys quarrel with interpreters over the interpretation of statements made by witnesses or defendants.

In their attempts at clarifying some grammatical aspect of witness testimony, interpreters can engage attorneys in lengthy interchanges. In 5.26 below, the interpreter's explanation of the witness's answer is more of an indirect criticism of the attorney's phrasing of the question. From her tone she is clearly vexed with him, perhaps because she knows that she has made this point before, and the attorney has not altered the wording of his questions in accordance with her suggestion. It should be noted that the dialogue occurs in the middle of the attorney's examination of a witness, and becomes, in effect, a conversation in its own right. Throughout the discussion neither one addresses the witness:

5.26 ATTORNEY: Has he said that he didn't, that he crossed the border 100 meters from the port of entry?
INTERPRETER: That's, that's what I understand that he said, that he crossed 100 meters from the port of entry, yes.
ATTORNEY: He didn't say Brownsville, Texas?
INTERPRETER: That's what I take it he said, yes.
ATTORNEY: And on the issue of the time, that he did not tell the border patrol agent "7:30"?
INTERPRETER: Uh, sir, the la-, the question that I was referring to that was mixed up was, "You wouldn't have told the border patrol agent something different from what you're telling us here?"
ATTORNEY: Uh, okay.
INTERPRETER: And he said, "No." You see, that doesn't mean anything. "Wouldn't," "No I wouldn't have" or "Yes, I would not have," it, it could mean either, and it's very ambiguous, so this is why I would appreciate it if you would make the questions in the affirmative.
ATTORNEY: I'll go along to the next question and answer. I'm going to ask him about Mr. Chavarría. I'm going to quote again to you from the question and answer that I have on this piece of paper, which says: "Question from the border patrol agent: Did you approach the men?"

In her subtle admonition of the attorney, the interpreter is not completely clear herself on the grammatical point that is troubling from the point of view of interpreting. Her claim is that the witness's answer of "no" to the question "You wouldn't have told the border patrol agent . . ." is ambiguous, meaning either that he wouldn't have told the agent or that he would have told the agent something different. She is, however, mistaken in finding ambiguity in the negative response, for it can only be taken to mean that he would not have told the agent. What she is confusing here is the response "no" with the alternative response "yes" to the negatively worded question. A response of "yes" could in fact be interpreted in two ways: as "Yes, I would have" or "Yes, it is the case that I wouldn't have," although the second sense of "yes" is a far less likely one in spoken American English. In effect, then, the interpreter is touching upon a question format that is indeed problematical for her as an interpreter, although the particular answer given by the witness was in fact not ambiguous. Thus, the outcome of the dialogue for the attorney was a persisting confusion. He could not see any ambiguity in the witness's answer, and rightfully so. The outcome for the interpreter was a sense of frustration, for she saw that she had not gotten through to the attorney, whom she considered to be grammatically dense for not grasping her point.

Even though interpreters ideally should add nothing of their own words to explain or clarify a witness's or defendant's answer, even when the answer seems meaningless, interpreters often do offer unsolicited explanations at such moments. It should be kept in mind, as has been pointed out above, that a nonsensical answer on the part of the witness or defendant casts doubt on the quality of the interpreter's interpretation. It may occur to those in the courtroom that the interpreter either has interpreted the question poorly into Spanish, or else has interpreted the answer incorrectly into English. In text 5.27 below, the witness's answer clearly bears no relation to the attorney's question, and the interpreter decides to clear up the confusion immediately:

5.27 ATTORNEY: Can you describe for us what he looked like ah, from your memory of that night?
INTERPRETER: *¿Puede Ud. describir la apariencia del chofer según recuerda Ud., según su memoria de esa noche?*
WITNESS: *¿Escribir? No, pos no sé escribir.* (Write? No, well I don't know how to write.)
INTERPRETER: You mean "write"?
INTERPRETER [addressing attorney]: *Descri-, escribir,* eh, eh, in Spanish "describe" and "write" are very similar. Um, he says, "I don't know how to write."
ATTORNEY: Can you tell us about his appearance on that night?

The attorney accepts the interpreter's explanation and takes it into consideration in rephrasing his question. He drops the word "describe" and refers instead to the "appearance" of the man in question.

The answers of Spanish-speaking witnesses or defendants may not necessarily be as completely off the mark as in 5.27 above. In the case of 5.28 below, the witness misunderstands the attorney's question, confusing point of departure for a job with location of the job:

5.28 DEFENSE ATTORNEY: And where was he going to take you to work from, from what point was he going to take you to work?
INTERPRETER: *¿Y de qué punto los iba él a llevar a trabajar?*
WITNESS: *Donde hubiera trabajo.*
INTERPRETER: Wherever there would be work.
INTERPRETER [addressing attorney]: Sir, excuse me, I asked "From what point would he take you to work?" and he answered, "Wherever there was work."

Interestingly, the sort of misunderstanding demonstrated by this witness is something that could just as easily have happened to a native speaker of English who had been asked the same question. A native English speaker testifying on the stand might have misunderstood the question for a variety of reasons: nervousness, lack of sufficient attention, deficiencies in the manner in which the attorney conveyed the question (e.g., mumbling, speaking in too low a volume), or incompetence on his own part (e.g., low level of intelligence, unfamiliarity with formal English speaking style). Finally, a native English speaker might have answered as did the Mexican illegal alien in 5.28 above, if he had been deliberately trying to conceal information from the Court.

In other words, a native English speaker's tangential answer might have made him appear either incompetent or deliberately evasive. The Mexican witness in this case might also have appeared incompetent or evasive to those in the courtroom. The interpreter's clarifying intervention, however, seems to be an accounting for his reply. Certainly in text 5.27, where the interpreter clearly does account for the witness's defective answer with an explanation of the sound similarity between *describir* and *escribir,* the interpreter achieves a certain degree of mitigation for the witness's defective reply. To some extent, because of the interpreter's interrupting, he comes off appearing less incompetent, less evasive.

There are times when the interpreter must make herself heard in order to add to a witness's testimony, which either has not been heard aloud, or has not been given clearance by the judge. In the case of the former, it is often a matter of the witness having added something to an answer, while the attorneys are engaged in the next verbal activity (e.g., formulating the next question, addressing the judge), or else while the interpreter is finishing rendering her interpretation. The three texts below, 5.29, 5.30, and 5.31, illustrate this type of interpreter clarification of a witness's or defendant's testimony.

5.29. Defense attorney: So you and Mr. White were the only two people in the car?
Interpreter: *De manera que Ud. y el señor White eran las únicas dos personas que venían en el carro?*
Witness: *Sí, porque él entró por donde se debe pasar, ¿no?*
Interpreter: Yes, because you see, he entered through where one should cross.
Interpreter [addressing attorney]: Excuse me. He added something I didn't hear.
Interpreter [addressing witness]: *¿A través de dónde?*
Witness: *O sea, por donde se pasa legal.*
Interpreter: Through where you, one crosses legally.

5.30 Witness: *No, no acordamos nada porque íbamos ya a arreglarnos acá ya llegando a la casa.*
Interpreter: We did not agree on a specific amount, because we were going to agree on the amount once we arrived at our home.
Witness: *A nuestra casa acá.*
Interpreter [addressing attorney]: Excuse me, she added, "At our home over here."

5.31 Prosecuting attorney: And do you recall meeting her once before in Juárez?
Interpreter: *¿Se acuerda Ud. de haberse encontrado Ud. con ella una vez antes en Juárez?*
Witness: *Mm, no.*
Prosecuting attorney: The first time you met her.
Interpreter: *¿La primera vez que la conoció? ¿La primera vez que la conoció?*

WITNESS: *Fue en Juárez.*
INTERPRETER [addressing attorney]: She answered "No" to the first part of your question and then she hasn't answered anything to the last part of the question. I repeated the last part of your question, "The first time you met her," and she answers, "It was in Juárez."

Text 5.31 is a rather complicated explanation, and rather difficult for a listener to follow. The reason the interpreter is able to refer to the "first part of your question" and "the last part of the question" is that she has noted down the entire question verbatim. Certainly a juror, and perhaps even a judge, who does not have the attorney's question written before him, would be confused by the interpreter's clarifying remarks.

In cases in which a question/answer sequence is halted by the opposing attorney's objection, and the interpreter either prevents the witness from answering or else refrains from interpreting the witness's answer until the objection has been overruled, the interpreter will speak for the witness in the third person. As soon as she refers to the witness as "he" or "the defendant," she is speaking as herself, the interpreter, and is no longer carrying out the interpreting role in the prescribed fashion. Thus, it is not the witness who is speaking into the court record, but the interpreter. A case in point, 5.32 below, is that of an objection that has been overruled:

5.32 DEFENSE ATTORNEY: And she has been living in San Diego for about six years?
INTERPRETER: *Y ella ha estado viviendo en San Diego como seis años?*
PROSECUTING ATTORNEY: I object your honor.
INTERPRETER [addressing witness]: *Momentito, objetó la licenciada Ellsworth.* (Just a moment, Miss Ellsworth has objected.)
JUDGE: The objection's overruled.
INTERPRETER: Overruled, sir?
JUDGE: Yes.
INTERPRETER [addressing the attorney]: Uh, the defendant answered "yes," sir.

During this objection sequence, because of the overlapping of attorney and interpreter speech, the witness's barely audible affirmative response, *sí*, is lost amid the loud objection and the concurrent Spanish interpreting that is going on. Thus, rather than wait for the question to be repeated to the witness, the interpreter speaks on her behalf, reporting to the Court the answer that had been given.

Accounting for the Side Comments of Witnesses and Defendants. There are many occasions on which a witness or defendant who is testifying speaks on the side to the interpreter, or begins addressing her personally and stops directing his answers to the examining attorney. It is the interpreter's obligation to inform the judge of any such comments when they occur. She must also account for any remarks that she herself may be making to the witness in return. For this reason, the interpreter must inform the judge, for the record, of any side conversations that may have occurred in the course of the examination procedure. It is an accounting of her own verbal behavior, and a clarification of the witness's speech as well. Texts 5.33, 5.34, 5.35, and 5.36 illustrate this type of clarifying procedure.

5.33 WITNESS: *¿Puede Ud. repetir la pregunta?*
INTERPRETER: Could you repeat the question please?
INTERPRETER [addressing witness]: *Yo no puedo repetirla sin que la repita la licenciada.* (I can't repeat it without the attorney's repeating it.)
INTERPRETER [addressing judge]: She means for me to repeat the question, your honor. And I advised her I cannot repeat it unless I'm given permission to do so and the attorney will do so.

5.34 INTERPRETER [addressing judge]: Uh, I, I just advised her that I had just translated what she had said.

5.35 DEFENSE ATTORNEY: All right. If they weren't questions do,—were ya, were ya asked just to tell what had happened as far as what you could remember as far as entering the country?
WITNESS [addressing interpreter]: *Ud. es la que estaba explicando.* (You're the one who was doing the explaining.)
INTERPRETER [addressing witness]: *O sea la intérprete, o sea ¿yo estaba presente?* (You mean the interpreter, you mean I was present?)
WITNESS [addressing interpreter]: *Mhm.*
INTERPRETER: Well, you see, you were the one,
INTERPRETER [addressing attorney]: Excuse me, sir, he's referring to me, the interpreter. "You were the one who was asking what had happened."

DEFENSE ATTORNEY: Okay. There was an interpreter present, is that right?

5.36 PROSECUTING ATTORNEY: Did you know you were entering the country illegally?
INTERPRETER: *Cuando Ud. entró a este país, señora, ¿sabía Ud. que estaba entrando ilegalmente?*
WITNESS: *Sí, señorita.*
INTERPRETER: Yes, sir.
INTERPRETER [addressing attorney]: Excuse me. I'm advising her not to answer "Yes, ma'am" or "No, ma'am" because I'm just the interpreter. Excuse me.

Texts 5.35 and 5.36 not only demonstrate how witnesses' comments to the interpreter cause the interpreter to halt the proceeding in order to make an accounting, but beyond that, they show that some witnesses in fact talk to the interpreter rather than to the attorney during the examination process. Text 5.35 also is illustrative of the interpreter's need to disentangle a confused situation. When she begins interpreting the answer with "Well, you see, you were the one . . . ," she realizes that those in the courtroom might assume that the pronoun "you" refers to the attorney who has asked the question. The interpreter, knowing that to untangle this misunderstanding would take several question/answer sequences, and would possibly produce irritation in the attorney and judge, forecloses such a possibility. She does so by setting matters straight immediately, before even completing the interpreting of the witness's answer. She thereby saves the Court time, and helps make the proceeding go more smoothly and with less frustration for the official participants. She also, however, has intruded into the proceeding, and in so doing, has saved the witness from an examination sequence that may have made him appear foolish.

There are times when the interpreter's interpreting of side comments are not welcomed by the Court, however. For example, in the episode below, in which a magistrate is warning material witnesses in a case not to discuss their testimony with anyone, one of the witnesses begins adding to his testimony. The interpreter, in the course of accounting for his additional remarks, is rather abruptly cut off by the judge. This is unsolicited commentary from the witness, and the judge apparently is not interested in hearing it:

5.37 JUDGE: Mr. Campos, I want you to remember the warning of the Court not to discuss this case or your testimony with anyone today, other than when you may be alone with any of the four attorneys in the case. You may step down.
WITNESS: *Mi declaración es que he llegado, y he llegado solo y estoy diciendo,* [. . .
INTERPRETER [addressing judge]: [He says, sir, that he has made his statement that he arrived alone and that was all, and I am telling . . .]
JUDGE: [There's no question con—]
INTERPRETER [addressing judge]: [No, I mean, . . .]
JUDGE [addressing witness]: [You may step down. We may have Juan Espinoza Fernández . . .

Thus, the willingness of judges to hear the explanatory remarks of interpreters is not limitless. Judges, as opposed to attorneys, have the power to curtail interpreters in midstream.

Controlling the Flow of Testimony

In all the cases that have been discussed in the preceding sections of this chapter, the intrusiveness of the court interpreter has been seen to derive from speech produced by her in reaction to problems she perceives as existing in the questions of lawyers and in the answers of witnesses and defendants. They constitute various sorts of clarification procedures. All the comments of the interpreter ought to be noted in the court record. Yet the interpreter exerts her influence in the courtroom in another way as well, a way that may appear far less obtrusive than the preceding cases to the attorneys and to the judge, both of whom are sensitive primarily to the court record. This type of verbal intervention does not enter the record, for it is carried out in Spanish.

The interpreter often plays a decisive role in controlling the speech of witnesses or defendants who are testifying on the stand. This additional and potentially decisive role is one of controlling the flow of testimony. The interpreter may achieve her own kind of pressure on witnesses or defendants in one of two ways: she can urge or prompt them to speak, and she can get them to be silent. Since the verbal mechanisms that the interpreter uses are in Spanish, the other court officials may be only dimly aware of them. In any event, judges and attorneys may not be very concerned about them, for they do not form part of the official record, and they do seem to be aimed at aiding the smooth flow of judicial process. To what extent these controlling mechanisms affect jurors' perceptions of the witness or defendant is an open question. How they affect the psyche of the person who is testifying is yet another.

Prompting the Witness or Defendant to Speak. Up to now the focus has been on intrusive effects on courtroom procedure resulting from the court interpreter's interpreting of witnesses' and defendants' speech. However, the interpreter also performs another function, one not intended to be part of her job description: managing the witnesses' or defendants' speech. This management can take the form of prompting the witness to speak, or alternatively, urging him to silence.

As can be seen in the texts below, interpreters use certain prompting mechanisms to speed up a witness's reply to an attorney's question, or to accelerate a response to the routine "Do you understand?" type of question used by judges to address defendants during arraignments, changes of plea, and sentencings. The principal method that interpreters use to prompt witnesses or defendants to answer an attorney's or judge's question is to order them to answer. Interpreters generally accomplish this by using the imperative mood of the verb *contestar,* "answer." It can be used by itself, *¡Conteste!* or, for a more polite, less commanding tone, it is followed by the phrase *por favor,* "please." The texts below, 5.38 through 5.40, illustrate the use of the more polite, less forceful, *Conteste, por favor,* and the commanding, *¡Conteste!*

5.38 JUDGE: You and Mr. Martin would be entitled to have at least thirty days. [pause] Do you understand?
INTERPRETER: *Ud. y el Licenciado Martin, o sea abogado, tendrían derecho a que se les concediere por lo menos treinta días. ¿Entiende Ud. señor?*
INTERPRETER [addressing defendant]: *Conteste por favor.* (Please answer.)
DEFENDANT: *Sí.*
INTERPRETER: Yes.

The desire on the part of the interpreter to prompt a response from someone being questioned by a judge is probably greater in the case of multiple witnesses or defendants. Perhaps because often no one defendant is singled out, but instead all are asked the same question at the same moment, defendants become reticent. In the following text, 5.39, the defendants are illegal aliens who are to serve as witnesses in the case against the "coyote," or smuggler, who was purportedly paid to bring them illegally into the United States:

5.39 JUDGE: As witnesses each of you is entitled to be represented by an attorney. Do any of you have an attorney?
INTERPRETER: *Como testigos que son, tienen Uds. el derecho de ser representados por un abogado. ¿Alguno de Uds. tiene abogado que los represente?*
INTERPRETER [addressing defendants]: *Contesten por favor.* (Please answer.)
DEFENDANTS: *No.*
INTERPRETER [addressing judge]: All answered "No" sir.

In text 5.40, the interpreter prompts the witness to answer the question of the examining attorney, even though the witness has in fact responded to the question with an affirmative "Mhm." What she is doing, in effect, is taking on the role typically played by the judge, who normally would admonish the witness to "answer 'yes' or 'no' " for the record, since "parasegmental" types of answers such as "mhm" are not acceptable for the court record:[10]

5.40 PROSECUTING ATTORNEY: And you had no papers or documents allowing you to come in lawfully, is that correct?
INTERPRETER: *¿Y Ud. no tenía documentos o papeles que lo autorizaran a entrar legalmente a los Estados Unidos? ¿Es esto correcto?*
WITNESS: *Mhm.*
INTERPRETER [addressing witness]: *¡Conteste!* (Answer!)
WITNESS: *¿Que no tenía papeles yo de migración de este lado?*
INTERPRETER: You mean I didn't have any immigration papers from this side?
PROSECUTING ATTORNEY: Right.
INTERPRETER: *Sí.*

The question that one must ask is how observers in the courtroom view the person who is being prompted. Does the witness look hesitant, unsure, or does he or she seem unwilling to answer? Does the interpreter's prompting give the judge, jury, or attorneys the impression that the witness is uncooperative? In the case of a defendant who is being asked a formalized set of questions by a judge, does he or she appear to the judge to be uncooperative? In reality, if a witness or defendant does not answer a question quickly, such hesitancy can often be a symptom of a failure to comprehend the question. A frightened witness or defendant may not feel confident enough to say, "I don't understand." Does the witness or defendant feel pressured by the interpreter into a premature response, when in fact he or she does not understand the question but is afraid to say so? These are areas of inquiry that need to be pursued.

A second way in which the interpreter prompts a witness or defendant to speak is to request a repetition of something he or she has already said. Apparently, most of the time this is done because the interpreter has forgotten part of the witness's testimony and needs to have it repeated so that she may give a complete interpretation. Sometimes the interpreter claims not to have heard the testimony well, but since she is physically very close to the witness on such occasions, the claim to not having heard may in fact often be a way of having the statement repeated when in reality she has forgotten a part of it. It should be kept in mind that consecutive interpreting, the mode of interpreting recommended for use with witnesses who are testifying, is perhaps the most difficult of the modes of interpreting. Memory plays a vital role in accurate consecutive interpreting, as do good note-taking skills. When an interpreter has not developed her note-taking ability to a sufficient degree, her need to have testimony repeated for her will be greater.

Interpreters use several verbal tactics for getting a witness or defendant to repeat an answer for them. Nearly all of them involve a query directly to the person testifying, in Spanish, rather than a formal request to the judge for a repetition. One common prompt is the term *¿Cómo?*, "What?" This is perhaps the bluntest, most direct way of getting the speaker to repeat his utterance. Another basic technique, the claim of not having heard well, can be accomplished by phrases such as *No lo oí*, "I didn't hear you," or *No oí, no oí*, "I didn't hear."

Variations on this type of mechanism involve additional explanatory statements, such as, *No puedo oírlo, ¿no puede hablar más alto?* "I can't hear you, can't you speak more loudly?" or *No lo oí, habla muy despacio y hay mucho que no lo oigo*, "I don't hear you; speak more slowly, there's a lot I don't hear from you." Finally, interpreters often use the expression *Por favor, repita*, "Please repeat." Often the request that the witness repeat the answer is done without consulting the judge or attorney. However, interpreters who are conscious of court protocol will inform the judge and attorney that they are asking for a repetition. The very act of informing them constitutes an indirect means of obtaining approval for such a verbal action. A typical way of handling this type of a request for a repetition is presented in 5.41:

5.41 PROSECUTING ATTORNEY: Where in Guatemala were you born?
INTERPRETER: *¿En dónde en Guatemala nació Ud.?*
WITNESS: *Santa Cruz de Solalá de Quetzaltenango.*
INTERPRETER [addressing witness]: *Por favor, repita.*
INTERPRETER [addressing attorney]: I'm asking her to repeat. It's quite long sir.

It should be noted that even in a text such as 5.41, where the interpreter does inform the court officials of her desire for a repetition, the request to the witness is made before the act of informing the judge, rather than the other way around. Thus, by the time the interpreter has informed the judge and attorney of her need to have the testimony repeated, the request is a fait accompli.

Silencing the Witness or Defendant: The Problem of Handling Objections. There are occasions in the courtroom when a witness or defendant is either interrupted midstream in a statement or is prevented from beginning a statement altogether. The interruption of a defendant commonly occurs at the initial appearance (or arraignment, in courts where the initial appearance is not a separate proceeding). There defendants frequently begin discursive explanations of why they are wrongfully being accused of the particular crime they believe they are charged with. As soon as defendants begin such speeches, judges will tend to cut them off, advising them not to say anything further at that time, and to wait until they have spoken to their defense counsel. In addition, judges warn defendants that anything they say at that time could be held against them in subsequent proceedings. When such admonitions come from judges, it is the interpreter's task both to interpret them and to successfully stop the defendant's stream of speech. In fact, judges typically instruct interpreters to get defendants to be quiet right away, before they incriminate themselves. Interpreters successfully stop the defendant's speech by interrupting with an interjection such as, *Señor, señor,* "Sir, sir," which serves to get the defendant's attention.

The second most common context in which a witness or defendant must be kept from speaking is during the course of an objection. From the vantage point of the court record, objections by nature are "messy" verbal exchanges: they usually involve an interruption of a speaker's speech, and thereby result in overlapping speech. The overlap occurs when the attorney who is objecting speaks simultaneously with either the opposing attorney—during the formation of a question—or simultaneously with the witness on the stand. When the witness is aided by an interpreter, an additional vocal element is added to the equation.

Objections that occur while an interpreter-assisted witness is testifying are highly confusing events for the spectator. Everyone seems to be speaking at once, and it is difficult for a moment to grasp what is being said, or even to know who is saying it. Unless the observer himself can tune in to two or three different sound tracks simultaneously, he will not understand all the speech that is going on when one attorney is asking a question, the other is raising an objection, the interpreter is finishing interpreting the question of the examining attorney, and the judge is beginning to verbalize his decision to either sustain or overrule the objection.

There are guidelines for interpreters on how to handle objections. In general, interpreters are expected to stop interpreting when an attorney makes an objection.[11] The guidelines of the Judiciary Interpreters Association of Texas state explicitly:

> If counsel objects to a question, the interpreter must await the judge's ruling, even if the non-English speaking person has already given the answer. If the objection is sustained, the interpreter does NOT give the answer: if the objection is overruled, then the interpreter can give the answer, or ask to have the question and answer repeated by the court reporter or counsel.

The intent behind this guideline, which is consistent with the intent of attorneys who raise an objection during an all-English examination, is to prevent the witness from answering. However, even in all-English proceedings, witnesses often complete their answer as the objection is being made, before the judge has had a chance to make a ruling. In such cases, if the objection is sustained, the court reporter is told to strike the answer from the record, and the jury, if there is one, is instructed to ignore the answer it may have heard. However, lawyers are well aware than an answer that has been heard is not automatically erased from the minds of jurors, simply because the judge has instructed the jurors to disregard it. A damaging bit of testimony can still leave its impact.

Despite the guidelines, however, observations of interpreter-assisted testifying show that there is a great deal of variation in the way that interpreters handle objections. Some interpreters stop interpreting the question in mid-course, at the moment at which the objection is made. Other interpreters not only complete the interpreting of the question, but also go on to interpret the Spanish-speaking witness's answer. Completing the interpreting of the question leaves the door open to the possibility of the witness's answering it, and even if that answer is not interpreted into English, it will be heard. In the case of yes/no answers, which can form a sizeable proportion of witness testimony, even non-Spanish-speaking jurors will be able to understand the meaning of Spanish *sí* and *no*. In the U.S. Southwest, where Hispanics make up a large part of the population, on any given jury several members may have a comprehension of Spanish, thereby having access even to narrative types of answers as well. In small towns on the U.S./Mexico border, the Hispanic population can constitute a large majority of the total number of residents, and juries are aimed at reflecting the demographic character of the locale. Thus, in most border towns a majority of the members of a given jury could well understand Spanish testimony.

Nevertheless, there is a built-in factor limiting the likelihood of a non-English-speaking witness's answering a question to which an objection is being raised. The fact that the question must be interpreted first—and this ideally in consecutive mode, so that the interpreter does not begin interpreting until the attorney has finished uttering his question—results in a lag time in which the judge can make his ruling. Such a lag can prevent the witness from answering. When proceedings are carried out as usual, entirely in English, there is no such lag time, and so the possibility of a witness's answering a question that has been objected to is far greater than in situations where an interpreter is working with a witness. If the attorney who has posed the objectionable question hopes for an answer before the judge's ruling, the presence of the interpreter can interfere with his strategy, in that the interpreter inadvertently can prevent the witness from answering his question. Thus, the interpreter unwittingly becomes an obstacle to one type of technique that attorneys employ in their questioning of witnesses.

Another element of variation introduced by the interpreter that can affect the outcome of an objection sequence is the use of simultaneous interpreting at the witness stand.[12] Many interpreters have not mastered the skill of consecutive interpreting, and therefore use simultaneous interpreting even when the consecutive mode is called for. Some interpreters use modified forms of consecutive interpreting. That is, they might allow half of a witness's utterance to be heard in Spanish, and then begin interpreting while the witness is finishing, thus overlapping onto the second part of his utterance. Others do the entire testimony in simultaneous mode, including the attorney's questions as well. When an interpreter is using the simultaneous mode for an attorney's question, it means that she will complete her interpretation within a few seconds of the moment when the attorney stops speaking. This technique, then, will put the Spanish-speaking witness in a position that is virtually identical to that of an English speaker: he will be ready to answer at virtually the same moment, minus a few seconds.

Thus, from the point of view of the attorney who has asked an objectionable question, the use of the simultaneous mode by the interpreter increases the likelihood of the witness's answering before the judge has made his ruling. Ironically, therefore, the interpreter who is unable to conform to the expected norm of using consecutive interpreting at the witness stand, ends up as a potential asset to the examining attorney: she opens up the possibility of the witness answering the lawyer's question.

Interpreters use a number of verbal means to prevent a witness from answering once an objection has been raised. Often they are successful, but sometimes they are not. In 5.43 and 5.44 below, the interpreter succeeds in keeping the witness from speaking. In 5.42, however, the monosyllabic answer, "No," is uttered before the interpreter can exercise her control over the speaker. Probably the most effective technique that an interpreter can use is the command *¡No conteste!,* as in 5.43. Interpreters often preface the command with a brief explanation to the witness of what is occurring, as in 5.42, *Hay una objeción, no conteste,* "There's an objection, don't answer." At other times interpreters will halt the witness with an expression such as *Un momentito,* "Just a moment," as in 5.44. This last type of control mechanism is probably just as effective as the command, *¡No conteste!,* but it is more polite.

In Spanish, direct commands would not normally be given to people whom one does not know. They are restricted to use between persons who are in a socially asymmetrical relationship to each other, and between whom power plays a significant role (e.g., parents/children, employers/employees). When Spanish-speaking persons use a direct command with someone they do not know, the social implication of this usage is that the person giving the command has authority over the addressee, as in the case of a policeman speaking to a motorist whom he has pulled over to the side of the road. Thus, the interpreter who uses a plain direct command without a prefatory explanation, is presenting herself as having authority over the witness. This type of verbal behavior exemplifies the highest form of linguistic coerciveness available to a Spanish speaker. Consequently, when the interpreter says to a witness, *Conteste,* or *No conteste,* the witness interprets the command as such, and probably assumes that there is some degree of authority behind such an order.

Texts 5.42 through 5.44, below, demonstrate how the interpreter controls the speech of witnesses in the course of objections by attorneys. Essentially, the interpreter orders the witness not to answer the question, and later, after receiving clearance from the judge, gives the witness permission to speak.

5.42 JUDGE [addressing defense attorney]: Mr. Langley.
DEFENSE ATTORNEY: Thank you your honor. [pause] Mrs. Cordero [pause], this individual that you mentioned earlier, uh, Felipe Guzmán, did, was he the one that told you and your husband to come to the United States?
INTERPRETER: *Señora Cordero, este individuo que Ud. mencionó anteriormente, este Felipe Guzmán, fue la, la persona que les mencionó a Ud. y a su marido que viniera acá a Estados Unidos?*
PROSECUTING ATTORNEY: Objection, [your honor. I believe it calls for hearsay.
WITNESS: [*No.*]
INTERPRETER [addressing witness]: [*Hay una objeción, no conteste.* (There's an objection; don't answer.)
JUDGE: The objection's overruled.
INTERPRETER [addressing witness]: *Puede Ud. contestar.* (You may answer.)
WITNESS: *No.*
INTERPRETER: No.

5.43 DEFENSE ATTORNEY: Have you ever been arrested, uh, by immigration or the border patrol in the United States?
PROSECUTING ATTORNEY: I object, your honor.
INTERPRETER: *¿Alguna, en alguna ocasión la ha arrestado a Ud., la han arrestado a Ud. los oficiales de immigración o la patrulla de la frontera de los Estados Unidos? ¡No conteste!* (Don't answer!)
JUDGE: The objection is overruled.

INTERPRETER [addressing witness]: *Hay una objeción, la denegaron, Ud. puede contestar.* (There's an objection, it was dismissed, you may answer.)
INTERPRETER: *¿En alguna ocasión la han arrestado a Ud. oficiales de inmigración u oficiales de patrulleros de la frontera en los Estados Unidos?*
WITNESS: *Sí.*
INTERPRETER: Yes.

5.44 PROSECUTING ATTORNEY: I want you to look all around the courtroom and look closely at everybody in the courtroom and tell me if the pilot's in this courtroom, okay?
INTERPRETER: *Quiero que busque Ud. cuidadosamente, y que busque si es que, si es que está el piloto aquí.*
DEFENSE ATTORNEY: Your honor, I object to this, uh, procedure. Uh, the witness *has* testified.
INTERPRETER [addressing witness]: *Un momentito.* (Just a moment.)
JUDGE: The objection's overruled.
INTERPRETER [addressing witness]: *Oké, puede Ud. contestar.* (Okay, you may answer.)

In trying to prevent a witness from answering a question that has been objected to, interpreters do not restrict themselves to verbal techniques. They often combine the linguistic mechanism with a nonverbal signal. That signal can be a raised hand motion, of the type used by traffic policemen to indicate a red light, or "STOP!" Another gesture used by some interpreters is putting their arm in front of the face of the witness, physically almost blocking his or her face from view. This is a very forceful technique and proves to be effective in both preventing a witness from speaking and stopping a witness who has already begun to speak. One wonders, however, how jurors perceive a witness whose speech must be blocked by another person's bodily intervention. Do such interventions cast a disparaging light on the witness? Do they make him appear timid and submissive, and consequently less competent than a monolingual English-speaking witness who would normally be cut off only verbally?

During an objection sequence, once the judge has overruled an objection, rather than to wait for the examining attorney to repeat his or her question, many interpreters take the initiative of prompting the witness to answer. This is done with the command, *!Conteste!* or the more polite, *Ud. puede contestar.* It should be kept in mind, however, that whether the interpreter is prompting a defendant or a witness to answer, or preventing the individual from answering, in either case she is exercising a measure of linguistic coercion over that person. From her point of view, and probably from the standpoint of the court, she is helping the proceeding run more smoothly and efficiently, and this is actually true. However, she is also to an extent controlling the speech of the testifying witness or defendant, and this is a role not intended for her by the judicial system.

Conclusion

This chapter has tried to demonstrate that the court interpreter is a new variable in the ecology of the American courtroom. She is an intrusive element, far from being the unobtrusive figure whom judges and attorneys would like her to be. Her intrusiveness is manifested in multiple ways: from the introduction of the interpreter to the jury by the judge, to the common practice resorted to by judges and attorneys of addressing the interpreter rather than the witness when they ask their questions, to the need on the part of interpreters to clarify attorneys' questions and witnesses' answers. Included as well are the tangential side-sequence conversations engaged in by interpreters and testifying witnesses, interpreter silencing of witnesses who have begun to verbalize their answers, and interpreter prodding of witnesses when they are not responding appropriately to a question. Together, these intrusions make for judicial proceedings of a different nature.

Perhaps the most important finding of this study is that the interpreter affects whatever power an interrogating attorney may have over a testifying witness or defendant. Through her interruptions, many of which may be subsumed under what have been called here "clarification procedures," the interpreter unwittingly usurps some of the power of the interrogating attorney. Finally, it has been shown that the interpreter brings to the judicial proceeding her own measure of coercion; whereas sometimes her coercion works in consonance with the efforts of examining attorneys, many times it works against them.

The following two chapters deal with alterations that interpreters make in the pragmatic aspects of a speaker's utterances. They show how the interpreter makes witness testimony lay more, or alternatively less, blame on agents of certain actions, and how she makes testimony become generally more "powerless" in O'Barr's (1982) terms.

6

Interpreter-Induced Alternation in Pragmatic Blame Avoidance Mechanisms

In the preceding two chapters it was shown that the court interpreter is a highly visible participant in judicial proceedings. It was shown, as well, that in a variety of verbal and nonverbal ways she exerts a measure of control over a testifying witness or defendant, and at the same time affects the progression of an examining attorney's questioning routine. In this chapter it will be demonstrated that interpreters exert an additional influence on the ultimate form of a question and of an answer: they can alter the pragmatic intent of an utterance. The changes made by interpreters affect the implication intended by speakers.

Specifically, this chapter will show how verb constructions uttered in syntactically passive form, without mention of agents, are frequently rendered in active form, sometimes naming agents, in their interpretation. Conversely, although less frequently, verb constructions uttered actively in the source language are sometimes rendered passively in the interpretation. These shifts in grammatical case can be seen as discourse strategies to place actors in the foreground or background of the activity being described, and concomitantly, to highlight the responsibility of certain participants in the speech situation, and to diminish responsibility from others who are present. Inasmuch as this chapter is somewhat technical in terms of its linguistic presentation, it may be of greater interest to linguists than to other social scientists. The latter might wish to read only the introductory sections and the textual analysis, beginning on page 107, omitting the intervening sections, beginning with "Verb Form and Blame Avoidance in Spanish."

Blame Avoidance/ Attribution Techniques

In the review of previous research on law and language presented in chapter 2, it was noted that features of speech are manipulated, both consciously and unconsciously, by parties involved in the adversary system of justice. Whereas many of these features have been studied from the point of view of attorneys' or judges' control over courtroom face-to-face interaction, particularly in regard to questioning (Danet and Kermish 1978; Danet and Rafn 1977; Philips 1979), linguistic resources are available to witnesses and defendants as well. To the extent that witnesses and defendants can manipulate these resources to their advantage, witnesses and defendants can be said to hold some measure of control over their replies to questions. And control over responses to questions is of crucial importance to those undergoing examination, as will be shown below.

If much of what is involved in a trial is the effort of prosecuting attorneys and their witnesses, on the one hand, and defense attorneys and their witnesses, on the other, to make defendants and even witnesses look blameworthy or blameless (Atkinson and Drew 1979), then it can be said that much of what is going on from the viewpoint of linguistic pragmatics is blame attribution and blame avoidance. Sociologists Atkinson and Drew (241) make an important distinction between blame and guilt, one worth quoting here:

> It is important to distinguish here between blame, and more formal notions of guilt. Witnesses who are in no formal sense accused of anything may nonetheless find themselves facing questions which can implicate that they were to blame for something, for example for some aspects of the defendant's behaviour, or for actions or events about which an investigation is being conducted (where the respect to which they may be to blame may not formally constitute a crime, etc.). Hence witnesses may detect blame implications in questions, even though they are not charged with an offence.

Atkinson and Drew demonstrate that speech acts such as blame allocations (i.e., blame ascriptions, or blamings), accusations, justifications, denials, challenges, and so on, are interactionally managed. All these speech acts are critically important in courtroom proceedings. Following the groundbreaking ethno-methodological work in conversational analysis by Sacks, Schegloff, and Jefferson (1974), Atkinson and Drew find that speech acts such as blamings are achieved over a series of conversational turns, specifically, a number of question-answer sequences, and that in the courtroom participants in the interaction are unconsciously aware of this, thereby constantly monitoring the speech around them in order to best plan out the strategy for their next turn at talk.

Looking at blaming in ordinary conversation, Pomerantz (1978) sees blamings (as well as excuses and denials) as "responsibility attributions," responsibility being associated with "unhappy incidents"—that is, adverse events. As do Atkinson and Drew, Pomerantz finds blamings to be interactionally managed, through a sequence of conversational turns. In addition to the turn-taking mechanism for achieving a blaming, Pomerantz observes, purely linguistic forces are at work. In utterances where responsibility is being attributed, the blamed party is referenced in subject position with an active predicate. That is, the blamed party is referred to as an actor-agent performing a blameworthy action (Pomerantz 1978:116). In reports of unhappy incidents, which normally precede blame allocations, actor-agents are not linked to events; rather, descriptions are formulated as "events that happened."

Pomerantz's conclusions regarding the relation between grammatical case and blame allocation in ordinary conversation is strikingly consonant with Danet's (1980) findings regarding the speech of prosecutors and defense attorneys. The conclusions of both scholars are supported further by my own work (Berk-Seligson 1983). In an empirical study of variation in Spanish verb construction usage, I demonstrate that nonactive verb forms—specifically, the dative of interest and the reflexive passive—are used by speaker/hearers to avoid attributing responsibility to agents for adverse events. These two verb constructions, together with other nonactive forms, are discussed in greater detail in the sections that follow.

Passive Voice for Blame Avoidance: A Cross-Cultural Universal

Linguistic evidence from languages other than English and Spanish points in the same direction—namely, that choice of case is used to create varying degrees of distance between actors and their actions. Japanese has something that has been termed an "adversative passive construction." The semantic function of this adversative passive is that of "connoting that the subject of the sentence was involuntarily subjected to something unpleasant" (Niyekawa-Howard 1968:2). When used in conjunction with a causative, the construction takes on the following connotation: "because the subject of the sentence 'was caused to' take the action expressed by the main verb, he is not responsible for the act nor for the outcome" (Niyekawa-Howard, 2).

In a pragmatic treatment of the so-called passive and the impersonal *si* constructions in Italian, Costa (1975) argues that they are actually passives in which generic human agents are demoted and deleted. She notes that a primary function of *si* constructions is to reduce the prominence of the agent, and that, "*si* constructions are exploited pragmatically as a means of shifting responsibility off a subject. This pragmatic use is typically a reflection of politeness and formality conventions which require that in potentially embarrassing situations speakers should avoid pinning down who is responsible for what action" (Costa 1975:120). The pragmatic coincidence of Italian *si* constructions with the Spanish dative of interest and reflexive passive is strikingly evident. They seem to be functionally identical.

Dutch, too, makes use of variation in case morphology to relate persons to acts. In a discourse analysis of the subjectless "pseudo-passive" in standard Dutch, Kirsner (1976) finds that the pseudo-passive construction is used to background the agentlike participant in an event more strongly than the true passive. However, common to both kinds of passive is the use of a linguistic sign to signal the single meaning, "high participant not focused," which is to say that in both types of passive the agentlike entity is not foregrounded as a grammatical subject (Kirsner, 389).

In sum, the linguistic findings alluded to above seem to indicate the operation of a cross-cultural universal. They all see grammatical case as functioning to establish linkages between actors and actions, and passivelike constructions in particular, as a means of diminishing responsibility from speakers for their own actions or for those of others. This mechanism fits under the rubric of what Brown and Levinson (1978) have termed "impersonalization mechanisms." Viewed from the broadest functional perspective, impersonalization mechanisms may be seen as a means of mitigation.

Verb Form and Blame Avoidance in Spanish: Ergativity, Agentless Passives, and Impersonal Constructions

A well-known fact among Hispanic linguists is that Spanish possesses a variety of passivelike and impersonal constructions, and that these constructions are exploited pragmatically in discourse contexts where agent-naming is considered by the speaker to be undesirable—that is, either unimportant to or potentially problematical for the social interaction. Two syntactically related constructions that substitute for the true passive, that is, the verb *ser* ["be"] + past participle of the verb in question, are the reflexive passive and the dative of interest. These two are defined as follows.

The term "reflexive passive" refers to the Spanish construction that uses the reflexive particle *se* and which is used in place of the true passive voice (Ramsey 1956:385). It is a reflexive construction that is used with an inanimate subject, and is considered passive because the grammatical subject—which is the logical object because inanimates do not act upon themselves—is not the actor but is acted upon by an agent (Solé and Solé 1977:81). Examples of the reflexive passive are the sentences *Se perdió la carta* ("The letter got lost"), *Se rompió el vaso* ("The glass broke"), and *Se contaminó el agua* ("The water became polluted").

A pragmatic analysis of the reflexive passive by Haverkate (1985), who prefers to refer to the reflexive pronoun as the "pseudo-reflexive *se*," demonstrates that this construction serves several functions, one of them being a strategy for avoiding a direct confrontation between interlocutors. Specifically, the pseudo-reflexive *se* is used:

> in those communicative situations in which the speaker wishes to hide specific referential information from the interlocutor. What happens, then, is that the speaker refrains from specifying his identity so as not to create an interactional context that could harm his social relationship with the hearer [translated from the Spanish, Haverkate 1985:17].

Haverkate adds that in this type of context, where the speaker is communicating information that he knows is in some way unpleasant for the hearer, in particular, where he is making assertions that indirectly criticize the behavior of the hearer, the pseudo-reflexive is one common type of discourse strategy. In short, the pseudo-reflexive serves as a defocusing agent, enabling the speaker to hide from the hearer the role that he, the speaker, plays in the state of affairs being described (Haverkate, 17).

The construction known alternatively as the "dative of interest," and "reflexive passive for accidental occurrences," and the "*se me* construction" (Lado and Blansitt 1967:63; Mujica 1982:35; Solé and Solé 1977:82; Soto 1969: 252) is considered to be used for referring to either accidental, unintentional, unplanned, or unexpected events. Sometimes called the "dative of participation," the dative of interest is a construction in which "the speaker is involved in the action or is emotionally affected by the action which the verb expresses; it introduces the hearer as a spectator to an event which unfolds before him" (Woehr, Barson, and Valadez 1974:156). It is also considered a "reflexive for a non-responsible subject," implying that "the one who is speaking makes the action more impersonal and makes himself less responsible" (Woehr et al. 1974:156). In fact, the doer of the action is portrayed as its unsuspecting victim. Typical constructions are the following. *Se me cayó* ("I dropped it" or "It fell on me"), *Se te rompió*

("You tore it" or "It got torn on you"), *Se le olvidó* ("He forgot it" or "It slipped his mind"), and *Se nos perdió* ("We lost it" or "It got lost on us").

What the dative of interest and reflexive passive for accidental occurrences have in common is the lack of any manifest, that is to say, overt agent. And in this respect they are similar to each other and to the true passive with an unstated agent in that rather than to connect a given action with a particular doer, they all leave that doer, or agent, unspecified. We can go further and say that there is one underlying syntactic function that the dative of interest and the reflexive passive share, and that is ergativity, in the sense of Lyons (1969:350–74) and Dixon (1979). Even though most European languages, including Spanish, are not considered to be ergative languages, many of them, including English and Spanish, possess elements of ergativity, or causativity. The ergative relationship can be seen in the three sets of related sentences below: (a), (b), and (c). The relationship between (a.1, a.2, a.3), on the one hand, and (b.1, b.2, b.3) and (c.1, c.2, c.3) on the other hand, is an ergative, or causative relationship. That is to say, "the subject of an intransitive verb 'becomes' the object of a corresponding transitive verb, and a new *ergative* subject is introduced as the 'agent' (or 'cause') of the action referred to" (Lyons 1969:352).

The notion of ergativity accounts well for the reflexive passive and the dative of participation. However, it is a relatively new theoretical concept in morphosyntax, and one that has not been applied to the analyses of passivelike constructions in Spanish. Rather, the majority of recent analyses of passive-substitutes in Spanish have been carried out within the paradigms of generative grammar (Hadlich 1971; Langacker 1970; Otero 1972; Perlmutter 1970), or case grammar (Goldin 1968). Syntacticians may disagree on what constitutes a correct analysis of these constructions, yet they ultimately arrive at conclusions that conform to a similar pragmatic analysis of their meaning. For example, Goldin (1968) characterizes the sentence *Se me olvidó el dinero* (I forgot to bring the money) as an impersonal one, arguing that the particle *se* can only be inserted into a sentence whose verb potentially takes an agent. Langacker (1970) rejects both the analysis of this sentence as impersonal, as well as the notion of a "potential agent"—that is, an agent that is potentially, but not actually, present. Instead, for sentences such as the one just cited, he posits the existence of an "unspecified" or "dummy agent." Nevertheless, the scholars agree on the absence of any agent in the surface structure of such sentences, and from the point of view of speaker meaning, a reflexive passive is far more agentless than a true (*ser*) passive that opts for not mentioning an agent.

It is proposed here that the relationship between an active construction, a dative of interest, and a reflexive passive be viewed as a continuum, where at one extreme one sees responsibility for an action manifestly attributed, at a point midway but closer to the opposite extreme there is no agent, and the individual most directly associated with the circumstances is not merely not its cause, but is viewed as its unsuspecting victim, and at the extreme point not only is the occurrence overtly dissociated from any agent, but the victim (who is potentially identifiable as the agent) is not referred to at all. Graphically, the relationship between the sentence types can be portrayed as in Figure 6.1.

(a) Active:
1. *Dejé caer el dinero.* (I dropped the money.)
2. *Perdí el dinero.* (I lost the money.)
3. *Rompí el vaso.* (I broke the glass.)

(b) Reflexive passive:
1. *Se cayó el dinero.* (The money fell down.)
2. *Se perdió el dinero.* (The money got (was) lost.)
3. *Se rompió el vaso.* (The glass broke.)

(c) Dative of interest:
1. *Se me cayó el dinero.* (The money fell down (on me).)
2. *Se me perdió el dinero.* (The money got lost (on me).)
3. *Se me rompió el vaso.* (The glass broke (got broken) on me.)

If one adds the true passive construction (d) to the continuum, one finds three alternative passives available to Spanish speakers. An example of the true passive is the following: *El vaso fue roto (por Juan)* (The glass was broken (by John)).

The grammatical picture is not yet complete, however. There is still

Figure 6.1. Attribution of Responsibility to an Agent

another passive-substitute in Spanish: the third person plural, usually called the "impersonal" construction. Examples would be those categorized under (e):

(e) Impersonal:
1. *Han robado un tranvía.* (A streetcar has been robbed [or stolen].)
2. *Dicen que eres buen pianista.* (It is said (They say) that you are a good pianist.)
3. *Hablan portugués en el Brasil.* (Portuguese is spoken in Brazil.)

According to Hadlich (1971), the impersonal construction is characterized syntactically by the fact that (1) there is no surface subject, (2) an agent of the action is *implicit,* (3) the agent of the action is *impersonal.* By impersonal he means specifically that the agent is not associated with any individual or group. Thus, the construction is comparable to the English impersonal use of "one" or "you" or "they" as in 4, 5, and 6 below:

4. One shouldn't smoke two packs a day.
5. You shouldn't smoke two packs a day.
6. They say that smoking two packs a day is bad for you.

Vázquez-Ayora, in his work on Spanish/English translation (1977:109), specifies that in the use of the third person plural impersonal for passive meaning, the agent is unknown. He suggests that the best translation, therefore, of sentence 7, below, is the Spanish gloss beneath it:

7. While they chatted about the flight, their luggage was brought around and they were taken to a side door. (*Mientras comentaban el vuelo, les trajeron el equipaje, y les acompañaron hacia una puerta lateral.*)

This construction belongs relatively close to the true passive on the continuum of responsibility attributed to an agent, for it entails the implication that an agent does exist, although his identity is not known. This is similar to the implied existence of an agent in the use of the true passive *ser* + past participle, although that agent appears on the surface only when the preposition *por* ("by") is used with the construction.

There is one major problem that the use of the third-person impersonal poses for interpretation/translation, and that is that it is inherently ambiguous. Without sufficient context, a sentence formulated by means of such a construction can be taken to have two meanings: (1) an active sentence, with a known third-person plural agent, (2) a passive sentence, with an impersonal subject, and therefore unknown agent. Consequently, in isolation—that is, without any further contextual information—sentences 8 and 9 have two meanings each, as indicated by (a) and (b):

8. *¿Lo detuvieron?*
   a. Did they arrest you?
   b. Were you arrested?
9. *Me interrogaron.*
   a. They questioned me.
   b. I was questioned.

Supposedly, with sufficient context, the sentences should be capable of disambiguation. One can imagine, however, the confused chain of questions and answers that might result if sentence 9 means gloss (b) for a Spanish-speaking witness, but is interpreted as gloss (a) by the interpreter. Interpretation (a) would very likely be followed by a question from the examining attorney along the lines of, "Who questioned you?" whereas interpretation (b) might not as readily provoke such a question.

The preceding example is merely a hypothetical example of "trouble," in sociologist Goffman's terms. Namely, it is a case of an inherent problem for interpreters: syntactic ambiguity. The discussion below presents data from actual courtroom situations that I have tape-recorded. The examples show how interpreters shift back and forth between active and passive voice, and within the passive voice,[1] among the several alternants available to them. It will be argued that interpreters manipulate grammatical case in order to achieve a particular pragmatic effect, sometimes consciously and sometimes not.

Intransitivity and Backgrounding in Legal Discourse

The pragmatic effect referred to above is backgrounding. Specifically, as Hopper and Thompson (1980) have found across languages, backgrounding in discourse can be achieved by the grammatical and semantic functioning of low transitivity. Foregrounding in discourse is achieved by high transitivity, transitivity itself being a scale, and high transitivity being characterized by the conscious activity of an agent, among other factors. It is argued here that the scale of attribution of responsibility to an agent, which appears in Figure 6.1, in effect reflects a scale of transitivity, high transitivity being found on the left-hand side, and low transitivity on the right.

The pragmatic connection between transitivity and grounding in discourse is related, in turn, to "decisions which speakers make, on the basis of their assessment of their hearers' situation, about how to present what they have to say" (Hopper and Thompson 1980:295). The linguistic situation of an examining attorney and a testifying witness or defendant is one in which the attorney must establish a set of facts, without appearing to put words into the witness's mouth, and the witness or defendant must portray himself and the events he witnessed in the most credible, convincing fashion possible. In an effort to avoid implicating specific persons in the adverse events around which a given trial revolves, until such time as the involvement of those persons has been properly established in court, lawyers make ample use of passive constructions—with or without agents. Witnesses and defendants, in turn, have their own reasons for wishing to put themselves and certain actors in the background, and to put other persons in the foreground. Intransitivity and passive voice are two effective grammatical ways of backgrounding agents, which in turn is a useful technique for achieving blame avoidance.

The reason why the alternation between active and passive is so important in the Spanish/English bilingual courtroom is not simply that this element of choice gives a speaker a linguistic mechanism for making himself appear more blameless and others more blameworthy. The significance of the role of case in the Spanish/English courtroom is that the use of the English passive is extremely high in American judicial settings. Just as it is characteristic of bureaucratic language in general, it has been found to be a characteristic of U.S. legalese in particular. However, as all Spanish translation texts will inform the reader, Spanish speakers assiduously avoid the true passive: one linguist from Spain has argued that the true passive construction is not used at all in spoken Spanish, and that it appears only in writing.[2]

Given the exceptionally high use of the passive in English legal contexts and the restricted use of the true passive in spoken Spanish, one might expect a built-in skewing of interpretations when one renders an English construction into Spanish. Specifically, it means that a Spanish speaker would avoid using the true passive in Spanish, and would use the several other alternatives available to him or her. However, it also means that the Spanish speaker would thereby do away with the only passive construction that implies a known agent.

What should be kept in mind throughout the following analysis is that Spanish speakers, in this case the interpreter and the Spanish-speaking witness or defendant, have several alternative constructions available to them, and that these can be used to describe one and the same situation. It is the fact that Spanish speakers have these options open to them whenever they describe an adverse situation that gives each construction its own implication in regard to the attribution of responsibility. Each of these constructions, then, colors a given situation in a particular way.

The Manipulation of Grammatical Case in the Bilingual Courtroom

In order to demonstrate the variety of ways in which an interpreter can render a series of questions that are constructed essentially in an identical fashion, using the passive voice in English, the following question/answer sequences have been taken from a single judicial proceeding, where the attorney, witness, judge, and interpreter are held constant—that is, the verbal participants remain the same. The context is the examination of a Mexican undocumented alien, who himself is not on trial in the particular case, but is a material witness against the defendant, the person who allegedly smuggled him across the Mexico/U.S. border for a fee. Such smugglers are known as *coyotes* in border Spanish/English slang.

Many of the question/answer sequences are temporally adjacent to each other, although some of the sequences are separated by other question/answer pairs not listed here (i.e., ones where the active/passive contrast does not enter the dialogue). Nevertheless, even where there is a temporal separation between one question/answer pair and another, the span of verbal interaction that intervenes is relatively brief. Thus, the text below represents a relatively continuous flow of questions and answers, and does in fact reflect the counterpart taped recording: a chunk of an attorney's examination of a witness.

6.1 (1) ATTORNEY: Sir, do you remember when you were apprehended[3] by the border patrol?
(2) INTERPRETER: *¿Se acuerda usted, señor, cuando lo aprehendieron a usted los patrulleros de la frontera?*
(3) WITNESS: *Sí.*
(4) INTERPRETER: Yes.
(5) ATTORNEY: Where was it that you were apprehended by the border patrol?

(6) Interpreter: *¿En qué lugar fue usted aprehendido por los patrulleros de la frontera?*
(7) Witness: *En la garita.*
(8) Interpreter: At, at the port of entry.
(9) Attorney: Sir, after you were apprehended by the border patrol, did ya give a sworn statement under oath to an agent of the border patrol?
(10) Interpreter: *Después de que fue usted apre-, aprehendido por los patrulleros de la frontera, dió usted una declaración jurada a uno de los patrulleros?*
(11) Witness: *Sí.*
(12) Interpreter: Yes.
(13) Attorney: Do you remember at that time being asked where and when you last entered the United States?
(14) Interpreter: *¿Se acuerda usted en el tiempo cuando el patrullero le hizo a usted las preguntas para su declaración jurada que le hicieron la pregunta, . . .*
(15) Attorney: Do you remember, sir, being asked this question:. . . .
(16) Interpreter: *¿Se acuerda usted, señor, que le preguntaron esta pregunta:. . . .*
(17) Attorney: Where were you going to be given a ride to, where was your destination?
(18) Interpreter: *¿Cuál era el destino de ustedes, hacia dónde les iba a dar el ride?*
(19) Attorney: Did you discuss with him where you were going to be taken?
(20) Interpreter: *¿Discutió usted con él adónde lo iba a llevar?*
(21) Attorney: When you were picked up by the car, did you, I take it that you got into the car, is that correct?
(22) Interpreter: *Cuando los levantó el carro, . . . cuando lo levantó a usted el carro. . . . Cuando a usted lo levantó el carro . . . estoy asumiendo que usted se subió al carro, ¿es esto correcto?*

To understand why there is variation in this interpreter's rendering of the attorney's passively constructed verb phrases, it is necessary to know something about her frame of mind and her attitudes regarding the case for which she is interpreting. Extensive conversations with the interpreter revealed a great sympathy on her part toward the undocumented aliens who daily are brought to the courthouse. In actuality, it is not they who are on trial, but the coyote, the person whom they pay to smuggle them into the United States. At the time of the ethnographic fieldwork, 1982–1983, whenever undocumented aliens were repeatedly caught by United States law enforcement officials, the magistrate in this particular court would give the illegal aliens three chances before he sentenced them to serve time in prison. In other words, no punitive action would be taken against these persons in the first few instances of illegal entry. In cases such as these, the aliens are probably unaware that they will be released the first two or three times. They have every reason to believe that they are in the courts to be punished, for they know that they have committed an illegal act and they realize that they are being held in custody by officials of the U.S. government. Consequently they are frightened.

The interpreter, and no doubt others in the courthouse, feel a sympathy for the undocumented Mexicans or Central Americans, and at the same time feel animosity toward the smuggler who is on trial. The particular interpreter who appears in the proceeding above held a strong feeling of rancor toward the coyotes. She explained that typically the coyotes exploit these unemployed Mexican peasants whom they bring across the border: they charge substantial fees for the service, and keep them in a type of indentured relationship. Thus, the illegal aliens become migrant workers quite far from the border, many heading toward Idaho and the Dakotas to pick potatoes during the harvest season there. At the same time, they must keep paying the coyotes until their debt to them is paid off. While they are working as migrant farm laborers they are threatened by the coyotes with physical reprisals if they consider not paying off their debts.

Finally, in addition to her feeling of sympathy for the undocumented alien and hostility toward the defendant coyote, the interpreter has a general antipathy toward the border patrol as a group, inasmuch as she has heard of systematic abuse of detained illegal aliens by border guards, and cites particular border crossing points as being notorious for the ill-treatment of arrestees. With all this background information in mind, the interpreter's shifting between grammatical cases can be more easily understood.

The attorney's questions, numbered 1, 5, and 9, have an identical structuring of the phrase containing a verb in the passive voice: they all repeat the phrase "you were apprehended by the border patrol."

This repetitive type of questioning pattern—that is, one in which a series of questions in close temporal proximity share a core of semantic substance—is very common in attorney examining routines. The attorney must elicit the information he seeks bit by bit, basing each question on the question he has asked prior to it, in order to establish the case he wishes to make. Thus, he needs to establish that the witness was in fact apprehended at a given time, in a given place, by certain law enforcement officials, and that he made certain declarations at the time of his arrest. For this reason, he will repeat the common core phrase, "you were apprehended" in questions relating to "when," "where," "by whom," and so on. Theoretically, that phrase ought to be interpreted in the same manner in each question. A look at question/answer sequences 1–10 reveals that that is not what happens in actuality. Of the three attorney questions, the second and third (utterances 5 and 9) are in fact interpreted correctly: English *be* + past participle + *by* + agent are rendered as Spanish *ser* + past participle + *por* + agent. Syntactically these happen to be parallel constructions in the two languages.

It is important to note that of the various passivelike constructions available to Spanish speakers, only the true passive admits the prepositional phrase *por* + agent—that is, agents cannot be mentioned with any of the other passives. Thus, to be true to the originally phrased question of the attorney in 1, 5, and 9, the interpreter should not use any of the other passives.[4] If she does, she automatically forfeits mentioning the agent ("the border patrol"), which is in fact a possibility available to her. Thus, agent-mentioning in the prepositional phrase "*por* + agent" is a linguistic constraint on choice of Spanish passive construction.

There are, in addition, further linguistic constraints related to the use of the true (*ser*) passive, constraints that may partially account for its limited use. The very comprehensive account of these constraints provided by Solé and Solé (1977:258) explains that "the passive with *ser* cannot be used with human subjects when the meaning of the verb implies the subject's deliberate or non-deliberate involvement or participation in the action." In addition, the *ser* passive cannot be used when the verb in question has an indirect object (Solé and Solé 1977:259). Nor can it be used with verbs of perception (see, hear, taste, smell), or when the mood of the verb is progressive (Valdés, Dvorak, Pagán Hannum 1984:61). Finally, there is a stylistic constraint on the *ser* passive, dictating that it not be used in informal speech, but that it be limited to formal speech contexts (Solé and Solé 1977:260).

Given these linguistic constraints on the use of the true passive, we find, nevertheless, that there is an ample number of instances where either the true passive or one of its substitutes should be used in the interpretation of attorney questions. Yet, in many instances the interpretations are rendered in the active voice. A case in point is the interpretation of sequence 1 in text 6.1.

In what way does the interpreter diverge syntactically from the English passive of utterance 1? She renders it, in 2, as an active voice construction, with the subject of the verb named (*cuando lo aprehendieron a usted los patrulleros de la frontera* = when the border patrol apprehended you). Pragmatically, what is the difference between the passive construction and its counterpart active one? Essentially it is a matter of focus. The passive construction places the focus on the receiver of the action, in this case "you," the undocumented alien who is testifying. The active voice focuses on the subject (the agent, or doer of the action) and the action itself. Thus, the interpreter's rendition in 2 shifts the focus away from the undocumented alien and aims it instead at the border patrol and its actions. The question is "why?"

It must be recalled that the testifying undocumented alien is himself *not* an accused party in this case, although admissions he makes regarding his own unlawful actions can be used against him on a subsequent occasion by the courts. Nevertheless, he is not being considered a possibly guilty party in the particular proceeding in which she is at the moment participating, and in addition the interpreter is sympathetic to his plight in the first place. What she has accomplished by shifting the focus of the attorney's question away from the Mexican witness and onto the border patrol is putting the witness somewhat more at ease, or, conversely, less on guard, and to a degree establishing some rapport with him. The witness is clearly intimidated and even frightened. It may not even be clear to him that it is not he who is being accused of a crime at the proceeding. All he knows is that he knowingly entered the United States illegally, in a covert way, was caught red-handed near the border by U.S. armed guards, is being kept incarcerated, and is now in a court of law before a federal magistrate. He has every reason to be frightened. The interpreter, by shifting the focus onto the border guard in her active-voice rendering of the question, lays the blame squarely on the guard for the adverse event, thereby moving it away from the witness.

One must then ask why the interpreter does not continue phrasing her subsequent interpretation (6 and 10) in the active voice—that is, why does she not stick to the same interpretation as in her first one

(2)? The answer would seem to be that 6 and 10, which are accurate renderings of the original English questions, are her basic interpretations. She is, in fact, a superb interpreter, and always aims at the highest quality of performance. Consciously or otherwise, she knows that 6 and 10 are the best equivalents of the attorney's repeated phrase. Consciously or unconsciously, however, she tries to set the witness at ease, perhaps, in Malinowski's (1923) terms, in an attempt to establish phatic communion with him, or perhaps an ethnic bonding. Furthermore, the border guards are for her the "bad guys," and portraying them in a blameworthy light is something she apparently cannot help doing.

Foregrounding the role of the border patrol is even more striking in 13–14 above. This time the attorney's passively worded question is asked in the progressive grammatical mood ("being asked . . ."), and there is no mention of an agent. Progressive mood is a linguistic constraint on the use of the true passive. Nevertheless, there are other passivelike constructions available for the interpretation. The interpreter, however, introduces an entire verb phrase that was not said by the attorney, using an active verb and agent in subject position, *el patrullero* (the patrolman). Hence, her interpretation in 14 should be glossed in English as follows: "Do you remember the time when *the patrolman asked you the questions for your sworn statement*, that you were asked. . . ." This is in contrast to the attorney's question: "Do you remember at that time being asked. . . ."

What is striking is the parallelism in the interpreter's shifting strategy. In both sequences 1–10 and 13–16 the interpreter begins interpreting a new question topic with an active verb form and subject of verb mentioned, contrary to the passive form used by the attorney. In her subsequent interpretations of the same verb phrase (see 16 in contrast to 14), she renders the interpretation accurately—that is, in a passive-type construction, and without an agent when there was no agent mentioned by the attorney (see 15 and 16).

It might be argued that one of the functions of inserting the actively worded phrase, *cuando el patrullero le hizo a usted las preguntas para su declaración jurada* (14), is to clarify for the witness the scene alluded to by the attorney, akin to refreshing his memory. It may be a type of clarification procedure for this interpreter. However, it serves equally to place into sharp focus the role of the border patrol on that occasion. Thus, whatever her motivation, within the verbal interaction, the border patrol is once again highlighted for the witness.

The correlation of active voice and blaming, and passive voice with backgrounding, is seen quite vividly in sequences 17–22. The topic here revolves around the mode of transportation by which the witness and the other undocumented aliens with him were brought across the border. Note that the attorney, in questions 17, 19, and 21, never once refers to the defendant, presumed to be the driver of the car. No person is ever mentioned, although his presence in the car is implied. The only agent ever mentioned is the car (21: "When you were picked up by the car, . . ."). All three questions by him are worded passively: "you were going to be given a ride," "you were going to be taken," "you were going to be picked up." All three are interpreted in the active voice: *hacia dónde les iba a dar el ride* (where was he going to give you a ride to?), *adónde lo iba a llevar* (where he was going to take you to?), *Cuando los levantó el carro, . . . cuando le levantó a usted el carro. . . . Cuando a usted lo levantó el carro* (when the car picked you [plural] up, . . . when the car picked you [singular] up. . . . When the car picked *you* [singular] up).

The interpretation of the attorney's last question (22) is a singularly vivid example of the interpreter's attention to detail and attempts at accuracy, with an apparent unconsciousness of the grammatical case of the English question. She engages in what is known in conversational analysis as a "repair mechanism," correcting herself twice in order to attain accuracy. The changes she makes are (1) a shift from second-person plural to second-person singular in reference to the object of the verb, and (2) a shifting in the position of that verb object to a more highlighted, or marked, place in the sentence (from "when you were picked up" to "when *you* were picked up"). Constant throughout her three attempts, however, is the role of the car as the subject of an active verb, whereas the attorney phrases his question passively, making the car the agent, but this time as object of the preposition, hence in a much less responsible role in the event.

The attorney's last question (21) stands in contrast to his first two in this sequence (17 and 19), in that it mentions an agent. In rendering her interpretation of 17 and 19 actively, however, the interpreter introduces an implicit agent, the unspoken subject of the active verb (*iba a dar, iba a llevar*). In Spanish subject pronouns are not needed in unmarked—that is, unemphasized or uncontrasted—verb phrases. The verb alone expresses grammatical person. Therefore, personal pronouns are usually omitted. They are used for clarity in potentially ambiguous contexts (e.g., third person, which uses the same grammatical form for "you" [formal, or polite form], "he," and "she"), and for certain pragmatic functions, such as emphasis or contrast. Thus, when the interpreter says, *¿Discutió con él adónde lo iba a llevar?*, the verb phrase *lo iba a llevar* necessarily means "*he* [emphasis added] was going to take you" since the verb *iba* must have some subject, and clearly it must be "he" since the third-person singular masculine subject pronoun *él* is referred to almost immediately before the verb phrase. The "he" in question is the defendant.

Thus, once again, by shifting from passive to active verb forms the interpreter has laid the blame on the subject of the active verb, in this case, the alleged coyote, the defendant. Even the defendant's car, the means by which he purportedly brought the witness across the border, is put into responsible, thus blameworthy, position.

The feeling of antipathy toward a defendant can be seen in other types of criminal cases, as well, to be the underlying cause of an interpreter's shifts in verb case. Texts 6.2–6.4 below come from a superior court murder trial in which a Cuban Marielito[5] defendant is accused of murdering a Mexican-American in a barroom brawl. To understand why the interpreter has rather negative feelings toward the defendant for whom she is interpreting, it must be pointed out that she is Mexican-American herself and has relatives living in the barrio, or Hispanic neighborhood, where the murder was committed.

More importantly, however, the defendant had shown himself on several prior occasions in court to be violent, and had lashed out at officials in the courtroom both verbally and physically. He had been placed under psychiatric examination to determine if he was mentally competent to stand trial. Thus, for a variety of reasons having to do with negative previous contact with the defendant, the interpreter feels a combination of fear of and dislike for him. Texts 6.2–6.4 are segments of the prosecuting attorney's opening statement at the trial.

6.2 (1) Attorney: As that bottle was thrown, Mr. Jiménez saw it, and tried to get a hand on it.
(2) Interpreter: *Cuando tiró la botella, el señor Jiménez la vió y trató de agarrarla.*

6.3 (1) Attorney: As I've indicated, the defendant has pleaded "not guilty."
(2) Interpreter: *Como se ha indicado el defendiente se ha declarado "no culpable" en esas acusaciones.*

6.4 (1) Attorney: And, uh, there are numerous versions of the facts that you will be concerning yourselves with.
(2) Interpreter: *Y hay nuevas cosas que ver entre las nuevas versiones en los hechos que se van a presentar a Uds.*

In statement 6.2(1), the attorney is referring to a bottle claimed to have been thrown by the defendant during the brawl that broke out in the bar. During an examination of a victim of the brawl who had survived a knife-stabbing, the attorney, in typical legalese, refers to the throwing of the bottle in the passive voice. The interpreter, however, changes the passive "that bottle was thrown" to the active counterpart, *tiró la botella* (he threw the bottle), thereby putting the defendant in a more responsible, and thus blameworthy, position.

In texts 6.3 and 6.4 the shifting of the interpretation is in the opposite direction. In both instances the attorney phrases a verb in the active voice with a personal pronoun identifying the subject of the verb, yet the interpreter renders the verb in a passive type of construction, specifically, the reflexive passive. The question is why, and what purpose does this shifting serve.

One of the problems that interpreters face is the possibility that the person for whom they are interpreting might misconstrue the subject pronouns "you" and "I" as referring to them—that is, the defendant or witness, and the interpreter, respectively. This is particularly likely to happen during simultaneous interpreting at the defense table. In effect, the use of the subject pronouns "you" and "I" might be taken by the defendant to mean that the interpreter is speaking for herself to him, personally—that is, engaging herself in a private side comment to him. To avoid implicating themselves by mistake, and to prevent the defendant's taking "you" to mean himself, interpreters will change an active verb form to a passive one, thereby doing away with the subject pronoun. This accounts for the interpreter's changing "as I've indicated" in 25 to *Como se ha indicado* (as it has been indicated), and "the facts that you will be concerning yourselves with" in 27 to *los hechos que se van a presentar a ustedes* (the facts that will be presented to you).[6] The avoidance of the subject pronouns "I" and "you" are particularly common in the interpretation of judges' speech to defendants, especially during the time of sentencing. Many interpreters systematically avoid these pronouns when the judge is declaring the sentence, and a common way to accomplish this is to use the passive voice. Some interpreters change active to passive voice when interpreting for a judge, even when the judge is not addressing the defendant. In the following case, the judge is explaining to the newly empaneled jury what the ensuing trial will be about. He says at one point, "As *I've indicated* [emphasis added] the defendant has pleaded guilty," using the present perfect tense and active case for the verb "indicate." The interpreter renders this as, *Como se ha indicado, el de-*

fendiente se ha declarado no culpable en esas acusaciones. She has used the Spanish dative of interest, meaning, "As *has been indicated*. . . ."

Other interpreters add to the first-person pronoun the word for "judge" (*juez*), so that when the judge says, "I am now remanding you to the authority of the federal marshalls," the interpreters will either say, *Yo, el juez* (I, the judge), to make it absolutely clear who the "I" refers to, or alternatively, they will use the noun phrase *El juez* by itself, thereby referring to the judge entirely in the third person.

The type of passive usage referred to above, which is a way of preventing the defendant from concluding that the interpreter is talking about herself, is thus a self-protective device. The protection is against the wrath of the defendant. Since interpreters are on many occasions assaulted in open court when the words they have uttered on behalf of a judge or an attorney or even a witness provoke the defendant's anger, the pronoun *yo* ("I") can be a dangerous word. The passive, because it can be stated in a variety of ways without an agent, avoids casting blame or responsibility on any person. It thus serves an important function for the interpreter, although by using it in place of an originally active sentence the interpreter somewhat alters the intention of the speaker whose speech she is interpreting.

Quantitative Evidence of Variation in the Interpretation of Verb Case

The kind of interpreter-induced variation in the interpretation of grammatical case of verbs presented above is by no means an isolated phenomenon. A quantitative analysis of the interpretation of verbs in two entire trials, both held in state-level courts, reveals that variation across all the verb phrase types discussed above is widespread. The analysis is based on a total of 228 instances in which either the source language or the target language verb phrase was uttered in some form of the passive voice. Table 6.1 displays the types of interpreter renditions that emerged in the transcriptions of the tape-recorded trials.

Perhaps most revealing, and reflective of the greatest discrepancy between source language and target language, is the interpretation of an active verb phrase as a passive one, and vice versa. This type of complete crossover of verb case occurred in 20.2 percent of the interpretations, 70 percent of them being changes of source language passive to target language active, and the remaining 30 percent being in the reverse direction. When active verb phrases were interpreted passively, in every case they were rendered in the reflexive passive.

Table 6.1. Variation in Interpreting Involving Verb Case (Instances of Nonactive Interpretation)

Changes in Verb Case	*N*	%
Active → Dative of Interest	14	6.1
Passive → Active	32	14.0
Passive → Reflexive Passive	44	19.3
Passive → Dative of Interest	17	7.5
Passive → 3rd Person Plural	40	17.5
Passive → ∅	16	7.0
Passive → Noun	3	1.3
Passive → Stative copula (*estar*) + adjectival participle	12	5.3
3rd Person Plural → Passive	1	0.4
Accurate Interpretation		
Passive → True Passive	48	21.1
Totals	228	100.0

Note: N represents all cases of interpreting where a nonactive verb form occurred in either the source language or the target language.

The interpretation of English passive verb phrases as Spanish true passives occurred in 21.1 percent of the instances. The Spanish true passive is the nearest equivalent of the English passive. Despite some claims that the true passive is not used at all or is used rarely in spoken Spanish, it is used with slightly greater frequency than the reflexive passive (19.3 percent), and with an even greater frequency than the third-person plural construction (17.5 percent). The rendering of English passive as Spanish dative of interest was far less preferred by the interpreters at work in these trials, accounting for only 7.5 percent of the interpretations. A sad commentary on the quality of the interpreting of one of the interpreters is that 7 percent of the verb phrases that were uttered in English in a passive form were not interpreted at all. In other words, the interpreter simply omitted chunks of source language speech when she provided the defendants and witnesses the interpretation.

Linguistic strategies that were unexpected were the rendering of passives as either (1) noun phrases or (2) as the stative copula *estar* followed by an adjectival participle—that is, an adjective derived from a past participle. An example of the former is the following source utterance and its interpretation: (1) the defense attorney, addressing the jury during the closing arguments of the trial, says, "before you allowed a certain operation to be conducted," which is rendered by the interpreter as *antes de permitir esa cirugía* [before allowing that surgery]. An instance of the latter is (2): the defense attorney, addressing the jury, says, "And I want you to know it's appreciated," which is rendered by the interpreter as *Y quiero que sepan que le estamos muy agradecidos* [And I want you to know that we're very grateful to you].

In the case of (1), the passive infinitive "to be conducted" is eliminated altogether, leaving in its place only the noun phrase *esa cirugía*, which the interpreter has rendered as the equivalent of the attorney's phrase, "a certain operation." In example (2), the passive "it's appreciated" is interpreted in Spanish as *le estamos agradecidos*, which consists of the copula verb *estar* and the adjectival participle *agradecidos*. Spanish uses this type of construction to indicate the *result* of passivization. Syntactically, there is a great similarity between this type of construction and the true passive, which uses the other copula, *ser*, followed by an adjectival participle. However, when *ser* is used with the adjectival participle, the verb retains the force of a passivized event, whereas when *estar* is used all that is conveyed is the end result of the event, which is some type of state of being.

Another major difference in pragmatic intention between the attorney's phrasing of his appreciation to the jury and the interpreter's rendition of the attorney's utterance is that the attorney for whatever reason has chosen not to refer directly to himself, as the agent of the verb, or to the jurors. The interpreter's rendition, however, contains an implicit verb subject, "we," and an overt indirect object, "to you" (*le*). In effect, the interpreter has converted a very impersonally phrased statement into one that manifestly links an agent of the verb with an indirect object of it.

What has been demonstrated in this chapter is that interpreters are unconsciously aware of the implications involved in the use of active and passive grammatical forms, and manipulate these forms for a variety of psychological reasons. To what extent a given interpreter alters the case of a verb knowingly in any specific instance cannot be known, short of asking her afterward why she had rendered her interpretation in that fashion. Questions of this nature are likely to provoke either defensive denials of having engaged in such manipulations, or genuine expressions of surprise and even disbelief. The best the observer can do is to note the association of certain verbal behaviors with particular situations or contexts, and to conclude from these repeated associations the social meaning of a particular linguistic usage. There is no doubt that interpreters make use of the passive to distance agents from actions and use the active case to link the two.

7

The Intersection of Testimony Styles in Interpreted Judicial Proceedings: Pragmatics and the Lengthening of Testimony

The manipulation of grammatical case is but one of the many pragmatic alterations that interpreters effectuate. This chapter demonstrates various other pragmatic shifts made in the course of interpreting, focusing directly on witness testimony. It will be shown that interpreters tend to lengthen testimony, and that in the process, they convert "fragmented" speech style into a more narrative testimony style. This lengthening is accomplished by the introduction of elements that are characteristic of "powerless" testimony style. The analysis is based upon the transcribed testimony of twenty-seven witnesses, comprising 2,470 answers as rendered by six court interpreters.

Length of Answer and Attorney Control

The distinction between narrative and fragmented testimony comes down to a distinction between long answers and short answers—that is, answer length. The length of a witness's answer to a question is in fact largely controlled by the examining attorney. Lind and O'Barr (1979: 74–75) have noted,

> the principle in Anglo-American legal procedure that most of the control over the substance and form of testimony is delegated to the interrogating attorney. Since this principle of attorney control is widely known, it seemed likely that narrative testimony would be seen by jurors as an instance of voluntary, partial transfer from the attorney to the witness of control over evidence presentation.

Danet et al. (1980), recognizing the relationship between length of witness answer and degree of attorney control, have used answer length as an index of an attorney's control over his witness. Both Danet et al. (1980) and Bresnahan (1979) have found that coercive questions result in a higher proportion of short answers than do noncoercive questions. By a process of deduction, if witness answers could be shown to be lengthened not by the operation of the examining attorney but by that of another participant in the interaction (e.g., the court interpreter), then it would mean that the attorney can be considered to have lost a measure of control over the witness whom he is questioning.

Spanish is Generally Longer than English in Translation

Those who are professional translators of Spanish and English are aware that the Spanish version of a text generally comes out longer than the English. Awareness of this difference stems from the fact that free-lance translators are generally paid by the page. One former federal court interpreter who currently does interpreting on a California Spanish/English bilingual news program estimates that, "Spanish takes 30 percent more words" (McEwan 1986:5).[1] It will be shown below why Spanish systematically is longer than English in translation/interpretation. Essentially, it is because large numbers of one-word English constructions are translated as phrases of two or more words in Spanish.

In his book on translating, Vázquez-Ayora (1977:336) notes that "all those who have practiced English/Spanish translating have the experience of the Spanish version tending to be much longer" than the English version. This difference in length, or "margin," he attributes to "the great economy of the English language." He points to a number of aspects of English and Spanish syntactic structure that necessitate an "amplification," or enlargement, when the translator goes from English to Spanish. By amplification Vázquez-Ayora (337) means the process by which the language of translation, or target language, uses more lexemes or morphemes than does the source language to express the same idea. Specifically, the structures of English that need amplification when rendered into Spanish are the following: (a) adverbs, (b) verbs, (c) adjectives, (d) pronouns, (e) demonstratives, and (f) prepositions.

Adverbs of frequency that end in *-ly* in English, on the whole, are best rendered in Spanish not in their adverbial form—that is, adverbs ending in the suffix *-mente*—but rather, as a prepositional phrase or some other periphrastic construction. Thus, the following English adverbs are best translated into Spanish as the phrases following each: angrily: *con furia;* suddenly: *de repente, de golpe;* instantly: *en el acto, al momento;* shortly: *a la mayor brevedad, en breve;* seriously: *con seriedad, de gravedad.*

There are many verbs in English that are usually expressed as periphrastic constructions in Spanish. For example, the translation of "mean" in the sentence, "I don't know what you mean," is *quieres decir,* as in *No sé lo que quieres decir.* Similarly, "to review" is usually translated as *pasar revista* or *dar una mirada;* "to surface" is *salir a la superficie;* "to endanger" is rendered as *poner en peligro.*

English adjectives when translated into Spanish behave in a manner similar to English adverbs: they become prepositional phrases. The following phrase from Vázquez-Ayora contains two instances of such adjectives. The adjectives and their corresponding translations have been underlined for clarity:

> Of the great outward movement from the inner city
> *Del gran movimiento desde el corazón* de *la ciudad hacia el exterior*

In the case above, the translator has transposed the equivalents of "outward" (*hacia el exterior*) and "inner" (*desde del corazón de*) so as to make them conform to Spanish stylistic expectations.

One of the most frequent sources of amplification of English pronouns in the translating process is the fact that the form of the third-person possessive pronoun, *su,* is ambiguous in Spanish, whereas English lexically distinguishes its pronouns in the third person. Thus, the equivalent of English "his," "her," "your," "its," and "their," is the Spanish pronoun *su.* The inherent ambiguity of *su* causes Spanish speakers to add clarifying phrases to it, so that the hearer knows what the pronoun refers to. In many colloquial registers of Spanish, both in Spain and in Latin America, added to the pronoun *su* are clarifying prepositional phrases, such as *de usted, de él, de ella, de ustedes, de ellos, de ellas* ("your," "his," "her," "your" [plural], "their" [masculine and feminine]). Thus, in colloquial Spanish speakers may say (b) for English (a), or, more standardly (c). In either event the English pronoun "your" is expanded into a phrase:

> (a) How is your mother?
> (b) *¿Cómo está su madre de usted?*
> (c) *¿Cómo está la madre de usted?*

Demonstratives are amplified in the translation of English to Spanish, according to Vázquez-Ayora (342), because the Spanish demonstrative has a weaker anaphoric reference than does the English demonstrative. Note Vázquez-Ayora's translation of "that" in the following example:

> A problem like that
> *un problema de ese género* (A problem of that type)

Prepositions are particularly subject to amplification in the translation of English into Spanish. What are single prepositions in English emerge as various sorts of phrases, phrases consisting of a preposition and either a noun, a verb, a part participle, or else relative clauses. The example below (Vázquez-Ayora, 342–46) illustrates the rendering of an English preposition as a Spanish phrase consisting of a preposition plus a noun:

PREPOSITION-NOUN
the night express for Birmingham
el expreso nocturno con destino a Birmingham

To sum up the argument that has been made in this section, then, there is a systematic difference in the way that various syntactic construction types are formed in English and Spanish, whereby what tend to be one-word constructions in English turn out to be phrases of two or more words in Spanish. This would lead one to the expectation that, overall, when a sentence is translated or interpreted from English into Spanish, the Spanish rendition will be longer than the English, and conversely, when a Spanish sentence is rendered in English, the translation or interpretation will emerge shorter than the original.

Lengthening of Testimony by the Court Interpreter

The discussion above has shown various factors that account for the generally greater length of Spanish textual material compared to its equivalent English. One would expect, therefore, that if we counted the length of Spanish utterances and their best rendition in English, the English would emerge as shorter. The ethnographic observation carried out by this investigator in federal, state, and city courts left her with the impression, however, that the interpreter's English version was longer than the original Spanish testimony. It is this hypothesis that has been tested here. What follows below is a quantitative analysis of the Spanish testimony of twenty-seven witnesses and the interpretation of that testimony into English by six court interpreters.

The testimony of the twenty-seven witnesses comes from six trials, one preliminary hearing, and fourteen depositions taken before a federal magistrate. Of the six trials, two took place in federal court, two in state-level courts, and two in municipal courts. The preliminary hearing took place in a justice of the peace court. It is a procedure used to determine if there is sufficient evidence against the defendant to bring him up for trial in the state-level court. The depositions all were taken in a federal courthouse before a magistrate, in the presence of an attorney for the defense, a federal prosecutor, and attorneys for the material witnesses who were testifying. In all the cases of depositions the witnesses were illegal aliens who themselves were not on trial, but who were testifying in regard to defendants who in the various cases pending were on trial for transporting them across the U.S./Mexico border. The two federal trials dealt with cocaine smuggling and bail jumping. In the superior court trials one had to do with purse-snatching and the other with murder. In the city court trials one dealt with shoplifting and the other with a traffic violation. The preliminary hearing had to do with a mugging in a liquor store.

Of the six court interpreters who did the interpreting in the cases examined, three of the four work full-time in their respective courts as interpreters, and two of the others work on a contractual basis as free-lancers in their courthouse. The sixth is a court clerk who used to do interpreting on a regular basis until a full-time interpreter was hired and took over her role. Of the six, two are men and four are women. Only two of the six interpreters have attained federal certification.

The analysis of the data is based on a total of 2,470 answers. It is important to note that an answer cannot be equated with a sentence, for answers can be as minimal as "Uh huh," and alternatively they can extend over a series of sentences. An answer, then, is a turn at talk, in the sense of Sacks, Schegloff, and Jefferson (1974). It is the talk produced by a witness that is bounded by either an attorney's or a judge's verbal intervention. Attorney interventions are usually in the form of next questions; however, sometimes they are objections from the attorney who is not the one carrying out the examination process. The interventions of judges are usually in the from of admonitions or signals permitting the witness to continue speaking.

Table 7.1 presents the number of answers per witness, and gives the mean length of those answers, both in the original Spanish and in the English interpretation. The mean is calculated as the total number of words produced by the witness, in both direct examination and cross-examination, divided by the total number of answer turns. The table is organized vertically according to the highest number of answers, at the top, to the lowest number of answers, at the bottom. What is of interest in this table is the extent to which the length of the English interpretations of the Spanish testimony is systematically

Table 7.1. Length of Witness Testimony in Spanish/English Interpreted Judicial Proceedings (Paired *t*-Test Results)

		Words per Answer				
Witness number	No. of Answers	Mean Spanish	Mean English	Diff. Mean	*t*-value	Sig.
1	203	9.2	10.6	1.40	5.60	<.001
2	196	7.1	7.2	.15	.74	NS
3	177	4.5	5.6	1.08	4.94	<.001
4	162	4.3	6.3	1.99	7.26	<.001
5	159	8.3	8.9	.60	.91	NS
6	130	3.0	4.4	1.45	6.65	<.001
7	114	11.6	13.9	2.29	4.73	<.001
8	112	7.7	8.4	.67	2.31	.022
9	108	8.2	11.1	2.88	6.81	<.001
10	95	2.7	3.9	1.20	6.18	<.001
11	92	3.1	4.3	1.27	5.24	<.001
12	86	8.2	8.5	.31	.90	NS
13	82	7.2	8.5	1.28	3.21	.002
14	77	4.8	5.7	.90	3.89	<.001
15	74	4.9	6.1	1.20	3.88	<.001
16	73	6.1	7.4	1.27	4.57	<.001
17	71	23.4	19.0	4.48	4.43	<.001
18	66	15.3	14.3	1.00	1.45	NS
19	56	6.1	8.5	2.34	4.18	<.001
20	52	9.6	13.5	3.90	5.92	<.001
21	52	5.8	5.6	.21	.22	NS
22	52	7.7	8.5	.75	1.01	NS
23	49	5.5	7.1	1.63	4.69	<.001
24	48	9.6	12.1	2.44	3.87	<.001
25	40	5.9	6.3	.43	.93	NS
26	25	7.1	9.7	2.60	.08	NS
27	19	15.6	17.9	2.37	1.70	NS
Total	2,470					

Note: NS = not significant at .05 or better.

different from the length of the original. It should be kept in mind that, all other things being equal, one would expect to find the English interpretations to be systematically shorter than the Spanish original answers.

Table 7.1 shows that with the exception of three cases, overwhelmingly the mean length of English interpretations is longer than the mean length of the Spanish answers. Given that the English interpretations would be expected to be significantly shorter, this finding is striking.

While 86 percent of the interpretations are longer than the original Spanish answers, these figures must be put to a test of statistical significance to see whether the difference in means is really meaningful. Thus a "paired *t*-test" was applied to the mean scores for each witness. This particular test of significance is appropriate in situations analogous to a "test-retest" situation—that is, in a situation where the same individual is taking the same test—let us say, before and after undergoing training for a given task. In the case being analyzed in this chapter, the test-retest situation involves, in the first instance, the answer to the question stated by the witness in Spanish, while the retest involves that same answer as interpreted by the interpreter.

As can be seen in the far-right column of Table 7.1, of the twenty-four pairs in which the English interpretation is longer than the Spanish original, the difference in means is statistically significant for seventeen. While this is encouraging insofar as confirming the hypothesis is concerned, one still wonders about the remaining seven for which the difference in means is not significant. Closer inspection of the pattern of Spanish and English answers in this group reveals that they have one thing in common—namely, a relatively high preponderance (35 percent or more) of very short answers (three words or fewer), or a very small percentage (5 percent or fewer) of long narrative answers (20 words or more). With the low percentage of lengthy narrative answers and the high percentage of what actually are yes/no answers (or their variants, "Yes, sir," "No, sir"; "Yes, I did," "No, I didn't"), there is little room for variation in interpretation. While there can indeed be variation in the interpretation of one-to-three word answers, for interpreters do in fact systematically either insert or omit the polite address forms "sir" and "ma'am" after "yes" and "no" answers in their interpretations, the difference in means that can result from such an alteration can only be small, since at most there will be a one-word difference at stake.

The question still remains as to why for three of the twenty-seven witnesses the length of the Spanish answers was greater than that of the English interpretations—that is, the relationship is in a direction opposite of that which was hypothesized. An examination of the transcripts and a review of the taped recordings explains the anomalies. In the case of witness #17, not only is the difference in means in the opposite direction, but the difference is statistically significant. Why is this so? The taped recording reveals that the interpreter in this case was performing primarily simultaneous interpreting at the witness stand, rather than the recommended consecutive mode. What happened during the proceeding is that since she was speaking as she was listening to the witness, and consequently could not take notes, as is customary during consecutive interpreting, she frequently omitted from her interpretation entire sentences that the witness had said. Thus, in comparing the total words of the English interpretation with the total words of the Spanish testimony, we find 1,346 words versus 1,664. This particular witness's testimony was laden with narrative-style testimony (about 47 percent of his testimony comprised answers of twenty words or more). In the interpreter's English rendition only 34 percent of the answers fit into this long narrative category. This interpreter made systematic changes at the short-answer level as well: every time the witness answered the questions with *Sí, señorita* (Yes, ma'am) the interpreter rendered it as a one-word "Yes." Thus, in the witness's replies there is no instance of a one-word answer. His shortest answers are two words in length, and these constitute 8.5 percent of his answers. Yet among the interpreter's interpretations exactly 8.5 percent comprise one-word answers. Clearly, then, the reason for the significantly briefer answers in English is the poor quality of interpreting on the interpreter's part: she did not interpret the entire content of the witness's answer.

The following set of questions, answers, and their interpretation illustrates how the English interpretation of the Spanish testimony omitted substance produced by the witness. They come from a preliminary hearing involving the alleged mugging of an elderly Mexican-American man in a liquor store. The testimony in text 7.1 below is given by the victim of the mugging. For the sake of clarity, those portions of the witness's testimony that were not interpreted have been underlined. This writer's own translation follows in parentheses, using lower-case letters, and underlining those segments that correspond to the underlined portions of the Spanish testimony found above it. Bracketed material represents nonverbal communication.

7.1 Prosecuting attorney: Mr. Gómez, when you were hit, what, what was taken from you?

Interpreter: *Que cuando fue golpeado ¿qué es lo que le quitaron, qué es lo que tomaron?*

Witness: *<u>Pues todo.</u> <u>Todo se llevaron con mi car-</u>. . . . El pasaporte, <u>este,</u> tarjetas que traíba de importancia, mi—<u>Una prueba, más prueba voy a darle, mire:</u> acabo de sacar el permiso de, del, de la emigración y aquí está,*

mire [as he pulls out his wallet], *ahí está, . . . porque se llevaron todo, ¡sss!*[2] [he shows the court his empty wallet]
INTERPRETER: Everything, my passport, important cards, important cards that I have. I've just, uh, I've just applied for immigration and this is it, because they took everything from me. (Well everything. Everything was taken with my wall—. . . . My passport, uh, important cards that I was carrying, my—Here's proof, I'm going to give you more proof, look: I've just gotten my permit from Immigration, and here it is, look [indicating his empty wallet], there it is! Because they took everything, jeez!)

It is important to realize that throughout the making of this statement, the witness is highly agitated and emotional. He is a retired man, and from his wallet had been stolen his monthly Social Security pension check along with another check, which together constituted his sole monthly earnings. Thus, as he testifies he speaks in a highly emphatic manner, frequently increasing the volume of his voice and the rapidity of his speech. He is trying to make his case as forcefully as he can, and in the process repeats phrases, uses many deictic expressions, and relies heavily on kinesics, making frequent use of gesture to demonstrate to the Court why he is justified in his outrage against the defendant. His reiteration that "everything was taken," and his attempt to offer evidence—his empty wallet—make him appear very sincere and justifiably indignant. Yet is it precisely this insistence on repeating that *everything* had been stolen from his wallet, and the attempt to demonstrate this to the Court, which are missing from the interpreter's rendition of his testimony. It should be kept in mind that the purpose of the preliminary hearing in lower-level courts is to determine whether there is sufficient evidence against a defendant to have him stand trial in a court of higher jurisdiction. The judge alone, hearing the testimony of witnesses, makes the decision in this regard. His understanding of the testimony comes entirely through the filter of the interpreter's interpretation of it.

In the particular case cited above, the witness was much more convincing in his Spanish testimony than was the interpreter in her English rendition of that testimony, and this is because she omitted some of the witness's testimony. It is possible that the interpreter considered the utterances that she omitted to be merely repetitions of something that she was about to interpret in one form anyway, and that she considered deictic expressions, such as "Look here," to convey no true information, since they serve largely to draw the attention of the listener. Nevertheless, both omissions corresponded to emphatic statements of the witness, and the fact that one was a reiteration and the other a supplication to view his evidence meant that the sense of indignation and urgency in his message was diminished by the interpreter.

In the two other instances where the mean length of the English interpretation is shorter than that of the Spanish, explanations once again can be found in the operation of the interpreter. In the case of witness #18, the interpreter had a great deal of difficulty retaining in memory the long stretches of narrative testimony that he was providing. She frequently had to interrupt him in midstream to ask him to repeat what he had just said. In effect then, the witness often doubled the length of his answer in order to satisfy the interpreter's request. She in turn would interpret only one version of his answer. Thus, her interpretation in several instances was about half as long as his entire Spanish turn at talk.

This particular interpreter was found to do this type of interrupting in many other instances in which she was observed at work. The examination sequence below, text 7.2, which is taken from a trial involving a purse-snatching incident, illustrates how an interpreter's interruptions of a witness can lead to a briefer English interpretation than the source language original. It also results in the lengthening of the witness's testimony in the source language. In this text the defense attorney is asking the defendant to recount his movements at the time when the purse-snatching was going on. The defendant is retracing his steps on a diagram that has been drawn for the benefit of the jury.

7.2 DEFENSE ATTORNEY: Okay, so you walked north on Clark Avenue, which would be off the map. Is that right?

INTERPRETER: *¿Así es que usted caminó norte de la, la Avenida Clark?*

DEFENDANT: *Sí, yo caminé por la Avenida Clark al norte, y de, y de aquí cuando agarré la Clark de oeste a este* (Yes, I walked along Clark Avenue heading north, and from, and from here when I took Clark going from west to east)

INTERPRETER: *¿Cómo? ¿Qué—*

DEFENDANT: *De oeste a este, y aquí entré al patio éste, y aquí fue cuando como a unas veinticinco yardas, fue cuando miré al bus y como no, no hay otra parada aquí* (From west to east, and here I entered this yard, and

it was here when, about twenty-five yards away, was when I saw the bus, and since there isn't any other bus stop here)
INTERPRETER: *¿Y cómo?* (What?)
DEFENDANT: *Y como no hay otra parada de bus, no quise que se me fuera y, eh, y corrí un momento pidiéndole al, al, al chofer que me esperara y él esperó por mí y me subí.* (And since there isn't any other bus stop, I didn't want it to get away from me, and, uh, and I ran for a moment, asking the, the, the driver to wait for me, and he waited for me, and I got on.)
INTERPRETER: I walked on Clark Avenue to the north, and here when I got from west to east and here I entered into this patio. And about some twenty-five yards from here was when I saw the bus and because there's not another bus stop there I didn't want the bus to go and I ran over there asking the chauffeur to wait for me and he waited for me and I got on.

As can be seen in text 7.2, each time the interpreter interrupts the witness in his testimony, using the expression *¿Cómo?* (What?), he begins his next utterance by repeating what he had just said before the interruption. Thus, after the first interruption, the witness reiterates, *De oeste a este* (from west to east), and after the second interruption, he repeats his explanation, *como no hay otra parada de bus* (since there's no other bus stop), to account for why he chased down the street after the bus.

Besides the factor of repetition provoked by interpreter queries, there is the element of witness hesitation and backtracking—that is, repeating one or two words that mark the beginning of a new phrase. Such brief backtracking repetitions tend not to be interpreted into English. Note the discrepancy between the Spanish repetitive, hesitant style (*Y de, y de aquí cuando agarré la Clark; y como no, no, hay otra parada; pidiéndole al, al, al chofer; Y, eh, y corri*), and the corresponding interpretations, which do not include the repeated elements: "and here,"[3] "and because there's not another bus stop there," "asking the chauffeur,"[4] "and I ran."

In the case of the third witness whose Spanish testimony emerged longer than the interpreter's rendition (witness #21), just as in the case of the nonsignificant differences in mean that were in the hypothesized direction, here too there was a preponderance of short answers (44 percent were three words or fewer), and a very low percentage (4 percent) of lengthy answers (20 words or more). If one looks at the two means, one finds that actually they are very similar (5.8 versus 5.6). the fact that one is higher than the other but in the wrong direction can be explained only by looking at the interpretations in the transcript.

What has happened in this case is that the witness frequently stops in mid-sentence, hesitates, backtracks, and either rephrases or repeats portions of his last few words. The interpreter, however, just as in the case of the interpreter for witness #18 above, does not replicate these false starts and hesitation phenomena in English. Thus, her interpretation gives a smoother, more coherent impression, and at the same time emerges shorter in length than the original Spanish testimony. The testimony is that of an illegal alien, who is being asked about the role played by the defendant in the case, the man accused off having brought him into the United States illegally, for a fee.

In text 7.3 below, the prosecuting attorney asks the witness if he had been met by anyone after crossing over to the United States side of the U.S./Mexico border, and the witness answers that a tall Mexican was there to meet him:

7.3. PROSECUTING ATTORNEY: And where did he meet you?
INTERPRETER: *¿Y en qué lugar se encontraron ustedes con este mexicano alto?*
WITNESS: *Yo recién lo había visto en la, en la cerca.*
INTERPRETER: I had seen him at the fence.

....

PROSECUTING ATTORNEY: Where were you at when you first saw Mr. Hawkins?
INTERPRETER: *¿Dónde estaba usted la primera vez que usted vio al señor Hawkins?*
WITNESS: *La primera vez, la primera vez estaba en la camioneta.*
INTERPRETER: The first time was at the station wagon or small truck.

The last answer and its interpretation happen to be equal in terms of length, despite the fact that the interpreter did not interpret a phrase that the witness had repeated (*la primera vez*), and this is because the interpreter uses a device that she often employs whenever a word in the source language has more than one gloss in the target language: rather than to stop the proceeding to inquire as to which meaning is the one that applies to the word, she provides both meanings ("station wagon" and "small truck"). Techniques such as this counterbalance the interpreter's failure to interpret repetitive backtrackings and hesitation phenomena.

How Testimony is Lengthened through Interpretation

Whereas a quantitative analysis has shown that the tendency among interpreters generally is to lengthen testimony, it does not tell us if there is any linguistic patterning to this lengthening process. A close look at pairs of Spanish/English answers reveals that in fact something systematic is going on in the conversion from Spanish to English. Specifically, the English interpretations (1) add hedges, (2) insert linguistic material that is perceived to be underlying or "understood" in the original utterances, (3) use uncontracted forms, (4) rephrase what the interpreter herself has just said in her interpretation, (5) add polite forms of address, and (6) add particles and hesitation forms. It is important to notice that most of these mechanisms turn out to be features of powerless testimony style. Examples of each follow below.

Hedges. In a case involving the transporting of illegal aliens across the U.S. border, the prosecuting attorney asks the witness who else had crossed the border with him:

7.4 ATTORNEY: Approximately how many?
INTERPRETER: *¿Aproximadamente cuántos?*
WITNESS: *Un promedio de veintiuno.*
INTERPRETER: Uh, probably an average of twenty-one people.

What the witness has actually said in Spanish is "an average of twenty-one." The interpreter has added three sorts of elements to her interpretation of the original answer: a hesitation form ("uh"), a hedge ("probably"), and a noun that can be construed by listeners as existing as the head of an underlying phrase whose English interpretation is "twenty-one people." In the question/answer given above, both the hesitation form and the hedge serve to make the answer less sure, less definite, and the witness less strongly committed to his affirmation. In fact, both hesitation forms and hedges are part of the constellation of features that constitute *powerless* testimony style. The net result is that the witness's answer in English sounds weaker in the strength of its affirmation than it did in Spanish.

The intrusion of hedges can be seen again in text 7.5, taken from another case involving the transporting of illegal aliens into the United States. Here the attorney asks the witness about his first contact with the defendant:

7.5 ATTORNEY: When did, when did you first see Mr. Rogers?
INTERPRETER: *¿Cuál fue la primera vez que usted vio al señor Rogers?*
WITNESS: *¿Acá en los Estados Unidos?*
INTERPRETER: <u>You mean</u> here in the United States?

The witness actually has said, "Here in the United States?" The insertion of the phrase "you mean" serves as a hedge on his question. It makes the witness appear to understand the attorney's question to a lesser extent than does his Spanish question. While an expression such as "you mean" is considered to be a meaningless phrase, it nevertheless serves to diminish the strength or power of the witness's question. In fact, those expressions that belong to the category of "meaningless phrase" can be considered to pertain to the larger category "hedges," if we use as our notion of hedging that developed by Brown and Levinson (1978:150–77). They define a hedge as ". . . a particle, word, or phrase that modifies the degree of membership of a predicate or noun phrase in a set; it says of that membership that it is *partial*, or true only in certain respects, or that it is *more* true and complete than perhaps might be expected" (Brown and Levinson, 150). The expression "sort of," is an archetypical form of a hedge. It is clear from the following description by an illegal alien of the airplane that flew him into Mexico that he is quite clear and definite in his characterization of the appearance of that plane. The interpreter, on the other hand, by adding the phrase "sort of," coupled with her rephrasing of the word *rayitos* (stripes), gives his description an element of vagueness and uncertainty.

7.6 WITNESS: *Una avioneta pequeña blanca con rayitos azules.*
INTERPRETER: It was a small airplane, white, with a sort of, a sort of blue lines, blue stripes.

Insertion of Substance considered to be "Understood" in the Meaning of Utterances. One of the most common ways in which interpreters lengthen testimony presented in the source language, a technique already alluded to in the analysis of text 7.4, is to insert linguistic material which they perceive is "understood" but is not explicitly stated in the utterances of witnesses. Thus, if one were to answer in the affirmative the question, "Did he have a beard at that time?" one would most typically say, "Yes, he did." This would be the linguistically unmarked, or expected, normal answer to a yes/no type of question phrased in the past tense. For one to answer, "Yes, he did have a beard," is to place special emphasis on the fact that he did. It stresses the fact that he had a beard. Spanish does not use an auxiliary such as 'do' in asking and answering yes/no type questions. It must employ the full verb. However, the verb need not be followed by a noun in the answer to a yes/no question.

If we examine the question/answer text below, in which the witness is asked to describe the defendant, we see that even though the witness is answering the questions in the unmarked form, omitting mention of a noun object of the verb, the interpreter renders his answer in a syntactic form that reveals the insertion of such a noun following the verb.

7.7 ATTORNEY: All right, do you remember whether or not he had a beard at that time?
INTERPRETER: *¿Se ac-, se acuerda usted, eh, señora, si entonces en ese tiempo tenía él barba?*
WITNESS: *Sí tenía.*
INTERPRETER: He <u>did</u> have <u>a beard.</u>
ATTORNEY: How about a mustache?
INTERPRETER: *¿Y bigote tenía, señora?*
WITNESS: *No me fijé si tenía bigote pero barba sí tenía.*
INTERPRETER: I did not, I did not notice if he had a mustache, but <u>I noticed though</u> that he had a beard.

The witness's first answer, as rendered by the interpreter, "he did have a beard," is much more emphatic and definite in its assertion than is the expected, normal response, "Yes, he did." Similarly, the addition of the phrase, "I noticed though" in the interpreter's rendition of *barba sí tenía* (best interpreted as "he did have a beard"), makes the witness's recollection more sure-sounding than it did in the Spanish. It tells the hearer that the witness had in fact taken note of this detail of the defendant's appearance. Witness descriptions of how the defendant had looked at the scene of the crime become vital pieces of evidence in later claiming or disclaiming that the person standing trial is in fact the same one who had been present at the scene of the crime. The degree of certainty with which a witness can describe the appearance of the defendant on that previous occasion can be a highly influential factor for a jury in its deliberations.

Two clear-cut additional examples of this type of interpreter lengthening mechanism, the insertion of what the interpreter considers to be understood in the witness's utterance, are texts 7.8 and 7.9 below. In the first, the attorney asks the witness to explain who drove the car to the airport where he was to board a plane that was to take him to a border town, and the witness answers:

7.8 WITNESS: *¿Al aeropuerto de Juárez?*
INTERPRETER: You mean, who drove to the airport at Juárez?

In text 7.9, the witness is asked if he has ever had a conversation with the defendant, and he answers:

7.9 WITNESS: *No, de ninguna manera.*
INTERPRETER: No, in no way did I ever have any conversation with him.

The interpretation in 7.9 is a particularly striking instance of this type of lengthening. Syntactically, the underlined portion of the sentence may be "understood" by the English speaker to be underlying the answer. However, to say what the interpreter did, as opposed to saying, "No, in no way," is to be absolutely, unequivocally sure of oneself in one's answer and to say so quite emphatically. This kind of emphatically expressed, absolute certainty is not conveyed by the briefer, more accurate interpretation.

Unfortunately, at times the filling in of material that the interpreter senses is "understood" in the statement of the witness goes too far—that is, it adds substance that cannot be seen by an observer to be underlying the witness's abbreviated answer. In a case involving the transporting of illegal aliens, for example, a witness answers the attorney's question with the one-word answer, "No." The interpreter renders it in English as, "I never did." When asked if he had expected to see the smuggler again, after paying him the fee for transporting him to the United States, the witness answers, "*No, no esperaba*" (meaning, "No, I didn't expect to"). The interpreter renders his answer as, "It is correct. I did not expect to see him again." Again, this kind of interpreter-induced lengthening results in an impression of greater certainty: the witness's interpreted testimony in English is far more sure-sounding than is his own Spanish testimony.

Uncontracted forms. A third way in which interpreters regularly lengthen a witness's testimony is to use uncontracted forms when normally English-speakers would use contracted forms. This usually involves the contraction of the auxiliaries "be" and "have," the modal "will," and the full verb "be." Normally, in spoken American English, when the auxiliary or modal is preceded by a subject pronoun and followed by a full verb, contraction will occur unless the speaker wishes to emphasize or stress the meaning of the auxiliary or modal. Thus, normally, in speaking one says: "I'll go," "He's going," "They're here," "She's seen it," "We've heard." The same type of contraction can occur with people's first names: "John'll go," "Mary's going," "Bill's here," "Tom's seen it." When these auxiliaries are not contracted, it is because either the auxiliary itself or the subject is being given extra stress in the sentence.

In most of the cases of interpreting that this investigator has observed, the absence of contraction coincides with the insertion of linguistic material that is normally deleted in surface syntax. The following answer, in 7.10, and its interpretation comprise a striking, but not uncommon example of this type of interpreter-induced lengthening of testimony:

7.10 ATTORNEY: Of what country are you a citizen?
INTERPRETER: *¿De qué país es usted ciudadano?*
WITNESS: *México.*
INTERPRETER: I am a citizen of Mexico.

The impression that this conveys is one of hyperformality. It is not the way that the witness answered, nor would it be the typical response of an English speaker. Neither the subject pronoun nor the verb is given heavy, or emphatic stress, so there is no ostensive reason for the lack of contraction of "I" and "am." Consequently, the answer in English emerges in a stilted, excessively formal style, one not usually used in spoken English, but largely restricted to written contexts. It is typical of the bookish grammar which O'Barr (1982) has found to produce negative social/psychological evaluations of witnesses.

Rephrasing and Repeating Interpretations. Interpreters regularly lengthen witness testimony by rephrasing portions of their own interpretation. That is to say, in the course of interpreting an answer into English, interpreters frequently backtrack and reword slightly what they themselves have just said, even though the witness did no such backtracking in his own utterance in Spanish. Interpreters often do this consciously for the sake of greater precision and accuracy in rendering the answer in the target language.

One instance of such interpreter rephrasing can be seen in text 7.3, where the interpreter renders *camioneta* as "station wagon or small truck." This interpreter consistently gives two interpretations to words that have more than one equivalent in the target language. Rather than stop the proceeding in order to inquire as to which meaning the witness has in mind, she offers both glosses as her interpretation. For the same reason she interprets the word *gafas* as "glasses or sunglasses," and, alternatively, "glasses or goggles." She gives the same double interpretation to the dialectal variant *lentes*.

Often interpreters merely repeat, in an unconscious way, something they have just rendered in English, because the repetition gives them time to formulate the interpretation of material that is about to come. It appears to be a type of cognitive mechanism to gain time to process the rest of the interpretation. It is similar to the mechanism that speakers use in a monolingual situation where they are answering a question, and repeat either the examiner's question or else a portion of their own utterance in order to collect their thoughts for the proper wording of their answer. This type of repetition can be seen in text 7.7 above, where the interpreter begins with "I did not," and then repeats the opening words: "I did not, I did not notice if he had a mustache, but I noticed though that he had a beard." Evidence coming from a study of juror perceptions of who is influential in jury decision-making indicates that repetitions in a person's speech are associated with a lack of persuasiveness (London 1973), leading one to conclude that repetitions in the interpreted testimony of a witness might similarly give jurors the impression that the witness is not persuasive.

Interpreter rephrasing for the sake of greater accuracy and fidelity to the source language utterance often occurs when syntactic problems arise. For example, in the answer presented in 7.11 below, in reference to a question regarding the manner in which the witness and his companions were to be picked up by the defendant for the purpose of crossing the U.S. border, the interpreter rephrases her interpretation, making the verb phrase active rather than passive. Actually, the interpreter's rephrased interpretation is not quite accurate in any event, since the subject of the Spanish verb *recoger* (pick up) is not "he," the driver, but rather "the car." Thus, the witness actually is referring to "the car that would pick us up":

7.11 WITNESS: *Que pasaría pitando en el momento que era el carro que nos recogiera.*
INTERPRETER: That the car would go by blowing its horn, when we were ready to be picked up, or when he was ready to pick us up.

Changes in case, from active to passive and vice versa, are a common reason for interpreters' rephrasing of their interpretations. Such changes often result in the misassigning of agents to verbs, as in the case above. Such secondary errors seem to be related to the fact that the interpreter is focusing her attention on one aspect of the sentence—namely, the grammatical case of the verb—and it may be difficult for her to give as much attention to other elements in the sentence as she makes her syntactic adjustment. Nevertheless, in the process of rephrasing, she has nearly doubled the length of the witness's answer.

Politeness. As has been mentioned earlier, politeness is one of the features characteristic of powerless testimony style, and persons who use powerless speech on the witness stand tend to be evaluated more negatively than do persons who use the powerful style. However, it is not clear whether politeness in itself, isolated from the other features of powerless speech, has a negative impact on simulated juries. In fact, there is some evidence indicating that the use of polite forms can have a positive impact on jurors. It has been shown by Parkinson (1979) that defendants who use polite forms and speak in complete sentences are more likely to be acquitted.

Of the most frequently used polite forms of speech heard in the courtroom are the terms for direct address, "sir" and "ma'am." They are used not only by testifying witnesses, but also by examining attorneys. Clearly there is variation in the frequency with which witnesses use such forms in answering attorneys. What determines whether a given individual will use "sir" or "ma'am" in addressing an attorney has not been explored to date. One might predict, however, that persons who come from social or geographical backgrounds where high use is generally made of such polite address forms will tend to use them more often in court than will persons who do not come from those backgrounds. What comes to mind in the case of American English is, first of all, the dialect zone known generally as "the south," or the southern states, a very broad term covering various important dialectal subdivisions, and secondly, professional military personnel and their families. These two groupings, one a geographically defined one and the other an occupationally distinguishable one, are known in the United States for their broad-scale use of polite address forms. The children of professional military personnel have long been known to use "sir" and "ma'am" in addressing adults in general, and their parents in particular. In addition to these two broad categories of speakers who make frequent use of "sir" and "ma'am" in addressing interlocutors, one can identify the occupational category of salesperson, for in over-the-counter transactions with clients, salespeople in the United States are expected to make regular use of polite address forms.

What is crucial to bear in mind is that whereas frequent use of polite address forms in American English is relatively restricted to a limited number of identifiable social groupings, the use of polite address is a prominent, regular feature of social interaction throughout Spanish-speaking Latin America.[5] One the whole, the Spanish equivalents of "sir," "ma'am," and "miss,"—namely, *señor, señora,* and *señorita*—are expected to be used in asymmetrical social relationships whenever a person of lower social standing addresses a person of higher standing. This is a basic rule for children addressing adults (although specific kinship titles are used for relatives, such as *papá* (Dad), *mamá* (Mom), *tía* (aunt), *abuelo* (grandfather). This rule also applies to household servants or low-status employees addressing employers. It is certainly the norm whenever a great power differential exists between two interlocutors. Consequently, it would be *normal* and *to be expected* that a Latin American of peasant or working-class background would use polite address forms in answer in the questions of a lawyer or judge.

If polite address is the norm for answering the question of a higher status, more powerful person in Latin America, it is even more strongly adhered to in making a request of the interlocutor. Thus, when a attorney asks a witness to step down from a witness stand for some reason (e.g., to walk over to a board that serves as an exhibit of evidence, or to leave the stand for the time being), in a Spanish-speaking setting such a request for action would have to be made using a polite form of address. The empirical evidence coming from this investigator's observations and from her checking of the Spanish transcripts shows that in fact when interpreters ask witnesses to perform some action, such as being sworn in or pointing out the defendant in the courtroom, the interpreters always address the witness with the polite address form, *señor, señora,* or *señorita.* Such polite address is often used by interpreters for interpreting questions even when a request is not being made.

The fact that interpreters are often those who initiate the use of polite address forms with witnesses is important, for it leads to a cycle of reciprocal polite address usage: that between the witness and the interpreter. In those cases where the attorney is male and the interpreter female, which most often is the case, it is clear when the witness is addressing the interpreter rather than the attorney, for the witness consistently replies: *Sí, señorita; No, señorita.* It is precisely this situation that leads some interpreters to omit the polite address word entirely from their interpretation in English. To interpret *Sí, señorita* accurately into English when the attorney is a man would be either to insult him or in some way to deprecate him, or else it would demonstrate to everyone in the courtroom that what the witness is doing is answering the interpreter rather than the attorney. In either event, the witness would be defective in his answer. For this reason, many interpreters prefer to omit the polite form altogether, in order to avoid the problematical situation that would result from a valid interpretation of the answer.

Other interpreters correct the witness's error, and change the gender reference of the polite form so as to match it up with the sex of the attorney, as in examination text 7.12 below:

7.12 Attorney [male]: Prior to boarding the aircraft, did you have to pay the pilot any more money?
Interpreter [female]: *Antes de abordar usted esa avioneta, de subirse, de montar en esa avioneta, ¿tuvo usted que pagarle al piloto alguna cantidad de dinero?*
Witness: *Sí, señorita.*
Interpreter: Yes, sir.

To show how the interpreter initiates a cycle of polite address, text 7.13 is presented. It should be noted, however, that when the witness responds to the question with a polite form, *Sí, señorita,* even though the attorney is male, the interpreter chooses not to interpret the polite form at all, rather than to change it to the masculine form:

7.13 Attorney [male]: At any time did you get scared?
Interpreter [female]: *¿En algún momento durante el transcurso del vuelo se asustó usted, señora?*
Witness: *Sí, señorita. Yo venía nerviosa porque como eso no es como el avión, eso da como vueltas y yo traía nervios.*
Interpreter: Uh, yes, I was, because you see I was very nervous,

because a small aircraft is not like a big airplane. It—it, uh, there is more movement, and I was scared.

Whereas polite forms sometimes are consistently not interpreted by some interpreters for a variety of reasons, at other times they are consistently *inserted* into the English interpretation when in fact they had not been said by the Spanish-speaking witness. This happens particularly frequently when defendants answer the questions of judges. Thus, the situations in which this is most likely to happen are during arraignments, changes of plea, and sentencings. The desire to make the defendant more deferential and polite before the examining judge may simply be due to the interpreter's own need to be polite as she speaks to the judge, for ultimately it is she, in lieu of the defendant, who is transmitting the English message to the judge.

Particles and Hesitation Forms. Interpreters are supposed to sound in the target language the way the speaker for whom they are interpreting sounded in the source language. Thus, if the Spanish speaker sounds hesitant and unsure, the interpreter should sound equally as hesitant and unsure in her English interpretation. Conversely, if the Spanish speaker is not hesitant sounding, then neither should the interpreter be. Unfortunately there is no consistent correspondence between source-language utterance and target-language interpretation in this regard. Interpreters often ignore what seem to them to be unimportant elements of discourse, leaving the Spanish *ah* (uh), *este* (uhm or uh), and *pues* (well) uninterpreted. However, they often insert these very forms into their interpretations, since the hesitation forms are a side effect of the great mental concentration and strain that interpreters experience when they are in the process of interpreting. The frequent "uhs" produced by interpreters are often their own, and not a rendering of Spanish hesitation forms.

Meaningless particles such as "well," and expressions such as "you know," and "so you see" can be considered to be hedges that serve a politeness function in discourse (Brown and Levinson 1978:172). An example from R. Lakoff (1973) illustrates the hedging function of "well":

7.14 A: How far is it?
B: <u>Well,</u> it's too far to walk.

The particle "well" is used the same way by one interpreter. In one case the defendant is asked about the house that he lives in:

7.15 Attorney: What kind of house is that?
Interpreter: *¿Qué tipo de casa es?*
Defendant: *Es una casa chica.*
Interpreter: Well, it's a small house.

The defendant's answer is a clear, definite statement. The interpreter's rendition, in contrast, is a hedged way of offering the information.

Similarly, from text 7.16, below, it can be seen how a witness's certain-sounding answers become hesitant, when the English interpretation includes "uhs" that were not uttered in the source-language testimony. In this instance the witness is being asked who else was present at the fence where he crossed over into the United States:

7.16 Attorney: Who else was with you?
Interpreter: *¿Quién más estaba con usted cuando usted cruzó?*
Witness: *Varios hondureños.*
Interpreter: Uh, uh, several other Hondurans.
Attorney: Approximately how many?
Interpreter: *¿Aproximadamente cuántos en total?*
Witness: *Un promedio de veintiuno.*
Interpreter: Uh, probably an average of twenty-one people.

What the witness actually has answered in reply to the first question is "Several Hondurans." His answer to the second, as first mentioned in text 7.16, is, "An average of twenty-one." The hesitation from "uh," coupled with the hedge, "probably," commits him to a far lesser degree to his calculation than does the English interpretation, and makes him much less confident-sounding about his recollection. At the same time, however, while his Spanish testimony is succinct and to the point, the English interpretation is more expansive and consequently less reticent-sounding in its overall impression. In other words, it has become more narrativelike in its style.

The conclusion that can be drawn as to the functioning of hesitation forms and meaningless particles and expressions is that whenever there is a discrepancy between the source-language utterance and the target-language interpretation in this regard, hesitation forms seem to be unconsciously introduced by the interpreter (or, alternatively, unconsciously omitted in the interpretation), whereas hedges in the category of meaningless forms serve a discourse function for the interpreter. Such hedges make the witness testimony more colloquial-sounding—perhaps from the interpreter's viewpoint, more natural—and give the answer a more logical connectedness to what the witness has just said in an immediately prior utterance. This is certainly the case for the tying expressions, "So, you see," "Well, you see," two favorite expressions of one interpreter, who uses them to connect utterances within a given answer turn or to introduce a new answer.

Conclusion: The Intersection of Testimony Styles

The preceding analysis of Spanish witness testimony and its English interpretation has shown that interpreters alter speech styles. It has revealed that when interpreters lengthen witness testimony in the English rendition, many of the elements that function as the lengthening agents turn out to be features that form part of the constellation comprising powerless speech style. Specifically, hedges, hesitation forms (pause fillers and meaningless particles), and polite forms have been shown to be elements that interpreters add to their English rendition of witness testimony. This leads one to the conclusion that as the testimony becomes more narrativelike in style, it also becomes powerless in style. This shifting of speech styles is important because of the psycho-linguistic implication that narrative speech style gives jurors a more positive impression of testifying witnesses than does fragmented style, and that powerful style has a similar impact on jurors in its opposition to powerless style. What this study has found, then, is a paradox: the shifting of fragmented style toward a more narrativelike style should result in a more favorable impression of the witness, yet the shifting of powerful to powerless style is a change in the direction of negative social/psychological attributes.

A second unexpected finding of this study is that when interpreters shorten witness testimony in the conversion of source language to target language, the elements that they fail to interpret tend to be precisely those used in the lengthening of testimony. Specifically, they are hedges, hesitation phenomena, and polite forms. This leads one to the conclusion that these linguistic categories are not salient enough for court interpreters to include them in their interpretations when they ought to be included, and to exclude them when they should be omitted. Perhaps because these elements seem extraneous to the "meat and potatoes" of the sentence—that is, the subject and predicate—for they do not refer to who did what to whom, they are not perceived as being sufficiently important for attention to be paid to them. Nevertheless, their presence or absence in the answer to a question in court can make the difference between a witness appearing hesitant, unsure, unwilling to commit himself fully to the assertion he is making, and obsequious to the examining attorney, as opposed to appearing to be just the contrary.

As far as the other lengthening mechanisms are concerned, both the insertion of linguistic substance that has been deleted syntactically in the utterances of the witness, and the use of uncontracted forms, would seem to make the English testimony sound excessively formal in register, a style akin to the style of written English. Although this highly formal register is not what is known as "hypercorrect" speech—that is, the misapplication of linguistic rules to a given form, or the attempt to use "bookish" grammar, but in a defective way—it is nonetheless a speech style not normally used even by highly educated native speakers of English, yet it is used by some interpreters to render into English the speech of working-class persons or peasants. Thus, there is an obvious mismatch between the social class of the Hispanic witness and the style of English used to represent his testimony. This mismatch might possibly have the equivalent impact of the use of hypercorrect speech by a monolingual English-speaking witness, and if this is so, then juror evaluations of a witness testifying in such a manner can be expected to be negative, judging by the experiments of O'Barr (1982) on witness use of hypercorrect testimony style.

One important pragmatic effect of using uncontracted forms and inserting linguistic substance that otherwise would be deleted from surface syntax is that the resulting statements convey a strong impression of definiteness. Much of this definiteness stems from the overt presence of nouns and verbs that otherwise would not be uttered in the sentence, for normally their existence would be "understood" by hearers to be underlying the words spoken.

Just what impression testimony makes when it contains backtracking and rephrasing is not known, although London's (1973) study of juror perceptions of other jurors in the decision-making process would lead one to suggest that these speech elements would convey an impression of uncertainty and hesitancy. To say that the defendant was wearing "glasses or goggles" indicates that the speaker is not sure which it was. It would not be at all clear to a monolingual English speaker that the motivation for such an ambivalent assertion is that the word uttered in Spanish has more than one gloss in English.

Only a bilingual Spanish/English speaker would understand what is really meant by such a statement. Thus, once again, it might be concluded that backtracking and rephrasing, insofar as they seem to indicate a lack of certainty, a kind of wavering or waffling in one's assertion, are similar to hedging. They therefore should be considered to form part of powerless speech style.

In conclusion, based on Spanish and English transcripts of tape-recorded proceedings that were conducted with the aid of a court-appointed interpreter, it has been shown that interpreters serve to lengthen witness testimony, and that in that lengthening process, as answers become narrativelike in style, they tend to become powerless in testimony style. It is suggested, furthermore, that such an intersection of testimony styles—that is, the cross-cutting of narrative and powerless styles—normally would happen even in monolingually conducted judicial proceedings, for various elements of powerless style serve important connecting functions in narrative discourse. Finally, the intersection of styles should not come as a surprise, since the dichotomies of narrative versus fragmented style and powerful versus powerless style need not be considered as mutually exclusively occurring speech styles. They are merely different dimensions of speech, which can be co-present in the utterances of one and the same speaker at one and the same moment. What is theoretically interesting is that a style in one dimension seems to be intimately linked to, and affected by, a style of another.

It would be worthwhile investigating this relationship in monolingually conducted judicial proceedings to see if the finding holds true, for the hypothesis is proposed here for monolingual testimony in general that narrative testimony tends to be characterized by a number of features of powerless speech style, particularly hedges and hesitation forms, for such elements form a normal part of connected discourse. As soon as a speaker goes beyond a terse utterance in his other turn at talk, and begins to talk in narrative fashion, various sorts of hesitation forms and hedges will normally begin to appear throughout the discourse. In fact, a scanning of the testimony of English-speaking witnesses in the transcripts of this researcher indicates that this is true for monolingual court talk in general. Perhaps it is only the expert witness who has had extensive experience in testifying on the stand (e.g., policemen, medical experts) or the professional who is used to public speaking (e.g., academics, trial lawyers) whose speech is relatively devoid of these features. The proposal that narrative testimony tends to intersect with powerless testimony style in general, even in a monolingual context, is one worth testing empirically. One must caution, however, against using the transcripts of court reporters, for as Walker (1985) has shown, the discrepancy between what witnesses actually say and what court reporters record is great, and the ill-fit is systematically discrepant, not randomly so. One would have to have linguistically trained transcribers, working with taped recordings, to produce accurate transcripts that do not omit particles such as "uh."

An additional finding of this study is that in the interpreting process various sorts of pragmatic elements are systematically added to the testimony of witnesses, while others are systematically deleted from it. Whereas some of these additions and deletions seem to be unconscious on the part of the interpreter, other types can be accounted for by problems inherent in the interpreting process. Nevertheless, consciously made or not, alternations in the interpretation of pragmatic features of utterances that are produced in a court of law as sworn testimony can make the difference between jurors having confidence in such testimony or not.

Finally, when viewed from the standpoint of an interactionally managed turn-taking system, the question/answer routines in which examining attorneys and testifying witnesses co-participate can be seen to be disturbed by the operation of an additional verbal participant: the court interpreter. What is apparent is that the interpreter removes some of the controlling power that is normally held by the examining attorney, by producing witness answers that are longer than were the witness's in the source language. This, together with the pragmatic changes that are made in the testimony, means that the interpreter is exerting a controlling force over the impression that the witness is making on the jurors. Together, these alterations make for a different type of verbal power relationship between interacting verbal participants in a courtroom setting.

The question that must be posed, however, is whether such alterations in testimony make any difference in the impressions that jurors might form of the testifying witness. In other words, to what extent are those who sit in judgment affected by the interpreter's rendition of testimony? The following chapter addresses this question, as it presents the findings of an experimentally designed psycholinguistic study of the impact of the court interpreter.

8
The Impact of the Interpreter on Mock Juror Evaluations of Witnesses

Linguists have known for some time now that listeners react subjectively to numerous aspects of a person's speech. Listeners attribute different sorts of social/psychological attributes to a speaker depending on that speaker's dialect, delivery style, and voice quality. This chapter examines the subjective reactions of persons listening to witness testimony, in particular, courtroom testimony given in Spanish and interpreted into English. It will show that various aspects of a witness's speech play an important role in the formation of impressions of witnesses. Specifically, the role of verbal politeness, speech register, hedging, and grammatical case, will be examined in the context of interpreted foreign language testimony. It will be demonstrated, in addition, that the court interpreter has the power to alter these aspects of a witness's testimony, and in so doing, influences the impression that mock jurors have of that witness. By the same token, the impact of interpreter interruptions of attorneys and witnesses will be examined.

Many studies have found that listeners react subjectively to speakers according to the dialect that they use. Studies conducted in the United States have revealed the preference of both majority- and minority-group members for speakers of standard English over Black Vernacular English (Tucker and Lambert 1969), and over Mexican-American accented English (Ryan and Carranza 1977). In Canada, where studies of this type were first developed by Lambert and his colleagues, it has been demonstrated that French Canadian listeners view speakers of European French more favorably than speakers of Canadian French (Lambert et al. 1960; d'Anglejan and Tucker 1973), and upper-class French Canadian speakers more favorable than lower-class French Canadian speakers (Brown 1969). Similar studies conducted in Great Britain by Giles and his associates demonstrate that persons speaking with a prestigious accent—in the case of Britain "received pronunciation"—are evaluated more positively on semantic differential scales than are persons who speak with either regional, foreign, or lower-class accents (Giles 1970, 1971; Giles and

Bourhis 1976; Bourhis et al. 1975). A comparable study by this investigator (Berk-Seligson 1984) of attitudes toward nonstandard pronunciation and perception of personality indicates that Spanish speakers, too, judge personality from dialect.

The general finding that listeners make evaluative social/psychological judgments about speakers comes from numerous studies that base themselves on speech communities where more than one language is spoken. For the case of Spanish and English alone, the evidence is overwhelming that listeners react subjectively to both the Spanish language in and of itself and to Spanish-accented English (Arnov 1978; Carranza and Ryan 1975; de la Zerda and Hopper 1979; Flores and Hopper 1975; Hopper and Williams 1973; Politzer and Ramirez 1973a, 1973b; Ramirez, Arce-Torres, and Politzer 1978; Rey 1977; Ryan and Carranza 1975; Ryan, Carranza, and Moffie 1975, 1977; Arthur, Farrar, and Bradford 1974; Ryan and Sebastian 1980; Wölck 1973).

Dialectal differences, cross-language differences, and accentedness are not the only speech variations that affect a listener's evaluations of a speaker's personality. Delivery styles, and even smaller-scale speech manipulations such as voice quality and nonfluency affect listeners' judgments of speakers. Thus, it has been found that dynamic delivery (Schweizer 1970; Pearce 1971; Pearce and Conklin 1971; Pearce and Brommel 1972), fast speech rate (Brown et al. 1973, 1974), relative lack of nonfluencies such as pauses and repetitions (Miller and Hewgill 1964; Sereno and Hawkins 1967; McCroskey and Mehrley 1969), and "normal" voice quality (Addington 1971) are positively correlated with higher ratings on attributes such as competence, dominance, and dynamism, and are related, although not as consistently or strongly, to ratings of trustworthiness, likability, and benevolence.

Scholars interested in socio-legal questions, particularly the relationship between law and language, have begun to notice the relevance of the relationship between speech cues and perceived personality characteristics. A number of such scholars (London 1973; Timney and London 1973; Scherer 1972, 1979) have examined the role of voice quality (for example, pitch height, pitch range, loudness, precision of articulation, breathiness, and so on), and what they refer to as "vocal cues" (length and frequency of pauses, rate of speech, speech "disturbances" such as slips of the tongue, omissions, sentence incompletions, repetitions, and such) in jurors' perceptions of the influence of other jurors in decision-making.

The work of O'Barr and his colleagues has been highly influential in its ability to isolate a number of recurring testimony styles in the speech of witnesses, and to demonstrate that each style has a different impact on those placing themselves in the role of jurors and evaluating the testifying witness. The finding that persons testifying in narrative style are generally rated more positively than are persons testifying in fragmented style, and that powerful style testimony is associated with better evaluations than is powerless testimony (Conley et al. 1978; Erickson et al. 1978; Lind et al. 1978; Lind and O'Barr 1979; O'Barr and Atkins 1980; O'Barr and Conley 1976; O'Barr and Lind 1981; O'Barr et al. 1976), leads one to wonder if the sorts of linguistic changes regularly made by court interpreters have any impact on persons who are assigned the duty of evaluating foreign language testimony. For the same reason, if speech formality, or register, used by a testifying witness affects listener social/psychological evaluations of him (O'Barr 1982), then might not interpreter-included variation in register also leave its impact on listeners, one wonders.

The experimental design employed by O'Barr and his colleagues, the one adapted for use in the study reported on here, involves the use of a subjective reaction type of test, a variant of what is known as the "matched guise technique." The classic version of the matched guise technique, developed by Lambert et al. (1960), consists of a series of recordings of a standardized passage, some of which are read by the same speaker, and some of which are produced by other speakers. Versions recorded by the same speaker differ systematically in some linguistic respect: they may be read in different languages entirely (e.g., Spanish versus English), or they may be read in different dialects of the same language (e.g., Black Vernacular English versus Standard Spoken American English), or they may be uttered using different vocal qualities (e.g., fluent versus hesitant). Since the different versions, or "verbal guises," of the text that are read by one and the same person are separated by readings produced by other speakers, investigators presuppose that the listeners participating in the study will not realize that some of the guises belong to the same speaker. Nevertheless, in using the classic matched guise technique the investigator runs the risk that a certain percentage of listeners will in fact recognize the guises as such.

For this reason, some scholars (Bourhis and Giles 1976; Carranza and Ryan 1975; Giles and Bourhis 1975, 1976; Labov 1966) have rejected the prototypical form of the matched guise technique, and have used one of two variants of it. In one version, a different person is used for every linguistic variant of the standardized text, so that there is no possibility of a listener's concluding that two of the versions were said by the same speaker.

The problem with this methodology is that by using different speakers to record the different versions of the text, one introduces a number of additional linguistic variables into the recordings, specifically, variability in paralinguistic vocal qualities such as relative pitch height, relative loudness, breathiness, huskiness, and so on. In other words, linguistic features other than the variables in question cannot be held constant. Some linguists reject this variant of the matched guise technique precisely for this reason.

Another way to approach the problem is to make two separate recordings, both of which employ the same set of speakers, but each of which is different from the other only with respect to the linguistic variable of interest. One recording is played to one group of listeners, and the other to a different group, holding constant for socioeconomic and demographic characteristics of the listeners—that is, the two groups should be similar in age, education, income, occupation, and so on. This type of methodology avoids the pitfalls of the other two. Its disadvantage is that it requires a much larger sample of listeners for the investigator to be able to determine statistically significant differences in subjective reactions to the two versions of the recording.

Subjects in verbal guise studies are typically asked to rate the speakers whom they have heard on the recording along various social/psychological dimensions (such as intelligence, strength, honesty, passivity, and so on). In the interest of comparability with the subjective reaction test used by O'Barr and his colleagues, the social/psychological traits chosen for use in the present study were competence, intelligence, trustworthiness, and convincingness.

Politeness in the Bilingual Courtroom

Politeness is one of the several defining characteristics of powerless testimony style. Since powerless style has been shown to produce negative evaluations of witnesses, it would seem that politeness, alone, would have a negative impact as well. The only findings known regarding the impact of politeness on jurors are those of Parkinson (1979), who reports that defendants who use polite forms and speak in complete sentences are more likely to be acquitted. This conclusion runs contrary to the implications of O'Barr's findings. The present study sets out to determine how important verbal politeness is for mock jurors listening to interpreted testimony.

The reason why politeness was chosen as a focus of investigation, aside from the fact that it represents one constitutive element of powerless testimony style, is that politeness was observed to be an important variable in the witness/interpreter/lawyer verbal relationship. Politeness enters into witness/interpreter/lawyer interaction in a variety of ways. If we focus on the use of polite address terms ("sir," "ma'am," and "miss"), we notice that lawyers use polite address in asking witnesses questions when they either esteem the witness (i.e., it is their witness, not that of the opposing attorney), or else when they simply want to show the jury that they are treating the witness fairly and courteously. Polite address can also be used facetiously by an aggressive lawyer who is carrying out a hostile examination of a witness. The use of polite address terms in such a context will obviously be understood by jurors as sarcasm, since the belligerent tone of the questioning will in such cases be the most salient aspect of the lawyer's speech.

Of greater interest to the present study is politeness in the testimony of the witness. Based on my six years of living in Latin America, I start out with the premise that Latin American Spanish speakers use politeness markers to a much greater extent than do Anglo-Americans, particularly in asymmetrical social relationships (student/teacher, child/older relative, worker/employer). The tendency would be for the person of low power or low social status to address the person of high power or status with a polite address marker.

What I observed in the ethnographic study of interpreted judicial proceedings, something alluded to in chapter 5, is that the court interpreter frequently initiates a cycle of mutual polite address when she directs her interpretation at the witness. This usually happens when the interpreter is trying to put the witness at ease, particularly when the witness is obviously frightened or nervous. Often, when the interpreter is someone who has been brought up in Latin America, and arrives in the United States as an adult, she will behave culturally with another Hispanic the way she would in a Hispanic setting—that is, with a higher use of polite verbal tokens than would an Anglo in the same context. The use of polite address by the interpreter begins a cycle of reciprocal polite address. Thus, once the interpreter has begun addressing the witness with *señor,* or *señora,* the witness will tend to use a polite address term in answering the interpreter.

What is clear is that most witnesses who testify through the mechanism of a court interpreter very quickly begin to answer the interpreter directly, as if it were she who was asking the question, rather than the attorney, who in fact is the person posing the question. That this occurs is evidenced by two common patterns: (1) in answering a question the witness tends to maintain eye contact not with the attorney, but with the interpreter, and (2) the polite address term frequently correlates with the sex of the interpreter rather than with that of the lawyer. The second pattern becomes easily noticeable in the commonly occurring situation where the interpreter is a woman and the attorney is a man.

It should be kept in mind that the rules of working with a court interpreter require that the witness speak directly to the examining attorney or judge, and not speak to the interpreter as a person. Thus, in theory, the two common occurrences just mentioned ought not happen. However, they do, repeatedly. When a mismatch occurs in the polite address term used by the witness and the sex of the examining attorney, interpreters are faced with the choice of (1) interpreting the witness's address term accurately, and thereby possibly embarrassing the attorney; (2) interpreting the address term incorrectly, so that the gender of the address term matches the sex of the lawyer; (3) dropping the address term altogether in the interpretation of the answer; and (4) raising the problem with the judge and lawyer. The first route is not very often taken. The second and third are the more common approaches taken by interpreters.

The following text, which comes from a case involving the transporting of undocumented aliens across the U.S. border, demonstrates the problems involved in interpreting polite address. It shows how the interpreter initiates the cycle of polite address, and demonstrates the various tactics she employs in dealing with the witness's failure to address the lawyer directly:

8.1 PROSECUTING ATTORNEY: Would you state your name, please?
INTERPRETER: *Señora, tenga la bondad de decir su nombre.*
WITNESS: *Mirta Chamorro.*
INTERPRETER: Mirta Chamorro.
PROSECUTING ATTORNEY: And, uh, what is your occupation?
INTERPRETER: *¿Cuál es su oficio? ¿De qué se ocupa usted, señora?*
WITNESS: *En Colombia vendía lotería.*
INTERPRETER: In Colombia I sold lottery tickets.
PROSECUTING ATTORNEY: And, uh, where were you born? In Columbia?

INTERPRETER: *¿Dónde nació usted? ¿Nació usted en Colombia, señora?*
WITNESS: *En Bogotá.*
INTERPRETER: *¿Colombia?*
WITNESS: *Colombia.*
INTERPRETER: I, uh, I was born in Bogotá, Colombia.
PROSECUTING ATTORNEY: And are you a citizen of Colombia?
INTERPRETER: *¿Es usted ciudadana de Colombia, señora?*
WITNESS: *Sí, señora.*
INTERPRETER: Yes, I am.
PROSECUTING ATTORNEY: Are you a citizen of the United States?
INTERPRETER: *¿Es usted ciudadana de los Estados Unidos?*
WITNESS: *No, señor.*
INTERPRETER: No, sir.
PROSECUTING ATTORNEY: Uh, did you enter the United States, uh, on May the fifteenth of nineteen eighty-three?
INTERPRETER: *¿Entró usted a Estados Unidos, señora, el día quince de mayo de mil novecientos ochenta y tres?*
WITNESS: *Sí, señora.*
INTERPRETER: Yes, I did.
PROSECUTING ATTORNEY: Uh, when you entered did you have any papers or documents that allowed you to enter or gave you permission to enter?
INTERPRETER: *Cuando usted entró, señora, ¿tenía usted documentos o papeles que la autorizaran a entrar legalmente a este país?*
WITNESS: *No, señorita.*
INTERPRETER: No, sir.
PROSECUTING ATTORNEY: Did you know you were entering the country illegally?
INTERPRETER: *¿Sabía usted,—puede usted contestarle al licenciado*—Excuse me, I'm advising her not to answer "yes, Ma'am" or "no, Ma'am" because I'm just the interpreter. Excuse me.—*Señora, cuando usted conteste, conteste al al licenciado porque yo no más como una mani, ma-, maquinita que le están traduciendo.—Cuando usted entró a este país, señora, ¿sabía usted que estaba entrando ilegalmente?*
WITNESS: *Sí, señorita.*
INTERPRETER: Yes, sir.
PROSECUTING ATTORNEY: And did you pay anybody money in Colombia to make arrangements for you?

INTERPRETER: *¿Y le pagó usted a alguien dinero en Colombia para hacer los arreglos para su entrada a Estados Unidos, señora?*
WITNESS: *Um, nos cobraron noventa y cinco mil.*
INTERPRETER: We were charged ninety-five thousand.
PROSECUTING ATTORNEY: Uh, that would be Colombian pesos?
INTERPRETER: *Noventa y cinco mil pesos colombianos, señora?*
WITNESS: *Colombianos.*
INTERPRETER: Yes, Colombian pesos.
PROSECUTING ATTORNEY: When you entered the United States, when you actually entered the United States, were you in an aircraft?
INTERPRETER: *Cuando usted entró a los Estados Unidos, cuando de hecho entró usted al territorio norteamericano, ¿estaba usted en un avión?*
WITNESS: *Sí, una avioneta era.*
INTERPRETER: It was a small airplane—a small aircraft.
PROSECUTING ATTORNEY: Was the girl that just testified here before you also in that aircraft?
INTERPRETER: *La, la señora o señorita que acaba de atestiguar aquí antes que usted, ¿también estaba en esa avioneta junto con usted?*
WITNESS: *Sí, señora.*
INTERPRETER: Yes, sir.

What this examination shows is that the interpreter's adherence to a cultural norm of politeness causes her to address the witness with the polite *señora* (ma'am), even though the lawyer has not used a polite address term in the phrasing of his question. Thus, it is because the interpreter feels the need to establish a relationship of respect and cordiality with the witness that she proffers the polite address term. It is she, the interpreter, who is creating a metalinguistic dimension of politeness in the verbal interaction. I believe the address term is used to soften the impact of the force of the questioning process—that is, it ameliorates the aggressiveness of the whole speech situation, for to be placed on the stand and to be required to answer questions on command is an inherently challenging, intimidating experience for a lay witness. The speech situation is even more challenging for a witness who himself is possibly subject to legal punishment, the situation of illegal aliens who are put on the witness stand.

Whereas text 8.1 exemplifies typical situations in which the court interpreter changes the gender of politeness markers or drops the markers altogether, it does not offer an example of interpreters adding politeness markers in the interpretation of testimony. The most prevalent pattern of interpreter addition of politeness is the situation of defendants answering the questions of judges. The speech situations that call for defendant/judge interaction are initial appearances, arraignments, changes of plea, and sentencings. In such judicial proceedings typically the judge asks the defendant a predesignated series of questions, many of which are yes/no type questions. Often when the defendant answers with a simple *sí* or *no* answer, the interpreter will render the responses as "Yes, sir" or "No, sir." Clearly, the interpreter wants the answer to be more polite.

The question is whether the politeness she is striving for is for the defendant's sake or for her own. Court interpreters, particularly those employed full-time in a courthouse, are highly sensitive to the fact that they are employees of the court, and that they are expected to act just as obsequiously before the judge as is any lawyer, defendant, or clerk. Thus, court interpreters feel the need to speak politely to the judge in their capacity of court employees. The addition of politeness markers to defendants' answers may simply be part of the sense that interpreters have that judges are listening to them as persons in their own right, and not merely mechanical vehicles for converting speech from one language into another. And even though ideally the interpreter is supposed not to have her own persona in the proceeding, in fact she is spoken to directly by witnesses, as was demonstrated above, and she often is addressed by lawyers and judges, even though she is there merely to be a medium through which court officials can communicate with the non-English-speaking and the hearing impaired. Since she is given a persona by the various parties present at a judicial proceeding, it is not surprising that she carries over the sense of persona when she facilitates communication between defendants and judges. It is the judge who more than any other party in the courtroom is delegated with the authority to evaluate her performance. It is no wonder, therefore, that she wishes to address the judge politely.

Politeness versus Lack of Politeness: What Difference does the Interpretation Make?

The preceding discussion has shown how court interpreters can and do make witness testimony systematically less polite, or alternatively, more polite than in the original. It must be asked, however, if the presence or absence of polite forms in a witness's testimony makes a differential impact on jurors listening to that testimony. That is to say, if a jury hears a witness sounding polite in his answers to a lawyer's question, what difference does it make? Would the jurors consider him to be any less convincing, less trustworthy, less competent, or less intelligent than if he answered questions without using polite markers?

We know from the work of O'Barr and his colleagues that powerless speech in a witness's testimony is associated with negative social/psychological evaluations of the witness, and politeness is one of the constituent elements in powerless style. We would therefore expect politeness in and of itself to result in negative evaluations by jurors, if it is to have any impact on them at all. In the case of the bilingual courtroom, that differential impact would be attributable to the functioning of the court interpreter. It is this research question that was posed as part of the larger study of mock juror evaluations of witnesses testifying in Spanish with the aid of a court interpreter.

A research design was devised that would be capable of testing if the presence or absence of politeness markers in the English interpreted testimony of Spanish-speaking witnesses would leave a significant impact on persons playing the role of jurors. If such a differential impact could be found to exist, then it would show not only that politeness makes a difference, but that the interpreter herself makes a difference, insofar as she constitutes a crucial factor in the formation of juror impressions of non-English-speaking witnesses.

Research Design

An experimental research design was set up along the lines of the verbal-guise technique. Two audio recordings were made of a witness testifying in Spanish through an interpreter, the recordings being identical in every way except that in one version the interpreter interpreted in English every instance of the polite address marker *señor* (sir) that occurred in the speech of the witness, whereas in the other version the interpreter failed to interpret the polite marker in every instance (see Appendix 6, text A.6.1 for the text of the two versions). Thus, the interpreter's interpretation of the witness's testimony in one tape recording was systematically polite, whereas her interpretation in the other version was devoid of politeness.

It should be stressed that the text of the recordings was based on the transcription of an actual case that I had recorded in the courts, during the ethnographic phase of this study of the bilingual courtroom. Thus, the text on the tapes used for the present study is drawn from an actual examination by a lawyer of an undocumented Mexican alien. The actors who played the roles of witness, interpreter, and lawyer were in real life similar socially and occupationally to the persons whom they were portraying in the recordings: the witness was a Mexican immigrant living in an urban barrio (neighborhood with a high concentration of Hispanics), who knew very little English; the woman who played the interpreter was a Mexican-American woman who was a full-time court interpreter at a major criminal trial court of a large midwestern city; and the lawyer was played by an Anglo male who had graduate-level university education.[1]

The experimental design used in this study was more challenging for the subjects of the experiment than was that used by O'Barr and his colleagues, and thus might be considered a "worst case scenario." O'Barr's testing of the powerless/powerful speech style hypothesis involved playing tapes that were 15–20 minutes in length, and included the totality of components that together comprise powerless or powerful speech. Thus,mock jurors had a great number of linguistic items to cue into. In the present study, in contrast, listeners were subjected to only four minutes of tape-recording, and only one linguistic variable was involved, the presence or absence of "sir" in the English interpretation of the witness's answers. Furthermore, O'Barr's subjects were given lengthier explanations prior to being allowed to hear the experimental tape, explanations regarding the facts of the judicial case they were about to hear. Thus, they had quite a bit of background knowledge of the issues surrounding the case.

In the study being reported on here, however, providing the subjects with a great deal of information was avoided. This was done because it was believed that the more that the subjects knew about the case before hearing the witness, the more preconceived notions (e.g., prejudices, formulated opinions) would they bring to the task of listening to the witness. The aim of the study was to determine whether the way in which the testimony was spoken—namely, politely or without politeness—in and of itself would affect the listener's impressions of the witness. The study deliberately wanted to avoid the confounding influence of detailed knowledge of the case, since this would then be an additional variable that might affect the listener's opinions, and would be related to the listeners' particular life experiences and biases, something that I could not determine without additional in-depth interviews with them. For this reason, the explanation that preceded the playing of the examination sequence was relatively brief.

The explanation, which was done on the tape recording itself so as to standardize the explanatory input that each mock juror in the study would be exposed to, consisted of the following facts: (1) they, the mock jurors, were about to hear a case involving the transporting of illegal aliens across the U.S./Mexico border. (2) They would be hearing the voices of three persons: a male lawyer, who would be asking questions in English; a male witness, who would be testifying in Spanish; and a woman, the court interpreter, who would be interpreting the lawyer's questions into Spanish, and the witness's testimony into English. (3) The person who was testifying was *not* the defendant in the case—that is, he was not the one being accused of anything in this particular proceeding—but was being asked to testify in regard to the man who was the defendant—that is, the person who was being accused of smuggling him and other people across the border for a fee. (4) They would be asked to pretend that they were members of the jury in this case, and to give their impressions of the witness based on what they had heard.

Each participant in the study was given a standardized questionnaire, on which there appeared four lines representing four seven-point scales. At one end of each line appeared an adjective ("convincing," "competent," "intelligent," "trustworthy"). At the other extreme lay the polar opposite of the evaluative term. In order to enable Hispanic respondents with greater proficiency in Spanish than in English to perform the task easily, everything written on the questionnaire, including general instructions, was written in Spanish as well as in English.

The participants were taught to use the scales with some easy-to-understand examples (e.g., a scale ranging from "sweet" at one end to "salty" on the other, where items such as "candy" and "potato chips" were provided to demonstrate the extreme ends of the scale, and "water" was given to demonstrate a neutral point. It was explained to the subjects that they would be given similar scales to score, but that they would be rating the persons whom they were about to hear on the recording. This type of preparatory teaching of how to work with a scale was felt to be necessary especially for per-

Figure 8.1. Intelligence Scale

Not Intelligent 1 : 2 : 3 : 4 : 5 : 6 : 7 Intelligent

sons in the study who had never attended college, and who therefore would have had less experience with standardized tests in general, and with psychological tests in particular, than would persons who had had some experience with American colleges.

The Sample

A total of 551 persons participated in the experiment. Of those who reported their sex (and only .7 percent did not), 55 percent were women and 44 percent were men. Their mean age was 27.3 years, 55 percent of the sample being of college age (17–22). A conscious effort was made to include in the sample as many adult nongraduates of a four-year college as possible—that is, persons who were already in the work force or who had life experience beyond that found in educational settings. For this reason church groups and adult education classes were included in the sample, as were community-based vocational training classes and high school equivalence (G.E.D.) classes for adults who for various reasons had never earned a high school diploma.

The educational levels of the 551 subjects varied widely. Twenty-nine percent fell into the group having no more than twelve years of education (i.e., U.S. high school); of the 29 percent, however, only 16.2 percent had completed twelve years of school. Those having between one and four years of college made up 62.6 percent of the sample. The remaining 9 percent of the population had attained more than the equivalent of a four-year baccalaureate. Interestingly, 30 percent of the sample had attended school outside of the United States. One-third of this group had completed high school abroad, and 7 percent had attended college in their native country. Since nearly the entire group of persons who had attended school abroad was Hispanic, this meant that at a minimum the 17 percent who had completed at least high school in Latin America would be somewhere between Spanish-dominant and balanced bilingual in their Spanish/English proficiency. As is explained below, comprehension of Spanish is an important variable in this study, for it turns out to be an important predictor in determining listener evaluations of the testifying witness.

Ethnically, the sample was 52.3 percent Anglo-American, 39.4 percent Hispanic, 6.7 percent Afro-American, .7 percent Oriental, and .4 percent Amerindian. To determine if Hispanic nationality or place of origin would affect the evaluations of the Hispanic subjects—since the witness in the recording stated his Mexican nationality, and in fact the man playing the role of the witness was a Mexican national with a distinctively Mexican intonation pattern recognizable to Latin Americans—the questionnaire asked subjects to fill in both their own country of birth and that of their mother.

It turned out that Mexican nationality constituted the largest subgroup among the Hispanic subjects. Puerto Rican background was second in importance. Thus, of the total sample of 551 persons, 16.3 percent were of Mexican background and 7.8 percent were of Puerto Rican background, as measured by the place of birth of their mother. These figures parallel the relative percentages of Hispanic subjects who themselves were not born in mainland U.S.A.: 11.4 percent were born in Mexico, 4.9 percent in Puerto Rico. The next most distinguishable Hispanic group constituted those whose mother was born in Colombia (3.6 percent of the sample). Smaller percentages of nationality background represented Ecuador, Guatemala, Honduras, El Salvador, Nicaragua, Peru, Chile, Uruguay, Argentina, and Cuba.

The income of the sample was rather evenly distributed across seven annual income categories. These categories ranged from less than $10,000 per year to $60,000 or more per year. The subjects were instructed to estimate their total family income, and that if they were students or did not work, to estimate their parents' combined income.

Three questions were included regarding the subjects' personal experiences with the court system. Subjects were asked (1) if they had ever been in a court of law in the United States, (2) if they had ever testified in a court of law in the United States, and (3) if they had ever served on a jury in the United States. It was expected that persons who had been in court themselves and had participated in the proceedings would have evaluations of the witness that would in some way by systematically different from those of persons who had no personal experience with the court system. Possibly because a substantial proportion of the respondents were immigrants, and thus must have had experience with the court system through immigration and naturalization proceedings, 55 percent of those who answered said that they had been in a court of law in the United States, and 21 percent had testified in court. Only 4.9 percent had ever served on a jury.

The ability to understand Spanish was deemed to be potentially an important variable in the input that the subjects brought to the experiment. As has already been mentioned, it was hypothesized that having access to the meaning of the witness's Spanish testimony would cancel out whatever effect the interpreter might have in creating in the minds of the mock jurors one sort of impression of him rather than another. Thus, it had to be determined to what extent the non-Hispanic population had understood the Spanish of the witness, and to what extent the Hispanic population had. For this reason, subjects were asked (1) if they had ever studied Spanish in school, (2) if they had, how many years had they studied it, and (3) if they had, how well had they understood the Spanish on the recording, on a 5-point scale ranging from "very well" to"hardly at all."

Hispanic subjects were asked an additional series of questions aimed at measuring their degree of bilingual proficiency. First, they were asked if they spoke Spanish. Of those who identified themselves as Hispanic, 96.7 percent said they did. They were then asked which language they spoke better, Spanish or English, or if they spoke them about the same. Of those who answered, 50.2 percent reported speaking Spanish better than English, 23.9 percent felt they spoke English better than Spanish, and 24.9 percent answered that they spoke them about the same. When asked which language they spoke at home most of the time, among those who answered, 70.8 percent answered "Spanish" and 28.7 percent said "English." Only .5 percent felt that they spoke both about the same amount at home. To uncover those Hispanics whose English was clearly the dominant language and Spanish was the far less proficient language, the subjects were asked, "If you do not speak Spanish but you understand it, do you understand it (1) very well, (2) well, (3) more-or-less, (4) hardly at all." Of this group, 80.8 percent considered themselves to understand Spanish between "very well" and "well," and only 6.4 percent (3 respondents) estimated that they "hardly understand Spanish at all." In other words, it was the unusual Hispanic respondent who judged him or herself to hardly understand Spanish.

In addition to these questions, which reflect the individual's appraisal of his or her Spanish or English proficiency. three questions were asked in relation to the subjects' use of the Spanish-language mass media. On a four-point scale ranging from "at least once a week" to "almost never," subjects were asked about their use of (1) Spanish-language newspapers or magazines, (2) Spanish-language television programs, and (3) Spanish-language radio programs. In addition, the subjects were asked about their ability to write Spanish versus English (which one did they write better in, or did they write in both to about the same degree). Finally, they were asked to rate their understanding of the English on the tape recording they had just heard, on a five-point scale ranging from "very well" to "hardly at all." Interestingly, whereas 50 percent of the Hispanic respondents consider their Spanish-speaking ability to be better than their English, only 5.9 percent of the Hispanic sample reported understanding the English on the recording either "badly" or "hardly at all." The overwhelming majority of the Hispanic subpopulation understood the English portions of the recording well (79.9 percent reported understanding the English either "very well" or "well").

Findings

One major hypothesis of this study is that politeness in the testimony of a witness makes a difference—that is, has an impact on the impression that jurors form of that witness. It was expected, given the findings of O'Barr and his colleagues regarding the negative impact of powerless speech style upon mock jurors and the fact that politeness is one feature of powerless speech, that the interpretation of politeness markers into English by the court interpreter would cause mock jurors to evaluate the witness more negatively than when the interpreter did not interpret the witness's Spanish politeness markers. Table 8.1 below, presents a summary of the findings in this regard.

Table 8.1 summarizes the output of a difference in means test (*t*-

Table 8.1. Politeness: Difference of Means (*t*-Test) for Entire Sample

Attribute	*N*[a]	Mean[b]	Std. Dev.	Sig.[c]
Convincingness				
polite interpretation	257	3.2	1.8	<.001
nonpolite interpretation	286	2.6	1.8	
Competence				
polite interpretation	257	3.2	1.7	<.001
nonpolite interpretation	286	2.4	1.5	
Intelligence				
polite interpretation	256	2.9	1.7	<.001
nonpolite interpretation	287	2.2	1.5	
Trustworthiness				
polite interpretation	255	3.1	1.8	<.001
nonpolite interpretation	288	2.5	1.8	

[a]*N* varies because of nonresponse.

[b]Scores for each attribute range between 1 and 7, 7 being the most positive evaluation and 1 being the most negative.

[c]Values of .05 or less are considered to be statistically significant.

test) of the answers of the entire sample of 551 subjects. The *t*-test was applied to the subjects' impressions regarding the degree to which the witness seemed convincing, competent, intelligent, and trustworthy, comparing the mean answers of those who heard the "polite version" of the English interpretation with the means of those who heard the interpretation lacking in politeness.

It should be recalled that the higher the number on the evaluations (numbers approaching 7), the more positive were the mock jurors; the lower the numbers (approaching 1), the more negative were the impressions. Looking down the column labeled "mean" we see that in every case where the witness's testimony was interpreted faithfully to the original—that is, with the politeness markers present—the means reflected a more positive evaluation, on each of the four social/psychological attribute continua. More importantly, the difference between the means for the polite version and those for the not polite version is statistically significant, for all four attributes. In other words, it is highly unlikely that the mock jurors reacted this way by chance.

Two important substantive conclusions emerge from an examination of Table 8.1. First, even though politeness has been considered to be one of the characteristics of powerless testimony style, and hence should have a negative impact on jurors, this study finds that just the opposite is true: politeness gives a witness an enhanced image. Secondly, what has made the difference between one version and another is the role played by the interpreter. The witness answered politely in Spanish in exactly the same way in both versions of the experimental tapes. It was merely the interpreter who rendered the testimony differently. And this difference, the absence of "sir" following an answer to an attorney's question was sufficient to cause mock jurors to evaluate the witness more negatively. The pivotal role of the interpreter is not surprising.

Table 8.1 represents the responses of Hispanic and non-Hispanic mock jurors alike. What it does not reveal is whether Hispanics, virtually all of whom reported understanding Spanish, are affected in anyway by the interpreting process. It was hypothesized that Hispanics, by virtue of being capable of tuning into the original Spanish testimony of the witness, would not make any distinction between the polite version and the version lacking politeness.

The expectation that Hispanics would pay attention to the Spanish testimony should not come as a surprise: it is similar to the effect experienced by bilingual moviegoers who read the subtitles even though they understand the language spoken by the actors. It should be kept firmly in mind, however, that jurors are regularly instructed by the judge to ignore the foreign language testimony of witnesses if they happen to understand the foreign language, and to pay attention solely to the English interpretation of the court interpreter.

To determine whether Hispanic mock jurors are affected in any way by the English interpretation of the witness's testimony, a *t*-test was computed on the responses of those Hispanics who had listened to the polite version of the testimony, comparing them with those of Hispanics who had heard the nonpolite version. The results of the *t*-test are presented in Table 8.2. This table shows that for two of the social/psychological attributes, convincingness and trustworthiness, there was no significant difference in the scores of those Hispanics who had heard the polite interpretation and those who had heard the nonpolite version. This was as expected. That is, it was expected that being able to understand the original language of the testimony would enable Hispanics to ignore the English rendition of the court interpreter.

What came as a surprise, however, is that on two of the four social/psychological attributes, competence and intelligence, the English interpretation clearly had an impact on the formation of evaluations by the Hispanic mock jurors. That is, on the attributes of competence and intelligence there were statistically significant differences in the means of those who had heard the polite version and those who had heard the nonpolite version.

Interestingly, but not unexpectedly, the Hispanic sample rated the witness whose interpreted testimony was polite as more competent and more intelligent than the witness whose testimony was interpreted without the politeness markers. If there was going to be any differential impact of the interpretation on the Hispanic subjects, it was anticipated that Hispanics would view polite speech more positively than speech lacking in politeness, because of the generally higher use of politeness in Hispanic verbal interaction compared to that in Anglo-American speech. Even the mean scores on convincingness and trustworthiness, although not statistically significant, were in the expected direction: the scores on the polite interpreted testimony were somewhat higher than were those on the interpretation lacking politeness.

The fact that the difference in means was significantly different on the qualities of competence and intelligence, but not on the attributes of convincingness and trustworthiness, would seem to indicate that

Table 8.2. Politeness: Difference of Means (*t*-Test) for Hispanic Sample

Attribute	*N*[a]	Mean[b]	Std. Dev.	Sig.[c]
Convincingness				
polite interpretation	106	3.3	1.9	NS
nonpolite interpretation	103	3.1	1.9	
Competence				
polite interpretation	106	3.3	1.8	.002
nonpolite interpretation	103	2.6	1.6	
Intelligence				
polite interpretation	105	3.1	1.9	.003
nonpolite interpretation	104	2.4	1.6	
Trustworthiness				
polite interpretation	104	3.4	1.8	NS
nonpolite interpretation	105	3.1	1.8	

[a]*N* varies because of nonresponse.
[b]Scores for each attribute range between 1 and 7, 7 being the most positive evaluation and 1 being the most negative.
[c]Values of .05 or less are considered to be statistically significant.

for Hispanics politeness in a witness's speech does not have much bearing on the evaluation of that witness in terms of his being convincing or trustworthy, two somewhat related characteristics that might be underlain by some common semantic dimension, possibly honesty. However, Hispanics apparently do give great weight to the factor of politeness in determining the competence and intelligence of a testifying witness, two traits that also seem to have some common semantic underpinning. Most importantly, even for a subgroup that understands the language of the testifying witness, the rendition of the court interpreter makes a difference in the impressions formed of the witness by that bilingual subgroup.

Whereas Table 8.1 provides the difference in means for the entire sample as a whole, with Hispanic subjects mixed in with non-Hispanics, and Table 8.2 presents the mean scores of the Hispanic subjects alone, we cannot determine from either table if persons who understand no Spanish at all, and who therefore rely entirely on the English interpretation of the court interpreter to understand the witness's testimony, react differentially to polite testimony versus testimony lacking in politeness markers. To sort out those respondents who knew no Spanish at all, a subgroup of a larger sample was drawn based on their answering that (1) they had never studied Spanish in school and (2) they were an ethnic category other than Hispanic. In other words, all those who had checked that they were Hispanic, and all those who had answered that they had had some formal study of Spanish in school, whether in high school or college, were eliminated from this analysis. This non-Spanish-comprehending group was then broken down into two subgroups: those who had heard the polite interpretation of the testimony and those who had heard the nonpolite version. The results of a difference in means test of their evaluations are presented in Table 8.3.

Table 8.3 demonstrates that for non-Spanish-comprehending non-Hispanics politeness in the interpreted testimony of the witness makes a significant difference. On all four social/psychological attribute scales, persons who had to rely entirely on the English interpretation of the testimony found the witness who had produced English politeness markers to be significantly more convincing, competent, intelligent, and trustworthy than was the witness whose testimony as rendered in English was lacking in such tokens of politeness.

One surprising finding is that there is no significant difference in the evaluations of men and women mock jurors. At a minimum, it was expected that women would be more greatly affected by the presence of politeness or the absence of it than would men. If, as Lakoff (1975) has claimed, women in the United States speak more politely than do men, then politeness in speech should be more important to women, and should be more noticeable to them. A look at *t*-tests of women's mean scores and men's means on the polite version and nonpolite version of the witness's testimony (see Table 8.4) reveals,

Table 8.3. Difference of Means (*t*-Test) for Non-Hispanic Informants Who Have Never Studied Spanish

Attribute	*N*[a]	Mean[b]	Std. Dev.	Sig.[c]
Convincingness				
polite interpretation	64	3.0	1.7	.036
nonpolite interpretation	66	2.3	1.5	
Competence				
polite interpretation	64	3.0	1.7	.028
nonpolite interpretation	66	2.3	1.4	
Intelligence				
polite interpretation	64	3.0	1.7	.001
nonpolite interpretation	66	2.1	1.4	
Trustworthiness				
polite interpretation	64	2.8	1.7	.036
nonpolite interpretation	66	2.2	1.7	

[a]*N* varies because of nonresponse.

[b]Scores for each item range between 1 and 7, 7 being the most positive evaluation and 1 being the most negative.

[c]Values of .05 or less are considered to be statistically significant.

Table 8.4. Women's and Men's Mean Scores on Polite and Nonpolite Versions of Testimony (*t*-Test)

	N[a]		Mean[b]		Std. Dev.		Sig.[c]	
Attribute	Women	Men	Women	Men	Women	Men	Women	Men
Convincing/Not convincing								
Polite version	140	113	3.8	4.0	1.9	1.8	.003	NS
Nonpolite version	157	129	4.4	4.4	1.8	1.8		
Competent/Not competent								
Polite version	140	113	3.8	3.9	1.7	1.7		
Nonpolite version	157	129	4.6	4.6	1.5	1.5	<.001	.001
Intelligent/Not intelligent								
Polite version	139	113	4.2	4.0	1.6	1.9	<.001	.001
Nonpolite version	158	129	4.9	4.8	1.5	1.6		
Trustworthy/Not trustworthy								
Polite version	138	113	4.0	3.8	1.7	1.9	.012	.002
Nonpolite version	158	130	4.5	4.5	1.8	1.9		

[a]*N* varies because of nonresponse.
[b]Scores for each item range between 1 and 7, 1 being the most positive evaluation and 7 being the most negative.
[c]NS = <.05.

however, that men and women alike react differentially to the two versions of the testimony, and they do so to the same degree and in the same direction: men, as do women, evaluate a witness more positively when his testimony is presented with politeness markers.

Interestingly, even the relatively more negative perceptions of the witness's intelligence is something shared by men and women (compare the mean scores of the two groups on intelligence, according to the version that was heard: for women, 2.85 versus 2.13; for men, 2.97 versus 2.19). Whatever it was in the witness's testimony that made him appear less intelligent than either competent, convincing, or trustworthy, it affected men and women to a similar degree. Most probably it was the witness's inability at several points in the examination process to answer the attorney's questions on the first asking.

Politeness: Discussion

The preceding analysis of the findings of this study has demonstrated that politeness in the testimony of a witness is associated with more favorable evaluations of that witness in terms of his convincingness, competence, intelligence, and trustworthiness. This finding is contrary to expectation, for politeness is one of the defining characteristics of powerless testimony style, a style that has been shown in experimental studies to be associated with more negative evaluations of witnesses. Thus, in and of itself, politeness in the testimony of a witness is an asset, from the point of view of jury impression-formation. Mock jurors have been shown here to give more positive ratings of a social/psychological nature to a witness whose speech contains politeness markers, than to a witness whose speech is lacking in such politeness.

Secondly, the fact that politeness in the testimony of a witness was controlled in an experimental fashion through the workings of a court interpreter demonstrates that the interpreter is a powerful filter through which a speaker's intended meaning is mediated. In effect, it was the interpreter who was producing the polite and nonpolite versions of the testimony. The witness's Spanish language testimony was a constant: it was identically polite in both versions of the experimental tapes. Thus, the different reactions to the witness were due entirely to the role of the court interpreter. It was she, in effect, who controlled the impressions of the witness, since for those mock jurors whose knowledge of Spanish was nil or quite limited, it was the interpreter's English rendition that had to be relied on for comprehension of the witness's testimony. Thus, the interpreter can be seen to play a pivotal role in how a jury perceives a non-English-testifying witness.

Whereas it was expected that bilingual mock jurors would "tune in" to the Spanish testimony, and the impact of the interpreter on these listeners would have been assumed to be minimal, the interpreter's failure to interpret politeness markers significantly affected the evaluations of bilingual mock jurors on two of the four social/psychological attributes examined in this study—competence and intelligence. Thus, the absence of politeness in the interpreter's English rendition of the witness's testimony led Hispanic mock jurors to rate the witness more negatively on those two attributes than they rated the witness whose interpreted testimony included the politeness markers. This means that bilingual mock jurors do in fact pay attention to the English rendition of the court interpreter (as they are instructed to by the presiding judge), and that in some social/psychological respects, the impact of the interpretation is the same on them as it is on non-Hispanics who know no Spanish.

What is interesting is that on the traits trustworthiness and convincingness, politeness in the English rendition of the interpreter has no impact on Hispanic mock jurors. Their evaluations of the witness in the polite version compared with those in the nonpolite version are not significantly different, which means that Hispanic listeners in fact do pay attention to Spanish testimony as given by a testifying witness. This is something the Court officially tells bilingual jurors not to do, something akin to a judge telling a jury to disregard testimony that it has heard but that has been ruled inadmissible after an attorney's objection has been sustained. Clearly, what jurors are told to disregard after they have heard it cannot be assumed to be wiped out entirely from their memory. Similarly, it would be highly difficult for a bilingual person to blot out speech he understands simply because he has been told to do so, especially since he knows that the *real* testimony is not that of the interpreter, but that coming from the lips of the person who is answering the attorney's questions.

Surprisingly, the sex of the mock jurors had no impact on the evaluations made of the witness. Men and women, alike, were favorably affected by politeness markers in the speech of the witness. It had been expected that women would be more greatly affected by the presence or absence of verbal tokens of politeness. This would mean that if American women are in fact more polite than men in their ways of speaking, it does not mean that women's regard for politeness in the speech of others is any different from men's. Perhaps in the context of a court of law, Americans of both sexes give the same weight to verbal politeness in testimony. That is, it may be a cultural expectation in the United States that people should speak politely on the witness stand, in the presence of a judge. If this is so, then the systematic alterations in politeness that often occur in the interpreting process can have important consequences in a jury's perceptions of a witness.

For practitioners of law, the finding that politeness in the answers of a witness enhances the image of that witness may be all the more salient for the context of cross-examination. In cross-examining a witness for the opposition, a lawyer will tend to limit the witness to short answers (typically answers to *yes/no* type questions), and will avoid eliciting lengthier, narrative-type answers. This strategy is used by lawyers for several reasons, one of them being the belief that witnesses who are allowed to answer with full, elaborated answers rather than with short, incisive, fragmented ones are viewed more positively by jurors (Morrill 1971). This belief in fact is supported by socio-legal research (Lind et al. 1978; O'Barr 1982).

The brief answers to *yes/no* type questions are precisely those that lend themselves to politeness marking—that is, they constitute a more favorable environment for the addition of "sir" and "ma'am" than do the lengthier answers that *wh-* type questions typically engender.[2] A bare "yes" or "no" in English, and *sí* or *no* in Spanish, are very blunt in nature, and lack any mitigating, or softening, illocutionary force, particularly when the "yes" or "no" answer of the witness implies that he is admitting to something that may make him look unfavorable in the eyes of the court. To answer "yes, sir" or "no, sir" is to soften the impact of the admission. At the same time it gives the impression of greater deference and politeness toward the questioner. If it is a Spanish-speaking witness who has used such politeness markers, and the interpreter has failed to include these markers in her interpretation, then in effect she is aiding the cross-examining attorney in his efforts to cast an unfavorable light on the witness. If, on the other hand, she inserts politeness markers in the interpretation when there were no such markers in the original Spanish testimony, then she has served to aid the attorney for whose side the witness is testifying. In either case she would be tampering with the intent of the witness. Beyond that, she would be affecting the impressions that jurors are forming of the person on the witness stand.

In conclusion, it has been shown that politeness is an important variable for persons listening to witness testimony. They judge witnesses more favorably, or alternatively less so, depending upon the presence or absence of politeness markers in the answers of witnesses. In addition, this study has found that for men and for women, as well as for Hispanics and for non-Hispanics, politeness is a positive attribute in a witness's speech. Finally, it has been demonstrated that the alterations in politeness made by the court interpreter have the power to affect the perceptions of those whose task it is to evaluate the testimony of witnesses, and that even when listeners understand the foreign language testimony of witnesses, the English rendition of the court interpreter has an influence on such evaluations. The implication of this finding is that bilinguals tune in both to foreign language testimony and to its interpreted rendition alike.

Hyperformality: A Shift Upward in Speech Register

Register, defined as "a variety that is not typically identified with any particular speech community but is tied to the communicative occasion" (Bolinger 1975:358), is generally conceived in terms of "formality levels." It is also alternatively referred to as "style" (Joos 1967) or "key" (Gleason 1965). Linguists are in agreement that English has five registers, or levels of formality: (1) oratorical, or frozen; (2) deliberative, or formal; (3) consultative; (4) casual; and (5) intimate (Gleason 1965; Joos 1967). From a variationist linguistic perspective, speech styles that vary according to formality level can be differentiated by the variable frequency with which standard and nonstandard linguistic forms are used (Labov 1972). This entails counting the tokens of prestigeful and stigmatized linguistic forms, be they phonological or morphosyntactic.

From a nonvariationist viewpoint, a speech style that varies according to formality of context can be identified by the co-occurrence of a number of linguistic features. For example, consultative style, the register used to conduct most transactions between strangers, is marked by the speaker's supplying background information to his or her interlocutor. This characteristic distinguishes consultative style from casual style speech, yet the two share an attribute—namely the use of contracted forms (Joos 1967). These two styles share enough features to be put together into the category of "colloquial speech" (Joos 1967). One clear marker of speech style is lexical choice. Words that have an overlapping semantic content can often best be distinguished by their position in the style continuum. Bolinger's (1975: 362) example of increasingly more formal vocabulary items is very effective in demonstrating the correlation between speech style and contextual formality: to guzzle, to swig, to drink, to imbibe, to quaff. For some linguistic anthropologists (O'Barr 1982), register is defined primarily in terms of vocabulary. Formal speech, for instance, is considered by some to be simply the standard variety of a given language, but one that uses a somewhat more formal lexicon than that used in everyday speech—in effect, the variety that is taught in schools as the "correct" variety (O'Barr 1982). It is this register that O'Barr finds is typical of the speech of most lawyers.

The preceding discussion makes no mention of one important speech style that is of particular significance to talk in a courtroom setting: hypercorrect speech. From one linguistic perspective, hypercorrect speech is a style that reflects the misapplication or overgeneralization of linguistic rules so as to produce nonstandard forms. Hypercorrection in terms of grammar is exemplified by construction such as "He gave it to she and I," which represents the speaker's effort to avoid accusative case pronouns in all contexts, even as objects of prepositions. This overgeneralization stems, in part, from attempts on the part of schoolteachers to stop their pupils from using object pronouns in subject position (e.g., "Joe and me found it"). Hypercorrection in this sense can be manifested in lexical usage as well. O'Barr's (1982) examples of hypercorrect use of lexicon in witness testimony include the use of "comatose" for "unconscious," and expressions such as "not cognizant" for "unaware."

The notion of hypercorrectness presented above contrasts with the conceptualization of variationists, in that the former implies the use of nonstandard forms, whereas the latter involves the use of standard, or prestigeful, forms more often than would normally be expected given the socio-economic status of the speaker and the formality level of the speech setting (Labov 1972). Thus, Labov found that the lower-middle-class sector of his sample of New York City English speakers used the prestigious variant of one phonological variable (postvocalic /r/)[3] more often than did speakers belonging to a higher socio-economic status, holding constant for contextual formality.

The present study departs from both of the previous two conceptions of hypercorrectness, focusing on a speech register that will be called "hyperformal" style. This is a style that neither uses nonstandard grammatical or lexical forms, nor is marked by a higher than expected use of prestigeful linguistic variants. Rather, it is a style that sounds bookish and stilted on account of two principal speech characteristics: (1) the lack of ellipsis or syntactic deletions in surface syntax, which produces overly-complete surface constructions (e.g., in answer to the question "How old are you?," a hyperformal response would be "I am twenty-one years old," rather than the more typical reply "I'm twenty-one" or, simply, "Twenty-one"); and (2) the failure to contract linguistic elements that are frequently contracted in consultative style (e.g., the copula *be* and the negative marker *not*, as in "am not" for "aren't" and "is not" for "isn't").

The failure to contract *be* and *not* is typical of written English. Labov (1969) has found that when *be* follows a pronoun, contraction of the copula is virtually categorical in spoken standard English (e.g., "I'm," "you're," "he's," "she's," "they're"). When lack of contraction occurs, it is because extra stress is placed on the copula, for the sake of emphasis or clarity. The same is true of the marker *not* when it follows either the auxiliary *do* or *did,* or modals ("can," "could," "must," "will," and so on): unless either the auxiliary or the marker *not* is given heavy stress, the tendency in American English is to contract the negative marker ("he didn't," "we don't," "I can't," "she couldn't," "you mustn't," "they won't").

The reason why I have targeted hyperformality for attention is that my ethnographic observations have discovered that some court interpreters systematically render the Spanish testimony of witnesses in hyperformal style English, even though the original Spanish is given in consultative style. In effect, these interpreters shift the Spanish-speaker's register up one notch in the ladder of formality. The following excerpt is taken from a case involving the transporting of undocumented persons across the U.S./Mexico border into the United States. The witness who is testifying is an undocumented Mexican farmworker who was brought into the United States by a smuggler, the defendant in the case:

8.2 PROSECUTING ATTORNEY: And how old are you?
INTERPRETER: *¿Qué edad tiene usted?*
WITNESS: *Veinte años.* (Twenty years old.)
INTERPRETER: I am twenty years old.
PROSECUTING ATTORNEY: And what is your occupation?
INTERPRETER: *¿Y cuál es su oficio de usted?*
WITNESS: *Trabajar en el campo.* (Working in the fields.)
INTERPRETER: I am a laborer in the fields.
PROSECUTING ATTORNEY: Of what country are you a citizen?
INTERPRETER: *¿De qué país es usted ciudadano?*
WITNESS: *De Michoacán.* (Of Michoacán.)
INTERPRETER: I am from the state of Michoacán.

In every case the Spanish-speaking witness answered in a register that must be considered to range between consultative and casual. The interpreter's rendition, however, can be seen to be hyperformal. It should be noted that court interpreters are expected to render interpretations that are as faithful to the source language original as possible. In striving for the goal of high-fidelity verbatim interpreting, they are supposed to preserve the register in which the source language utterance emerged (Almeida and Zahler 1981). The type of interpreting presented above clearly fails to meet these expectations.

Given that systematic changes in register are often made in the interpreting process, the research question that was posed was this: Does an alteration in speech register make a difference? Specifically, do listeners placing themselves in the position of jurors form a different impression of the witness depending upon the register in which his or her testimony is interpreted? The findings of O'Barr (1982) and his colleagues lead us to expect an affirmative answer to this question. Two of the styles that they have isolated in court talk, formal testimony style and hypercorrect style, were found to result in opposite evaluations: witnesses who testified in formal style were judged to be more convincing, competent, intelligent, and qualified, than were witnesses who presented their testimony in hypercorrect style (O'Barr 1982).

It was hypothesized, therefore, that a witness whose Spanish testimony was interpreted in English in hyperformal style, which is a bookish, stilted, written style of English, would be evaluated more negatively than one whose testimony was rendered in a consultative register. The hyperformal style is considered here to be a "marked" style, while the consultative style is thought of as "unmarked," or the expected norm for transactions between strangers.

Using the same experimental research design that was devised to test whether the use of politeness markers by the court interpreter left a differential impact on mock jurors, two interpreted versions of the same testimony were played to the participants of the study, one of which had the interpreter rendering the witness's testimony in a marked, hyperformal speech style, the other of which contained a different English rendition of the same Spanish testimony, one in consultative style. (See Appendix 6, text A.6.2 for the transcripts of the experimental recordings.) As in the study of politeness, the interpreter, the witness, and the examining attorney were identical on the two tapes.

The questions of the attorney, the Spanish interpretation of the questions, as well as the Spanish answers of the witness were identical in the two versions. Only the English interpretation of the witness's answers varied. In the hyperformal version the interpreter inserted material that she felt was implicit in the Spanish answers, and in addition refrained from using contracted forms. Thus, the interpreter's rendition of the witness's testimony in one tape recording was systematically hyperformal, whereas her interpretation in the other version was devoid of constructions that reflect hyperformal style, and thereby corresponded closely to the consultative style in which the Spanish testimony was uttered. If a differential impact could be found to exist in the reactions of the two groups of mock jurors who had heard the different versions of the recordings, it would show not only that speech register makes a difference, but that the interpreter herself makes a difference, insofar as she would be shown to comprise a crucial factor in the process whereby listeners form impressions of non-English-speaking witnesses.

Findings

The hypothesis being tested is that a difference in speech register (i.e., hyperformality versus the lack of it) in the testimony of a witness makes a difference—that is, has an impact on the impression that jurors form of that witness. It was expected, given the findings of O'Barr and his colleagues regarding the negative impact of hyper-

Table 8.5. Register: Difference of Means (t-Test) for Entire Sample

Attribute	N[a]	Mean[b]	Std. Dev.	Sig.[c]
Convincingness				
consultative	286	3.7	1.7	NS
hyperformal	259	3.9	1.8	
Competence				
consultative	283	3.2	1.6	.004
hyperformal	256	3.7	1.7	
Intelligence				
consultative	283	2.6	1.6	<.001
hyperformal	258	3.3	1.7	
Trustworthiness				
consultative	285	3.2	1.7	.009
hyperformal	258	3.6	1.8	

[a]*N* varies because of nonresponse.

[b]Scores for each attribute range between 1 and 7, 7 being the most positive evaluation and 1 being the most negative.

[c]Values of .05 or less are considered to be statistically significant.

correct speech style upon mock jurors, that the interpretation of hyperformal speech in English by the court interpreter would cause mock jurors to evaluate the witness more negatively than when the interpreter did not interpret the witness's Spanish in the hyperformal style. Table 8.5 presents a summary of the findings.

Table 8.5 summarizes the output of a difference in means test (t-test) of the answers of the entire sample of 551 subjects. The t-test was applied to the subjects' impressions regarding the degree to which the witness seemed convincing, competent, intelligent, and trustworthy, comparing the mean answers of those who heard the "hyperformal version" of the English interpretation with the means of those who heard the consultative interpretation. It should be recalled that the higher the number on the evaluations (numbers approaching 7), the more positive were the mock jurors; the lower the numbers (approaching 1), the more negative were the impressions. Looking down the column labeled "mean" we see that in every case when the witness's testimony was not interpreted faithfully to the original—that is, where the interpretation was hyperformal rather than consultative—the means reflected a more positive evaluation, on each of the four social/psychological attribute continua. More importantly, the difference between the means for the hyperformal version and those for the consultative version is statistically significant for three of the four attributes: competence, intelligence, and trustworthiness. In other words, it is highly unlikely that the mock jurors reacted this way by chance.

Two important substantive conclusions emerge from an examination of Table 8.5. First, even though the hyperformal English interpretation contrasts with the low socio-economic status of the witness, and hence should have a negative impact on jurors, this study finds that just the opposite is true: hyperformality gives the witness an enhanced image. Secondly, what has made the difference between one version and another is the role played by the interpreter. The witness answered in Spanish in exactly the same way in both versions of the experimental tapes—that is, in consultative style. It was only the interpreter who rendered the testimony differently. And this difference, the presence of contractions, of relatively short, unwordy responses to questions, was sufficient to cause mock jurors to evaluate the witness more negatively.

Table 8.5 represents the responses of Hispanic and non-Hispanic mock jurors combined. What it does not reveal is whether Hispanics alone, virtually all of whom reported understanding Spanish, are affected in any way by the interpreting process. Once again, as in the case of politeness, it was hypothesized that Hispanics, by virtue of being capable of tuning into the original Spanish testimony of the witness, would not make any distinction between the hyperformal version and the consultative version.

To determine whether Hispanic mock jurors are affected in any way by the English interpretation of the witness's testimony, a *t*-test was computed on the responses of those Hispanics who had listened to the hyperformal version of the testimony, comparing them with those of Hispanics who had heard the consultative version. The results of the *t*-test are presented in Table 8.6. This table shows that for one of the social/psychological attributes, convincingness, there was no significant difference in the scores of those Hispanics who had heard the hyperformal interpretation and those who had heard the consultative version. This was as expected. That is, it was expected that being able to understand the original language of the testimony would enable Hispanics to ignore the English rendition of the court interpreter.

However, Table 8.6 also shows that Hispanic mock jurors clearly were affected by the register of the interpreter's English rendition of the testimony. On three of the four social/psychological attributes—competence, intelligence, and trustworthiness—there were statistically significant differences in the means of those who had heard the hyperformal version and those who had heard the consultative version. Once again, when the witness's Spanish testimony was interpreted in hyperformal style, the ratings he received on these three

Table 8.6. Register: Difference of Means (*t*-Test) for Hispanic Sample

Attribute	N[a]	Mean[b]	Std. Dev.	Sig.[c]
Convincingness				
consultative	103	3.9	1.8	NS
hyperformal	108	4.1	1.9	
Competence				
consultative	100	2.9	1.8	.021
hyperformal	105	3.5	1.9	
Intelligence				
consultative	100	2.5	1.8	.010
hyperformal	107	3.2	1.9	
Trustworthiness				
consultative	102	3.3	1.9	.049
hyperformal	107	3.9	1.8	

[a] *N* varies because of nonresponse.
[b] Scores for each attribute range between 1 and 7, 7 being the most positive evaluation and 1 being the most negative.
[c] Values of .05 or less are considered to be statistically significant.

attribute scales were more positive than were the ones he received when his testimony was interpreted in consultative style.

Register: Discussion

This analysis has demonstrated that speech register is important to those evaluating witness testimony. Specifically, hyperformality is regarded positively by mock jurors, so much so that it improves the impression made by a witness testifying in Spanish: it makes him appear more competent, more intelligent, and more trustworthy than he does when his testimony is rendered in English in a less formal style.

This finding is contrary to expectation, for hypercorrection in the Labovian variationist sense—which most closely parallels hyperformality—is poorly regarded by judges who are of the same socioeconomic status as is the hypercorrect speaker. Similarly, hypercorrection in the traditional sense of the misapplication of linguistic rules on the part of the speaker in order to make him/herself give a better impression is likewise poorly received, according to the studies of O'Barr and his colleagues.

From the standpoint of a linguist-observer, it would seem that a hyperformal rendition of this particular witness's testimony would be given a more unfavorable rating than would a less formal style rendition, for two reasons. First, there is a mismatch between the socioeconomic status of the witness and the excessively formal speaking style of his answers in English. That is, we would not expect a Mexican farmworker to be speaking in a style that in the United States is equated with persons of very high educational attainment. We would tend to assume that a person who reports having obtained less than a complete elementary school education would not have in his repertoire a speech style associated with bookishness and formal learning. In other words, there is a cognitive dissonance between what we know of the speaker and his social background, and the English utterances that are being attributed to him by the interpreter.

Secondly, as O'Barr (1982) confirms in his ethnographic observation in the courts, lawyers shift registers—upward and downward—as they speak in court. Their speaking style varies between formal and colloquial, including consultative as an intermediary style. This is normal for lawyers' court talk. The interpreter's rendition of the testimony of the witness in question, however, is carried out in an unvarying style. That is, it is uniformly hyperformal. It thus stands in marked contrast to the speech of most lawyers, who do normally engage in style-shifting.

It is puzzling, therefore, to find that mock jurors give a higher, more positive rating to a witness who sounds as if he were speaking in a homogeneously hyperformal style of English than they do the same witness when he speaks in an unmarked speech style. One possible explanation for this unexpected finding is that Americans, both Hispanic and non-Hispanic alike, consider hyperformal speech style to be appropriate to this particular speech setting and speech situation. In other words, they apparently feel that a courtroom setting and the giving of testimony under oath constitute an eminently formal context for speech. Thus, in Hymes's (1972) terms, to speak "appropriately" while one is being examined by an attorney on the witness stand is to speak bookishly.

What seems to be underlying this notion of communicative appropriateness in a legal setting is the notion of politeness. To speak hyperformally on the witness stand is to be polite to the examining attorney and to the court in general. This form of politeness, which consists of maintaining a highly formal style, and, consequently, not shifting downward, is a manifestation of deference to the interlocutor and to the listeners who are not direct addressees (i.e., the judge and the jury). The very ability of lawyers to shift their styles upward and downward in court is evidence of their sense of power and control over their interlocutors. It is akin to the greater sense of freedom of action that a host feels in his/her home, as opposed to the sense that a guest has of needing to keep up his or her good manners throughout a visit. The courtroom is, in the end, the lawyer's territory. In some sense he/she is at home there. The testifying witness in every sense of the word is nothing but a temporary guest whose length of stay in the lawyer's turf is beyond his or her control.

An additional explanation as to why hyperformal testimony is given more positive evaluations than is an unmarked speech style is that hyperformal utterances tend to be wordy. That is, testimony given in hyperformal style is longer, in terms of words per answer, than is testimony spoken in consultative style. Longer answers, or "narrative style" testimony, have been shown to evoke more positive social/psychological evaluation than do short, incisive answers, or "fragmented style" testimony (O'Barr 1982). What may have gone on in the present study is an interactive effect between utterance length and hyperformality, for hyperformality turns out to be manifested by wordier, more elaborate, answers.

A third possible reason for why hyperformal testimony is well received is that hyperformally worded answers convey a sense of certainty and definiteness, something absent from colloquial registers. The lack of contraction and the inclusion of linguistic material that otherwise could be interpreted as "being understood," or being implicit, in a short utterance, together produce answers that convey a sense of definiteness and deliberateness ("I am from the state of Michoacán" versus "From Michoacán").

Whereas it was expected that bilingual mock jurors would "tune in" to the Spanish testimony, and it was therefore assumed that the impact of the interpreter on these listeners would be minimal, in reality the interpreter's addition of linguistic substance to the source testimony significantly affected the evaluations of bilingual mock jurors on three of the four social/psychological attributes examined: competence, intelligence, and trustworthiness. Thus, the lack of hyperformality in the interpreter's English rendition of the witness's testimony led Hispanic mock jurors to rate the witness more negatively on those three attributes than they did the witness whose interpreted testimony was realized in a hyperformal register. This demonstrates once again that bilingual mock jurors do in fact pay attention to the English rendition of the court interpreter—as they are instructed to do by the presiding judge—and that in some social/psychological respects, the impact of the interpretation on them is the same as it is on non-Hispanics.

On one trait, however, the hyperformal English rendition of the interpreter had no influence on Hispanic respondents: convincingness. There is no significant difference between their evaluations of the witness in the hyperformal experimental tape and their judgments of the same witness when his testimony was interpreted in consultative style. This means that Hispanic listeners do in fact pay attention to the Spanish language testimony of the witness.

In conclusion, it has been shown that speech register is an influential variable for listeners who are assigned the task of evaluating witnesses. Apparently, one can never speak too formally on the witness stand, so long as one does not end up producing hypercorrections. Moreover, hyperformal testimony style in English is as highly regarded by Hispanic-Americans as it is by Anglo-Americans. Finally, the implication of these findings is that Spanish/English bilinguals are very much affected by the English interpretation of the court interpreter, despite their having aural access to Spanish source language testimony.

Hedging

Hedging has been defined differently by different linguists. As we have seen in chapter 7, Brown and Levinson (1978:150) define a hedge as "a particle, word, or phrase in a set; it says of that membership that it is *partial,* or true only in certain respects."[4] Lakoff (1975:66), who has analyzed hedging as a feature of women's speech, finds that hedges "leave the addressee the option of deciding how seriously to take what the speaker is saying. It is for this reason that 'John is sorta short' may be in the right context, a polite way of saying 'John is short,' rather than a scaled-down comment on John's actual height."

The reason why hedging is so important in the courtroom is that it can be used by witnesses to mitigate, or soften the impact of, the point they are making. Danet (1980:525), analyzing the question/answer sequences of the Watergate hearings, finds:

> It is obviously in the interest of defendants to mitigate the illocutionary force or point of damaging assertions ("I guess I killed her") but to avoid mitigating neutral or positive assertions ("I didn't do it" rather than "I guess I didn't do it"). "I guess" is a kind of hedge (Lakoff 1970). John Erlichman's testimony during the Watergate hearings was full of hedges on potentially damaging admissions.

Brown and Levinson (1978:151) find that the Watergate transcripts as a whole "contain a formidable array of hedges designed to limit criminal culpability." Using the analytical framework of conversational implicature as developed by Grice (1975), with its notion of "conversational maxims," or a set of general conditions determining the proper conduct of conversation, Brown and Levinson find that persons who testified at the Watergate hearings employed various types of hedges on Grice's maxims. For example, hedges on the maxim of "quality,"[5] "suggest that the speaker is not taking full responsibility for the truth of his utterance" (Brown and Levinson, 169). Examples of quality hedges found in the Watergate transcripts are the following: "to the best of my recollection," "as I recall," "you might say," "quite frankly" (Brown and Levinson, 169–70).

A study of hedges reveals that even seemingly "meaningless" words such as "well" can be seen as adding a layer of meaning to an utterance, in a way that may not be as obvious as the semantic content carried by nouns, adjectives, and verbs. A number of linguists and sociologists have analyzed the function of "well" in conversation and have discovered several generalizations. Sacks et al. (1974) found that "well" often begins turns at talk as a way of introducing what a speaker is going to say. Lakoff (1973) has shown that "well" prefaces responses that are insufficient to questions. Pomerantz (1975) finds that "well" prefaces disagreements, alternating with "yes but" and silences, in this capacity. Owen (1983) has found that "well" can precede an answer in which a speaker cancels a presupposition of a prior question, or "well" may express the speaker's noncompliance with a request or a rejection of an offer. Wootton (1981) has shown that "well" precedes parents' responses to their children's requests more often when those responses reject, rather than grant, the children's requests. Thus, a number of scholars have found that "well" signals that something is about to be said that is in some way negative, or dispreferred. Finally, Schiffrin (1985) has discovered that "well" serves as a discourse marker that is used by speakers to try to build coherence into the discourse. Schiffrin concludes that "well" "anchors the speaker in a conversation precisely at those points where upcoming coherence is not guaranteed" (662).

Because discourse markers such as "well" seem meaningless to the average speaker or hearer, they are easily overlooked by interpreters in two respects. A Spanish-speaker's *pues* ("well") may be deleted in the interpreter's English rendition, or, alternatively, the interpreter's English rendition might include "well" when the Spanish-speaker's utterance did not. The presence of hedges such as "well" and the ones referred to above weakens the certainty and which an assertion is made. Hedges create the impression that the speaker is hesitant. They therefore make the listener lack confidence in the surety of the speaker. In a court of law, hesitancy on the part of the speaker might even be misconstrued as an attempt at obfuscation or deception—that is, the speaker might be assumed to be hedging because he or she does not want to tell the plain truth outright.

Hedging is one of the defining components of powerless testimony style.[6] Since powerless style is associated with negative social/psychological qualities being attributed to a testifying witness (O'Barr 1982), hedging in and of itself can be expected to produce similar negative results in mock jurors listening to interpreted testimony. This hypothesis was tested experimentally in the study of the bilingual courtroom.

Findings

Using the verbal guise technique experiment described previously, two recordings were made, in which the variable of interest was the presence or absence of hedging in the English rendition of the court interpreter. (See Appendix 6, text A.6.3. for the transcripts.) The case was drawn from a trial involving a traffic accident. The person testifying is a Mexican-American man, who answers the attorney's questions in narrative style testimony, but a style that at the same time is filled with instances of hedging. In one version of the experimental tape recording, the interpreter renders the testimony in English in a similar, hedged fashion. In the other experimental recording the same interpreter interprets the same witness's answers in a way that systematically omits the hedges used by the witness.

A *t*-test analysis performed on the responses of all those who participated in the study (*N* varies between 526 and 529) reveals that for the sample as a whole—that is, Hispanics and non-Hispanics alike—the presence of hedging in the English interpretation of the witness's testimony made a significant impact on the mock jurors. (See Table 8.7.) Those listeners who had heard the hedged interpretation were significantly more negative toward the witness than were those who had heard the interpretation that lacked hedges. This finding is true for all four social/psychological traits: convincingness, competence, intelligence, and trustworthiness. Thus, when the witness's testimony was rendered faithfully—that is, the English interpretation included hedges as had his original Spanish testimony—the witness was judged to be significantly less convincing, less competent, less intelligent, and less trustworthy than when his testimony was inter-

Table 8.7. Hedging: Difference of Means (*t*-Test) for Entire Sample

Attribute	*N*[a]	Mean[b]	Std. Dev.	Sig.[c]
Convincingness				
hedging in interpretation	285	3.5	1.8	.032
no hedging in interpretation	244	3.8	1.9	
Competence				
hedging in interpretation	283	3.4	1.6	<.001
no hedging in interpretation	245	3.9	1.6	
Intelligence				
hedging in interpretation	283	3.2	1.6	<.001
no hedging in interpretation	243	3.8	1.6	
Trustworthiness				
hedging in interpretation	285	3.6	1.7	.028
no hedging in interpretation	244	3.9	1.7	

[a]*N* varies because of nonresponse.

[b]Scores for each attribute range between 1 and 7, 1 being the most positive evaluation and 7 being the most negative.

[c]Significance = .05 or less.

preted in English without the hedges. This finding is consistent with expectations, given the findings of O'Barr (1982) and his colleagues that hedging is one constituent of powerless testimony style, which in turn is generally evaluated negatively.

In the reactions of Hispanic mock jurors, however, no significant differences emerged. (See Table 8.8.) Why this is so can be explained by several possible factors. One is a cultural factor. Hispanic culture is more likely to be amenable to hedged ways of speaking than is the culture of North American Anglos. Hedging is one manifestation of speaking indirectly, and indirection is a positive attribute in Latin America. North Americans are considered by Latin Americans to be blunt and even brusque in their desire to get to the point. This cultural difference is frequently noted by persons in the diplomatic corps and businessmen who have international dealings. While North Americans often perceive Latin Americans as being roundabout and slow in getting to the heart of a business matter, both in face-to-face business meetings and in business letters, Latin Americans often consider North Americans rude or lacking in feeling in the way they conduct a transaction. Speaking succinctly and directly has no high value in Latin America. For this reason, a hedged but narrative series of answers might not sound evasive to Hispanics, while it would to Anglos.

Another possible explanation for the lack of differentiation among Hispanic listeners is the potentially confounding influence of

Table 8.8. Hedging: Difference of Means (*t*-Test) for Hispanic Sample

Attribute	*N*[a]	Mean[b]	Std. Dev.	Sig.[c]
Convincingness				
hedging in interpretation	105	3.7	2.0	NS
no hedging in interpretation	94	3.7	2.0	
Competence				
hedging in interpretation	103	3.5	1.8	NS
no hedging in interpretation	95	3.8	1.7	
Intelligence				
hedging in interpretation	103	3.4	1.8	NS
no hedging in interpretation	93	3.7	1.8	
Trustworthiness				
hedging in interpretation	105	3.8	1.9	NS
no hedging in interpretation	94	3.8	1.8	

[a]*N* varies because of nonresponse.
[b]Scores for each attribute range between 1 and 7, 1 being the most positive evaluation and 7 being the most negative.
[c]Significance = .05 or less.

narrative-style speech. Perhaps for the Hispanic mock jurors the fact that both versions of the testimony were spoken in narrative style—both in the Spanish source and in the English target—overrode any effects of an additional variable. In other words, if the testimony had been given in a fragmented manner in both the hedged and non-hedged versions, the hedging might have stood out more sharply for the Hispanic mock jurors. The most likely explanation is the first one proposed—namely, that hedging does not have the pejorative cultural connotation in Hispanic culture that it has in Anglo-American culture. However, other studies would need to be undertaken to verify this.

Active versus Passive Voice

We have seen in chapter 6 that interpreters can and do alter the case of verbs. We have seen, too, that many languages, Spanish included, use passive verb forms to avoid laying blame for adversative events, or to distance agents from such events. With this notion in mind, a verbal guise experiment was devised to determine whether the use of active versus passive voice in the English interpretations of the court interpreter would leave a different impact on mock jurors evaluating a Spanish-speaking witness. It was hypothesized that the use of passive voice would be associated with more negative social/psychological attributions than would the use of active voice.

As in the previous three experiments, a pair of nearly identical re-

Table 8.9. Active vs. Passive: Difference of Means (*t*-Test) for Entire Sample

Attribute	*N*[a]	Mean[b]	Std. Dev.	Sig.[c]
Convincingness				
passive interpretation	290	3.0	1.6	NS
active interpretation	249	3.0	1.8	
Competence				
passive interpretation	287	3.1	1.4	NS
active interpretation	248	3.3	1.6	
Intelligence				
passive interpretation	288	2.9	1.4	.003
active interpretation	247	3.3	1.6	
Trustworthiness				
passive interpretation	288	2.6	1.7	.020
active interpretation	247	2.9	1.8	

[a]*N* varies because of nonresponse.
[b]Scores for each attribute range between 1 and 7, 1 being the most positive evaluation and 7 being the most negative.
[c]Significance = .05 or less.

cordings was taped, the only difference between the two being the interpreter's English rendition of verbs used by the witness in his testimony. (See Appendix 6, text A.6.4 for the transcripts.) Whenever the attorney worded his question in the passive voice, the witness would answer with some form of the passive: either the true passive, the dative of interest, the reflexive passive, or the third-person plural construction. In one version of the recording the interpreter would consistently render these verbs in the English passive, and in the other recording she would interpret these verbs in the active voice. The Spanish-speaking witness was a Mexican man testifying in regard to the defendant in the case, a man accused of smuggling the witness across the U.S./Mexico border.

Findings

A *t*-test performed on the responses of the entire sample of mock jurors reveals that the use of passive voice in the English interpretation of testimony is associated with negative evaluations of the witness's intelligence and trustworthiness. (See Table 8.9.) That is, on those two traits the impact of hearing testimony spoken in the passive voice versus the active was sufficiently great so as to significantly lower the listeners' estimation of the witness. The evaluations of the mock jurors with respect to the witness's convincingness and competence were also in the same direction—namely, the passively worded testimony was associated with more negative estimations of the witness on those two traits. However, the differences in ratings between the groups who heard the different versions was not great enough to reach statistical significance. The hypothesis, then, that testimony worded in the passive voice rather than in the active voice produces lower estimations by mock jurors is confirmed, but not as strongly as with the other pragmatic variables.

The reactions of the Hispanic subsample are similar to those of the sample as a whole: on every social/psychological characteristic the witness was evaluated more negatively when his testimony was interpreted in the passive voice than when it was worded in the active voice. (See Table 8.10.) The differences in the ratings, however, do not reach statistical significance. Why the difference is not significant is unclear. It seems to have to do with the generally negative reaction of Hispanic listeners to this witness, particularly on the dimension of honesty. On both convincingness and trustworthiness, Hispanic listeners were decidedly more negative regarding the witness than they were on the attributes of competence and intelligence. There may have been some paralinguistic feature of this witness's speech that intervened (e.g., his tone of voice was somewhat nasal) that struck them as dishonest. Perhaps, too, Hispanic listeners found his rather lengthy answers to *yes/no* questions to be an indication of trying to hard to appear truthful. His answers included much of the wording of the attorney's question, rather than being short "yes, sir" "no, sir" types of answers. What is important, nonetheless, is that the direc-

Table 8.10. Active vs. Passive: Difference of Means (*t*-test) for Hispanic Sample

Attribute	N[a]	Mean[b]	Std. Dev.	Sig.[c]
Convincingness				
passive interpretation	107	3.3	0.2	NS
active interpretation	102	3.2	0.2	
Competence				
passive interpretation	104	3.1	0.2	NS
active interpretation	101	3.4	0.2	
Intelligence				
passive interpretation	105	3.0	1.6	NS
active interpretation	100	3.5	1.7	(.07)
Trustworthiness				
passive interpretation	105	3.0	1.9	NS
active interpretation	100	3.2	1.9	

[a] *N* varies because of nonresponse.

[b] Scores for each attribute range between 1 and 7, 1 being the most positive evaluation and 7 being the most negative.

[c] Significance = .05 or less.

tion of the difference in evaluations between those Hispanics who heard the passive version and those who heard the active one is that the passive wording consistently produced more negative judgments of the witness.

The Impact of Interpreter Intrusiveness: The Consequences of Interrupting and Prodding

The ethnographic analysis presented in chapter 5 revealed that interpreters intrude upon judicial proceedings in various ways, many of them being engendered by other parties present in the courtroom. Three types of interpreter-induced intrusions are (1) interrupting the attorney, (2) interrupting the witness, and (3) prodding or prompting the witness. A subjective reaction test on these variables shows that each of them has an impact on the evaluations of certain social/psychological traits. However, no one intrusive device is uniformly powerful in creating in the minds of mock jurors one sort of impression rather than another.

Interrupting the Attorney

It was believed that both the interpreter's interrupting the attorney during an examination, and her interrupting a witness in the course of an answer, would result in negative impressions overall. That is to say, it was hypothesized that when an interpreter regularly interrupted a lawyer while he was questioning a witness, persons acting as jurors would find the lawyer less competent, intelligent, and persuasive than when his examination routine went uninterrupted. Similarly, it was thought that when an interpreter regularly interrupted a witness as he was giving his testimony, evaluations of that witness would be lower than when the same witness was permitted to speak in an unimpeded fashion. In addition, interrupting a witness in the course of testimony was believed to result in lower estimations of the attorney conducting the examination. These expectations are based upon the findings of O'Barr (1982:87–91) and his colleagues, which indicate that interruptions and simultaneous speech between attorney and witness are associated with poor judgments regarding the attorney, whether that attorney has won the verbal clash or not. That is, no matter who dominated or acquiesced, the attorney was perceived as having less control over the presentation of testimony.

To test whether interpreter interruptions of an attorney made any differential impact on mock jurors' evaluations of that attorney's competence, two experimental tapes were recorded based upon a case involving an undocumented Mexican alien.[7] (See Appendix 6, text A.6.5 for the text of the transcripts.) In one experimental tape there were no interruptions by the interpreter. In the other, the interpreter questioned the attorney on four occasions. These interruptions were not of the type where the interpreter's speech overlaps onto the attorney's ongoing speech, since this type of interruption is not very common among interpreters. Rather, these interruptions interrupt in the larger sense of the examination sequence, in that they halt the flow of the question/answer pairs. Typically, in such instances interpreters refrain from interpreting the attorney's question in Spanish, and instead question the attorney about the question that he has just formulated.

In the experimental tape that contained interpreter-induced interruptions, the interruptions were mainly clarification procedures, ones that either (1) requested that the attorney repeat some portion of his question because the interpreter either had not heard or had forgotten that segment, (2) informed the attorney of how the question was going to be interpreted in terms of its grammatical structure, or (3) asked the judge for permission to clarify a dialectal problem with the witness. In two of the instances the interpreter implies that the attorney is at fault in her inability to carry out the interpretation of his question. In asking for a repetition of the question, she begins her request by saying, "That's about the limit of my retention, sir." She is implying that the attorney is either insensitive to or unaware of her needs as an interpreter: he has formulated his question in too long a chunk for her to reproduce via consecutive interpreting. Consecutive interpreting, after all, requires a straining of the interpreter's powers of recall. The interaction between the attorney and the interpreter is clearly tense, as evidenced by his reply to her statement to him that she has rendered his question in an affirmative fashion rather than a negative one. He interrupts her statement, overlapping onto her utterance with an irritated retort: "I want the question exactly as I stated it."

Finally, when the interpreter asks the judge permission to clarify the meaning of the Spanish verb *cancelar,* which can mean either "cancel" or "complete," the attorney asks the judge if they can "discuss this off the record" since he does not think that the issue is a proper one for the jury to hear. Clearly, the attorney and interpreter are engaged in a verbal clash. However, it must be kept in mind that the interpreter at all times is verbally very polite to the attorney. Every question of hers is phrased with politeness markers, prefaced by such expressions as, "Excuse me, sir," and ending with the polite request opener, "May I." The verbal clash is not one in which the interpreter is openly hostile or nasty to the attorney, but is perceived as a clash because of the attorney's clear irritation with the interpreter, and her veiled, indirect, and always polite criticism of him.

After listening to the experimental tapes, the mock jurors were asked to rate the attorney on how competent, intelligent, and persuasive he was. Those who had heard the recording that included the interpreter interruptions ($N=255$) found the attorney to be significantly less competent (sig. = .009) than did those who had heard the experimental tape that contained no interpreter interruptions ($N=285$), the mean scores for the two subsamples of listeners being 3.6 and 4.0, respectively. Whereas the evaluations of the attorney's intelligence and persuasiveness were in the expected direction, they failed to reach a level of statistical significance, and therefore cannot be counted as conclusive in this regard.

Hispanic mock jurors also were affected by the interpreter's interruptions of the attorney. Those who had heard the version that included the interruptions ($N=105$) also found the attorney to be significantly less competent (mean of 3.5 versus 4.1; sig. = .02) than did those who had heard the version lacking in interruptions ($N=102$). In addition, when the attorney was interrupted by the interpreter, Hispanic listeners found him significantly less intelligent (sig. = .05), their mean ratings on intelligence being 3.8, versus a mean of 4.3 by those Hispanics who had heard the version devoid of interruptions. Their judgments regarding the attorney's persuasiveness were in the anticipated direction, but they failed to be sufficiently different to be statistically significant.

Interrupting the Witness

Keeping in mind the findings of O'Barr and his colleagues in regard to the negative impact of simultaneous speech and interruptions, it was hypothesized that when the interpreter interrupted a testifying witness, the evaluations of both the witness and the examining attorney would be adversely affected by the interference of that third party. On the whole, this hypothesis was only weakly borne out. As will be explained below, the impact of the interpreter's interrupting the witness has a negligible impact on listeners' evaluations of the examining attorney. It has somewhat of an impact on mock jurors' estimations of the witness, although that impact is more strongly felt by Hispanic mock jurors than by the sample as a whole.

Once again, the participants in this study were asked to evaluate the witness who would be heard testifying on a tape recording. As in the other cases, the traits on which they were asked to rate the witness were convincingness, competence, intelligence, and trustworthiness. The mock jurors also were asked to give their opinion of the interrogating attorney in terms of his competence, intelligence, and persuasiveness. The case that they heard on the experimental tapes was drawn from a preliminary hearing dealing with the mugging of an elderly Mexican-American man. (See Appendix 6, text A.6.6 for transcripts of the tapes.) In one version of the tape the interpreter never interrupted the witness during the presentation of his testimony. In the other version she interrupted him seven times. As opposed to the type of interruption typically carried out by interpreters in relation to examining attorneys, in which case interpreters tend to wait for the attorneys to complete their question before they address the attorney or the judge, when interpreters interrupt testifying witnesses it is generally in the middle of the witness's answer. There is a real cutting off of the witness's speech.

In the experimental tape the interpreter stopped the witness for two reasons: (1) to request that he repeat a portion of his answer, and (2) to prevent him from continuing with a lengthy narrative answer so that she might render an interpretation in consecutive mode without losing any substance. She closely controlled the flow of his testimony by stopping with him phrases such as *Un momentito, por favor* (One moment, please), and *¿Cómo?* (What?), and by repeating the last word he had uttered, but with a question intonation. She would allow him to continue by using commands such as *Siga* (Go on), or by saying more politely *Puede seguir* (You may continue). This case is typical of the progression of a witness's testimony when it is tightly constrained by the external pressure placed upon it by the court interpreter.

Using a difference of means test once again, the responses of those who had heard the version that included the interruptions ($N=247$) were compared with the responses of those who had heard the version devoid of interruptions ($N=287$). For the mock jurors as a whole, the only judgment affected by the presence or absence of interpreter interruptions of the witness was intelligence. Quite unexpectedly, the version that contained the interpreter interruptions was associated with an enhanced evaluation of the witness's intelligence (a mean score of 3.8, compared to a mean of 3.4; sig. = .014 for the version that was lacking in interpreter interruptions). The mean scores on the three other social/psychological characteristics were in the same direction—that is, the witness whose testimony was interrupted frequently by the interpreter was viewed more favorably in terms of his being convincing, competent, and trustworthy. However, the difference in the mean scores for the two versions was not significant in these three areas.

While this finding is counter-intuitive and, at first, puzzling, there is an explanation for the enhanced impression given by the witness who was interrupted over and over again. This particular witness was testifying in narrative style to begin with, and the interruptions allowed him to hold the floor even longer than he would have held it had he not been interrupted. Thus, the interpreter unwittingly was affording him a chance to express himself even more fully than he might have done if she had not made requests for repetitions and pauses. In effect, she was making an already narrative-style answer even more narrative.

What is puzzling, however, is the fact that Hispanic mock jurors drew an opposite conclusion regarding this witness. Their reactions were as hypothesized: those who had heard the witness being interrupted by the interpreter ($N=99$) found him to be significantly less convincing and less competent than did those who had heard the uninterrupted version of the testimony ($N=106$). The mean scores for convincingness were 3.8 and 4.5, respectively; sig. = .009; for competence the means were 3.6 and 4.1; sig. = .035). The difference in means on both intelligence and trustworthiness were not significant.

Interestingly, whereas the reactions of the Hispanic mock jurors were the opposite of those of the sample as a whole on three of the four social/psychological traits, when it came to evaluating the witness's intelligence, the impressions of the Hispanic listeners were similar to those of the larger sample: they found the witness to be slightly more intelligent when his testimony was interrupted by the interpreter, although not sufficiently more intelligent to leave one confident that the difference between the mean scores was not by chance (3.61 for the interrupted version and 3.55 for the version lacking interruptions). Nevertheless, the Hispanic sample clearly was not left with a negative impression of the witness's intelligence when his testimony was repeatedly interrupted, while it was indeed unfavorably impressed with his convincingness and competence under the same circumstances. One can conclude that for all the participants in this study, perceptions of intelligence of the testifying witness were not affected by interpreter interruptions of his testimony. The question arises as to whether the interpreter's frequent interruptions of a witness affect mock juror evaluations of the examining attorney. Given that interpreter interruptions of an attorney make the attorney seem less competent than he would otherwise, and from the standpoint of Hispanic listeners, less intelligent, it was anticipated that an interpreter's repeated interruptions of a witness would make the attorney appear less in control of the examination. For this reason, participants in the experiment were asked not only to evaluate the witnesses whose testimony was repeatedly interrupted, but also the attorney who was carrying out the questioning. Mock jurors were asked to rate the attorney's competence, intelligence, and persuasiveness.

Contrary to expectation, whatever negative impressions of the witness were caused by the interpreter's interruptions of his testimony, no negative attributions spilled over into the mock jurors' appraisals of the attorney. Neither the sample of listeners as a whole, nor the Hispanic listeners as a subgroup, found the attorney to be any less competent, intelligent, or persuasive when the witness he was questioning was frequently interrupted by the interpreter. Clearly, persons acting as jurors separate their opinion of the attorney from that of the witness when the interpreter is not simply interpreting interruptions, but rather, is initiating them herself.

It is evident, then, that those who observe interpreted proceedings make a distinction between an interpreter who interrupts an attorney and one who interrupts a witness on her own behalf. An interpreter's interruptions of an attorney often can be perceived as veiled criticism of the attorney's performance, and if the interpreter is conveying to others in the courtroom that the attorney, in some sense, is not formulating the questions adequately, then those listening will be contaminated to a certain extent by the dissatisfaction that she has expressed. However, when an interpreter interrupts a witness, mock jurors seem to see this partially as a problem of the interpreter's and partially a defectiveness in the witness. Clearly they do not see such interruptions as connected to the attorney's professional capabilities. This distinction is an important one, given that interpreters commonly interrupt attorneys and witnesses alike. A recent poll of federally certified interpreters (Mikkelson 1989:11) finds that of 127 interpreters who were asked to what extent they interrupt witnesses or attorneys, 85 percent said they did so either "sometimes," "often," or at "every interpreting event," whereas only 33 percent claimed to do so only "rarely" or "never." Unfortunately, the poll does not break down the question into its two component parts. The differential impact of an interpreter's interrupting an attorney rather than a witness is important, something which both trial lawyers and interpreter trainers need to keep in mind.

Prodding the Witness

The ethnography of the bilingual courtroom has demonstrated that among the ways that interpreted proceedings are different from monolingually conducted ones is that interpreters commonly prompt witnesses or defendants to answer questions when for a variety of reasons they are hesitant about doing so. Whereas this type of prompting or prodding is most frequently seen during examinations carried out by judges, it can also be seen in attorney/witness interrogation sequences.

The prodding of a witness or defendant to answer a question is considered here to be the most coercive type of intrusive behavior by the interpreter. When a person who is testifying under oath is not ready to answer a question, it may be that he or she has not understood the question but is afraid to say so, or the person may be formulating his or her answer with some care. The latter possibility, in turn, may be due either to the witness's or defendant's desire to be truthful and accurate in his or her statements, or it may be out of a desire to obfuscate and deceive. In the context of interpreter-assisted testifying, it was considered important to determine whether an interpreter's prodding a witness to answer an attorney's question left mock jurors with a negative impression of that witness.

The experimental tapes in this study dealt with another case of illegal entry into the United States by a Mexican (see Appendix 6, text A.6.7 for the transcripts of the tapes). The witness in this particular case answered in highly fragmented style. In addition to answering yes/no type questions in the affirmative, he often would utter the expression *mhm* or *ajá* ("uhuh"). This type of affirmative response is usually not accepted by lawyers and judges, and witnesses who answer in this way are warned by the examiner to answer with a "yes" or a "no." In one version of the tape the interpreter would replicate such paralinguistic utterances in the equivalent English form. In the case of *mhm*, the Spanish and English forms are virtually identical. In the case of Spanish *ajá*, the English equivalent is quite similar in pronunciation. Therefore, when the interpreter renders her interpretation of these affirmative responses in English, they sound almost like a repetition of what the witness has just said.

In the other tape-recorded version, rather than to render these paralinguistic responses in English, the interpreter would say to the witness ¡*Conteste*! (Answer!), which is the command form of the verb. In other words, the interpreter did not accept the terms *mhm* and *ajá* as an answer to the question. In effect, the interpreter was functioning in lieu of the attorney, since it was the attorney who normally would not accept such an answer for the record. This type of coercive behavior on the part of the interpreter is considered in this study to be a form of prodding.

Interestingly, and unexpectedly, when prodding did not occur, and the interpreter rendered the paralinguistic Spanish answers in the equivalent paralinguistic English form, the persons acting as jurors would erupt in laughter. Clearly they found the interpreter's mimicking of paralinguistic utterances to be comical. Thus, while the version that lacked prodding was originally conceived of as the unmarked version, it turned out to have an unexpected variable with its own independent effect on the listeners.

An analysis of the mean scores of all the mock jurors reveals that a witness is more highly regarded when an interpreter prods him into answering a question in an appropriate manner than when she renders his paralinguistic answers in an equivalent paralinguistic fashion. Those who had heard the version that was marked by the interpreter's prodding ($N = 248$) found the witness significantly more intelligent (sig. = .025) than did those who had heard the version in which the interpreter mimicked the witness's paralinguistic answers ($N = 285$). The mean scores of the two groups of mock jurors were 2.9 and 2.6, respectively. This was the only witness attribute for which a difference in the behavior of the interpreter had a significant impact on the mock jurors as a whole.

It was suspected that when an interpreter took on a lawyerlike role—that is, when she prodded the witness to answer when his responses were not acceptable in court—the attorney conducting the examination would appear less competent, intelligent, and persuasive than when the interpreter did not act in a way normally associated with lawyers. Apparently, because of the intervening variable of laughter-provoking behavior by the interpreter, just the opposite turned out to be the case. On two of the three attributes—competence and persuasiveness—the attorney was found to be significantly inferior when there was no prodding of the witness, but there was interpreter mimicry of the witness's inappropriate answers (the mean scores on competence were 4.5 and 4.1, respectively; sig. = .010, $N=438$). On the trait persuasiveness, the mean scores were 4.0 and 3.7; sig. = .055). Apparently, the perception of the listeners that the interpreter's virtual repetition of the expressions *mhm* and *uhuh* was ludicrous adversely affected their estimation of the interrogating attorney as well.

In contrast to the reactions of the sample of listeners as a whole, the Hispanic subsample was impervious to the effects of both interpreter prodding and interpreter mimicking of paralanguage. For the Hispanic mock jurors, there were not statistically significant differences in response to the witness. Nor did they judge the attorney any differently depending upon the experimental tape that they had heard. This is surprising in light of the fact that they, too, had laughed at the interpreter's mimicry of the witness's unacceptable responses.

It appears that whereas both Hispanic and non-Hispanic mock jurors alike considered the interpreter's repetition of paralinguistic utterances to be laughable, Hispanic listeners did not allow their perception of the situation to spill over onto their evaluation of the witness. Nor did they allow it to color their estimation of the lawyer. In the case of paralinguistic mimicry, the Hispanic listeners seemed to be able to separate out the interpreter as a separate speaker, whereas the overall sample treated her more as a surrogate for the witness and for the attorney. She is, after all, supposed to be their mouthpiece, and for nonbilinguals she is much more the focus of attention than she is for bilingual evaluators.

Conclusions

This chapter has demonstrated in a number of different ways that pragmatic alterations made by the court interpreter count a great deal in shaping the impressions that mock jurors form, both of the testifying witness and of the examining attorney. This is true not only of monolingual English speakers, but of Hispanic bilinguals as well.

Clearly the impact of the interpreter is greater on non-Hispanic listeners. They must rely entirely on the English rendition of the interpreter to be able to understand a witness's testimony. Hispanic listeners do tune in to the Spanish source testimony; however, they are also to a large degree affected by the interpreter's version of the testimony as well.

Of the pragmatic variables that have been explored as the focus of experimental study, the ones having to do with the interpreter's intrusive verbal acts—that is, interrupting the attorney, interrupting the testifying witness, and prodding the witness—seem to have less of a large-scale impact than do those dealing with the interpreter's pragmatic alterations of some aspect of the testimony itself (i.e., making it less polite, excessively formal, introducing hedges, or changing the case of the verb). The intrusive actions of the interpreter do leave their own measure of influence on the way that mock jurors evaluate witnesses and attorneys. However, the impact is not as far-reaching as the impact left by interpreter alterations in some pragmatic aspect of a witness's answer.

Why this is so is not self-evident. It is believed, however, that there is a fundamental difference between interpreter actions in which the interpreter acts as an independent party to the interaction between the examiner and the witness, and those in which she is merely replicating the examiner and the witness. When she intrudes to clarify a point with either one, or halts the examination process to request that something that has been said in the source language be repeated for her benefit, she becomes the center of attention in her own right. Clearly, this has less of an impact on listeners's impressions of the witness than when the interpreter is simply speaking in lieu of the witness, taking his place.

Perceptions of the competence of the attorney, however, are adversely affected by interpreter interruptions of the attorney's questioning. Both Hispanic mock jurors and the entire sample as a whole consider an attorney to be less competent when the interpreter stops him repeatedly in order to clarify some point in reference to her impending interpretation, or to request that he repeat a portion of his question for her. Such interruptions often can justifiably be interpreted by the listener as an indirect criticism of the attorney by the interpreter. When an interpreter states that the attorney's question is so long that it exceeds the limits of her retention, she is in effect complaining to him that he is not being sensitive to her professional needs. It is to imply that he should know better. When she asks permission to change the grammatical form of the question so that the witness may better comprehend the question, she is indirectly criticizing the lawyer for not being more sensitive to the linguistic needs of the witness. Apparently, mock jurors, particularly Hispanic mock jurors, judging by their evaluations of the attorney who is interrupted, sympathize with the veiled criticism made by the interpreter. For Hispanic listeners an attorney who repeatedly is interrupted by an interpreter is perceived as not only less competent, but also less intelligent.

In addition, this set of studies has shown that politeness on the witness stand is well received. A witness whose answers are interpreted in English with politeness markers such as "sir" and "ma'am" will be judged more competent, intelligent, trustworthy, and convincing than is one whose interpreted testimony lacks such overt politeness signals.

These studies have shown, furthermore, that speaking in a hyperformal manner is an advantage for witnesses. In contrast to hypercorrect speech, which reflects the nonstandard use of lexical items and grammatical constructions, hyperformal speech is well received in interpreted testimony. The enhancing impact of hyperformal speech style may be due to its pragmatic sense of definiteness and precision, on the one hand, and to the air of politeness that it conveys, on the other.

Hedging in the interpreted testimony of a Spanish-speaking witness is uniformly perceived in a negative light by mock jurors, in general. However, Hispanic mock jurors are consistently unaffected by the presence of hedges in the English interpretation of testimony. This is surprising in light of the finding that politeness and hyperformality in interpreted testimony leave an impact on Hispanic listeners that is virtually identical to that found among an undifferentiated group of listeners.

It has been shown that the use of passive rather than active voice in the interpretation of Spanish testimony leaves no significant impact at all on Hispanic mock jurors, and affects only the perceptions of intelligence and trustworthiness among a larger group of non-Hispanic and Hispanic evaluators together.

This set of experimental studies has shown that the involvement of the court interpreter in the examination of a witness affects the impressions of that witness by listeners playing the role of jurors. It has demonstrated that perceptions of some of the witness's social/psychological attributes—namely, convincingness, truthfulness, intelligence, and competence—are affected by pragmatic alterations made by the interpreter. In addition, it has revealed that even bilingual evaluators are affected by the English interpretations that they hear, which means that to a large extent they are able to minimize the effects of tuning in to the foreign language testimony. In effect, they are able to comply with the desire of the Court in so doing.

Finally, these studies have shown that the interpreter has the powerful capability of changing the intent of what non-English-speaking witness wishes to say in the way that he or she would like to say it. The implication of this is that interpreters and court administrators alike need to be made aware of the power that resides in the interpreter's role, and that interpreter training programs should look to linguistics in general, and to the field of pragmatics in particular, to sensitize persons entering this profession as to the multiple ways in which they can affect a jury.

9

Conclusion: An Appellate View of Interpreting Issues

The series of experimental studies reported on in the preceding chapter has demonstrated empirically that the variety of alterations that interpreters make in the testimony of witnesses and in the questioning routines of lawyers has a significant impact on the way in which persons listening to these proceedings perceive the testifying witness, and to some extent, on the way they perceive the interrogating attorney. Those studies show that the court interpreter does indeed make a difference in the impressions formed of speakers in the courtroom. Whereas the evidence for this conclusion is based upon an experimentally designed investigation, there is evidence of a different sort as well: appellate cases grounded in claims of poor interpreting. The following discussion sets out to show that the judicial system as a whole has become increasingly more aware of the problems associated with the use of foreign language interpreters in the courts, and of the need for high quality interpreting. A clear reflection of this new consciousness is an increase in the rate of appeals.

To discover how many and what type of appeals have been made on the basis of some issue regarding court interpreting, a *Lexis Nexis* computerized search was carried out, using as key search words "interpreter," "interpretation," "translate," "translation," and "Spanish." No starting date was given the *Lexis* search program, so that the earliest possible appeals could be uncovered.[1] The search ended with the most current date available, February 1987, covering all case reporter books normally housed in law school libraries. It therefore covered all geographical areas of the United States. Whereas the only language to be used as a search word was Spanish, the other key words found cases involving interpreting issues for other languages as well. The vast majority that emerged, however, dealt with Spanish.

The computerized search retrieved 48 cases altogether: 23 cases in which errors of interpreting or translating themselves were a cause of either an appeal or a trial court decision, and 25 cases in which issues other than interpreting/translating errors were singled out. Altogether five major themes emerged, excluding the highly frequent appeals based on the failure of the court to appoint an official interpreter to a party:[2] (1) inaccuracies in interpreting, or interpreting errors; (2) bias on the part of the interpreter, and the insinuation that there had existed a conflict of interest on the interpreter's part; (3) the improper use of interpreting procedures and techniques; (4) the intervention of jurors in the course of interpreting; and (5) the issue of whether an interpreter's testimony is hearsay. These five areas of appellate review and trial court decision are presented in the order mentioned because they represent the frequency with which these types of cases have occurred. However, the second and the fifth themes will not be analyzed, for they do not deal directly with linguistic issues or with the mechanics of interpreting. They are more on the plane of legal and ethical matters.

Interpreting errors comprise by far the most common reason for appeal or judicial decision: the 23 cases in this category represent 48 percent of all the cases.

Figures 9.1 and 9.2 show the dramatic rise in interpreter-related appeals in recent years. In the 6-year period from 1981 to 1987 there were more appeals and decisions grounded on interpreting inaccuracy than there were cases of this type in the 21-year period from 1948 to 1969. Similarly, in the category of interpreter-related appeals/deci-

Figure 9.1. Appeals Based on Interpreter Errors/Inaccuracies, from 1945 to February 1987 ($N = 23$; · = one case)

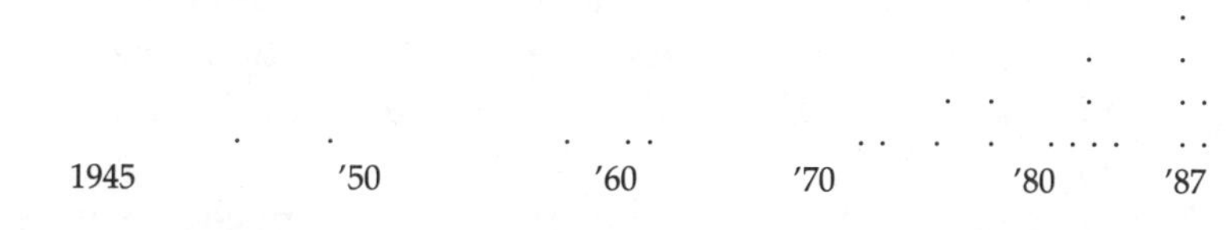

Figure 9.2. Appeals Based on Grounds Related to Interpreting other than Interpreter Errors/Inaccuracies, from 1945 to February 1987 ($N = 26$; · = one case)

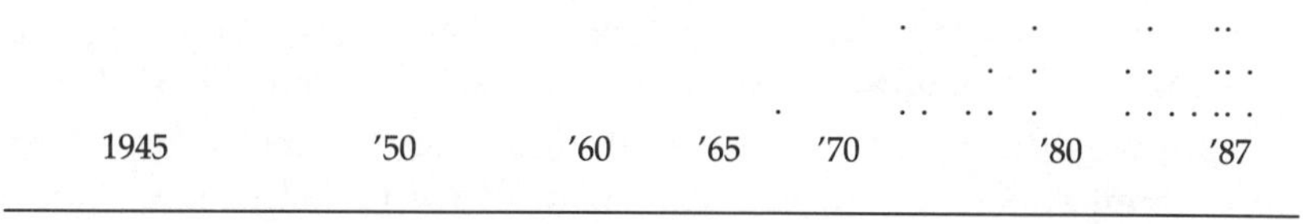

1945 '50 '60 '65 '70 '80 '87

sions that did not have to do with interpreting errors or inaccuracy, there was only *one* case prior to 1970, whereas there were 15 cases in the 6-year period from 1981 to 1987, and 9 cases between 1973 and 1979. Clearly the *rate* of appeals made on these grounds is increasing rapidly. Clearly, too, this trend becomes most noticeable beginning in 1977. The sudden sharp rise in interpreter-related appeal cases in the late 1970s is obviously linked to the prevailing line of thought and legal argumentation that gave rise to the Court Interpreters Act in 1978. One can safely assume that defense attorneys, hearing about the impending congressional legislation and knowing the arguments that were leading to the passage of the law, were using these arguments to appeal the convictions of their clients.

The Appellate Cases

Appeals Based on Interpreter Errors/Inaccuracies

A review of all the cases in which interpreter inaccuracy or error was used as a ground for appealing a prior ruling uncovers one overwhelmingly predominant pattern: appellate judges generally uphold the rulings of lower courts, rejecting appellant claims that their trial had been unfairly conducted. The major reason why appellate judges can and do rule in this way is that usually the appellant cannot provide concrete evidence of poor quality interpreter performance. This is so because proceedings conducted with the aid of a court interpreter are transcribed in the court record in English alone, as if they were monolingually conducted in English. In other words, because foreign language testimony is not entered into the court record in the source language, there is no way that alleged errors of interpretation can be directly verified or discounted on appeal. The only situation in which this would be possible is if the proceedings were tape-recorded, and the taped recording existed intact at the time of the appeal.

The most commonly made arguments used by appellate judges to reject the requests of appellants that the ruling made in the lower courts be overturned is that there is nothing in the court record to indicate faulty interpreting. Appellate judges argue that they would legitimately accept two types of evidence of inaccurate interpreting: (1) the presence in the court record of English answers provided by the interpretater that are unresponsive, confusing, or unintelligible; and (2) attorney or defendant objections to the interpreter's renditions, given during the course of foreign language testimony. In effect, when appellate judges decide against overturning a lower court ruling, an appellant claiming that the interpreter had made errors in her interpretations, they are saying that the objections to the quality of the interpretations should have been made at the trial itself, not after the trial was over.[3]

Typical of this type of appellate reasoning are the following cases. In the case of People v. Molina (418 N.E.2d 831 [Ill. App. 1981]), the appellate court of Illinois ruled that the court record failed to sustain the state's contention that the Serbian interpreter, who had interpreted the testimony of the state's chief witness, was incompetent. The defendant-appellant, Gilberto Molina, who had been convicted of armed robbery, argued, among other grounds, that the incompetence of the interpreter assigned by the court to interpret for Sefki Emiui, the state's chief witness, denied him his Sixth Amendment right to confront witnesses and his right to due process.

Citing case law, the appellate court conceded that a defendant's constitutional rights were indeed denied in cases where "the witness's testimony was 'incomprehensible' or 'unintelligible,' or where the witness displayed a 'lack of comprehension' of the English language to the extent that he could not be understood." However, the appellate court judged, these criteria did not fit this case. The court argued:

> While certain of Mr. Emiui's answers were confusing and unresponsive, an analysis of the entire segment reveals that as a whole his testimony was *sufficiently understandable* [emphasis added]. Moreover, we believe that the trial judge who had the opportunity to hear the witness's testimony, with its inflections, and observe his gestures and general demeanor, would have a better understanding of Mr. Emiui's testimony. Indeed, there is no indication in the record that the trial judge or either counsel had any *major difficulty* [emphasis added] understanding Mr. Emiui.

The appellate court went on to say that, judging by the court record, the trial judge had given the defense attorney a full opportunity to question the interpreter prior to the trial, and that the attorney had declined to do so, stating that if he noticed any problems related to the interpreter during the trial, he would raise objections at that point. The appellate court noted that apparently the defense attorney had not seen any need for objecting to the competency of the interpreter, for the attorney had never raised any objections. The court concluded that it found no "abuse of discretion" by the trial judge in appointing the interpreter, for when viewed in its entirety, the witness's testimony was found to be "sufficiently comprehensible."

The reasoning used in this appellate ruling is typical of appellate decisions that reject the argument that inaccurate interpreting during a defendant's trial deprived him of his constitutional right to confront a witness testifying against him. The basis for rejecting the defendant's grounds for appeal is the relative comprehensibility of the witness's testimony as interpreted into English. So long as the examining attorney and the presiding judge found that the witness's answers made sense and were relevant to the questions asked (i.e., they found the interpreted testimony to be sufficiently comprehensible), the interpreter's rendition would be assumed to be accurate.

The line of reasoning illustrated above is a very peculiar way of measuring interpreter accuracy. There is no attempt to determine if there is a semantic correspondence, or congruence, between what the foreign language testimony says and what its English interpretation says. Conceivably, the interpreter might be adding to, subtracting from, or altogether changing the meaning of the witness's answer, yet still be producing English answers that make sense in relation to the questions being asked. Clearly, the criterion of "comprehensibility to attorney and judge" is a highly questionable measure of interpreter accuracy.

Secondly, the prevailing thinking that the absence of objections by attorneys to interpretations of testimony is another good indication of accurate interpreting is also highly flawed. Undoubtedly, bilingual attorneys are capable of recognizing interpreting errors, and the ethnographic phase of the present study shows that in fact they do frequently object to interpreter renditions of testimony. However, this type of objection cannot come from an attorney who does not understand the language of the witness. Some defendants, those in the category of "low English proficient," rather than "non-English-speaking" have a sufficient comprehension of English to enable them to follow a great deal of the English spoken in the courtroom. Such defendants to a certain degree have the capability of informing their lawyer of discrepancies between what the witness said and how the interpreter rendered it. This would be the case of Hispanic-Americans who have lived in mainland U.S.A. for a number of years.

However, persons newly arrived in the United States may have no comprehension of English at all (e.g., the case of undocumented aliens) or very little proficiency (e.g., recent immigrants). Such persons do not have the ability to detect even grossly inaccurate interpretations. If the defendant is a speaker of one of the many "exotic" languages, it is highly unlikely that anyone in the courtroom other than members of the defendant's family will understand that language. It is therefore unlikely that in cases involving the low-English proficient who are speakers of exotic languages, the defendant or defense counsel would be in a position to recognize inaccurate interpreting when it did occur.

Successful Appeals. On occasion, appeals based on claims of erroneous interpreting are successful. However, when prior convictions are overturned, it is not on the basis of the poor interpreting argument alone that appellate courts reverse a prior judicial ruling. Nevertheless, it is important to note the line of reasoning of appellate judges who do support the appellant's contention that the interpreting carried out during the trial and in pretrial proceedings was erroneous.

One case in which the appellant was successful in having a prior conviction reversed on the grounds of poor interpreting is People v. Starling (315 N.E.2d. 163 [1974]). This case is highly unusual in that the issue of erroneous interpreting was the defendant's *sole* ground for appeal. The appellant, Willie Starling, had been convicted in Chicago of simple robbery. During his trial, a Spanish-speaking witness for the prosecution, Sergio Bolañis, testified through an interpreter that he had been robbed of $480 by the defendant and his girlfriend, whom Bolañis had just met in a bar. Bolañis was the state's sole "occurrence" witness—that is, no other witness had been present at the scene where the alleged robbery had occurred.

Willie Starling appealed his conviction on the grounds that he had been denied his rights to be confronted by the witnesses against him, arguing that (1) the complaining witness, Bolañis, spoke only Spanish; (2) the interpreter was incompetent; and (3) the interpreter frequently engaged in unrecorded discussions with the complaining witness. For the appellate court, the central question was whether the witness's testimony, as presented through the interpreter, was "understandable, comprehensible, intelligible. And if it was not, did that lack of intelligibility, brought about by an ineffective and incompetent interpreter, deny defendant the right to be confronted by the witnesses against him?"

The appellate judge found that the defendant had been denied his right, and gave the following arguments to support his ruling. First of all, at one point in the trial, even the assistant state's attorney had commented on the difficulty of understanding what the witness was saying as related by the interpreter and said that the witness should testify in *narrative*. Second, on the second day of the trial the defense attorney brought with him a new interpreter, who was supposed to interpret for Bolañis. However, Bolañis did not appear in court that day, and so the trial was postponed until the following day, at which time the original interpreter was again sworn in to duty, and the second one apparently was not present. Third, there was evidence in the court record of repeated complaints from the defense counsel, and at least one complaint from the prosecuting attorney, about the interpreter's ineffectiveness. Fourth, the record showed that the trial judge was aware of the problem regarding the interpreter, for he admonished the interpreter about his conversations with the witness and, in addition, attempted to clarify the witness's testimony. According to the court record, both the defense attorney and the prosecuting attorney made similar attempts to clarify the testimony.

For the appellate court, at the heart of the matter in this case is the fact that with the exception of the witness, none of the principal players involved in the trial understood the language of the witness. The opinion of the Court in this regard is worth quoting:

> It appears from the record that neither the trial judge, nor the attorneys or defendant understood Spanish. Thus, the accuracy of the questions and answers rested solely in the hands of the interpreter. It is obvious the interpreter was not fully, completely or accurately translating the questions and answers. When an interpreter is employed, that practice must be strictly followed; otherwise the possibility of editing, and error, rests solely with the interpreter. Due process rights of persons charged with crimes cannot be short-cut by avoiding the ritual of translating each question and answer as required in chapter 38, paragraph 165-12. In our view, the only cure for the unfortunate situation would have been another interpreter, one who would translate truly, competently, and effectively, each question and answer with due regard for his or her oath to do so.

Clearly it is naive of the judge to believe that swearing an oath to accurate interpreting will guarantee accurate interpreting. Interpreters generally do the best they can, and are sincere in their effort to be precise and faithful to the foreign language testimony. Yet if they are not highly qualified to do their job, the product of their efforts is bound to be faulty. No amount of oath-swearing can guarantee high quality interpreting from an interpreter who does not have the necessary competency.

More typical of the appeals that succeed in reversing a lower court ruling is the case of State v. Mitjans (394 N.W.2d 221 [Minn. App.

1986]). Here the issue of mistranslations at a trial is only one of several grounds for appealing a lower court decision. Another issue deals with the qualifications of the person first assigned to interpret for the defendant-appellant after his arrest. The interpreter at this point was a police officer helping to conduct an interrogation of the defendant. The particular issue regarding the policeman-interpreter is not his ability to interpret, but the fact that upon beginning to interpret for the defendant, he did not swear an oath stating that he would interpret accurately, a requirement established by a Minnesota statute. The appellate court's opinion was that police officers who are working actively on a case, such as the one who served as interpreter following the defendant's arrest:

> stand at the outer limits of the statutory definition of qualified interpreter. Interpreters should be neutral and objective if at all possible. Globa [the policeman-interpreter] had a built-in conflict of interest. He and the others had actively focused on appellant as a serious suspect in a murder and felony assault and were working to gather evidence against appellant. The police at that point should have invested time and work in attempting to find someone outside the department to translate. Because of the close relationship and natural empathy between a translator and a defendant dependent on that translator to communicate his thoughts and feelings, a translator should be someone a defendant can place trust in and rely on to protect his interests. This is an unnatural burden to place on the shoulders of a peace officer actively working to gather evidence to help convict a defendant.

A possible conflict of interest on the part of the policeman-interpreter was just one of the issues brought up by the appellant. Mistranslations were a separate issue, these having to do not with the policeman-translator, Anatoli Globa, but with the person appointed by the court to interpret at the trial, Luis Borges. Borges had learned Spanish growing up in Puerto Rico. The defendant, Luis Candalario Mitjans, was from Cuba, and knew very little English. The defense attorney had requested before the trial that the court appoint another interpreter, Danelia Savino, to interpret the defendant's testimony to the jury, since she was known to be familiar with the dialect of Spanish spoken by the defendant. The judge had denied this request, but allowed Savino to do simultaneous interpreting for the defendant at the defense counsel table.[4] Both interpreters were sworn in.

Savino testified in regard to a number of inaccuracies that she had detected in Borges's interpretation of the defendant's testimony. The defendant had been describing the events leading up to his shooting a man during a fight that broke out in a Minneapolis bar. Savino testified that the other interpreter had omitted some portions of the defendant's testimony. She testified that, for example, Borges's interpretations had omitted saying that before the shooting, the deceased victim had gone over to the defendant, had grabbed his neck, squeezing it. Similarly, Borges had omitted a portion of the testimony in which the defendant said that he was afraid that the man with whom he was having the altercation would come back toward him and take the defendant's gun away from him and use it on him. The defendant's phrase, "using it on me" (uttered in Spanish), had not been interpreted at the trial. In addition, Savino testified, Borges had omitted an entire utterance of the defendant, in which he described the deceased victim as having come at him "with his head bent like this, like a charge, with his head bent down." There was also a criticism by Savino of Borges's interpretation of two words used by the defendant: *causionarlo* and *embestir.* In describing his intent in drawing his gun during the initial dispute with the friend of the dead victim, the defendant had testified that he wanted to *causionarlo.* Borges had interpreted this as "I want to coerce him." At a hearing held after the trial was over, Borges testified that the word only had a meaning in context, and that it meant "to advise him some event" [*sic*]. Savino testified that it meant "to caution somebody." At the trial, however, neither meaning had been used.

Similarly, Savino testified to the inaccuracy of Borges's interpretation of the word *embestir.* Borges had rendered it as "tackle": "He came to tackle me," referring to the victim's actions toward the defendant before the shooting. Savino testified that what the defendant really had meant was that the victim had come "charging like a bull." Borges, at the appeal, agreed with Savino's interpretation, but defended his previous rendition, saying he had thought originally that the meaning of *embestir* in the sense of "animal fighting" was an inappropriate one.

The appellate court felt that the alleged errors in interpretation did not in isolation warrant a new trial. However, when added to other errors that had been made in the course of the trial, they made for an unfair trial. The court held that the translation problems were significant because they had occurred during some very crucial testimony—specifically, the defendant's account of what was going on immediately before he fired his gun. This portion of the testimony was crucial to the defendant's portrayal of his shots being accidental in the case of the man who was killed, and self-defense in the case of another man who was assaulted.

As additional evidence of mistranslations, the appellate court cited the trial court judge, who had admonished the interpreter for paraphrasing and giving obviously incomplete interpretations, telling Borges, "It appears that you may be summarizing from time to time." The appellate court explained its ruling in regard to the interpreting in the following way: "We hold that whether or not the translation errors by themselves amount to reversible error, they contribute to the cumulative effect of errors which denied appellant his right to a fair trial." If on appeal, therefore, an appellant can show that there were errors in interpretation, *and in addition* can make a good case for reversal on other grounds as well, the appellant stands a good chance of winning the appeal. To date, appealing solely on the grounds of inaccurate interpreting has not been very successful in cases of criminal convictions.

It is worthwhile noting that the appellant in State v. Mitjans was able to prove his assertions that the interpreter had not interpreted his testimony accurately, because there existed an audio tape of the trial. At the hearing on his motion for a new trial, there was no trial transcript available as yet, and only the audio tape was available for analysis. Thus, when Savino was asked to testify in regard to the accuracy of Borges's interpretations, she had the Spanish answers of the appellant, together with the interpretations of Borges to work with. While the appellate judge does not say this, he seems to be implying that had there been a trial transcript in English, then the transcript would have been used as the basis for Savino's evaluation. Clearly, the existence of an audio tape of the trial, together with the absence of a court transcript, made it possible for the appellant to produce "hard evidence" of erroneous interpreting. The more typical appellate approach, to look for instances of attorney objections and trial judge admonitions of the interpreter, are merely *indirect* reflections of allegedly erroneous interpreting.[5]

The conclusion that one can draw from all this is that for the purposes of appeal, the non-English-speaking defendant, teamed up with a monolingual English-speaking attorney, is at a distinct disadvantage over a defendant who has a relatively good comprehension of English and is represented by a lawyer who can comprehend the foreign language of the defendant and of the witnesses testifying against him. A lawyer in the latter category stands a good chance of knowing when to raise an objection to inaccurate interpreter renditions. Lawyers who are not in this advantageous position would be well advised to have their own competent interpreter sit at the trial, to serve as a check on the accuracy of the court-appointed interpreter. Clearly, indigent defendants represented by public defenders cannot afford the luxury of such privately paid interpreting services. As the ethnographic phase of this study has shown, well-to-do defendants (e.g., persons involved in the narcotics trade) do precisely that.[6]

Appeals Based on Unqualified Interpreters

Within the category of interpreting errors is the issue of whether an "unqualified interpreter" had been used to interpret for the defendant. Typically, the issue is raised whenever friends or family related to the defendant have served as interpreters—that is, whenever an official court-appointed interpreter was not utilized at the proceedings. Appellate ruling in such cases shows that if the appellant can demonstrate that the presiding trial judge had not inquired into the prospective interpreter's ability to adequately interpret, then the appellant has a solid ground for reversal of the lower court decision.

A good illustration of a successful reversal of a lower court decision is People v. Medrano (N.Y.S.2d 375 [Co. Ct. 1986]). The defendant/appellant, Manuel Medrano, had changed his plea to guilty on a drug offense. At the change of plea hearing, the presiding judge appointed Medrano's wife to serve as his interpreter, upon the recommendation of the assistant district attorney, who told the judge that the defendant's wife was fluent in both English and Spanish.

At the heart of this appeal is the issue of whether the defendant had "knowingly, voluntarily, and intelligently" waived his right to a jury trial by pleading guilty.[7] In all changes of plea from "not guilty" to "guilty" it is the obligation of the judge to make sure that the defendant understands what he is doing by changing his plea. The appellate court found the judge to be in error in using the defendant's wife as an interpreter since she was not a "public official who must subscribe to an oath of office" as prescribed in a New York State law. The defendant's wife had never filed such an oath. Thus, there was no assurance that her interpreting was accurate, and consequently, that her husband had knowingly and intelligently given up his constitutional rights. Using this line of reasoning, the New York State appellate court overturned the lower court's sentencing of the appellant.

It is not merely unofficial court interpreters whose overall competency is questioned during a trial. Court-appointed interpreters are challenged as well. An excellent example of an appeal based largely on the issue of overall interpreter competency is United States v. Anguloa (598 F.2d 1182 [1979]). The specific issue was court policy over the hiring and replacement of court interpreters. The appellate court had to decide whether the prosecution's unilateral dismissal of the court-appointed interpreter and its substituting another one in the course of the trial was improper. The appellate court decided that this was in fact an error. It is the duty of the trial judge to appoint replacement interpreters. Secondly, at issue was whether an interpreter's disparaging remarks about the defendant in open court were sufficiently prejudicial to him. The appellate court ruled that there was no prejudice done to the defendant by the interpreter's remark, since the trial judge had given the jury "prompt and forceful instructions to disregard" them. The appellate court upheld the lower court's conviction.

The defendant/appellant, Cesar Rosario Anguloa, was a Mexican national, caught crossing the U.S./Mexico border with heroin hidden in his car, and was convicted in Arizona of possession and importation of heroin with the intent to distribute it. During the trial he was represented by a privately retained attorney who did not speak Spanish, and by an attorney from the public defenders office, who did speak Spanish. The prosecutor did not speak Spanish, but he was assisted throughout the trial by a Spanish-speaking case agent. The judge did not speak Spanish.

After the first day of trial, the prosecutor asked the clerk of the court to replace the interpreter, explaining that his Spanish-speaking case agent had noticed that the interpreter was rendering mistranslations. A new interpreter was assigned, and on the second day of the trial, the prosecutor began objecting to her interpretations as well. So, too, did the defense attorney. The objections were made based on (1) the accuracy of the translations and (2) the following disparaging remarks made by the interpreter about the defendant:

> "It's not necessarily the questions. It's the way the defendant changes the subjects into different things at different times."
>
> "He says a lot of mumbo-jumbo that doesn't mean a lot of things."

These comments were stricken from the record by the judge. In addition, the judge gave the jury a cautionary instruction, and did so promptly and forcefully.

The judge's instruction is worth quoting since it reflects the general judicial view on the role of the court interpreter:

> All right. Ladies and gentlemen, sorry for the delay, but an emergency involving legal matters arose and, as you know, we have a new court interpreter. I want to instruct you as follows.
>
> While the Court has no personal feelings about the Interpreter, we had prior to the recess—are you interpreting for him now?—nevertheless, there seemed to be conflict among counsel, some of which you noted, and I just want to instruct you as follows. We have a new interpreter now and, apparently, agreeable to all counsel. I want you to take this instruction very seriously I will give you now. You are not to draw any factual or legal or any kind of inference from any statements made by the previous Interpreter today, earlier in the day—I forgot her name.
>
> [The Clerk: Juanita Martin.]
>
> With respect to the state of mind, intent or way or manner or methodology, if you will, of answering the questions if, indeed, she did make any such remarks or you think she did. *Obviously, an Interpreter is not a participant in the trial. An Interpreter really only acts as a transmission belt or telephone* [emphasis added]. In one ear should come in English and out comes Spanish, but just as the transmission belt—transmission wire so that the questions can be asked in English and asked in Spanish and whatever the witness desires to say, he says that in Spanish and she translates that into English for the benefit of those who can not speak Spanish, but any remarks, if any she did make, with respect to the witness other than translate his answers or his statements as best she could or as best she thought she could, you must disregard entirely.

Perhaps one of the most cogent observations made by the appellate judge is his acknowledgment, "that there is an inherent difficulty in attempting to evaluate the accuracy of interpretations on appellate review. The reporter's transcript can only contain the questions in English and the answers after they have been translated into English." This judge goes on to cite the statement made in the legislative history to the Court Interpreters Act, something he finds is the heart of the problem: "nobody knows how accurate the interpretation may have been except the interpreter. And he is the wrong person to look for an impartial assessment of his performance." If this is true, and it seems abundantly clear that it is, then there can be little substance behind the oath of accuracy that interpreters must swear before they start interpreting. Nor can testimony by interpreters regarding the accuracy of interpretations that they themselves have already made have much credibility, or at a minimum, any objectivity. Yet the fact that an interpreter either did or did not swear an oath before beginning to interpret will count heavily in appellate review.

Appeals Based on Mode of Interpreting

One common ground for appeals related to interpreting is the use of the summary mode rather than the consecutive or simultaneous mode of interpreting. This becomes a concern in cases where foreign language testimony is involved. There are many cases in which interpreters are seated next to the defendant and use the summary mode throughout the trial, and this is not usually viewed as a cause for complaint.[8] Thus, the defendant is deprived of a full knowledge of what witnesses are saying against him. What concerns most courts, however, is not this situation, but the situation in which a witness's testimony is summarized rather than rendered verbatim. Nevertheless, there are cases in which appellate judges have rules that "spasmodic interpretation and ex post facto résumés of English testimony deprive the non-English speaking defendant of the constitutionally guaranteed right to understand the precise nature of testimony against him" (e.g., United States v. ex rel. Negrón v. New York, 434 F.2d 386, 388–90 [2d Cir. 1970]). In the case of United States v. Torres (793 F.2d 436 [1st Cir. 1986]), the appellate court agreed with this view, yet did not reverse the lower court's ruling. The defendant/appellant, Gilbert Torres, had pleaded guilty to possessing cocaine with the intent to distribute it and to distributing cocaine, and in a jury trial was found guilty of assaulting, resisting, and interfering with federal officers in the performance of their official duties by using a deadly and dangerous weapon. During his jury trial, Torres acted as his own defense counsel, participating in the jury selection, delivering his own opening statement, cross-examining witnesses, testifying in his own defense, and delivering a closing argument, all this with the assistance of a court interpreter.

The grounds on which Torres appealed his conviction is that on two occasions, during his cross-examination of officials of the Drug Enforcement Agency, Torres went beyond asking questions, and instead made statements. Each time this happened, the judge instructed the interpreter not to interpret Torres's statements. The first time that this happened, during the defendant's examination of a government witness, the judge said to the interpreter: "Miss Interpreter, he is there to ask questions, not to make statements, so don't translate any affirmative representation he makes as to the facts. He will have a chance to testify if he wants to exercise that right." During

Torres's cross-examination of another government witness, the prosecuting attorney raised an objection to a statement that Torres had made, the judge then intervened, and Torres made an additional statement to the effect that the government witness was lying. At this point, the judge instructed the interpreter once again, as follows:

JUDGE: I'll instruct the jury to disregard that. Miss Easman, please do not translate those can [*sic*] statements. He is only entitled at this stage of the game to make comments, not make statements.
INTERPRETER: When the defendant starts to speak, I don't know if it is a question or a statement. I don't have any way of knowing.
JUDGE: Wait until you hear the end of it. Don't start translating until you know it's a question or a statement. When the government's putting in its case, he's entitled to ask him questions on it, but not make statements. If he wants to take the statement and make the statement when the government is finished, he can do it.
INTERPRETER: Your Honor, may I wait until he finishes, then you will instruct me if I should state it?
JUDGE: If you can't tell whether it's a question or a statement, then come up here and I will instruct you.

The appellate court ruled that the trial court judge had erred in directing the interpreter to use the summary mode of interpretation without obtaining the consent of all parties, saying that, "we are satisfied that the interpreter's duty is to translate all statements, without restriction by the court." The appellate judge then cites the report of the House Judiciary Committee, which had served as input into the 1978 Court Interpreters Act: "all interpretations are to be made in the consecutive mode except in those limited situations where the court determines, *and all the parties agree,* that the simultaneous or summary mode will aid in the efficient administration of justice." In sum, the appellate court felt that the interpretation of Torres's statements should not have been limited. Nevertheless, it did not overturn the lower court conviction, saying that "the error was indisputably harmless," since in reality, all of Torres's statements had been interpreted, despite the judge's intervention.

Jurors and the Interpreter

Bilingual jurors who understand the language of the non-English-speaking defendant or witness sometimes voice disagreement with the English renditions of the interpreter. According to one legal scholar,[9] who has worked under a judge in Puerto Rico for an extended period of time, whenever judicial proceedings were carried out with the assistance of an interpreter in this particular courtroom, jurors became actively involved throughout a trial, criticizing and correcting the interpreter's interpretations. According to this professor of law, this type of juror intervention in the interpreting process is quite common in Puerto Rico. One recent appeal based on problems emanating from juror criticism of the interpreter reflects just this issue (United States v. Perez, 658 F.2d 654 [1981]).

The case of United States v. Perez deals with the co-defendants/appellants Inocencio Gutierrez Perez and Jose de Ruvalcaba-Villalobos, who were convicted in California of conspiracy to distribute cocaine and of distributing it. During the testimony of a witness who was testifying in Spanish through an interpreter, one of the jurors burst out, asking the judge permission to question the interpreter regarding her interpretation of a word that the witness had used, *La Vado* (*sic*). The interpreter had rendered it in English as "bar" and the juror believed it meant "restroom." The testimony dealt with the circumstances of a meeting between the witness and an undercover narcotics agent. In her discussion with the judge over her confusion as to the meaning of the testimony, the juror, Dorothy Kim, and the interpreter, Ms. Ianziti, had a verbal altercation:

JUROR: I understand the word *La Vado*—I thought it meant restroom. She translates it as bar.
INTERPRETER: In the first place, the jurors are not to listen to the Spanish but to the English. I am a certified interpreter.
JUROR: You're an idiot.

The judge admonished the juror for trying to address the witness and the interpreter directly, and instructed the juror to direct her queries to him whenever there was something about the witness's answers that she could not understand. However, after conferring with the defense attorney, the defendant, and the prosecutor, the judge decided to dismiss the juror from jury duty the following day. The judge felt that the juror had developed certain strong opinions and feelings of anger toward some of the principal actors in the courtroom, and her attitude might infect the other jurors during their deliberations.

One of the co-defendants, Ruvalcaba, appealed on the ground that the dismissal of the juror was improper, for two reasons: (1) there was insufficient cause to dismiss her, and (2) by dismissing the juror, the judge had inhibited the rest of the jurors, which deprived Ruvalcaba of an impartial jury. The appellate court rejected both contentions. Even though the issue instigated by the juror's criticism of the interpreter was not the sole contention of the defendant/appellant, the appeal was unsuccessful.

The Implications of Appellate Review for Interpreting in the Courts

The preceding overview of appellant claims and court rulings shows us that the legal community is becoming increasingly aware of the fact that (1) interpreters make errors, and that some interpreters basically are incompetent and should not be permitted to serve the court in an official capacity; (2) the use of the summary mode of interpreting as the basic mode of interpreting for a witness at the stand, or for a defendant at the defense table is fundamentally unfair to the defendant, yet some interpreters do follow this practice; and (3) bilingual jurors sometimes intervene when they perceive mistakes in interpretations.

The ethnographic study has shown that principal players beyond the interpreter herself often compel her to perform functions that in reality belong to the domain of the attorney or the judge. The interpreter herself contributes to this problem when she prompts witnesses to answer or prevents them from doing so.

From a linguistic point of view, the focus of this book has not be on lexical equivalence. The attention has not been on whether or not, or to what extent, interpreters "get the right word" in their interpretations. Rather than focus on problems such as the one pointed out by the juror in United States v. Perez, as to whether *la vado* meant "restroom" or "bar,"[10] the focus in this book has been on regularly occurring pragmatic alterations that interpreters make in court, alterations that do not appear as "errors" since they form part of grammatically well-formed sentences, and meaningful utterances. They would not attract the attention of a lawyer or judge who did not understand the language of the testifying witness. Only a bilingual attorney or judge would notice such discrepancies, and be capable of commenting on them.

This study has focused also on some of the intrusive behaviors of the interpreter: interrupting the examining attorney, interrupting the testifying witness, prompting the witness to answer in a responsive manner. The experimentally designed set of studies has shown that these pragmatic shifts and interactional interventions by the interpreter to varying degrees leave their impact on persons putting themselves in the position of jurors. And these sorts of interpreter-induced alterations in the way a proceeding is conducted are quite subtle compared to the more blatant errors that are the ones most readily noticeable to the monolingual English-speaker.

Some legal analysts might despair at the power of court interpreters, and at their potential for altering the intended meaning of witnesses' answers. One group in Canada, the Freedom of Choice Movement, has come to the conclusion that it is prejudicial to the defendant to have the proceedings interpreted for him, since interpreting can never be perfectly accurate. The position of this group is that a defendant should have the right to a trial conducted in the language that he understands. In an appeal taken to the Supreme Court of Canada (Mercure v. A.G. Saskatchewan), involving a French-speaking Canadian priest, Father André Mercure, who had been involved in a traffic violation in the English-speaking province of Saskatchewan, the supreme court ruled that a defendant did not have such a right. Thus, the supreme court of Canada upheld, in February 1988, the normal state of affairs in what is an officially bilingual country: if a defendant ends up in court in a jurisdiction whose predominant language is not his dominant language, he will go through the judicial process in that jurisdiction with the aid of a court-appointed interpreter. The position of Father Mercure (who died before the case reached the supreme court) and that of Freedom of Choice, is that a defendant should have the right to be tried in a court where the proceedings are conducted in the language of his choice. Furthermore, he argued, the defendant should have the "right to be understood by the Judge or Judge and jury without the assistance of an interpreter or simultaneous translation." The Canadian supreme court ruled that the defendant did not have such a right.

Whereas this is an extreme reaction to the problems of court interpreting, and the position of Freedom of Choice might possibly be feasible in Canada, where there are in fact two official national languages, to take such a position in the United States would be not only unfeasible, but also perhaps undesirable. While one can admit that the quality of court interpreting varies tremendously from courtroom to courtroom within any given city in the United States, it does not mean that one's hands are tied and that we cannot do something to improve the existing situation.

The certification of court interpreters is one crucial step in the right direction. The standards set by the federal certification exam are the highest of any of the existing examinations. With a 96 percent failure rate among test-takers, no test is as stringent. The state certification tests of California, New Mexico, and New York, although not as difficult to pass as the federal exam, also are beneficial to the state system of courts. They ensure a substantial level of interpreter competence. Yet the types of pragmatic linguistic changes described in this book are made by practicing federally certified interpreters. These certification exams need to look more closely at pragmatics for their test items. At the moment they are heavily skewed in the direction of testing knowledge of vocabulary, whether it is specialized jargons of different social groups or college-level lexicon perceived to be prevalent in court talk. While vocabulary is indeed important, there are other linguistic realms to which interpreters need to be made sensitive. Even when grammar is covered on these certification tests, it is the testing of formal, written style that is of interest to testmakers.[11]

In addition to certification exams, training programs would be vital in upgrading the competency of those interpreters who are currently employed as interpreters in courthouses, and those who wish to enter the profession. The programs referred to in chapter 3 are good examples of such training programs. Finally, there is a crying need for the courts themselves to provide their staff interpreters with guidelines on what constitutes good and bad interpreting. One director of interpreting services in a southwestern state court for a number of years has been giving his staff written guidelines in this regard. In the absence of a state-mandated certification test, he has devised one for his courthouse, as a way of determining whether applicants for full- or part-time positions are competent enough to work in the courthouse. Whereas it is the job of the presiding judge to determine in any given case whether an interpreter is "qualified" to perform the job of interpreting,[12] judges in effect rely on the office of court interpreting services within the courthouse to provide them with lists of qualified persons available locally. In the absence of a state certification exam, what this chief interpreter has been doing, given his credentials as a federally certified interpreter, can only be an improvement over a state of affairs where bilingual court secretaries and bailiffs are used as interpreters whenever the need arises.

The justification of one appellate court for turning down an appeal based on ineffective interpreting stands out as perhaps one common attitude of judges regarding this problem (State v. Casipe, 686 P.2d 28 [Hawaii App. 1984]): the federal and state constitutional guarantee of due process is not a guarantee of a perfect trial. While this may be so, it does not mean that we should yield to complacent inaction. The judicial system has every right to insist on high quality interpreting services for defendants and plaintiffs at every judicial tier. After all, this country has federally legislated the right of the non-English-speaking and the hearing-impaired to be "linguistically present" at their own trial. With states following suit, it is time that the highest possible quality interpreting services be guaranteed as well. Only then can the bilingual American courtroom truly live up to its constitutional promise.

One way to help ensure high quality interpreting is to tape-record—and in the case of the deaf and hearing-impaired, video-record—and transcribe all non-English language testimony. Providing access to testimony uttered in its source language is the only legitimate vehicle for ascertaining the fit between foreign language testimony and its English interpretation. For attorneys who do not understand the language of the defendant or plaintiff whom they represent, and who are doubtful of the quality of the interpreting services that the court has provided them, access to bilingual transcripts of proceedings is the only accurate way to assess whether the questions of attorneys and judges, and the answers of witnesses or defendants, have been interpreted with high fidelity. Appellate criteria that are currently in use fall woefully short of the mark in this regard. For the purposes of appeals, only bilingual recordings and bilingual transcripts can provide sufficient evidence as to whether or not there is in fact a basis for appeal. Providing lawyers with such bilingual transcripts is one test of the seriousness of the commitment of the American legal system to due process for the non-English-speaking.

It is worthwhile noting that whereas the focal point of this book has been the Spanish-English bilingual courtroom, the issues regarding interpreting that have been raised here apply equally to the numerous other languages that every year are heard in American courtrooms. The United States has always been a magnet for immigrants from around the globe, and for this reason linguistic heterogeneity has been a sociological fact of American life. If we are to afford due process to the multitudes of persons who either have only recently arrived on our shores, or who have already attained American citizenship but are nevertheless struggling to master English while they are in the throes of incipient bilingualism, then standards for the bilingual courtroom must be set high, and for every linguistic group.[13] If the American judicial system is to render justice to this nation's linguistic minorities, then it will have to pay greater attention to the interpreting services that it provides these groups, because for those millions of persons whose ability to speak and understand English is limited, the American courtroom in effect is a bilingual courtroom.

Appendix 1: State Legislation Regarding Rights to Court Interpreting

Selected state legislation regarding interpreting for the non-English-speaking and for the deaf and hearing-impaired

Alabama	Ala. Code (§12–21–131 [criminal and probate]) Rules of Civil Proceedings 43(f) (1978)
Alaska	Alaska Administrative Rules 6 [fees] (1981)
Arizona	Ariz. Rev. Stat. Ann. (§11–601 [compensation]; §12–241 [penal sanction]; §12–242 [criminal] [pre-trial] [administrative]; §36–1946 [interpreters for the deaf and their duties]) Arizona Rules for Criminal Proceedings (Rule 12.5 [grand jury]) (1982)
Arkansas	Ark. Stat. Ann. (§5–715 [administrative]; §5–715.1 *et seq.* [qualifications]; §27–835; §43–2101.1 [criminal]; §22–148 to 153 [court interpreter program]) (1981)
California	Cal. Evid. Code (§750–54 [criminal, juvenile, mental, administrative]) (West) Cal. Govt. Code (§68560–64) (West 1978)
Colorado	Colo. Rev. Stat. (§13–90–113; §13–90–114; §13–90–201 to 205) (1978)
Connecticut	Conn. Gen. Stat. Ann. (§17–137[k] thru [p]; §K[a] [criminal and civil]; §K[b] [administrative]; §K[c] [employee grievance]; §K[d] [any school or college, human services agency]; §P[a] & [b] [compensation]; §1–25 [oath]) (West 1983)
Delaware	Del. Code Ann. 10 (§8907) (1976)
District of Columbia	D.C. Code Ann. (§1–1509; §1–1511) (1982)
Florida	Fla. Stat. Ann. (§90.606; §905.15 [grand jury]; 90.606.3; 901.245 [arrest]) (West 1981)
Georgia	Ga. Code Ann. (§24–9–100 thru 108; §24–9–107 [oath]; §24–9–108 [compensation]; §24–1–5 [arrest]; Art. 5 [evidence]) (1983)
Hawaii	Hawaii Rev. Stat. (§606–9) (1979)

For a comprehensive summary of the scope of these statutes, including the manner of payment to interpreters and the qualifications required of interpreters, see the "Compilation of State Interpreter Laws," published by the National Center for Law and the Deaf (1984). The data presented in this appendix is derived from that source.

Idaho	Idaho Code (§9–205 [criminal and civil]; §19–1111 [grand jury]; §9–1603 [fees]) (1975)
Illinois	Ill. Ann. Stat. (ch. 38, §165–11 thru 13 [criminal]; 51, §47; 51, §48.01 [criminal and civil]) (Smith-Hurd 1971) Ill. Code Civ. Proc. (ch. 110, §8–1402) (1982)
Indiana	Ind. Code Ann. (§4–22–1–22.5 [administrative]; §34–1–14–3 [civil]) Ind. R. Tr. P. 43 (f) (West 1984)
Iowa	Iowa Code Ann. (§622A.1 *et seq.*; §622B.1 *et seq.*; §622B appendix) (West 1980)
Kansas	Kan. Stat. Ann. (§60–243 [appointment and fee]; §60–243(e); §75–4351 through 4355 [all cases] [deaf mute]; §60–417 [Rules of Evidence] [qualifications of interpreter]) (1972)
Kentucky	Ky. Rev. Stat. (§30A.400 to .435) (1978)
Louisiana	La. Rev. Stat. Ann. (15, §270 [criminal]; 49, §181 [administrative]) La. Code Crim. Proc. Ann. (Art. 433, 441 [grand jury]) La. Code Civ. Pro. Ann. (Art. 192.1) La. R.S. (46:2361 to R.A. 46:2372) La. Rev. Stat. Ann. (West 1982)
Maine	Me. Rev. Stat. Ann. tit. (5, §48 [all proceedings]) Rules of Civ. Proc. (§43 [L]) Rules of Crim. Proc. (§6 [D] [grand jury]; §28 [criminal]) (1979)
Maryland	Md. Crs. and Jud. Proc. (§9–114) Md. Ann. Code (Art. 27, §623A [criminal]; Art. 30, §1 [administrative]; Art. 30, §2A [employee grievance]) (1979)
Massachusetts	Mass. Gen. Laws Ann. (ch. 221, §§92 to 92A) Mass. Gen. Laws Ann. (ch. 234A, §69 [interpreter for deaf juror]) (West 1983)
Michigan	Mich. Comp. Laws Ann. (§393.501–509) (West 1982) (deaf persons' interpreter act)
Minnesota	Minn. Stat. Ann. (§546.42–546.44 [civil]; §611.30–611.34 [criminal, grand jury, time of arrest, preliminary proceedings]; §15.4 [state meetings]; §204 C.15[voters]) (West 1984)
Mississippi	Miss. Code Ann. (§13–1–16; §99–17–7 [criminal cases]; §11–7–153 [oath]) (1972)
Missouri	Mo. Ann. Stat. (§476.060 [civil]; §490.630 [evidence]; §491.300 [fees]; §540.150 [grand jury]; §546.035 [criminal and mental proceedings]) (Vernon 1965)
Montana	Mont. Code Ann. (§§49–4–501 to 49–4–511; §25–404, 25–413, 93–514, M.R. Civ. Pr. Rule 43(f) Montana Code Ann. (ch. 245, §§1–14) (1979)
Nebraska	Neb. Rev. Stat. (§25–2401 to 25–2406) (1973)
Nevada	Nev. Rev. Stat. (§50.045 [qualifications]; §50.050 [criminal

	and civil]; §171.1535 [definition]; §171.1536 [time of arrest]; §171.1537–171.1538 [waiver of rights]) Rules of Civ. Pro. 43(f) (1977)
New Hampshire	N.H. Rev. Stat. Ann. (§§521–A: 1 *et seq.*, 521–A: 2, 521–A: 3 [criminal], 521–A: 4 [competency], 521–A: 5 [administrative hearings], 521–A: 8 [compensation], 521–A: 11 [privileged communication]) (1977)
New Jersey	N.J. Stat. Ann. (§2A: 11–28.1) (West 1971) (repealed and replaced by ch. 564, approved Jan. 1984)
New Mexico	N.M. Stat. Ann. (§38–9–1–1 to 38–9–10) (1979)
New York	N.Y. Jud. Law (§390) N.Y. A.P.A. (§301) N.Y. Exec. (§259 (i) [parole]) N.Y. Lab. (§620 (4)) N.Y. Work. Comp. (§150 (b); §927) (McKinney 1981)
North Carolina	N.C. Gen. Stat. (§§8B-1 through 8B-8) (1981)
North Dakota	N.D. Cent. Code (§28–33–01 to 28–33–08 [deaf parties]; §31–01–11 [deaf witnesses; oath of interpreter]; §31–01–12 [fees]) (1979) Rules of evidence (604 [oath])
Ohio	Ohio Rev. Code Ann. (§2311.14, §2335.09 [courts]; §3501.22 [elections]) (Baldwin 1976)
Oklahoma	Okla. Stat. Ann. (tit. 12, §2604 [oath]; tit. 63, §2407 to 2412; tit. 22, §340 [grand jury]; tit. 22 §344 [grand jury]; tit. 22, §1278 [criminal and mental]) (West 1982)
Oregon	Or. Rev. Stat. (§44.095 [criminal and civil], repealed C.892, §98; §132.090 [grand jury]; §133.515 [time of arrest]; §183.310 [administrative definition]; §183.418 [administrative]; §151.050 [public defender's staff]; §151.240 [administrative powers of public defender's staff]) (1973)
Pennsylvania	Pa. Stat. Ann. (tit. 16, §1608; §3101) Rules of Crim. Proc. (209 [grand jury]; tit. 42; §§1726, 2301, 3722 [fees]; tit. 42, §8701 [criminal, arrest]; tit. 43, §476 [employee-note of hazards]; tit. 72, §3191; tit. 72, §5020 = 309 [assessors]) (Purdon 1978)
Rhode Island	R.I. Gen. Laws (§§8–5–8 [civil and criminal]; §9–29–7 [fees]) Superior Court Rule of Crim. Proc. 28 District Court Rule of Crim. Proc. 28 (1969)
South Carolina	S.C. Code Ann. (§15–27–110) (Law. Co-op. 1972)
South Dakota	S.D. Comp. Laws Ann. (§15–6–43 f [civil]; §19–3–7 through 19–3–14; §19–3–10 [grand jury, penal sanction and criminal]) (1974)
Tennessee	Tenn. Code Ann. (§24–1–103) Rules of criminal procedure (Rule 28) (1977)
Texas	Tex. Stat. Ann. (Art. 6252–18 to 18a) Tex. Rev. Civ. Stat. Ann. (art. 3712[a]) (Vernon 1979)

	Tex. Code Crim. Proc. Ann. (art. 38.31; art. 15.17; art. 38.22) Rules of Civ. Proc. (183)
Utah	Utah Code Ann. (§21–5–17 [fees]; §77–35–15; §77–35–14 [subpoena]; §78–24a–1 through 11 [interpreters for hearing impaired—any action]) (1983)
Vermont	VRCP (43 (f)) VRCrP (28)
Virginia	Va. Code (2.1–570–§§573 [agency proceeding]; 19.2–164.1 [1982 Amend. Crim.]; 63.1–85.4 [V.C.D. Law]; 8.01–400.1 [priv. comm.]; 37.1–67.5 [commitment]; 8.01–384.1 [civil 1982]) (1982)
Virgin Islands	T.4 (§323 [interpreters]; ch. 19)
Washington	Wash. Rev. Code Ann. (§2.42.010 through 2.42.050) (1973)
West Virginia	W.Va. Code (§57–5–7) (1982)
Wisconsin	Wis. Stat. Ann. (§§59.77 [fee]; §879.41 [probate]; §85.05 [fee]; §814.67; §885.37 [criminal, commitment, administrative]) (West 1978)
Wyoming	Wyo. Stat. (§5–1–109 [civil, criminal, arrest]) Rules of Civ. Proc. (§43 (f)) Rules of Crim. Proc. (29) (1979)

Appendix 2: Public Law 95–539 Court Interpreters Act (Effective October 28, 1978)

§1827. *Interpreters in the courts of the United States.*

(a) The Director of the Administrative Office of the United States Courts shall establish a program to facilitate the use of interpreters in courts of the United States.

(b) The Director shall prescribe, determine, and certify the qualifications of persons who may serve as certified interpreters in courts of the United States in bilingual proceedings and proceedings involving the hearing impaired (whether or not also speech impaired), and in so doing, the Director shall consider the education, training, and experience of those persons. The Director shall maintain a current master list of all interpreters certified by the Director and shall report annually on the frequency of requests for, and the use and effectiveness of, interpreters. The Director shall prescribe a schedule of fees for services rendered by interpreters.

(c) Each United States district court shall maintain on file in the office of the clerk of the court a list of all persons who have been certified as interpreters, including bilingual interpreters and oral or manual interpreters for the hearing impaired (whether or not also speech impaired), by the Director of the Administrative Office of the United States Courts in accordance with the certification program established pursuant to subsection (b) of this section.

(d) The presiding judicial officer, with the assistance of the Director of the Administrative Office of the United States Courts, shall utilize the services of the most available certified interpreter, or when no certified interpreter is reasonably available, as determined by the presiding judicial officer, the services of an otherwise competent interpreter, in any criminal or civil action initiated by the United States in a United States district court (including a petition for a writ of habeas corpus initiated in the name of the United States by a relator), if the presiding judicial officer determines on such officer's own motion or on the motion of a party that such party (including a defendant in a criminal case), or a witness who may present testimony in such action—

(1) speaks only or primarily a language other than the English language; or: (2) suffers from a hearing impairment (whether or not suffering also from a speech impairment)

The text of the act appears in *United States Code Annotated,* Title 28, Judiciary and Judiciary Procedure.

so as to inhibit such party's comprehension of the proceedings or communication with counsel or the presiding judicial officer, or so as to inhibit such witness' comprehension of questions and the presentation of such testimony.

(e) (1) If any interpreter is unable to communicate effectively with the presiding judicial officer, the United States attorney, a party (including a defendant in a criminal case), or a witness, the presiding judicial officer shall dismiss such interpreter and obtain the services of another interpreter in accordance with this section.

(2) In any criminal or civil action in a United States district court, if the presiding judicial officer does not appoint an interpreter under subsection (d) of this section, an individual requiring the services of an interpreter may seek assistance of the clerk of court or the Director of the Administrative Office of the United States Courts in obtaining the assistance of a certified interpreter.

(f) (1) Any individual other than a witness who is entitled to interpretation under subsection (d) of this section may waive such interpretation in whole or in part. Such a waiver shall be effective only if approved by the presiding judicial officer and made expressly by such individual on the record after opportunity to consult with counsel and after the presiding judicial officer has explained to such individual, utilizing the services of the most available certified interpreter, or when no certified interpreter is reasonably available, as determined by the presiding judicial officer, the services of an otherwise competent interpreter, the nature and effect of the waiver.

(2) An individual who waives under paragraph (1) of this subsection the right to an interpreter may utilize the services of a noncertified interpreter of such individual's choice whose fees, expenses, and costs of an interpreter appointed under subsection (d) of this section.

(g) (1) Except as otherwise provided in this subsection or section 1828 of this title, the salaries, fees, expenses, and costs incident to providing the services of interpreters under subsection (d) of this section shall be paid by the Director of the Administrative Office of the United States Courts from sums appropriated to the Federal judiciary.

(2) Such salaries, fees, expenses, and costs that are incurred with respect to Government witnesses shall, unless direction is made under paragraph (3) of the subsection, be paid by the Attorney General from sums appropriated to the Department of Justice.

(3) The presiding judicial officer may in such officer's discretion direct that all or part of such salaries, fees, expenses, and costs shall be apportioned between or among the parties or shall be taxed as costs in a civil action.

(4) Any moneys collected under this subsection may be used to reimburse the appropriations obligated and disbursed in payment for such services.

(h) In any action in a court of the United States where the presiding judicial officer establishes, fixes, or approves the compensation and expenses payable to any interpreter from funds appropriated to the Federal judiciary, the presiding judicial officer shall not establish, fix, or approve compensation and expenses in excess of the maximum under the schedule of fees for services prescribed pursuant to subsection (b) of this section.

(i) The term "presiding judicial officer" as used in this section and section 1828 of this title includes a judge of a United States district court, a United States magistrate, and a referee in bankruptcy.

(j) The term "United States district court" as used in this section and section 1828 of this title includes any court created by Act of Congress in a territory which is invested with any jurisdiction of a district court of the United States established by section 132 of this title.

(k) The interpretation provided by certified interpreters pursuant to this section shall be in the consecutive mode except that the presiding judicial officer, with the approval of all interested parties, may authorize a simultaneous or summary interpretation when such officer determines that such interpretation will aid in the efficient administration of justice. The presiding judicial officer on such officer's motion or on the motion of a party may order that special interpretation services as authorized in section 1828 of this title be provided if such officer determines that the provision of such services will aid in the efficient administration of justice.

Amendment
(1982)

§1828. *Special interpretation services.*

(a) The Director of the Administrative Office of the United States Courts shall establish a program for the provision of special interpretation services in criminal actions and in civil actions initiated by the United States (including petitions for writs of habeas corpus initiated in the name of the United States by relators) in a United States district court. The program shall provide a capacity for simultaneous interpretation services in multidefendant criminal actions and multidefendant civil actions.

(b) Upon the request of any person in any action for which special interpretation services established pursuant to subsection (a) are not otherwise provided, the Director, with the approval of the presiding judicial officer, may make such services available to the person requesting the services on a reimbursable basis at rates established in conformity with section 9701 of title 31, but the Director may require the prepayment of the estimated expenses of providing the services by the person requesting them.

(c) Except as otherwise provided in this subsection, the expenses incident to providing services under subsection (a) of this section shall be paid by the Director from sums appropriated to the Federal judiciary. A presiding judicial officer, in such officer's discretion, may order that all or part of the expenses shall be apportioned between or among the parties or shall be taxed as costs in a civil action, and any moneys collected as a result of such order may be used to reimburse the appropriations obligated and disbursed in payment for such services.

(d) Appropriations available to the Director shall be available to provide services in accordance with subsection (b) of this section, and moneys collected by the Director under that subsection may be used to reimburse the appropriations charged for such services. A presiding judicial officer, in such officer's discretion, may order that all or part of the expenses shall be apportioned between or among the parties or shall be taxed as costs in the action.

Amendment
(1984)

§602. *Employees.*

(b) Notwithstanding any other law, the Director may appoint certified interpreters in accordance with section 604(a) (15) (B) of this title without regard to the provisions of chapter 51 and subchapter III of chapter 53 of title 5, relating to classification and General Schedule pay rates, but the compensation of any person appointed under this subsection shall not exceed the appropriate equivalent of the highest rate of pay payable for the highest grade established in the General Schedule, section 5332 of title 5.

§604. *Duties of Director generally.*

(14) Pursuant to section 1827 of this title, establish a program for the certification and utilization of interpreters in courts of the United States.

(14.1) Pursuant to section 1828 of this title, establish a program for the provision of special interpretation services in courts of the United States.

(15) (A) In those districts where the Director considers it advisable based on the need for interpreters, authorize the full-time or part-time employment by the court of certified interpreters; (B) where the Director considers it advisable based on the need for interpreters, appoint certified interpreters on a full-time or part-time basis, for services in various courts when he determines that such appointments will result in the economical provision of interpretation services; and (C) pay out moneys appropriated for the judiciary interpreters' salaries, fees, and expenses, and other costs which may accrue in accordance with the provisions of sections 1827 and 1828 of this title.

Appendix 3: Suggested Interpreter's Written Oath

ON MY WORD OF HONOR, AS OFFICIAL COURT INTERPRETER AND OFFICER OF THE [Insert name of court] ________, I, [name of interpreter] ________, swear (or affirm) to be true to the Code of Ethics of my profession, and to discharge faithfully the following solemn duties and obligations:

I WILL interpret accurately and faithfully to the best of my ability. I will convey the true meaning of the words, phrases, and statements of the speaker, and I will pay special attention to variations of the target language due to educational, cultural and regional differences.

I WILL never interject my own words, phrases, or views, and if the need arises to paraphrase any statements in order to convey the proper meaning, I will do so only after the presiding judicial officer has granted permission.

I WILL familiarize myself with the case as much as possible prior to going into the courtroom. I will inquire whether the language in the case will involve terminology of a technical nature or a particular vernacular that would require special preparation. I will study the indictments or charges to avoid possible interpretation problems during formal court proceedings.

I WILL speak in a clear, firm, and well modulated voice, and when using inflections, I will be particularly careful not to allow them to be interpreted as partiality. I will employ the techniques of interpretation best suited to the situation at hand or according to the needs or wishes of those utilizing my services.

I WILL maintain an impartial attitude during the course of interpreting and will guard any confidential information entrusted to me. I will not discuss the testimony or the merits of the case under any circumstances, with anyone, particularly not with those for whom I interpret.

I WILL attempt to establish rapport with the persons needing my services and will explain to them my position as an impartial officer of the court, serving both the courts and the individuals involved in the case. I will also inquire whether any person involved suffers from a hearing impairment or any physical or psychological problem that could interfere with the effectiveness of my services, and I will make adjustments accordingly.

I WILL adopt a conservative manner of dress and conduct in upholding the dignity of the Court and of my profession, particularly when attention is

These ethical guidelines are provided to the federal district courts by the Administrative Office of the United States Courts, which is charged with the implementation of the Federal Court Interpreters Act.

upon me in the courtroom. I will familiarize myself thoroughly with all the local court rules and I will abide by them.

I WILL strive constantly to improve my knowledge of legal terminology in English and in the language I interpret, and to be familiar with general courtroom procedures, so that in addition to interpreting, I may, when time and conditions permit and with the permission of the presiding judicial officer, explain to those for whom I interpret what is occurring in the courtroom.

I WILL be personally responsible for having the proper dictionaries and other linguistic reference materials readily available for consultation when needed.

So Help Me God.

[Signature]

Appendix 4: Standards of Professional Conduct and Responsibilities for Members of the Judiciary Interpreters Association of Texas

METHOD OR MODE OF INTERPRETATION

• Simultaneous Verbatim—This mode signifies the concurrent communication of words from one language to another. The interpretation occurs as proximately in time, or simultaneously, as the interpreter can make the transfer from one language to another. This mode is used when interpreting for a non-English speaking person seated at the counsel table in the courtroom. This mode is utilized to keep said person completely and fully informed of the testimony, information or instructions being given by others, and provides the client with the opportunity of communicating to his/her attorney any discrepancies in the testimony, thereby assisting in his/her own defense. Simultaneous interpretations shall be executed by a team of two interpreters who shall alternate every 30 minutes or so. This mode of interpretation is very exhausting, and accuracy, speed and concentration cannot be physically sustained for more than 45 minutes at a time, thus, over the years, the team approach has been found to be the only viable method.

Until such time as simultaneous interpreting equipment becomes available in the courts, this mode of interpretation shall have to be executed in a low voice, so as not to interfere with the hearing of others.

• Consecutive Verbatim—This mode signifies a sequential communication of statements or sentences from one language to another. The successive nature of the consecutive mode does not preclude a verbatim interpretation. This mode is the best, and least confusing way of interpreting for a non-English speaking person who must participate in a dialogue or cross-examination.

CODE OF ETHICS

• To interpret and to translate with the greatest fidelity and accuracy he/she can command, endeavoring at all times, to communicate the impression of the original.

• To maintain professional discretion and in particular, to respect the rights of clients and employers by not divulging any information learned through the performance of duties and assignments; nor to derive personal profit or advantage from any confidential information acquired during the exercise of the profession.

• To not accept an assignment for which he/she is unqualified, in terms of language or subject matter.

• To share professional knowledge on a reciprocal basis.

• To refrain from any action likely to discredit the profession and in particular, to abstain from engaging in unfair competition.

• To be loyal to colleagues and to the profession.

• To agree to settle professional differences by arbitration whenever possible.

• To constantly strive to maintain and upgrade the professional knowledge required to perform the task of assignment accurately.

GENERAL CONDUCT OF INTERPRETERS

• Instances may arise where knowledge of special terminology is needed in a particular case, or the interpreter may be required to understand uncommon dialects or regionalisms. These instances may cause an otherwise qualified interpreter to be unsuitable for that particular case. Should these conditions arise, and the interpreter has not been given sufficient information or time to study terminology ahead of time, then it is the interpreter's responsibility to critically assess his/her own ability to perform, and to disqualify him/herself if not fully capable of performing high-quality interpretation.

• The interpreter shall maintain a professional relationship with the non-English speaking person needing his/her services. While rapport built on compassion and understanding should be established, every effort should be made to avoid personal dependency on the interpreter.

• The interpreter should strive for professional detachment. Displays of emotion, bias or personal opinion should definitely be avoided.

• The interpreter and the non-English speaking person should refrain from addressing one another on a first name basis. Familiar forms of address, such as the "tú" in Spanish, shall be avoided. Obviously, the same holds true with respect to any other parties involved.

• The interpreter must inform the Court whenever an actual conflict of interest, or the appearance of a conflict of interest, arises. Any condition which may infringe upon the objectivity of the interpreter, or affect his/her professional independence constitutes a conflict of interest. It shall be assumed that such a conflict of interest exists when any of the following instances arise:

a) The interpreter is acquainted with any party to the action (excluding judges and lawyers).

b) The interpreter has, in any way, an interest in the outcome of the case.

c) The interpreter is not a free-lancer and is employed full-time by other than a Court or Clerk's Office.

d) The interpreter performed professionally in the case during the prosecutorial or law enforcement phases, in any capacity other than as an interpreter.

• The interpreter must keep confidential all conversations overheard or interpreted between counsel and client. By law (Court Interpreter's Act, PL 95–539), the interpreter may not be used as a witness to anything that was said between counsel and client, whether interpreted or not.

• To avoid the appearance of prejudice, the interpreter should avoid unnecessary discussions with counsel, the parties to the action, witnesses, jurors, or any other interested parties inside or outside of the courtroom.

• The interpreter shall NEVER give advice of any kind to the non-English speaking person, even when requested to do so. Instead, the client should be referred to his/her counsel.

• Should the interpreter be privately and separately contacted by any of the parties to a suit (i.e., by phone or personally at home or private office), he/she should try to discontinue the conversation as quickly as possible, and immediately notify the court or counsel of said occurrence.

• During cross-examination, the interpreter should speak in a loud, clear voice, so that he/she may be properly heard in the whole room.

• If the interpreter believes that the quality of his/her interpretation is faltering due, for instance, to fatigue or illness, the court should be so informed.

• Interpreters shall be totally impartial in judicial proceedings, and shall act and conduct themselves so that there can be no question as to said impartiality, and they shall give no reason to distrust or doubt their integrity.

• Interpreters shall not accept payment from anyone other than the specific party that hired them; nor shall interpreters accept any gifts, gratuities or favors of any kind which might reasonably be interpreted as an attempt to influence their actions with respect to the court or any other party to the action.

• The interpreter shall not disclose confidential information acquired by or made available to him/her in the course of carrying out his/her professional duties.

• The interpreter should never discuss the case in progress, either inside or outside the courtroom.

• An interpreter should never render opinions or make subjective statements of any kind through, or in connection with, newspapers, radio or other public media regarding any legal matter in which the interpreter is or was professionally involved.

• The interpreter shall have the responsibility of engaging in continuing education to keep him/herself abreast of matters which can improve his/her skills and performance.

• The interpreter shall appear at the appointed time, and shall immediately report to the court clerk, or other designated person.

• The interpreter should wear appropriate clothing and be properly groomed.

• The interpreter shall provide his/her correct name and address, when requested, for the court record, as well as the language to be interpreted.

• The interpreter should be sworn in prior to the commencement of any proceeding.

• The interpreter should not leave the courtroom until the proceedings are officially terminated or until he/she is officially excused. The same applies when in a conference room or elsewhere for a deposition.

• If the interpreter should become ill or fatigued, he/she shall so inform the parties involved.

• Proper names should not be interpreted, they are to remain in their original language.

• The interpreter shall not emulate the gestures made by his/her client—they have already been seen—emulating the tone of voice is sufficient.

• The non-English speaking person's name should be spelled out exactly as stated by same, particularly for the benefit of the court reporter. The same applies to any other proper nouns, indicating names or places.

• The interpreter shall provide an accurate interpretation of what is said, without embellishments, omissions or editing (i.e., epithets should also be interpreted). An interpreter should not hesitate to provide the most accurate form of a word in spite of a possibly vulgar meaning or sexual connotation.

• Non-English speaking persons should be informed prior to the proceedings that their testimony will be interpreted in full, even when they say something obviously not meant for interpretation. The point being, that if said person spoke only English, the remark would have been understood or not made.

• In personal injury cases, medical cases or rape cases that involve testimony that may be socially embarrassing to a male non-English speaking person with a female interpreter, or conversely, a female non-English speaking person with a male interpreter, it should be made known to the court or to counsel, as it may affect the content of the testimony given, and measures should be taken to put said person at ease. Ideally, the interpreter is "sexless," but in reality, it sometimes presents a serious stumbling block.

• The interpretation should be as close to verbatim and literal in content and meaning as possible. When idioms or other terms are used that are not co-definitional and the speaker's intent is clear to the interpreter, then the closest appropriate term or phrase should be used. If a term or phrase can reasonably have more than one meaning, or if the interpreter is unfamiliar with the term or phrase, he/she should inform the court of this fact. With the court's permission, the interpreter may inquire further from the speaker to determine the exact meaning. This should occur very infrequently, if the interpreter has had time to prepare for the case.

• The interpreter shall NOT correct an erroneous fact or statement that may occur in a question posed to the non-English speaking person, even though the error is obviously unintentional or simply a slip of the tongue: likewise, the interpreter shall not correct an obvious error in the testimony of a non-English speaking person. Neither shall the interpreter infer a response, that is, if the non-English speaking person is asked to clarify a prior response, the interpreter should pose the question as asked and not volunteer what he/she thought said person had meant.

• If a term or phrase is used which the interpreter believes may confuse the non-English speaking person, the interpreter should so inform the court. These instances may arise when a particular concept is unknown in the client's native culture or when certain English terms are ambiguous in translation, i.e., "you" may be either singular or plural.

• The interpretation shall be conducted in the first and second person, as if the interpreter did not exist. The non-English speaking client should be informed of this, so as to avoid confusion. For instance, the question should be "What is your name?" NOT "Ask him what his name is." Likewise, the interpreter shall respond for the client "My name is. . . ." NOT "He says his name is. . . ."

• If a serious communication problem arises between the interpreter and the non-English speaking person, the interpreter should bring this to the immediate attention of the court or counsel, then may request time to resolve the problem, or ask to be replaced.

• When at the witness stand or in front of the bench, the interpreter should stand close to his/her client, but not so as to block the view of judge, jury or counsel.

• The interpreter shall, at all times, emulate the inflections and intonations of the speaker, in order to reinforce the meaning and stresses of the speaker's words.

• During cross-examination, should a very lengthy question or answer arise, the interpreter may request that it be broken down into reasonable segments to allow a verbatim interpretation.

• If the client speaks just a little English, enough to understand part but not all of what is being said, the interpreter should insist on everything being interpreted, regardless of whether he/she understood the English or not. This will avoid a great deal of confusion for all and unintentional inaccuracies on the part of the non-English speaking person.

• If counsel objects to a question, the interpreter must await the Judge's ruling, even if the non-English speaking person has already given the answer. If the objection is sustained, the interpreter does NOT give the answer; if the objection is overruled, then the interpreter can give the answer, or ask to have the question and answer repeated by the court reporter or counsel.

• Should the interpreter find that at some point in the testimony, he/she has made an inadvertent mistake that was not immediately noticed (i.e., in the case of two meanings for a given word: the interpreter chose one and subsequently found that it should have been the other), he/she shall immediately advise the court or counsel that the interpreter made an error and that he/she wishes to correct it.

Appendix 5: Code of Professional Responsibility for Court Interpreters and Legal Translators

Purposes

The purposes of this code are to support the administration of justice and promote the public's confidence in the Judiciary's ability to administer justice for all persons by clarifying the ethical responsibilities of court interpreters and legal translators and upgrading the quality of these services.

Scope

This code shall be binding upon all persons who perform interpreting or translating services in connection with—

(1) any matter that is before or to be brought before any court of this State;

(2) any proceedings or hearings of a Surrogate or any arm of the Judiciary, including but not limited to grand juries, Juvenile Conference Committees, Intensive Supervision Program Panel, Child Placement Review Board, attorney and judicial disciplinary committees and hearing officers; and

(3) any court support service.

Enforcement

A court interpreter or legal translator who violates any of the provisions of this code is subject to the charge of contempt, disciplinary action or any other sanction that may be imposed by law.

Canon 1 Court interpreters and legal translators, as assistants to the courts, should maintain high standards of personal and professional conduct that promote public confidence in the administration of justice.

Canon 2 Court interpreters and legal translators should know and observe all statutes, rules of court and policies of the Administrative Office of the Court which relate to the delivery of their professional services.

This is a proposed code of ethics for court interpreters and translators, formulated by the New Jersey Supreme Court Task Force on Interpreter and Translation Services, and published by the New Jersey Supreme Court. In its final report, *Equal Access to Justice for Linguistic Minorities* (1985), the task force recommended that the New Jersey Supreme Court adopt such a code of ethics.

Canon 3 Court interpreters and legal translators should maintain an impartial disposition in all matters and toward all parties and should avoid any appearance of bias. They should also avoid conflicts of interest or the appearance thereof in matters in which they serve.

A. Court interpreters and legal translators should not render services in any matter in which—
   (1) they are associates, friends, or relatives of a party or of counsel for a party;
   (2) they know that they, their spouse or child has a financial interest in the subject matter in controversy or in a party to the proceeding, or any other interest that would be affected by the outcome; or
   (3) they have been involved in the choice of counsel.

   Prior to serving in a proceeding, court interpreters and legal translators should disclose any of the foregoing relationships, interests or involvements to the presiding judge, to all counsel and any pro se party appearing in the case.

B. Prior to providing professional services in a matter, court interpreters and legal translators should disclose to the attorney or party who has requested their services the nature and extent of all professional services they have rendered to all parties and counsel for any party involved in the matter.

C. Court interpreters and legal translators should disclose to the court and contending parties all instances in which they are acquainted with or related to any juror or witness and the extent of such acquaintance.

D. The fees and remuneration of a court interpreter or legal translator should never be contingent upon the success or failure of the cause in which she or he has been engaged.

E. Prior to providing professional services to any attorney or pro se party, court interpreters and legal translators should divulge to all participating counsel any and all professional services which they have previously provided in connection with that matter.

F. Prior to providing professional services in a proceeding in court, court interpreters and legal translators should first divulge to the presiding judge, all participating counsel and pro se parties any and all professional services which they previously provided in connection with the matter.

G. Prior to providing professional services in a proceeding in court, court interpreters and legal translators should divulge to the presiding judge, all participating counsel and pro se parties anything else that might affect their ability to serve impartially or might constitute a conflict of interest.

Canon 4 Court interpreters should be unobtrusive during court proceedings so that their presence permits an atmosphere as close as is possible to one in which there is no language barrier.

A. Court interpreters should not engage in any behavior that draws attention to themselves (e.g., imitating gestures or emotions, pointing, or engaging in other paralinguistic conduct).

B. Court interpreters should dress in a manner that does not attract attention.

C. Court interpreters should position themselves so that—

1. When interpreting witness testimony, they stand in a place where they do not obstruct the view of the witness by the judge, jury or attorneys and they speak at a rate, quality and volume of speech that can easily be heard and understood throughout the courtroom and does not attract attention;
2. When interpreting proceedings for a party at counsel table, they speak or sign in the most unobtrusive manner possible that enables the party for whom they are interpreting to understand all of their interpretation.

Canon 5 Court interpreters and legal translators should protect confidential information and refrain from commenting about cases.

A. Court interpreters and legal translators should not communicate information which has been obtained in the course of their duties but not been made public, including grand jury proceedings and all confidential communications (e.g., counsel and client, *RPC* 1.6; *Evid. R.* 26; psychologist and client, *Evid. R.* 26A-1 *et seq.*; and others), to anybody at any time, except as is required of attorneys under *RPC* 1.6 or as may be otherwise required by law.

B. Court interpreters and legal translators should neither discuss nor report upon a matter in which they are engaged with or to any person, except in their official capacity. Accordingly, they should not have contact with parties, witnesses, jurors, attorneys, friends or relatives of any party during the pendency of any cause in which they are engaged, except as may be required for the proper discharge of official functions or as may be required by law.

C. Court interpreters and legal translators should not comment or render an opinion on the propriety or impropriety of a verdict in any matter in which they have served. Nor should they comment at any time upon the conduct of such proceedings, except as may be required by law.

Canon 6 Once having accepted or undertaken an assignment in any court, court interpreters and legal translators should be prompt in arriving in the courtroom or other place where services are to be rendered or in completing the translation. When they cannot fulfill such obligation due to anything beyond their control, they should immediately report to the appropriate person their inability to perform as agreed.

Canon 7 Court interpreters and legal translators should accept assignments only when they are confident of their capacity to perform in accordance with this code and standards promulgated by the Administrative Office of the Courts.

Canon 8 Court interpreters and legal translators should convey all of the meaning of the source language in the target language without adding to, leaving out or modifying anything given the cultural, syntactic and lexical limits of the target language.

A. A statement in the source language should not be paraphrased.

B. A statement in the source language should be interpreted into the target language using the same persons of pronouns and verbs as were used by the speaker (e.g., "I live at 123 Baker Road" should not be rendered as, "He says he lives at 123 Baker Road." Rather, the first person used in the source should be preserved in the interpretation or translation).

C. The level or style of language used in the source language should be preserved in the target language. Simple, crude or obscene language should not be dressed up nor should sophisticated and erudite language be simplified. Slang terms and phrases should be rendered in equivalent slang in the target language.

D. Court interpreters should never interject or reveal their own feelings (e.g., sympathy, disbelief, outrage, disgust, embarrassment or surprise), moods, attitudes or beliefs while performing their duties.

E. Court interpreters and legal translators may explain or clarify the meaning of a word or phrase only when directed to do so by a judge or according to standards promulgated by the Administrative Office of the Courts.

F. Court interpreters should not explain paralinguistic gestures or other features of body language except when directed to do so by a judge.

G. When court interpreters discover that they have made an error, they should, if still interpreting for a witness, correct the error at once, first identifying themselves for the record. If they realize an error after the testimony has been completed, they should discreetly request a bench or lobby conference with the judge and attorney(s) and make the correction on the record.

Canon 9 Since the only function of court interpreters is to provide a medium for enabling speakers of different languages to communicate with one another, they should not be active participants in connection with any interpreting assignment, except as provided in E of this Canon, G of Canon 8, Canon 11 or as may be provided by standards promulgated by the Administrative Office of the Courts.

A. At no time should court interpreters converse with a juror, a witness, a party or an attorney except as permitted by standards promulgated by the Administrative Office of the Courts.

B. Court interpreters and legal translators should not engage in activities which may be reasonably construed to constitute the practice of law such as providing legal advice and explaining legal rights or obligations. A court interpreter may convey legal advice from an attorney to a person only while that attorney is giving it. A court interpreter who is also an attorney may not serve in both capacities in the same matter.

C. Court interpreters and legal translators should not explain forms, services or otherwise act as counselors or advisors. A court interpreter or legal translator may translate language on a form for a person who is filling out the form, but may not explain or interpret the form for such a person.

D. When interpreting for a sworn witness, court interpreters should interpret each statement even if it appears non-responsive or confusing and even if the witness thinks he or she is making a statement to be heard only by the interpreter.

E. Court interpreters may be active participants only when they are unable to understand the meaning of a source message or to convey the meaning in the target language, when they believe they are no longer able to serve in a manner completely free of bias, when they find that continuing to serve would violate a law or a provision of this code; or when, while interpreting in the simultaneous mode, the rate of the speaker exceeds the interpreter's ability to keep up; or when, while interpreting in the consecutive mode, the length of a statement to be interpreted approaches the interpreter's maximum capacity for recall. Should any of the foregoing situations arise, court interpreters should immediately advise the parties and the judge, if any, thereof and await the judge's direction.

Canon 10 Court interpreters and legal translators should accurately and completely represent their certifications, training and pertinent experience accurately and completely and be prepared to produce evidence of same upon request.

A. Court interpreters and legal translators should not indicate or imply that they have a certificate unless they have passed all parts of the certifying examination.

B. Court interpreters and legal translators should not imply that they enjoy a certain status (e.g., official Superior Court or United States District Court interpreter) unless they can produce evidence of such designation by an authority.

Canon 11 Court interpreters and legal translators should immediately report to the presiding judge any solicitation or effort by another to induce or encourage them to violate any law, any provision of this code, or any provision of standards governing court interpreting and legal translating promulgated by the Administrative Office of the Courts.

Appendix 6: Text of Experimental Tape Recordings

A.6.1 (Polite Interpretation of Testimony)

PROSECUTING ATTORNEY: Sir, would you state your name, please?
INTERPRETER: *Señor, dé su nombre por favor.*
WITNESS: *Roberto Quesada Murillo.*[1]
INTERPRETER: Roberto Quesada Murillo.
PROSECUTING ATTORNEY: Where were you born?
INTERPRETER: *¿En dónde nació?*
WITNESS: *En Saltillo.*
INTERPRETER: In Saltillo.
PROSECUTING ATTORNEY: And of what country are you a citizen?
INTERPRETER: *¿De qué país es usted ciudadano?*
WITNESS: *¿Cómo?*
INTERPRETER: Uh, what's that?
PROSECUTING ATTORNEY: Of what country are you a citizen?
INTERPRETER: *¿De qué país es usted ciudadano?*
WITNESS: *De México, señor.*
INTERPRETER: Of Mexico, sir.
PROSECUTING ATTORNEY: I call your attention to the night of March 23rd and the morning of March 24th. Were you in the United States at that time?
INTERPRETER: *Le llamo su atención a la noche del veintitrés de marzo y la mañana del veinticuatro de marzo. ¿Estuvo usted en los Estados Unidos en ese día?*
WITNESS: *¿El veinticuatro de marzo?*
INTERPRETATOR: March 24th?
PROSECUTING ATTORNEY: Yes.
INTERPRETER: *Sí.*
WITNESS: *No, señor.*

[1] All names of persons and places that appear in the text are fictitious—that is, they do not correspond in any way to the persons and locations that were named in the actual judicial proceeding that was taped. Such changes were intentionally made in order to protect the privacy of defendants, witnesses, court interpreters, and lawyers, alike.

INTERPRETER: No, sir.

PROSECUTING ATTORNEY: Do you recall entering the United States during the month of March at all?

INTERPRETER: *¿Recuerda haber entrado a los Estados Unidos durante el mes de marzo?*

WITNESS: *No, señor.*

INTERPRETER: No, sir.

PROSECUTING ATTORNEY: When did you last enter this country?

INTERPRETER: *¿Cuándo fue la última vez que entró usted a este país?*

WITNESS: *Esta es la primera vez.*

INTERPRETER: This is the first time.

PROSECUTING ATTORNEY: When was that, sir?

INTERPRETER: *¿Cuándo fue esto, señor?*

WITNESS: *Um,no recuerdo, como el veintidós.*

INTERPRETER: I don't remember, around the twenty-second.

PROSECUTING ATTORNEY: Did you have any documents or papers to authorize your entry?

INTERPRETER: *¿Tenía sus documentos, o papeles autorizando su entrada?*

WITNESS: *No, señor.*

INTERPRETER: No, sir.

PROSECUTING ATTORNEY: Were you inspected by immigration officials when you entered the United States?

INTERPRETER: *¿Fue usted inspeccionado por un oficial de inmigración cuando entró usted a los Estados Unidos?*

WITNESS: *¿Inspeccionado? No entiendo, señor.*

INTERPRETER: Inspected? I don't understand that word, sir.

PROSECUTING ATTORNEY: Did you enter through a port of entry?

INTERPRETER: *¿Entró usted por la garita?*

WITNESS: *No, señor.*

INTERPRETER: No, sir.

PROSECUTING ATTORNEY: Did you enter illegally?

INTERPRETER: *¿Entró usted ilegalmente?*

WITNESS: *Sí.*

INTERPRETER: Yes.

PROSECUTING ATTORNEY: Would you explain for the court the circumstances surrounding that entry?

INTERPRETER: *¿Puede usted explicarle a la corte las circunstancias de por cómo usted entró usted?*

WITNESS: *Sí, señor. Pues entré, . . .* [pause] *¿Cómo entré?*

INTERPRETER: Yes, sir. Well I entered, . . . [pause] Uh, you mean the way I came in?

PROSECUTING ATTORNEY: Yes, sir. Did you cross through a fence or . . . ?

INTERPRETER: *Sí, señor. ¿Cruzó usted por un cerco?*
WITNESS: *Sí, por uno.*
INTERPRETER: Yes, through a fence.
PROSECUTING ATTORNEY: Had you made any arrangements for a ride before you left Mexico?
INTERPRETER: *¿Había hecho usted, ah, arreglos para obtener un raite antes de salir de México?*
WITNESS: *Sí, señor.*
INTERPRETER: Yes, sir.
PROSECUTING ATTORNEY: How did that come about?
INTERPRETER: *¿Cómo fue que sucedió eso?*
WITNESS: *Bueno, pues, es como no traía yo dinero, busqué un raite.*
INTERPRETER: Well, since I didn't have any money, I, I asked for a ride.

(Non-Polite Interpretation)

PROSECUTING ATTORNEY: Sir, would you state your name, please?
INTERPRETER: *Señor, dé su nombre por favor.*
WITNESS: *Roberto Quesada Murillo.*
INTERPRETER: Roberto Quesada Murillo.
PROSECUTING ATTORNEY: How old are you?
INTERPRETER: *¿Qué edad tiene Ud.?*
WITNESS: *Veintiséis años.*
INTERPRETER: Twenty-six years old.
PROSECUTING ATTORNEY: Have you ever used any other name?
INTERPRETER: *¿Ha usado Ud. algún otro nombre?*
WITNESS: *No, señor.*
INTERPRETER: No.
PROSECUTING ATTORNEY: Where were you born?
INTERPRETER: *¿En dónde nació?*
WITNESS: *En Saltillo.*
INTERPRETER: In Saltillo.
PROSECUTING ATTORNEY: And of what country are you a citizen?
INTERPRETER: *¿De qué país es Ud.ciudadano?*
WITNESS: *¿Cómo?*
INTERPRETER: Uh, what's that?
PROSECUTING ATTORNEY: Of what country are you a citizen?
INTERPRETER: *¿De qué país es Ud. ciudadano?*
WITNESS: *De México, señor.*
INTERPRETER: Of Mexico.
PROSECUTING ATTORNEY: I call your attention to the night of March 23rd and the morning of March 24th. Were you in the United States at that time?

INTERPRETER: *Le llamo su atención a la noche del veintitrés de marzo y la mañana del veinticuatro de marzo. ¿Estuvo Ud. en los Estados Unidos en ese día?*
WITNESS: *¿El veinticuatro de marzo?*
INTERPRETER: March 24th?
PROSECUTING ATTORNEY: Yes.
INTERPRETER: *Sí.*
WITNESS: *No, señor.*
INTERPRETER: No.
PROSECUTING ATTORNEY: Do you recall entering the United States during the month of March at all?
INTERPRETER: *¿Recuerda haber entrado a los Estados Unidos durante el mes de marzo?*
WITNESS: *No, señor.*
INTERPRETER: No.
PROSECUTING ATTORNEY: When did you last enter this country?
INTERPRETER: *¿Cuándo fue la última vez que entró Ud. a este país?*
WITNESS: *Esta es la primera vez.*
INTERPRETER: This is the first time.
PROSECUTING ATTORNEY: When was that, sir?
INTERPRETER: *¿Cuándo fue esto?*
WITNESS: *Um,no recuerdo, como el veintidós.*
INTERPRETER: I don't remember, around the twenty-second.
PROSECUTING ATTORNEY: Did you have any documents or papers to authorize your entry?
INTERPRETER: *¿Tenía sus documentos, o papeles autorizando su entrada?*
WITNESS: *No, señor.*
INTERPRETER: No.
PROSECUTING ATTORNEY: Were you inspected by immigration officials when you entered the United States?
INTERPRETER: *¿Fue Ud. inspeccionado por un oficial de inmigración cuando entró Ud. a los Estados Unidos?*
WITNESS: *¿Inspeccionado? No entiendo, señor.*
INTERPRETER: Inspected? I don't understand that word.
PROSECUTING ATTORNEY: Did you enter through a port of entry?
INTERPRETER: *¿Entró Ud. por la garita?*
WITNESS: *No, señor.*
INTERPRETER: No.
PROSECUTING ATTORNEY: Did you enter illegally?
INTERPRETER: *¿Entró Ud. ilegalmente?*
WITNESS: *Sí.*
INTERPRETER: Yes.

PROSECUTING ATTORNEY: Would you explain for the court the circumstances surrounding that entry?
INTERPRETER: *¿Puede Ud. explicarle a la corte las circunstancias de por cómo Ud. entró Ud.?*
WITNESS: *Sí, señor. Pues entré, . . .* [pause]. *¿Cómo entré?*
INTERPRETER: Yes. Well I entered [pause]. Uh, you mean the way I came in?
PROSECUTING ATTORNEY: Yes, sir. Did you cross through a fence or . . . ?
INTERPRETER: *¿Sí. Cruzó Ud. por un cerco?*
WITNESS: *Sí, por uno.*
INTERPRETER: Yes, through a fence.
PROSECUTING ATTORNEY: Had you made any arrangements for a ride before you left Mexico?
INTERPRETER: *¿Había hecho Ud., ah, arreglos para obtener un raite antes de salir de México?*
WITNESS: *Sí, señor.*
INTERPRETER: Yes.
PROSECUTING ATTORNEY: How did that come about?
INTERPRETER: *¿Cómo fue que sucedió eso?*
WITNESS: *Bueno, pues, es que como no traía yo dinero, busqué un raite.*
INTERPRETER: Well, since I didn't have any money, I, I asked for a ride.
PROSECUTING ATTORNEY: Who did you ask?
INTERPRETER: *¿A quién le pidió?*
WITNESS: *Al señor Humberto.*
INTERPRETER: Mr. Humberto.
PROSECUTING ATTORNEY: Mr. Humberto?
INTERPRETER: *¿El señor Humberto?*
WITNESS: *Sí, señor.*
INTERPRETER: Yes.
PROSECUTING ATTORNEY: Do you see Mr. Humberto here in the courtroom now?
INTERPRETER: *¿Ve, ve Ud. al señor Humberto aquí en la sala? ¿Está aquí aquí en la corte?*
WITNESS: *Sí, señor.*
INTERPRETER: Yes.

A.6.2 (Consultative Style Interpretation)

PROSECUTING ATTORNEY: Would you state your name please?
INTERPRETER: *Diga Ud. su nombre por favor.*
WITNESS: *José Alvarez Urruña.*

INTERPRETER: José Alvarez Umaña.
PROSECUTING ATTORNEY: And how old are you?
INTERPRETER: *¿Qué edad tiene Ud.?*
WITNESS: *Veinte años.*
INTERPRETER: Twenty years old.
PROSECUTING ATTORNEY: And what is your occupation?
INTERPRETER: *¿Y cuál es su oficio de Ud.?*
WITNESS: *Trabajar en el campo.*
INTERPRETER: Working in the fields.
PROSECUTING ATTORNEY: Of what country are you a citizen?
INTERPRETER: *¿De qué pais es Ud. ciudadano?*
WITNESS: *De Michoacán.*
INTERPRETER: Of Michoacán.
PROSECUTING ATTORNEY: In Mexico?
INTERPRETER: *¿En México?*
WITNESS: *Sí.*
INTERPRETER: Yes.
PROSECUTING ATTORNEY: And where were you born?
INTERPRETER: *¿En qué lugar nació Ud.?*
WITNESS: *En Michoacán.*
INTERPRETER: In Michoacán.
PROSECUTING ATTORNEY: And that's also in Mexico?
INTERPRETER: *¿Y eso se, ese lugar se encuentra ubicado en México?*
WITNESS: *Sí.*
INTERPRETER: Yes.
PROSECUTING ATTORNEY: Are you a citizen of the United States?
INTERPRETER: *¿Es Ud. ciudadano de los Estados Unidos?*
WITNESS: *¿Ciudadano? ¿Qué es ciudadano?*
INTERPRETER: What do you mean "citizen"?
PROSECUTING ATTORNEY: Do you have any papers that would allow you to remain in the United States?
INTERPRETER: *¿Tiene Ud. algún documento o papel que le autorice a estar aquí en los Estados Unidos?*
WITNESS: *No.*
INTERPRETER: No.
PROSECUTING ATTORNEY: Have you ever applied for citizenship to become a citizen of the United States?
INTERPRETER: *¿En algún momento ha puesto Ud. solicitud para convertirse en ciudadano de los Estados Unidos, en persona que pueda vivir y trabajar aquí en territorio norteamericano?*
WITNESS: *No.*

INTERPRETER: No.
PROSECUTING ATTORNEY: When did you last enter the United States?
INTERPRETER: *¿Cuál fue la última vez que entró Ud. a los Estados Unidos?*
WITNESS: *El año pasado.*
INTERPRETER: Last year.
PROSECUTING ATTORNEY: All right. Were you in a motor home that was stopped by agents of the United States border patrol on October 15th of this year?
INTERPRETER: *¿Estaba Ud. en una casa rodante que fue detenida por agentes de los Estados Unidos de la patrulla de la frontera el día quince de octubre ahora de este año?*
WITNESS: *Sí.*
INTERPRETER: Yes.
PROSECUTING ATTORNEY: And how long before you were stopped in that motor home had you entered, had it been since you had crossed into the United States illegally?
INTERPRETER: *¿Y cuánto tiempo transcurrió desde el momento en que Ud. cruzó la frontera al momento en que los levantó la casa remolque, desde que cruzaron ilegalmente la frontera hasta el momento en que los recogió la casa remolque, cuántas horas transcurrieron?*
WITNESS: *Unas catorce.*
INTERPRETER: About fourteen hours.
PROSECUTING ATTORNEY: And where did you cross into the United States at?
INTERPRETER: *¿En qué lugar cruzó Ud. a los Estados Unidos?*
WITNESS: *Por Matamoros.*
INTERPRETER: Through Matamoros.
PROSECUTING ATTORNEY: All right, when you started your journey to the United States were you walking or in a vehicle?
INTERPRETER: *Cuando Ud. comenzó su viaje para los Estados Unidos, ¿venían a pie o venían en algún carro?*
WITNESS: *En un carro.*
INTERPRETER: In a car.
PROSECUTING ATTORNEY: All right, and did there come a time when you got out of the car and began walking?
INTERPRETER: *¿Y llegó un momento en que Uds. se bajaron del carro y comenzaron a caminar?*
WITNESS: *Sí.*
INTERPRETER: Yes.
PROSECUTING ATTORNEY: When you began walking were you still in Mexico?
INTERPRETER: *Cuando Uds. comenzaron a caminar ¿todavía estaban caminando en terreno de México?*

WITNESS: *Casi un pedacito allí.*
INTERPRETER: Only for a short distance.
PROSECUTING ATTORNEY: All right, was there a fence where you crossed into the United States?
INTERPRETER: *¿Había un cerco por donde Uds. cruzaron a los Estados Unidos?*
WITNESS: *Sí, un alambre.*
INTERPRETER: Yes, a wire fence.
PROSECUTING ATTORNEY: Barbed-wire fence?
INTERPRETER: *¿Era de alambre de púas?*
WITNESS: *No, era liso.*
INTERPRETER: No, it was plain.
PROSECUTING ATTORNEY: All right, was there a gate there with an immigration inspection station?
INTERPRETER: *¿En ese lugar por donde cruzaron había una garita, una puerta de entrada con un inspector de inmigración?*
WITNESS: *No.*
INTERPRETER: No.
PROSECUTING ATTORNEY: As you were walking into the United States did you present yourself to an immigration officer for inspection?
INTERPRETER: *Mientras venían Uds. caminando hacia los Estados Unidos, ¿se encontraron Uds. con algún oficial de inmigración?*
WITNESS: *No.*
INTERPRETER: No.
PROSECUTING ATTORNEY: Those are all the questions I have for the moment.

(Hyperformal Interpretation)

PROSECUTING ATTORNEY: Would you state your name please?
INTERPRETER: *Diga Ud. su nombre por favor.*
WITNESS: *José Alvarez Umaña.*
INTERPRETER: José Alvarez Umaña.
PROSECUTING ATTORNEY: And how old are you?
INTERPRETER: *¿Qué edad tiene Ud.?*
WITNESS: *Veinte años.*
INTERPRETER: I am twenty years old.
PROSECUTING ATTORNEY: And what is your occupation?
INTERPRETER: *¿Y cuál es su oficio de Ud.?*
WITNESS: *Trabajar en el campo.*
INTERPRETER: I am a laborer in the fields.
PROSECUTING ATTORNEY: Of what country are you a citizen?
INTERPRETER: *¿De qué país es Ud. ciudadano?*

WITNESS: *De Michoacán.*
INTERPRETER: I am from the state of Michoacán.
PROSECUTING ATTORNEY: In Mexico?
INTERPRETER: *¿En México?*
WITNESS: *Sí.*
INTERPRETER: Yes.
PROSECUTING ATTORNEY: And where were you born?
INTERPRETER: *¿En qué lugar nació Ud.?*
WITNESS: *En Michoacán.*
INTERPRETER: *¿En qué lugar de Michoacán?*
WITNESS: *Colonia Agua Buena.*
INTERPRETER: I was born in Michoacán, and I asked him, "What spot in Michoacán were you born in?": Colonia Agua Buena.
PROSECUTING ATTORNEY: And that's also in Mexico?
INTERPRETER: *¿Y eso se, ese lugar se encuentra ubicado en México?*
WITNESS: *Sí.*
INTERPRETER: Yes, it is.
PROSECUTING ATTORNEY: Are you a citizen of the United States?
INTERPRETER: *¿Es Ud. ciudadano de los Estados Unidos?*
WITNESS: *¿Ciudadano? ¿Qué es ciudadano?*
INTERPRETER: What do you mean "citizen"?
PROSECUTING ATTORNEY: Do you have any papers that would allow you to remain in the United States?
INTERPRETER: *¿Tiene Ud. algún documento o papel que le autorice a estar aquí en los Estados Unidos?*
WITNESS: *No.*
INTERPRETER: No, I do not.
PROSECUTING ATTORNEY: Have you ever applied for citizenship to become a citizen of the United States?
INTERPRETER: *¿En algún momento ha puesto Ud. solicitud para convertirse en ciudadano de los Estados Unidos, en persona que pueda vivir y trabajar aquí en territorio norteamericano?*
WITNESS: *No.*
INTERPRETER: No, I have not.
PROSECUTING ATTORNEY: When did you last enter the United States?
INTERPRETER: *¿Cuál fue la última vez que entró Ud. a los Estados Unidos?*
WITNESS: *El año pasado.*
INTERPRETER: Last year.
PROSECUTING ATTORNEY: All right. Were you in a motor home that was stopped by agents of the United States border patrol on October 15th of this year?

Interpreter: *¿Estaba Ud. en una casa rodante que fue detenida por agentes de los Estados Unidos de la patrulla de la frontera el día quince de octubre ahora de este año?*
Witness: *Sí.*
Interpreter: Yes, I was.
Prosecuting attorney: And how long before you were stopped in that motor home had you entered, had it been since you had crossed into the United States illegally?
Interpreter: *¿Y cuánto tiempo transcurrió desde el momento en que Ud. cruzó la frontera al momento en que los levantó la casa remolque, desde que cruzaron ilegalmente la frontera hasta el momento en que los recogió la casa remolque, cuántas horas transcurrieron?*
Witness: *Unas catorce.*
Interpreter: It was about fourteen hours since we had crossed over.
Prosecuting attorney: And where did you cross into the United States at?
Interpreter: *¿En qué lugar cruzó Ud. a los Estados Unidos?*
Witness: *Por Matamoros.*
Interpreter: I crossed through Matamoros.
Prosecuting attorney: All right, when you started your journey to the United States were you walking or in a vehicle?
Interpreter: *Cuando Ud. comenzó su viaje para los Estados Unidos, ¿venían a pie o venían en algún carro?*
Witness: *En un carro.*
Interpreter: We were in a car.
Prosecuting attorney: All right, and did there come a time when you got out of the car and began walking?
Interpreter: *¿Y llegó un momento en que Uds. se bajaron del carro y comenzaron a caminar?*
Witness: *Sí.*
Interpreter: Yes, there did.
Prosecuting attorney: When you began walking were you still in Mexico?
Interpreter: *Cuando Uds. comenzaron a caminar ¿todavía estaban caminando en terreno de México?*
Witness: *Casi un pedacito allí.*
Interpreter: Only for a short distance.
Prosecuting attorney: All right, was there a fence where you crossed into the United States?
Interpreter: *¿Había un cerco por donde Uds. cruzaron a los Estados Unidos?*
Witness: *Sí, un alambre.*
Interpreter: Yes, there was a wire fence.
Prosecuting attorney: Barbed-wire fence?

INTERPRETER: *¿Era de alambre de púas?*
WITNESS: *No, era liso.*
INTERPRETER: I believe it was just a plain wire.
PROSECUTING ATTORNEY: All right, was there a gate there with an immigration inspection station?
INTERPRETER: *¿En ese lugar por donde cruzaron había una garita, una puerta de entrada con un inspector de inmigración?*
WITNESS: *No.*
INTERPRETER: No, there was not.
PROSECUTING ATTORNEY: As you were walking into the United States did you present yourself to an immigration officer for inspection?
INTERPRETER: *Mientras venían Uds. caminando hacia los Estados Unidos, ¿se encontraron Uds. con algún oficial de inmigración?*
WITNESS: *No.*
INTERPRETER: No, we did not.
PROSECUTING ATTORNEY: Those are all the questions I have for the moment.

A.6.3 (Non-Hedged Interpretation of Testimony)

PROSECUTING ATTORNEY: Mr. Domínguez, I would like you to, to remember back to February 18th of this year at about ten minutes after midnight. [pause] Do you remember where you were on that day at that time?
INTERPRETER: *Señor Domínguez, quisiera que recuerde Ud. dónde estuvo Ud. en esa noche, en ese día.*
WITNESS: *Sí, estaba trabajando.*
INTERPRETER: Yes, I was working.
PROSECUTING ATTORNEY: Do you remember driving your car that night?
INTERPRETER: *¿Recuerda haber manejado su carro en esa noche?*
WITNESS: *Sí.*
INTERPRETER: Yes.
PROSECUTING ATTORNEY: Do you remember being involved in an accident at First Avenue and Creedmore Road?
INTERPRETER: *¿Se acuerda Ud. haber estado en un accidente en la Creedmore y la Primera?*
WITNESS: *Sí.*
INTERPRETER: Yes.
PROSECUTING ATTORNEY: And can you tell us what happened at First Avenue and Creedmore Road that night?
INTERPRETER: *¿Y nos puede decir qué le pasó en la Primera Avenida y la Creedmore esa noche?*

WITNESS: *Pues, yo estaba esperando pasar. O sea que le habían robado el carro al muchacho y entonces, cuando habían terminado todo y vi que venía en la segunda línea y esperé. Entonces yo creo que se venía durmiendo cuando salió y me dio con el carro.*

INTERPRETER: I was waiting there because they had stolen a young fellow's car,—and I was gonna leave—I saw the vehicle coming along in the second lane, and I waited. So I think he must have been sleeping as he was coming along and he came directly at my car.

PROSECUTING ATTORNEY: And what did the vehicle do?

INTERPRETER: *¿Y qué hizo el vehículo?*

WITNESS: *Pues se vino derecho hacia mi carro.*

INTERPRETER: It came straight toward my car.

PROSECUTING ATTORNEY: Did it hit your car?

INTERPRETER: *¿Lo chocó?*

WITNESS: *Sí.*

INTERPRETER: Yes.

PROSECUTING ATTORNEY: Where?

INTERPRETER: *¿Dónde?*

WITNESS: *En el puro frente y en el borde, y me voltió así.*

INTERPRETER: On the front part. Then it hit me in one corner and it turned me this way.

PROSECUTING ATTORNEY: What happened to the vehicle after it hit your car?

INTERPRETER: *¿Qué pasó con el vehículo después que chocó con su carro?*

WITNESS: *El iba, iba a parar por un momento pero no paró, y, y se fue y, pero llevaba dos llantas ponchadas y tuvo que pararse como a un bloque y medio.*

INTERPRETER: He was gonna stop for a moment but he didn't stop and he left. But he had two flat tires and he had to stop around a block and half away from me.

PROSECUTING ATTORNEY: Mr. Domínguez, what did you do after, uh, you saw the van drive away?

INTERPRETER: *¿Qué hizo Ud. después de que vio irse el van?*

WITNESS: *Porque yo lo que traté de hacer, Ud. sabe, por el momento me puse muy nervioso, y como él corrió yo traté, y lo seguí. Entonces yo paré, él paró y, y llegó la policía; entonces ya fue cuando salieron.*

INTERPRETER: What I tried to do,—for the moment I became very nervous, and since he ran away, I followed him. So then I stopped, he stopped, and the police came. And that was when they got out.

PROSECUTING ATTORNEY: And had you seen police officers there before the accident?

INTERPRETER: *¿Había visto oficiales de policía allí antes del accidente?*

WITNESS: *Sí, allí estaban enfrente no más que como, como cuando me pegó, yo vi que corrió y traté de seguirlo. Entonces, sí entonces, este, salieron, ellos salieron de una puerta, de este lado de acá, la grande. Entonces lo que pasó es él no se quería bajar. Entonces el policía, ya cuando se bajó, entonces aventó al policía, y luego comenzaron a agarrarlo y lo detuvieron.*

INTERPRETER: Yes, they were there in front of me, when he hit me. I saw that he was running away and I tried to follow him. So then, they got out, they got out through the door on this side, the big door. So what happened was that he didn't want to get out. So then, when he finally got out, he pushed the policeman and then they started grabbing him and they arrested him.

(Hedged Interpretation)

PROSECUTING ATTORNEY: Would you please state your full name for the record?

INTERPRETER: *Diga su nombre completo por favor.*

WITNESS: *Rafael Domínguez.*

INTERPRETER: Rafael Domínguez.

PROSECUTING ATTORNEY: Mr Domínguez, I would like you to, to remember back to February 18th of this year at about ten minutes after midnight. [pause] Do you remember where you were on that day at that time?

INTERPRETER: *Señor Domínguez, quisiera que recuerde Ud. dónde estuvo Ud. en esa noche, en ese día.*

WITNESS: *Sí, estaba trabajando.*

INTERPRETER: Yes, I guess I was working.

PROSECUTING ATTORNEY: Do you remember driving your car that night?

INTERPRETER: *¿Recuerda haber manejado su carro en esa noche?*

WITNESS: *Sí.*

INTERPRETER: Why, yes.

PROSECUTING ATTORNEY: Do you remember being involved in an accident at First Avenue and Creedmore Road?

INTERPRETER: *¿Se acuerda Ud. haber estado en un accidente en la Creedmore y la primera?*

WITNES: *Sí.*

INTERPRETER: Well, yes.

PROSECUTING ATTORNEY: And can you tell us what happened at First Avenue and Creedmore Road that night?

INTERPRETER: *¿Y nos puede decir qué le pasó en la Primera Avenida y la Creedmore esa noche?*

WITNESS: *Pues, yo estaba esperando pasar. O sea que le habían robado el carro al muchacho y entonces, cuando habían terminado todo y vi que venía en la segunda línea y esperé. Entonces yo creo que se venía durmiendo cuando salió y me dio con el carro.*

INTERPRETER: Uh, I was waiting there, ah, because uh, in other words, because they had stolen a young fellow's car,—and I was gonna leave—I, uh, saw the van coming along in the second lane, and I waited. So I think he must have been, uh, he must have been sleeping as he was coming along and he came directly at my car.
PROSECUTING ATTORNEY: And where was the vehicle when you first saw it?
INTERPRETER: *¿Y dónde estaba el vehículo cuando lo vio por la primera vez?*
WITNESS: *Pues venía como, no recuerdo a cuántos pies, no podía, no me podía meter.*
INTERPRETER: Well, I was coming along about, I don't remember how many feet away it was but I couldn't, I couldn't get out of the way.
PROSECUTING ATTORNEY: Were you in the intersection or behind it?
INTERPRETER: *¿Andaba Ud. dentro de la incrucijada o . . .*
WITNESS: *No, no ya estaba haciendo alto.*
INTERPRETER: No, I was already making a stop.
PROSECUTING ATTORNEY: And what did the van do?
INTERPRETER: *¿Y qué hizo el van?*
WITNESS: *Pues se vino derecho hacia mi carro.*
INTERPRETER: Well, it came straight up to my car.
PROSECUTING ATTORNEY: Did it hit your car?
INTERPRETER: *¿Lo chocó?*
WITNESS: *Sí.*
INTERPRETER: Oh, yes.
PROSECUTING ATTORNEY: Where?
INTERPRETER: *¿Dónde?*
WITNESS: *En el puro frente y en el borde, y me voltió así.*
INTERPRETER: Right on the front part. Then it hit me in one corner and it turned me sort of this way.
PROSECUTING ATTORNEY: What happened to the van after it hit your car?
INTERPRETER: *¿Qué pasó con el van después que chocó con su carro?*
WITNESS: *El iba, iba a parar por un momento pero no paró, y, y se fue y, pero llevaba dos llantas ponchadas y tuvo que pararse como a un bloque y medio.*
INTERPRETER: Well he was gonna stop for a moment but he didn't really stop, and he left. But he had two flat tires and he had to stop, say, around a block and a half away from me.
PROSECUTING ATTORNEY: Mr. Domínguez, what did you do after, uh, you saw the van drive away?
INTERPRETER: *¿Qué hizo Ud. después de que vio irse el van?*
WITNESS: *Porque yo lo que traté de hacer, Ud. sabe, por el momento me puse muy nervioso, y como él corrió yo traté, y lo seguí. Entonces yo paré, él paró y, y llegó la policía; entonces ya fue cuando salieron.*

INTERPRETER: Well, because what I tried to do,—you know, for the moment I became very nervous,—and since he ran away, I tried to follow him. So then I stopped, and he stopped, and the police came. And I suppose that was when they got out.
PROSECUTING ATTORNEY: And had you seen police officers there before the accident?
INTERPRETER: *¿Había visto oficiales de policía allí antes del accidente?*
WITNESS: *Sí, allí estaban enfrente no más que como, como cuando me pegó, yo vi que corrió y traté de seguirlo. Entonces, sí entonces, este, salieron, ellos salieron de una puerta, de este lado de acá, la grande. Entonces lo que pasó es él no se quería bajar. Entonces el policía ya cuando se bajó, entonces aventó al policía, y luego comenzaron a agarralo y lo detuvieron.*
INTERPRETER: Yes, they were right there in front of me, just when he hit me. Well, I saw that he was running away, and, well, I guess I tried to follow him. So then, they got out, they got out through a door over on this side, the big door. So what happened was that I guess he just didn't want to get out. So then, uh when he finally got out, he pushed the policeman and then they kind of started grabbing a hold of him and, well, they arrested him.

A.6.4 (Active Interpretation of Testimony)

PROSECUTING ATTORNEY: How was it that you happened to be in a vehicle apprehended by the border patrol?
INTERPRETER: *¿Cómo es que estaba Ud. en un vehículo de motor cuando fueron aprehendidos por la patrulla de la frontera?*
WITNESS: *Cuando fuimos aprehendidos estábamos pidiendo raite.*
INTERPRETER: When they apprehended us we were asking for a ride.
PROSECUTING ATTORNEY: And did you give a sworn statement to the border patrol after you had been taken into custody?
INTERPRETER: *¿Le dio Ud. una declaración jurada a los patrulleros de la frontera una vez que los cogieron presos?*
WITNESS: *Sí, después que nos cogieron presos hicimos una declaración jurada.*
INTERPRETER: Yes, after they took us into custody we made a sworn statement.
PROSECUTING ATTORNEY: Did you tell the truth to the border patrol agent when you were being interviewed for that sworn statement?
INTERPRETER: *¿Le dijo Ud. la verdad al agente patrullero cuando le estaban entrevistando para dar esa declaración?*
WITNESS: *Sí. Yo dije nada más que la verdad cuando me estaban entrevistando.*

Interpreter: Yes. I told only the truth when they were interviewing me.

Prosecuting attorney: Did you put your initials or in some way sign that statement after it had been typed up?

Interpreter: *¿Puso Ud. sus iniciales o firmó como pudo esa declaración después de que había sido escrita a máquina?*

Witness: *¿Después de que había sido escrita a máquina? No recuerdo.*

Interpreter: After they had typed it up? I don't remember.

Prosecuting attorney: When you were being interviewed by the border patrol agent was he typing the questions on a typewriter and then typing your answers, at the same time?

Interpreter: *Cuando estaba Ud. siendo entrevistado por el agente patrullero ¿estaba él escribiendo sus contestaciones y las preguntas en una máquina de escribir al mismo tiempo que lo interrogaba a Ud.?*

Witness: *Creo que sí. Sí, usaba una máquina de escribir mientras que me entrevistaba.*

Interpreter: I believe he was. Yes, he was using a typewriter while he was interviewing me.

Prosecuting attorney: Do you remember being asked this question and giving this answer. The question was: "What arrangements did you make to be transported into the United States," and giving this answer: "Nothing more than for him to bring us to pay him $35. We gave it to him last night in Matamoros." Do you remember being asked that question and giving that answer?

Interpreter: *¿Se acuerda Ud. haber dado esta respuesta a esta pregunta: "¿Qué arreglos hizo Ud. para ser transportado a los Estados Unidos?" Su respuesta: "Nada más que nos traía y que le pagábamos treinta-cinco dólares y se lo dimos anoche en Matamoros." ¿Se acuerda Ud. que le hicieron esa pregunta y dio Ud. esa respuesta?*

Witness: *Ha pasado mucho tiempo, no me acuerdo bien. Sí me acuerdo de que me hicieron muchas preguntas.*

Interpreter: A lot of time has gone by, I don't remember well. I do remember that they asked me a lot of questions.

Prosecuting attorney: Okay, going back to the day you crossed the border into the United States, how long after you walked across the border were you picked up by that vehicle?

Interpreter: *Bien, volviéndose al día en que vino através de la frontera a los Estados Unidos, ¿cuánto tiempo después de atravesar la frontera los recogió ese vehículo?*

Witness: *Ah, pues como estábamos muy cansados, dormimos un ratito, una hora, pues sí.*

Interpreter: Well, since we were very tired we slept for a while, for about an hour I believe.

Prosecuting attorney: How long had you traveled in the vehicle before you were stopped by the border patrol?

INTERPRETER: *¿Qué tanto tiempo habían viajado Uds. en el vehículo antes de que los pararan, los detuvieran la patrulla fronteriza?*
WITNESS: *Fue un ratito después que nos detuvieron.*
INTERPRETER: It was a short while later that they stopped us.
PROSECUTING ATTORNEY: Was it still dark at the time that you were stopped, or was it getting light?
INTERPRETER: *¿Ya había luz del día cuando los pararon o todavía estaba medio obscuro?*
WITNESS: *No, se veía ya claro cuando nos pararon.*
INTERPRETER: It was already light when they stopped us.

(Passive Interpretation)

PROSECUTING ATTORNEY: How was it that you happened to be in a vehicle apprehended by the border patrol?
INTERPRETER: *¿Cómo es que estaba Ud. en un vehículo de motor cuando fueron aprehendidos por la patrulla de la frontera?*
WITNESS: *Cuando fuimos aprehendidos estábamos pidiendo raite.*
INTERPRETER: When we were apprehended we were asking for a ride.
PROSECUTING ATTORNEY: And did you give a sworn statement to the border patrol after you had been taken into custody?
INTERPRETER: *¿Le dio Ud. una declaración jurada a los patrulleros de la frontera una vez que los cogieron presos?*
WITNESS: *Sí, después que nos cogieron presos hicimos una declaración jurada.*
INTERPRETER: Yes, after we were taken into custody we made a sworn statement.
PROSECUTING ATTORNEY: Did you tell the truth to the border patrol agent when you were being interviewed for that sworn statement?
INTERPRETER: *¿Le dijo Ud. la verdad al agente patrullero cuando le estaban entrevistando para dar esa declaración?*
WITNESS: *Sí. Yo dije nada más que la verdad cuando me estaban entrevistando.*
INTERPRETER: Yes. I told only the truth when I was being interviewed.
PROSECUTING ATTORNEY: Did you put your initials or in some way sign that statement after it had been typed up?
INTERPRETER: *¿Puso Ud. sus iniciales o firmó como pudo esa declaración después de que había sido escrita a máquina?*
WITNESS: *¿Después de que había sido escrita a máquina? No recuerdo.*
INTERPRETER: After it had been typed? I don't remember.
PROSECUTING ATTORNEY: When you were being interviewed by the border patrol agent was he typing the questions on a typewriter and then typing your answers, at the same time?
INTERPRETER: *Cuando estaba Ud. siendo entrevistado por el agente patrullero ¿es-*

taba él escribiendo sus contestaciones y las preguntas en una máquina de escribir al mismo tiempo que lo interrogaba a Ud.?

Witness: *Creo que sí. Sí, usaba una máquina de escribir mientras que me entrevistaba.*

Interpreter: I believe he was. Yes, he was using a typewriter while I was being interviewed.

Prosecuting attorney: Do you remember being asked this question and giving this answer? The question was: "What arrangements did you make to be transported into the United States," and giving this answer: "Nothing more than for him to bring us to pay him $35. We gave it to him last night in Matamoros." Do you remember being asked that question and giving that answer?

Interpreter: *¿Se acuerda Ud. haber dado esta respuesta a esta pregunta: "¿Qué arreglos hizo Ud. para ser transportado a los Estados Unidos?" Su respuesta: "Nada más que nos traía y que le pagábamos treinta-cinco dólares y se lo dimos anoche en Matamoros." ¿Se acuerda Ud. que le hicieron esa pregunta y dio Ud. esa respuesta?*

Witness: *Ha pasado mucho tiempo, no me acuerdo bien. Sí me acuerdo de que me hicieron muchas preguntas.*

Interpreter: A lot of time has gone by, I don't remember well. I do remember that I was asked a lot of questions.

Prosecuting attorney: Okay, going back to the day you crossed the border into the United States, how long after you walked across the border were you picked up by that vehicle?

Interpreter: *Bien, volviéndose al día en que vino através de la frontera a los Estados Unidos, ¿cuánto tiempo después de atravesar la frontera los recogió ese vehículo?*

Witness: *Ah, pues como estábamos muy cansados, dormimos un ratito, una hora, pues sí.*

Interpreter: Well, since we were very tired we slept for a while, for about an hour I believe.

Prosecuting attorney: How long had you traveled in the vehicle before you were stopped by the border patrol?

Interpreter: *¿Qué tanto tiempo habían viajado Uds. en el vehículo antes de que los pararan, los detuvieran la patrulla fronteriza?*

Witness: *Un ratito después nos detuvieron.*

Interpreter: A short while later we were stopped.

Prosecuting attorney: Was it still dark at the time that you were stopped, or was it getting light?

Interpreter: *¿Ya había luz del día cuando los pararon o todavía estaba medio obscuro?*

Witness: *No, se veía ya claro cuando nos pararon.*

Interpreter: It was already light when we were stopped.

A.6.5 (Interrupting the Attorney)

Defense attorney: Mr. Chavarría, um, when you met Mr. Lobo Arce in Mexico, you paid him five-hundred dollars in Mexico?
Interpreter: Excuse me sir, was that *five* hundred dollars?
Defense attorney: Yes.
Interpreter: *Señor Chavarría, cuando Ud. conoció al señor Lobo Arce en México ¿le pagó Ud. quinientos dólares en México?*
Witness: *Sí.*
Interpreter: Yes.
Defense attorney: And isn't it true, sir, that this was for, this money was for the purchase of airline tickets and travel expenses for you?
Interpreter: Uh, I'm going to change that to the, uh, to the affirmative. Is that, sir, is that all right sir, instead of ["isn't"
Defense attorney: [I want the question exactly as I stated it.
Interpreter: *¿Y no es cierto, señor, que este dinero era para pagar boletos de avión y, y gastos de viaje?*
Witness: *No, porque él me hizo un presupuesto de cuánto me costaba todo. Entonces me quedaron a mí seiscientos dólares. Aparte de los quinientos que le di. Y con esos seiscientos yo pagué todos mis viajes y hoteles hasta llegar a Juárez con lo cual tengo depositado, doscientos dólares de mis seiscientos.*
Interpreter: No, because he made an estimate for me of how much everything was gonna cost me. Then six-hundred dollars remained for me, separate from the five-hundred dollars that I gave him, and with those six-hundred I paid all my trips and hotels until I arrived in El Paso, and in El Paso I have deposited, I have two-hundred dollars deposited from the six-hundred dollars that I had.
Defense attorney: Two-hundred dollars deposited where?
Interpreter: *¿Dónde están depositados los doscientos dólares?*
Witness: *En inmigración.*
Interpreter: At inmigration.
Defense attorney: So you, when you were, when you were arrested, you had two-hundred dollars on your possession, correct?
Interpreter: *De manera que ¿cuando lo arrestaron a Ud. tenía los doscientos dólares en posesión de su persona?*
Witness: *Sí, doscientos catorce, doscientos trece dólares.*
Interpreter: Yes, two-hundred and fourteen dollars, two-hundred and thirteen dollars.
Defense attorney: So the two-hundred approximate dollars you used for airline tickets from Mexico City to Juárez, correct?

INTERPRETER: Could you repeat that sir, so I can do it justice sir?
DEFENSE ATTORNEY: The two-hundred approximate dollars you used for airline tickets from Mexico City to Juárez, correct?
INTERPRETER: *¿Los aproximadamente doscientos dólares los usó Ud. en boletos de avión de la Ciudad de México a Juárez, correcto?*
WITNESS: *Sí.*
INTERPRETER: Yes.
DEFENSE ATTORNEY: Mr. Chavarría, you testified yesterday that your father had paid Mr. Lobo Arce a sum of money in Mexico City. Were you present when the money was paid by your father, to the man you've identified in court today?
INTERPRETER: That's about the limit of my retention, sir. Could you please repeat that?
DEFENSE ATTORNEY: Mr. Chavarría, were you present when the money was paid by your father to the man you've identified in court today?
INTERPRETER: *Señor Chavarría, ¿estaba Ud. presente cuando el padre de Ud. le pagó dinero al hombre que Ud. ha identificado aquí en este cuarto de la corte en el día de hoy?*
WITNESS: *Sí.*
INTERPRETER: Yes.
DEFENSE ATTORNEY: And when the money was paid by your father to this man was there any conversation? [pause] I'm just asking if there was any conversation.
INTERPRETER: *Y cuando el dinero fue pagado por el padre de Ud., ¿hubo alguna conversación entre ellos? Se llevó a cabo alguna conversación?*
WITNESS: *Sí.*
INTERPRETER: Yes.
DEFENSE ATTORNEY: Would you relate the conversation you overheard?
INTERPRETER: *¿Puede Ud. relatarnos la conversación que Ud. oyó?*
WITNESS: *Que le daba el dinero, o sea, que le daba el dinero porque él había hecho un presupuesto de todo mi viaje* [pause]. *Y él había dado una parte y con esa, . . . y con esa parte, la cancelaba ya.*
INTERPRETER: That he was giving him the money because he had made an estimate of my whole trip. And he had already given him a portion, and this portion would cancel the debt.
INTERPRETER: Excuse me, sir, the Mexicans I believe, and I would like to pursue this, but in my past experience they use the verb "cancelar," cancel, as "to complete." May I pursue if this is what he means?
DEFENSE ATTORNEY: Your honor, can, can we discuss this, uh, off the record? I don't think it's proper for the jury to hear this.
JUDGE: Very well.

(Not Interrupting the Attorney)

DEFENSE ATTORNEY: Mr. Chavarría, um, when you met Mr. Lobo Arce in Mexico, you paid him five-hundred dollars in Mexico?
INTERPRETER: *Señor Chavarría, cuando Ud. conoció al señor Lobo Arce en México, ¿le pagó Ud. quinientos dólares en México?*
WITNESS: *Sí.*
INTERPRETER: Yes.
DEFENSE ATTORNEY: And isn't it true, sir, that this was for, this money was for the purchase of airline tickets and travel expenses for you?
INTERPRETER: *¿Y no es cierto, señor, que este dinero era para pagar boletos de avión y, y gastos de viaje?*
WITNESS: *No, porque él me hizo un presupuesto de cuánto me costaba todo. Entonces me quedaron a mí seiscientos dólares. Aparte de los quinientos que le di. Y con esos seiscientos yo pagué todos mis viajes y hoteles hasta llegar a Juárez con lo cual tengo depositado, doscientos dólares de mis seiscientos.*
INTERPRETER: No, because he made an estimate for me of how much everything was gonna cost me. Then six-hundred dollars remained for me, separate from the five-hundred dollars that I gave him, and with those six-hundred I paid all my trips and hotels until I arrived in El Paso, and in El Paso I have deposited, I have two-hundred dollars deposited from the six-hundred dollars that I had.
DEFENSE ATTORNEY: Two-hundred dollars deposited where?
INTERPRETER: *¿Dónde están depositados los doscientos dólares?*
WITNESS: *En inmigración.*
INTERPRETER: At immigration.
DEFENSE ATTORNEY: So you, when you were, when you were arrested, you had two-hundred dollars on your possession, correct?
INTERPRETER: *De manera que ¿cuando lo arrestaron a Ud. tenía los doscientos dólares en posesión de su persona?*
WITNESS: *Sí, doscientos catorce, doscientos trece dólares.*
INTERPRETER: Yes, two-hundred and fourteen dollars, two-hundred and thirteen dollars.
DEFENSE ATTORNEY: So the two-hundred approximate dollars you used for airline tickets from Mexico City to Juárez, correct?
INTERPRETER: *¿Los aproximadamente doscientos dólares los usó Ud. en boletos de avión de la Ciudad de México a Juárez, correcto?*
WITNESS: *Sí.*
INTERPRETER: Yes.
DEFENSE ATTORNEY: Mr. Chavarría, were you present when the money was paid by your father, to the man you've identified in court today?

INTERPRETER: *Señor Chavarría, ¿estaba Ud. presente cuando el padre de Ud. le pagó dinero al hombre que Ud. ha identificado aquí en este cuarto de la corte en el día de hoy?*
WITNESS: *Sí.*
INTERPRETER: Yes.
DEFENSE ATTORNEY: And when the money was paid by your father to this man was there any conversation? [pause] I'm just asking if there was any conversation.
INTERPRETER: *Y cuando el dinero fue pagado por el padre de Ud., ¿hubo alguna conversación entre ellos? ¿Se llevó a cabo alguna conversación?*
WITNESS: *Sí.*
INTERPRETER: Yes.
DEFENSE ATTORNEY: Would you relate the conversation you overheard?
INTERPRETER: *¿Puede Ud. relatarnos la conversación que Ud. oyó?*
WITNESS: *Que le daba el dinero, o sea, que le daba el dinero porque el había hecho un presupuesto de todo mi viaje* [pause] *Y él había dado una parte y con esa, . . . y con esa parte, la cancelaba ya.*
INTERPRETER: That he was giving him the money because he had made an estimate of my whole trip. And he had already given him a portion, and this portion would cancel the debt.

A.6.6 (Interrupting the Witness)

PROSECUTING ATTORNEY: Directing your attention to June twenty-eighth of this year, did you have occasion, in the evening hours of that day, to go to a liquor store located on St. Mary's Road, at about eleven hundred sixteen?
INTERPRETER: *Hablando del día veintiocho de junio de este año, si Ud. tuvo la oportunidad de, de estar en una licorería que está ubicada en el 1116 al oeste de la calle St. Mary?*
WITNESS: *Sí, señor.*
INTERPRETER: Yes, sir.
PROSECUTING ATTORNEY: And when you arrived there, sir, were you carrying certain cash on your person?
INTERPRETER: *Y cuando Ud. llegó ahí, ¿si Ud. traía en su posesión algún dinero en efectivo?*
WITNESS: *Sí, señor.*
INTERPRETER: Yes, sir.
PROSECUTING ATTORNEY: And do you recall, sir, about how much money that amounted to that night?

INTERPRETER: *¿Si se acuerda Ud. como cuánto fue la cantidad aproximadamente?*

WITNESS: *Traía yo, mil doscientos dólares, traía yo, señor.* (I was carrying, twelve-hundred dollars was what I was carrying, sir.)

INTERPRETER: *¿Cómo? ¿Cuántos dólares?* (What? How many dollars?)

WITNESS: *Mil doscientos.*

INTERPRETER: I had, uh, twelve-hundred dollars.

PROSECUTING ATTORNEY: And, how was it that you know the amount of money that you had?

INTERPRETER: *¿Cómo sabe Ud. que, que, ¿cómo sabe Ud. que ésa fue la cantidad que Ud. traía esa noche?*

WITNESS: *Porque ese dinero lo tenía yo guardado: primero, de los cheques que me llegaban de la pensión. Segundo,*

INTERPRETER: *Un momentito.* (Just a moment.) I, I know I had that amount of money because, first of all, I had saved that money from checks that I, from pension checks that I had been receiving.

WITNESS: *Segundo, de un dinero que me mandaron de Sacramento de la cambiada de mi casa, porque me hicieron una casa nueva aquí en . . . la ciudad, señor.*

INTERPRETER: And second, um, I had a receipt from money, um, some other money from Sacramento, in exchange for a house that I was having built here in the city.

PROSECUTING ATTORNEY: Mr. Rivera, previously you had testified that you had been talking to the clerk in the liquor store, Francisco. While you were there talking with Francisco, did another man come into the liquor store who is Mr. Durán, the man who owns the restaurant next door?

INTERPRETER: *Señor Rivera, anteriormente Ud. había atestiguado que Ud. había estado conversando con el empleado de la licorería, Francisco. Y mientras Ud. estaba hablando con el señor, con Francisco ahí, este, en la, en la tienda, ¿tuvo la ocasión de presentarse ahí, con quien Ud. estaba hablando, el señor Durán?*

WITNESS: *Estaba yo precisamente con el,el señor, del del que despacha ahí, mhm. Cuando el señor, en seguida en-, entraron ellos, . . . el señor Durán, y los otros. . . .*

INTERPRETER: *Un Momentito, por favor.* Just wait a minute, please. I was there when the other gentleman, the clerk, when, when the other gentleman, Mr., uh, Durán, and the others. . . . *Siga.* (Go on.)

WITNESS: *Cuando entraron los otros, las otras personas, yo no les vi la cara, señor, yo no me di cuenta.*

INTERPRETER: When the others entered, the other persons, I did not see their faces, I did not notice them.

WITNESS: *Exacto, así fue, . . . mhm. Fíjense.* (Exactly; that's how it was. Mhm. Imagine!)

PROSECUTING ATTORNEY: After Mr. Durán entered, and these two other gentlemen, approximately the same time, did he have a conversation with Mr. Durán as to who had the most money?
INTERPRETER: *Bueno, entonces cuando esas, estos dos, cuando estos dos otros hombres, este, entraron, este, con el señor Durán, si Ud. tuvo una conversación con el señor Durán acerca de, del dinero que Ud. estaba, del dinero que Ud. traía.*
WITNESS: *Eh, estábamos precisamente que yo iba a pagar la cerveza del paquete, y el, el empleado me pedía quince dólares, prestados, y, y se lo, se los di.*
INTERPRETER: *Perdón, ¿cuántos dólares pidió?* (Excuse me, how many dollars did he ask for?)
WITNESS: *Me pidió quince.* (He asked me for fifteen.)
INTERPRETER: *Puede seguir.* (You may continue.)
WITNESS: *Entonces, saqué yo mi cartera, cuando se dieron cuenta que traiba yo el dinero. Iba yo a salir ya para, irme para la casa, iba a agarrar yo el paquete, y que le había pagado ya la cerveza, y de repente, el golpe, y zaz azoté, así fue.*
INTERPRETER: We were there, I was going to pay for the beer, the pack of beer, the clerk asked me for fifteen dollars, to borrow fifteen dollars from me, and I gave them to him. I took out my wallet, and they realized that I had money on me. I was going to leave. I was going to go home, getting ready to leave, I was going to pick up the bag with the beer that I had bought. And all of a sudden I got hit and pow, and I fell to the floor.
PROSECUTING ATTORNEY: At the time you were struck, where were you standing?
INTERPRETER: *Que cuando le pegaron a Ud. señor, ¿dónde estaba parado Ud.?*
WITNESS: *Pues en seguida ahí de la ventanilla, donde me estaba despachando el, . . . Sí, fue adentro, fue adentro de la tienda.*
INTERPRETER: Right next to the window where they were standing. It was inside the store.
PROSECUTING ATTORNEY: And which way were you facing in regard to the door?
INTERPRETER: *¿En qué, en qué dirección Ud. estaba dando, en relación con la puerta?*
WITNESS: *Pues, exactamente yo estaba con el empleado, sss. Eh, en cuanto di yo vuelta para venirme ya fue cuando me dieron el golpe, exactamente en la cabeza, y azoté.*
INTERPRETER: *¿Cómo?* (What?)
WITNESS: *Azoté. Por cierto todavía estando, todavía ando mal del golpe.*
INTERPRETER: Well, I was right there with the, uh, clerk, when I turned around to leave is when I got hit, right here on my head, and I fell. Not only that but I'm still feeling bad from the blow.

PROSECUTING ATTORNEY: Mr. Rivera, when you were hit, what, what was taken from you?
INTERPRETER: *Que cuando fue golpeado ¿qué es lo que le quitaron, qué es lo que tomaron?*
WITNESS: *Pues todo. Todo se llevaron con mi car- . . . el pasaporte, este, tarjetas que traíba de importancia, mi . . . una prueba,*
INTERPRETER: *Un momentito por favor.* (Just a moment, please.) Everything, my passport, important cards, important cards that I have. *Siga.* (Go on.)
WITNESS: *Más prueba voy a darle, mire, acabo de sacar el permiso de, de la emigración y aquí está mire, . . . ahí está . . . porque se llevaron todo, sss.*
INTERPRETER: I'll give you more proof. I've just, uh, I've just applied for immigration and this is it, because they took everything from me.
PROSECUTING ATTORNEY: What about your wallet?
INTERPRETER: *¿Y de su cartera?*
WITNESS: *Pues, pues con todo y todo, se llevaron todo, pss todo.*
INTERPRETER: Yeah, they took everything, everything with it.

(Not Interrupting the Witness)

PROSECUTING ATTORNEY: Directing your attention to June twenty-eighth of this year, did you have occasion, in the evening hours of that day, to go to a liquor store located on St. Mary's Road, at about eleven hundred sixteen?
INTERPRETER: *Hablando del día veintiocho de junio de este año, si Ud. tuvo la oportunidad de, de estar en una licorería que está ubicada en el 1116 al oeste de la calle St. Mary?*
WITNESS: *Sí, señor.*
INTERPRETER: Yes, sir.
PROSECUTING ATTORNEY: And when you arrived there, sir, were you carrying certain cash on your person?
INTERPRETER: *Y cuando Ud. llegó ahí, ¿si Ud. traía en su posesión algún dinero en efectivo?*
WITNESS: *Sí, señor.*
INTERPRETER: Yes, sir.
PROSECUTING ATTORNEY: And do you recall, sir, about how much money that amounted to that night?
INTERPRETER: *Si se acuerda Ud. como cuánto fue la cantidad aproximadamente.*
WITNESS: *Traía yo, mil doscientos dólares, traía yo, señor.*
INTERPRETER: I had, uh, twelve-hundred dollars.
PROSECUTING ATTORNEY: And, how was it that you know the amount of money that you had?

INTERPRETER: *¿Cómo sabe Ud. que, que, ¿cómo sabe Ud. que ésa fue la cantidad que Ud. traía esa noche?*
WITNESS: *Porque ese dinero lo tenía yo guardado: primero, de los cheques que me llegaban de la pensión. Segundo, de un dinero que me mandaron de Sacramento de la cambiada de mi casa, porque me hicieron una casa nueva aquí en . . . la ciudad, señor.*
INTERPRETER: I, I know I had that amount of money because, first of all, I had saved that money from checks that I, from pension checks that I had been receiving and second, um, I had a receipt from money, um, some other money from Sacramento, in exchange for a house that I was having built here in the city.
PROSECUTING ATTORNEY: Mr. Rivera, previously you had testified that you had been talking to the clerk in the liquor store, Francisco. While you were there talking with Francisco, did another man come into the liquor store who is Mr. Durán, the man who owns the restaurant next door?
INTERPRETER: *Señor Rivera, anteriormente Ud. había atestiguado que Ud. había estado conversando con el empleado de la licorería, Francisco. Y mientras Ud. estaba hablando con el señor, con Francisco ahí, este, en la, en la tienda, ¿tuvo la ocasión de presentarse ahí, con quien Ud. estaba hablando, el señor Durán?*
WITNESS: *Estaba yo precisamente con el, el señor, del del que despacha ahí, mhm. Cuando el señor, en seguida en-, entraron ellos, . . . el señor Durán, y los otros, las otras dos personas, yo no les vi la cara, señor, yo no me di cuenta. . . .*
INTERPRETER: I was there when, when the gentleman, the clerk, when the other gentleman, Mr., uh, Durán, and the others entered. And the two other people, I did not see their faces, I did not notice them.
WITNESS: *Exacto, así fue, . . . mhm. Fíjense.*
PROSECUTING ATTORNEY: After Mr. Durán entered, and these two other gentlemen, approximately the same time, did he have a conversation with Mr. Durán as to who had the most money?
INTERPRETER: *Bueno, entonces cuando esas, estos dos, cuando estos dos otros hombres, este, entraron, este, con el señor Durán, si Ud. tuvo una conversación con el señor Durán acerca de, del dinero que Ud. estaba, del dinero que Ud. traía.*
WITNESS: *Eh, estábamos precisamente que yo iba a pagar la cerveza del paquete, y el, el empleado me pedía quince dólares, prestados, y, y se lo, se los di. Saqué yo mi cartera, cuando se dieron cuenta que traiba yo el dinero. Iba yo a salir ya para, irme para la casa, iba a agarrar yo el paquete, y que le había pagaedo ya la cerveza, y de repente, el golpe, y zaz azoté, así fue.*
INTERPRETER: We were there, I was going to pay for the beer, the pack of beer, the clerk asked me for fifteen dollars, to borrow fifteen dollars from me, and I gave them to him. I took out my wallet, and they realized that I

had money on me. I was going to leave. I was going to go home, getting ready to leave, I was going to pick up the bag with the beer that I had bought. And all of a sudden I got hit and pow, and I fell to the floor.
PROSECUTING ATTORNEY: At the time you were struck, where were you standing?
INTERPRETER: *Que cuando le pegaron a Ud. señor, ¿dónde estaba parado Ud.?*
WITNESS: *Pues en seguida ahí de la ventanilla, donde me estaba despachando el, . . . Sí, fue adentro, fue adentro de la tienda.*
INTERPRETER: Right next to the window where they were standing. It was inside the store.
PROSECUTING ATTORNEY: And which way were you facing in regard to the door?
INTERPRETER: *¿En qué, en qué dirección Ud. estaba dando, en relación con la puerta?*
WITNESS: *Pues, exactamente yo estaba con el empleado, sss. Eh, en cuanto di yo vuelta para venirme ya fue cuando me dieron el golpe, exactamente en la cabeza, y azoté. Por cierto todavía estando, todavía ando mal del golpe.*
INTERPRETER: Well, I was right there with the, uh, when I turned around to leave is when I got hit, right here on my head, and I fell. Not only that but I'm still feeling bad from the blow.
PROSECUTING ATTORNEY: Mr. Rivera, when you were hit, what, what was taken from you?
INTERPRETER: *Que cuando fue golpeado ¿qué es lo que le quitaron, qué es lo que tomaron?*
WITNESS: *Pues todo. Todo se llevaron con mi car- . . . el pasaporte, este, tarjetas que traiba de importancia, mi . . . una prueba,—Más prueba voy a darle, mire, acabo de sacar el permiso de, de la emigración y aquí está mire, . . . ahí está . . . porque se llevaron todo, sss.*
INTERPRETER: Everything, my passport, important cards, important cards that I have. I've just, uh, I've just applied for immigration and this is it, because they took everything from me.

A.6.7 (Prodding the Witness to Answer)

JUDGE: May we have Francisco Araya Zúñiga.
PROSECUTING ATTORNEY: What is your name sir?
INTERPRETER: *¿Cómo se llama Ud. señor?*
WITNESS: *Francisco Araya Zúñiga.*
INTERPRETER: Francisco Araya Zúñiga.

PROSECUTING ATTORNEY: How old are you Mr. Araya?

INTERPRETER: *¿Qué edad tiene Ud., señor Araya?*

WITNESS: *Veinticinco años.*

INTERPRETER: Twenty-five.

PROSECUTING ATTORNEY: Where were you born?

INTERPRETER: *¿En qué lugar nació?*

WITNESS: *En Dolores de Guanajuato.*

INTERPRETER: In Dolores, Guanajuato.

PROSECUTING ATTORNEY: Is that in Mexico?

INTERPRETER: *¿Eso queda en México?*

WITNESS: *Sí, México.*

INTERPRETER: Yes, Mexico.

PROSECUTING ATTORNEY: And are you a citizen of Mexico?

INTERPRETER: *¿Es Ud. ciudadano de México?*

WITNESS: *Mhm.*

INTERPRETER: *Pero conteste.* (But, answer.)

WITNESS: *Sí.*

INTERPRETER: Yes.

PROSECUTING ATTORNEY: Do you remember when you were arrested by Brownsville police and the border patrol?

INTERPRETER: *¿Se acuerda Ud. cuando lo arrestó la policía de Brownsville y la patrulla fronteriza?*

WITNESS: *Ajá.*

INTERPRETER: *Conteste.* (Answer.)

WITNESS: *Sí.*

INTERPRETER: Yes.

PROSECUTING ATTORNEY: And was that at about midnight on November the ninth of this year?

INTERPRETER: *¿Y fue como a medianoche del nueve de noviembre de este año?*

WITNESS: *Mhm.*

INTERPRETER: *Conteste por favor.* (Please answer.)

WITNESS: *Sí.*

INTERPRETER: Yes.

PROSECUTING ATTORNEY: And that was in Brownsville, Texas, wasn't it?

INTERPRETER: *Y fue en Brownsville, Texas, ¿verdad?*

WITNESS: *Mhm.*

INTERPRETER: *Conteste.* (Answer.)

WITNESS: *Sí.*

INTERPRETER: Yes.

PROSECUTING ATTORNEY: How did you get into Brownsville, Texas?

INTERPRETER: *¿En qué forma entró Ud. a Brownsville, Texas?*

WITNESS: *Por el túnel.*
INTERPRETER: Through the tunnel.
PROSECUTING ATTORNEY: Did you come with someone else?
INTERPRETER: *¿Entró Ud. con alguien más?*
WITNESS: *Sí.*
INTERPRETER: Yes.
PROSECUTING ATTORNEY: And was that, uh, what was that person's name?
INTERPRETER: *Y el, . . . ¿Cuál era el nombre de esa otra persona?*
WITNESS: *Miguel Ríos.*
INTERPRETER: Miguel Ríos.
PROSECUTING ATTORNEY: Are you and Miguel Ríos from the same town in Mexico?
INTERPRETER: *¿Ud. y Miguel Ríos son originarios del mismo pueblo de México?*
WITNESS: *Ajá.*
INTERPRETER: *Conteste.* (Answer.)
WITNESS: *Sí.*
INTERPRETER: Yes.
PROSECUTING ATTORNEY: Did you come together to Brownsville, Texas?
INTERPRETER: *¿Y vinieron juntos a Brownsville, Texas?*
WITNESS: *Sí.*
INTERPRETER: Yes.
PROSECUTING ATTORNEY: When you went through that tunnel did, did the tunnel begin in Matamoros?
INTERPRETER: *Cuando Uds. se metieron a ese túnel, ¿el principio del túnel estaba en Matamoros?*
WITNESS: *Mhm.*
INTERPRETER: *Conteste por favor.* (Please answer.)
WITNESS: *Sí.*
INTERPRETER: Yes.
PROSECUTING ATTORNEY: Was there an immigration guard or an officer where you, uh, entered through that tunnel into the United States?
INTERPRETER: *¿Y había alguna guardia de inmigración o algún oficial de, de la patrulla o de la inmigración ahí en el lugar donde Uds. cruzaron a los Estados Unidos?*
WITNESS: *Pues no, no, no. No se sabría decir.*
INTERPRETER: No, I, I, I just couldn't tell you.
PROSECUTING ATTORNEY: Did you have any papers or documents that would lawfully entitle you to come into the United States?
INTERPRETER: *¿Tenía Ud. documentos o papeles que legalmente lo autorizaban a estar en los Estados Unidos?*
WITNESS: *No.*
INTERPRETER: No.

PROSECUTING ATTORNEY: So you came in illegally.
INTERPRETER: *De modo que entró Ud. ilegalmente.*
WITNESS: [pause]
INTERPRETER: *Conteste.* (Answer.)
WITNESS: *Sí.*
INTERPRETER: Yes.

(Not Prodding the Witness)

JUDGE: May we have Francisco Araya Zúñiga.
PROSECUTING ATTORNEY: What is your name sir?
INTERPRETER: *¿Cómo se llama Ud. señor?*
WITNESS: *Francisco Araya Zúñiga.*
INTERPRETER: Francisco Araya Zúñiga.
PROSECUTING ATTORNEY: How old are you Mr. Araya?
INTERPRETER: *¿Qué edad tiene Ud., señor Araya?*
WITNESS: *Veinticinco años.*
INTERPRETER: Twenty-five.
PROSECUTING ATTORNEY: Where were you born?
INTERPRETER: *¿En qué lugar nació?*
WITNESS: *En Dolores de Guanajuato.*
INTERPRETER: In Dolores, Guanajuato.
PROSECUTING ATTORNEY: Is that in Mexico?
INTERPRETER: *¿Eso queda en México?*
WITNESS: *Sí, México.*
INTERPRETER: Yes, Mexico.
PROSECUTING ATTORNEY: And are you a citizen of Mexico?
INTERPRETER: *¿Es Ud. ciudadano de México?*
WITNESS: *Mhm.*
INTERPRETER: Mhm.
PROSECUTING ATTORNEY: Do you remember when you were arrested by Brownsville police and the border patrol?
INTERPRETER: *¿Se acuerda Ud. cuando lo arrestó la policía de Brownsville y la patrulla fronteriza?*
WITNESS: *Ajá.*
INTERPRETER: Aha.
PROSECUTING ATTORNEY: And was that at about midnight on November the ninth of this year?
INTERPRETER: *¿Y fue como a medianoche del nueve de noviembre de este año?*
WITNESS: *Mhm.*

INTERPRETER: Mhm.
PROSECUTING ATTORNEY: And that was in Brownsville, Texas, wasn't it?
INTERPRETER: *Y fue en Brownsville, Texas, ¿verdad?*
WITNESS: *Mhm.*
INTERPRETER: Mhm.
PROSECUTING ATTORNEY: How did you get into Brownsville, Texas?
INTERPRETER: *¿En qué forma entró Ud. a Brownsville, Texas?*
WITNESS: *Por el túnel.*
INTERPRETER: Through the tunnel.
PROSECUTING ATTORNEY: Did you come with someone else?
INTERPRETER: *¿Entró Ud. con alguien más?*
WITNESS: *Sí.*
INTERPRETER: Yes.
PROSECUTING ATTORNEY: And was that, uh, what was that person's name?
INTERPRETER: *Y el, . . . ¿Cuál era el nombre de esa otra persona?*
WITNESS: *Miguel Ríos.*
INTERPRETER: Miguel Ríos.
PROSECUTING ATTORNEY: Are you and Miguel Ríos from the same town in Mexico?
INTERPRETER: *¿Ud. y Miguel Ríos son originarios del mismo pueblo de México?*
WITNESS: *Ajá.*
INTERPRETER: Aha.
PROSECUTING ATTORNEY: Did you come together to Brownsville, Texas?
INTERPRETER: *¿Y vinieron juntos a Brownsville, Texas?*
WITNESS: *Sí.*
INTERPRETER: Yes.
PROSECUTING ATTORNEY: When you went through that tunnel did, did the tunnel begin in Matamoros?
INTERPRETER: *Cuando Uds. se metieron a ese túnel, ¿el principio del túnel estaba en Matamoros?*
WITNESS: *Mhm.*
INTERPRETER: Mhm.
PROSECUTING ATTORNEY: Was there an immigration guard or an officer where you, uh, entered through that tunnel into the United States?
INTERPRETER: *¿Y había alguna guardia de inmigración o algún oficial de, de la patrulla o de la inmigración ahí en el lugar donde Uds. cruzaron a los Estados Unidos?*
WITNESS: *Pues no, no, no. No se sabría decir.*
INTERPRETER: No, I, I, I just couldn't tell you.
PROSECUTING ATTORNEY: Did you have any papers or documents that would lawfully entitle you to come into the United States?

INTERPRETER: *¿Tenía Ud. documentos o papeles que legalmente lo autorizaban a estar en los Estados Unidos?*
WITNESS: *No.*
INTERPRETER: No.
PROSECUTING ATTORNEY: So you came in illegally.
INTERPRETER: *De modo que entró Ud. ilegalmente.*
WITNESS: [pause] . . . *Sí.*
INTERPRETER: Yes.

Notes

Chapter One

1. Throughout this book interpreters are referred to by the feminine pronoun, since this study has found that nationwide the majority of court interpreters are women.

2. Loosely defined, "pragmatics" is the use of language to do things, focusing on what a person is doing with words in particular situations. In effect, it focuses on "the intentions, purposes, beliefs, and wants that a speaker has in speaking—in performing *speech acts*" (Akmajian, Demers, and Harnish 1979:268). The theory of speech acts, in turn, was developed by Austin (1962) and Searle (1969), and says that speakers do things with words via four basic categories of speech acts: utterance acts, illocutionary acts, perlocutionary acts, and propositional acts. Utterance acts are simply acts of uttering sounds, syllables, words, phrases, and sentences. Illocutionary acts are acts performed *in* uttering something, examples of which are promising, reporting, asking, stating, threatening, intimidating, deceiving, embarrassing, and misleading. Propositional acts deal with the content of utterances. Thus, they consist largely of referring and predicating.

3. The term "exotic languages" most recently has been used by court interpreting offices to refer to any foreign language other than Spanish.

4. When foreign sign language interpreting is called for, two interpreters often need to be used: one who will "sign" directly for the foreign language signing person, and one who will then interpret the foreign language signing into American Sign Language for the second interpreter, who in turn will interpret the American Sign Language interpretation into English for the court. Problems can arise when the foreign language called for itself is not a common one in American courts. The chief interpreter of a large midwestern state courthouse cites the problematical case of a Hungarian deaf defendant, to whom two interpreters had to be assigned simultaneously. Clearly, the two-stage process of interpreting must entail a built-in probability of distortion that is higher than when a source language is converted directly into a single target language.

5. Throughout this book the identity of courthouses, interpreters, judges, attorneys, defendants, witnesses, and any other participants in the legal proceedings to be referred to will be kept anonymous in order to help ensure the privacy of all those involved in the data-gathering for this study.

6. It should be noted that figures on the use of non-Spanish interpreters in this courthouse were not available for 1982. Thus, figures for 1987 were used

instead, as these were the only ones available. The lack of up-to-date, adequate records on the workload of court interpreters is one of the problems that one will encounter in getting such "hard data" from a courthouse. This is not a reflection on the administrative abilities of court-appointed interpreters per se, but rather, it is merely symptomatic of the general lack of awareness of court administrative offices of the need for generating statistics. Among the judicial tiers, federal courts generally keep the best records on the use of interpreters, and are generally the most highly organized in terms of keeping track of interpreter utilization on a day-to-day basis. This is probably due to the financing role that the Office of U.S. Courts Administration plays in paying the salaries of per diem interpreters in U.S. district courts, a role established by the Court Interpreters Act.

7. The 1980 U.S. Census reveals that there are 14.6 million persons of Spanish/Hispanic origin or descent living in the United States (Bills 1987:3). The actual number of persons in this category is in fact far greater, for undocumented aliens generally avoid participating in the census. Among legal U.S. residents who were born outside the United States, Spanish-speaking Mexico leads the other 155 countries with a total of 2,199,221 persons, the second largest contributor; Germany, comprising 849,384, or not even half that figure (America's Melting Pot 1984:B7). So long as Mexicans and other Latin Americans continue to immigrate to the United States, legally or otherwise, Spanish will continue to be numerically the most important non-English language spoken in the United States. Evidence that Spanish is the main language spoken at home among U.S. Hispanics comes from one analysis of the 1980 U.S. Census (Bills 1987:21). This study finds that of the 8,787,795 Hispanics who live in the five states known as "the southwest"—Arizona, California, Colorado, New Mexico, and Texas—73.7 percent of those who are five-years old or older are reported as speaking Spanish at home.

8. In the fiscal year 1986, there were 46,501 proceedings conducted with the aid of an interpreter in federal courts alone (see Table 1.2). Although data are not available from all states, if one can assume that the use of interpreting in state and municipal courts is basically comparable, and if it can be assumed as well that the proportion of Spanish interpreting compared to that of other languages is similar to that demonstrated in Tables 1.1 and 1.2, then one can estimate that the number of appearances of Spanish interpreters in American courtrooms as a whole totals well over 120,000 per year.

9. The initial appearance is a defendant's first appearance before a judge, at which time he is informed of his rights and of the charges pending against him. In courthouses where the initial appearance is a separate proceeding, the arraignment is the proceeding at which the defendant must enter a plea. Some courts have no separate initial appearance proceeding, however. In such courts the arraignment entails both functions, that of the initial appearance before a judge or magistrate, combined with the entering of a plea.

10. The exception to the rule is the case of deaf parties. They are guaranteed the right to free interpreting services in both criminal and civil cases alike in New Jersey state courts.

11. The current New Jersey law, which for the last few years has been the target of legislative change, actually does allow for the appointment of free

court-appointed interpreters to civil cases. However, such a decision is up to the discretion of the judge, and depends upon the availability of staff interpreters at the moment. According to Robert Joe Lee, Chief of the Court Interpreting, Legal Translating, and Bilingual Services Section of the Administrative Office of the New Jersey Courts, in practice there is tremendous variation from one county court to another. In the Hudson County court, approximately 80 percent of interpreting carried out by court-appointed staff interpreters deals with criminal law, about 15 percent with family law, and 5 percent with "special civil" law—that is, small claims. In the Pasaic County court, however, one full-time interpreter is assigned exclusively to family court. Thus, while the state law does not guarantee free court-interpreting services to civil cases, in practice, the courts do assign staff interpreters to such cases. Apparently, state courts make a major distinction between "pure civil" (i.e., cases involving litigation) and other types of civil law (e.g., family law), the latter more often being considered worthy of court-paid interpreting services.

Chapter Two

1. The voir dire procedure is the questioning routine used by judges and attorneys to decide on the acceptability of individuals to serve on a given jury.

2. A "register," is a speech variety associated not with any particular group of speakers, but with a communicative occasion. The notion of register is examined in greater depth in chapter 8.

3. The linguistic status of legalese is open to dispute among persons working within the field of law and language. It is considered by some (Charrow and Crandall 1978; O'Barr n.d.) to be a dialect in its own right. It can alternatively be viewed as a register of English, a form of jargon—that is, a speech variety restricted to an occupational group, or a form of diglossia, as Danet (1980) has suggested, diglossia being a distinct speech variety restricted to use on formal, public occasions, contrasting with speech varieties used for everyday purposes.

4. The examples of narrative and fragmented style presented here do not demonstrate attorney control over the witness, since they represent alternative versions of one and the same examination sequence.

5. *Wh-* questions are questions that begin with question words, such as "who," "what," "why," "when," "which," and "how." Such questions are contrasted with *yes/no* type questions, which are questions that are meant to elicit either a "yes" or "no" in the addressee's answer.

Chapter Three

1. The notion of "stable bilingualism" originates with J. Fishman (1966), who distinguished stable foreign mother tongue maintenance from the typical pattern of immigrant mother tongue loss. Fishman noted that the normal pattern of language maintenance in the United States was the loss of the foreign language by the third generation. Spanish has stood in marked contrast to this typical pattern, maintaining a stable bilingualism in various areas of the nation, the southwest being foremost among them. Christian and

Christian (1966) have given a number of reasons why Spanish bilingualism has become a permanent feature of various speech communities in the United States, not the least important of which is the contiguity of the United States to Mexico, and the proximity of the United States to Central America. The economic and political difficulties of these Spanish-speaking areas guarantee the continuous migration, legal and otherwise, of Spanish-speaking persons across the U.S. border.

2. See Appendix 1 for a summary of state legislation regarding the right to a court-appointed interpreter.

3. As of July 1988, only three states had established state certification procedures for court interpreters: California, New Mexico, and New York. While none of these is as rigorous as the Federal Court Interpreters Examination, judging by the rate of passing in two of the states for which data have been collected, the examinations do aim for a certification of the most highly qualified interpreters. Of the 500–600 persons who take the California Court Interpreters Examination each year, only 9 percent pass (McMorinne 1987), compared to the 4 percent who pass the Federal Court Interpreters Examination. Among the test takers in New York State, approximately 7.5 percent (120 out of 2,000 persons) are considered eligible to qualify for full-time court interpreter positions in state courts (Ferrara 1987). The New Mexico certification exam went into effect officially only in July 1986 (Valdés and Wilcox, n.d.), and so no data have been made available regarding rate of passing. All of these exams involve a written testing procedure followed by an oral testing of interpreting skills and a knowledge of judicial procedures.

4. Case law shows that it is generally within the discretion of the trial judge to determine whether there is a need for an interpreter (People v. Soldat, 32 Ill. 2d 478, 207 N.E.2d 449 [1965]; People v. Bragg, 68 Ill. App. 3d 622, 25 Ill. Dec. 214, 386 N.E.2d 485 [1979]; People v. Shok, 12 Ill. 2d 93, 95, 145 N.E.2d 86 [1957]; People v. Rivera, 13 Ill. App. 3d 264, 267, 300 N.E.2d 869 [1st Dist. 1973]).

5. See Appendix 2 for the full text of the Federal Court Interpreters Act.

6. In 1984 the schedule of fees was set at $175 per day (Farmer 1983). By 1987 the fee rate had been raised to $210 per day (Vidal 1988). These are fees paid to per diem federally certified interpreters. Certified staff interpreters who work full-time in their courthouse are paid a flat yearly salary, also determined by the Administrative Office.

7. The passing point has fluctuated with each administration of the test. The description of the written portion of the test that is presented here is based upon the 1983 exam. For a description of how the certification exam was designed see Arjona (1985).

8. Up until 1983 there were some inherent problems in the Spanish written test, in that Spanish subsumes so many geographic dialects, and the test made no effort to exclude lexical items that vary from one Spanish-speaking dialectal area to another. In recent years, however, a conscious attempt has been made to exclude such items from the exam (Leeth 1986). Thus, a word such as *espumador,* which may be familiar to a person with little formal schooling in one Latin American country, may be totally meaningless to a college-educated person coming from another part of Latin America. Words such as these are now being avoided on the exam.

9. Unfortunately, by gearing knowledge of grammar to the highest level of written language, the tests test grammatical forms that rarely occur during spoken judicial proceedings, and that would sound odd even to persons who normally use a standard spoken style. The inclusion of two alternating forms within one test item, one from a very formal written style and one from a standard *spoken* style, certainly leaves test-takers confused as to which is "correct" since both may in fact be standard forms in the test-taker's dialect.

10. The relative importance given to simultaneous interpreting has changed. In 1983, the portion of the oral exam that tested the simultaneous mode of interpreting was seven minutes long, as opposed to fifteen-to-eighteen minutes that were devoted to consecutive interpreting. In 1986, the time allotted to testing simultaneous and consecutive interpreting was much more equal: ten minutes and twelve-to-fifteen minutes, respectively (Leeth 1986).

11. In 1983, 220 items were scored. The allowable number of errors reported here are based upon the 1983 test.

Chapter Four

1. According to the regulations of the Administrative Office of the U.S. Courts, whenever an interpreter is needed in a federal U.S. district court, priority must be given to federally certified interpreters. Noncertified interpreters may be used only when certified interpreters are not available, and only after the defendant has signed a waiver releasing the court of its obligation to provide him with a certified interpreter. However, these guidelines are not always followed by federal judges. The chief of interpreting/translating services in one metropolitan state court reports, in a personal communication to this investigator, that a federal court in that city uniformly employs nonfederally certified interpreters, knowingly violating the policy of the Administrative Office of the U.S. Courts.

Chapter Five

1. The transcription style used here to some extent follows the format developed by conversational analyst pioneers Sacks, Schegloff, and Jefferson (1974). Thus, all hesitation phenomena are transcribed, extra heavy word stress is indicated by italics, and simultaneous speech is indicated by a latching symbol [.

2. For a complete listing of court interpreting guidelines and codes of ethics, see Appendices 3, 4, and 5.

3. Throughout this book whenever English translations appear in square brackets they represent this writer's renditions of Spanish utterances that have not been interpreted into English by the interpreter. Sometimes the uninterpreted Spanish textual material represents testimony of the witness or defendant, and at other times it comprises side comments made by the interpreter to the person testifying.

4. Note that the judge is uttering the Spanish word [kulpáble] at this point. The spelling in Spanish happens to be homographic with the English word "culpable."

5. The notion that court interpreting must be verbatim—that is, precise and a hi-fidelity rendition of the source language utterance—is emphasized

in court interpreter training workshops and seminars. At sessions of the California Court Interpreters Association conferences, for example, and at intensive court interpreting institutes such as the University of Arizona Summer Institute for Court Interpretation, which this investigator attended in June-July 1983, the need for hi-fidelity accuracy is stressed constantly. It is precisely the verbatim quality of court interpreting that distinguishes it from conference interpreting and escort interpreting. The former chief interpreter of the United Nations, Theodore Fagan, commented (University of Arizona Summer Institute for Court Interpretation, June 1983) on the distinction between the type of interpreting done at the United Nations and that expected in court—namely, that the former regularly involves the interpreter's embellishment and improvement upon source language statements, whereas the latter does not allow for any alterations on the source language utterance. Fagan ultimately came to serve as a consultant on the team that created the first Federal Court Interpreters certification examination.

Written guidelines provided by the Administrative Office of the U.S. Courts, in the form of an interpreter's oath, together with guidelines provided by organizations whose aim is to improve the quality of interpreting in state courts, specifically state that interpreters are obligated to interpret accurately and faithfully, without adding to, omitting from, or changing the meaning of what the speaker has said in the source language. These guidelines are found in Appendices 3, 4, and 5 of this book.

6. Note-taking is a crucial element in consecutive interpreting, for interpreters know that they cannot rely entirely on memory alone for accurate interpreting in this mode. Note-taking skills, therefore, are a regular feature of court interpreter training programs.

7. This sequence is taken from a deposition of a material witness before a federal magistrate in federal court. Whereas the witness himself has done something illegal—namely, entering the United States without papers authorizing such entry—the case in which he is testifying is that of the person accused of smuggling him and other undocumented aliens into the United States. Thus, the testimony of this witness becomes part of the court record of the upcoming trial. The magistrate who presided over this and most of the other depositions of illegal aliens usually allowed the aliens to return to Mexico, their point of entry, and prosecuted only those who had been habitual offenders of the crime of illegal entry.

8. Polysemy is a term used in semantics to refer to a word having more than one sense, or meaning.

9. Ethnographic observation of court interpreters in the variety of courthouses that were visited by this investigator has revealed that the interpreter is considered to hold an occupational status on a par with court reporters—that is, persons whose status falls well below that of a lawyer or judge, yet is somewhat higher than that of a clerk or bailiff. Evidence of this occupational standing is the fact that interpreters' offices are generally placed within or alongside of offices of court clerks, and that overwhelmingly they socialize with clerks, bailiffs, and law enforcement officers, rather than with lawyers or judges. Thus, court interpreters tend to eat lunch, share birthday celebrations, and even hold lunch-hour Tupperware parties with court clerks, re-

porters, and other secretarial-type staff. One reason for the relatively low occupational categorization that interpreters are placed into is the fact that many court interpreters are former clerks themselves. Through their bilingual capacity they often find a more specialized niche in the courthouse occupational structure.

10. The term "parasegmental," coined by Walker (1985:123), refers to "any feature of *speech* which either (1) coexists with (para) a word (segment) or stretch of words; or (2) takes the place of a word, or both."

11. The issue of whether the objection itself should be interpreted for the witness is highly debated. The guidelines provided by expert Zahler (1985:5) state that both the objection and the judge's ruling should be interpreted: "There is controversy as to whether these objections and rulings should be interpreted at all to the witness. There are strong convictions on either side of the question. However, the non-English speaking witness should be in the same situation as the English speaking witness and the interpreter should interpret here simultaneously for the witness."

12. Evidence of the high variability in the use of consecutive versus simultaneous mode for interpreting at the witness stand comes from a recent poll of federally certified interpreters (Mikkelson 1989). Of the 127 interpreters who answered a question regarding whether they used the simultaneous mode for testifying witnesses, 67 percent admitted to using it either "sometimes," "often,"or "always." Only 33 percent stated that they "rarely" or "never" used the simultaneous mode for witnesses testifying on the stand.

Chapter Six

1. The label "passive voice" is used here as a cover term, comprising the several alternatives to the true passive, as defined in the preceding discussion. Whereas "passive voice" may not be the most accurate category to encompass all the syntactic constructions that have been included under it, it is nevertheless a convenient shorthand for referring to functionally related forms.

2. This is a personal communication from Ignacio Roca, professor of Spanish linguistics at the University of Essex, England. My own findings, based on an empirical study of the active and passive in Costa Rican speech (Berk-Seligson 1983), are that the true passive is used to some extent by speakers, although in a very restricted fashion. An empirical study of the frequency of passive constructions in Spanish (Green 1975) comes to a similar conclusion.

3. Throughout the transcription, key segments, revealing the passive and active constructions in question, have been underlined for emphasis.

4. This restriction in agent-mentioning in passive constructions is a rule of standard Spanish. In some vernacular Spanish varieties, however, the reflexive passive construction does allow the prepositional phrase *por* + agent. Given that the interpreter is interpreting standard spoken English, she should render her interpretation in standard Spanish.

5. The term "Marielito" refers to the group of Cubans freed by Fidel Castro from Cuban prisons and sent to the United States, where they have been living in various predesignated sites throughout the nation.

6. Note that the interpreter has changed the verb itself in her interpreta-

tion. Actually, in the interpretation that she has rendered, there are various sorts of deviations from the original.

Chapter Seven

1. The following discussion, together with the examples from English and Spanish, are taken from Vázquez-Ayora (1977:116–19, 337–46).

2. The parakinesic sound produced by the witness is an elongated hissing sound, which serves as a commentary on what he has just said; it is an expression of disgust. It is similar in force and tone to the American English exclamation "jeez!" or to certain clicking sounds that indicate exasperation or disgust.

3. In this particular segment of the interpretation, the interpreter omits some substance. She fails to say, "*I took Clark* from west to east."

4. Nonstandard forms in the Spanish of the witness or in the English of the interpreter have not been pointed out here. For example, the witness's use of the expression *él esperó por mí,* meaning "he waited for me," shows the influence of English syntax on Spanish structure. Standard Spanish would be *él me esperó.* Similarly, the interpreter uses a "false friend" when she interprets the Spanish word *chofer* as "chauffeur," for actually in the context of someone who drives a bus, the word means "driver."

5. Clearly when one talks about "Latin America" one will have to make generalizations that will not apply to all the countries contained within it, as they will not apply to all social groupings within even one given Latin American nation. It is expected that urbanites will have very different speech forms from rural dwellers, as would the highly educated elites compared to social strata grappling with the problem of illiteracy. Nevertheless, it is possible to find cultural characteristics that are prevalent throughout Latin America, possibly because they derive historically from a common peninsular Spanish ancestry, characteristics which are clearly distinct from North American norms of behavior. Thus, the average student from the United States who lives for a time with any Latin American family, of whatever socio-economic level, will find Latin Americans more "polite" in their day-to-day speech, in the sense that verbal customs which in the United States might be considered "formal," will be a daily norm even among members of the same household. The U.S. appreciation for casualness, conversely, is often interpreted as lack of manners by Latin Americans, for the absence of small verbal tokens of respect.

Chapter Eight

1. Whereas it could be argued that a video-recording would have been preferable to an audio-recording, there are several reasons why an audio-recording was decided on. First, it seemed unlikely that the kinesic behavior, or body language, of the three actors would be perfectly identical on the two versions. Unless one is a skilled professional actor, it would be highly difficult for a person to perfectly replicate his or her facial expressions. Secondly, no professional actors could have been as convincing as the interpreter and the witness who were chosen for the roles, since these people were merely being themselves, and not playing a role different from that embodied in their own

social and occupational station. In O'Barr's experimental studies, too, professional actors were rejected after repeated attempts were made to make the actors sound like the true witnesses and lawyers in the tape recordings of the actual judicial proceedings. O'Barr (1982:59) explains that because the professional actors had been trained to project their voices, in general to "play act," the experimental tapes that they produced were too artificial sounding and dramatic to replicate a real courtroom. He found that lay people who were not trained in drama reproduced the court transcripts much more faithfully. The Mexican man who played the witness read his lines the way Mexican illegal aliens tend to speak in court: quietly, looking somewhat frightened, and sounding like a *humilde campesino* ("poor peasant"). Thirdly, from the point of view of experimental design, it was desirable that as many variables as possible that were not linguistic be excluded from the stimulus recordings. The subjects of the study were to listen to eight recordings in addition to the one testing the impact of politeness, and it was feared that the physical appearance of the different actors playing the witnesses would be an additional intervening variable affecting the subjective reactions of the mock jurors. Specifically, it was assumed that the actors' degree of attractiveness and friendliness (the quality of being *simpático* versus *antipático*) would have their own independent impact on the impressions of the mock jurors. By removing the possibility that a witness's looks and friendliness might confound the impact of language, it was decided that an audio-tape would serve the experiment best, for then it could only be vocal qualities that the listeners could be reacting to.

2. *Wh-* type questions begin with words such as "who," "what," "why," "when," "where," "which," and "how." Questions that begin with "how" and "why" in particular lend themselves to lengthier answers.

3. Postvocalic /*r*/ is the *r*-sound that follows vowels, as in the words "car," "beard," and "her."

4. For Brown and Levinson this is the colloquial sense of hedging, and the one used in this book. Their definition of hedging extends, in addition, to linguistic forms that indicate that membership of a predicate or noun phrase in a set is *more* true and complete than perhaps might be expected. Thus, the words "quite" and "absolutely" in the following examples would be hedges of this type.

You're *quite* right.
You're *absolutely* right.

5. Grice's conversational maxims are categorized under four headings: quality, quantity, relation, and manner. The maxim of quality says, Try to make your contribution one that is true: (a) Do not say what you believe to be false; (b) Do not say that for which you lack adequate evidence. The maxim of quantity says, (a) Make your contribution as informative as is required (for the current purposes of the dialogue); (b) Do not make your contribution more informative than is required. Hedges on the maxim of quantity convey to the hearer that information that the speaker is providing is not as much or as precise as might be expected. Expressions such as "roughly," "more or less," "or so," and "to some extent" are examples of hedges of quantity (Brown and Levinson 1978:171). Grice's third maxim, that of relation,

says simply: Be relevant. When speakers know that what they are going to say is not relevant to the topic currently underway, they can use a variety of hedges that mark the change in topic, and partially apologize for the change. Typical of such hedges are the following (Brown and Levinson 1978:174): This may not be relevant, but; by the way; while I remember it; all right, now. Finally, Grice's fourth maxim, that of manner, says: Be perspicuous: (a) avoid obscurity of expression; (b) avoid ambiguity; (c) be brief; and (d) be orderly. To hedge on the maxim of manner is to use expressions such as the following: "if you see what (I'm getting at, I'm driving at, I mean)," "you see," "what I meant was" (Brown and Levinson 1978:176).

6. It should be noted that the notion of hedging used in the present study is somewhat broader than the one used by O'Barr (1982:67) and his colleagues. The concept of hedging used here, which is based upon the conceptualization of Brown and Levinson (1978), encompasses two of the features of powerless testimony style: hedging and hesitation forms.

7. Each pair of audio-recordings used in the series of experiments reported on in this book involved a different witness. Thus, even though several of the cases involve the transporting of illegal aliens across the U.S./Mexico border, each case used a different person playing the role of the witness. The woman acting as court interpreter in the tapes remained the same. Most of the cases employed the same actor in the role of attorney. Two additional men were employed to play the attorney role when the question of attorney-competence became a focal point of the individual study. Thus, in order to avoid asking the mock jurors to rate the same attorney three times, in each of the three cases where questions were asked regarding the attorney, the attorney was played by a different person. All the experimental tapes used the same sexual configuration of actors in order to standardize for listener reactions to sex of speaker: the interpreter was always a woman, the attorney always a man, and the witness, similarly, a man.

Chapter Nine

1. The *Lexis* search found primarily appellate cases (over 90 percent of the cases listed), but reported trial court decisions as well.

2. This area of appellate review is not included in the present discussion because a review of the relevant arguments and important cases regarding the right to an interpreter has been provided in chapter 3.

3. Nevertheless, even in cases where the defense attorney repeatedly goes to the extreme of asking for a mistrial in the course of a trial because of "ineffective translating," appellate courts can uphold the convictions that have come out of such trials (e.g., State v. Casipe, 686 P.2d 28 [Hawaii App. 1984]). In State v. Casipe, the appellant contended that the court-appointed interpreter had been ineffective because he had (1) failed to use simultaneous interpreting in rendering a witness's testimony for the benefit of the appellant; (2) had not interpreted the appellant's testimony accurately, insofar as he had omitted portions of it; and (3) had used an irregular technique in answering in the third person, and in some instances had edited, explained, or interpolated the questions and answers.

4. The appellate judge notes that Borges had been employed by the court-

house since 1981, and had interpreted over 1,000 hearings by the time this trial began. Included among the persons for whom he had interpreted were many Cubans.

5. Even when there is such indirect evidence of interpreting difficulties in the court record, appellate judges sometimes reject the significance of these interpreting problems. In People v. De Larco (190 Cal. Rptr. 757 [App. 1983]), the defendant appealed his burglary conviction on the ground that the transcript of his preliminary hearing, which contained the testimony of the chief prosecution witness for impeachment purposes, was excluded from use at his trial. The transcript had been excluded by the prosecution on the grounds that the interpretation of the Spanish-speaking witness's testimony was inaccurate. The prosecution's claims to interpreter inaccuracy had rested on the following evidence: in two instances the interpreter had interrupted the preliminary hearing because of the witness's Cuban accent and because of the witness's quickness of speech (the case took place in Claremont, California, and most likely the interpreter was Mexican-American). The interpreter is on record as having interrupted the proceeding in these three ways:

> "And then a few words I didn't understand."
> "Would you repeat? I'm sorry, I'm having a hard time keeping up because I'm not used to his Cuban manner of speaking and accent."
> "Okay, I'm having a little trouble with the witness because he goes on and on and on and I can't keep up with all of it."

In addition, the interpreter acknowledged under oath that he had had some trouble interpreting what the witness said, but on those occasions had informed the judge of his difficulty, and the proceedings were stopped. The interpreter also testified that he had accurately interpreted what the witness said, and that the witness had not expressed any difficulty in understanding the questions.

The California appellate court ruled that the trial court had been wrong to exclude the preliminary hearing on the basis of erroneous interpreting, arguing that "an interpreter's problems in translating are not in themselves sufficient to rebutt a presumption that his 'official duty' was regularly performed" in accordance with the California Evidence Code. This case, then, represents a reversal of most appeal situations involving the issue of interpreter accuracy: the appellant felt that he had not been given a fair trial precisely because testimony that had been judged to be inaccurately interpreted had been excluded from his trial.

6. In People v. Mendes (210 P.2d 1 [1950]), one of the grounds for appeal was the series of affidavits of private interpreters hired by the defendant/appellant, which stated that the court-appointed interpreter had been incompetent. The appellate court upheld the lower court ruling.

7. In a Texas case involving the improper judicial acceptance of a change of plea (United States v. Aleman, 417 F. Supp. 117 [1976]), the defendant successfully had his case remanded to the lower court for a retaking of the plea, on the sole ground that his interpreter had mistranslated the charges to which he had to respond.

8. This investigator sat through an entire murder trial, and observed that throughout, the court interpreter did only summary interpreting for the defendant while witnesses were testifying both in his behalf and against him. This occurred because the interpreter worked in the courthouse in multiple capacities: as interpreter, as bailiff, and as probation officer—thereby working closely with the prosecutor's office. The defense counsel admitted that he did not trust the interpreter, and therefore did not employ him for attorney/client conferences, preferring to use his bilingual secretary instead. Whereas the preferred mode of interpreting for defendants at the defense table is the simultaneous mode, the sole court interpreter in this small court regularly used the summary mode for this defendant and for others as well, he explained to me.

9. This observation was made by an anonymous professor of law of the Northwestern University School of Law, at a talk given by this writer to the American Bar Foundation, in October 1986.

10. Actually, the juror was confusing *lavado* ("wash," or "laundry") with *lavabo* ("washroom," or "lavatory"). We cannot tell what the witness actually said in Spanish, for we have available only the court reporter's transcript, which spells the term, "La Vado."

11. It is possible that the very act of taking the certification tests repeatedly, as is customary among those who fail on the first test-taking, may be indirectly responsible for the use of hyperformal English testimony style by some interpreters. It would only be a reasonable, yet unfounded, conclusion for interpreters to jump to that if the exam is heavily oriented toward a knowledge of bookish forms and college level vocabulary, then that is the sort of English that would routinely be expected of them on the job.

12. This policy has been decided time and time again (e.g., People v. Valencia, 27 Cal. App. 407, 408, 150 P. 68; People v. Salas, 2 Cal. App. 537, 539, 84 P. 285).

13. Ironically, at the time of this writing, the United States is facing a quickly spreading linguaphobia, encapsulated in what is known as the "English-only movement." This is an effort on the part of monolingual English-speaking groups to legislate English as the official language both at the state and federal levels of government. Its goals are to restrict the use of languages other than English for public purposes. This movement, therefore, seeks to repeal such rights as the right to bilingual voting ballots, bilingual social security application forms, bilingual applications for welfare assistance, to name just a few. Laws making English the official language of the state have been successfully passed in seventeen states, as of January 1989. Those states are: Arizona, Arkansas, California, Colorado, Florida, Georgia, Hawaii, Illinois, Indiana, Kentucky, Mississippi, Nebraska, North Carolina, North Dakota, South Carolina, Tennessee, and Virginia.

References

Books and Articles

Addington, D. W. 1971. The effect of vocal variations on ratings of source credibility. *Speech Monographs* 38:242–47.

Aiken, R. J. 1960. Let's not simplify legal language. *Rocky Mountain Law Review* 32:358–64.

Akmajian, A., R. A. Demers, and R. M. Harnish. 1979. *Linguistics: An Introduction to Language and Communication.* Cambridge, Mass.: The MIT Press.

Almeida, F., and S. Zahler. 1977; revised 1981. *Los Angeles Superior Court Interpreters Manual.* Los Angeles: Los Angeles Superior Court.

Almeida, F., A. Rainof, and S. Zahler. 1979. *Glossary of Terms Most Often Used in Court Interpretation.* California Court Interpreters Association.

Arjona, E. 1985. The Court Interpreters Certification Test design. In L. Elías-Olivares, E. A. Leone, R. Cisneros, and J. Gutiérrez, eds., *Spanish Language Use and Public Life in the USA.* Berlin: Mouton de Gruyter.

Arnov, V. B. (1978). Analysis of the effects of language on impression formation: Evaluation reactions of Miami-Dade Community College students to the voices of Cuban-Americans speaking English and in Spanish. Doctoral dissertation, Florida Atlantic University.

Arthur, B., D. Farrar, and G. Bradford. 1974. Evaluation reactions of college students to dialect differences in the English of Mexican-Americans. *Language and Speech* 17:255–70.

Atkinson, M., and P. Drew. 1979. *Order in Court: The Organization of Verbal Behavior in Judicial Settings.* London: MacMillan.

Austin, J. L. 1962. *How to Do Things with Words.* Oxford: Clarendon Press.

Berk-Seligson, S. 1983. Sources of variation in Spanish verb construction usage: The active, the dative, and the reflexive passive. *Journal of Pragmatics* 7:145–68.

———. 1984. Subjective reactions to phonological variation in Costa Rican Spanish. *The Journal of Psycholinguistic Research* 13:415–42.

———. 1985. Fallacies in judicial assumptions about bilingual court proceedings: The role of the court interpreter. Paper presented at the Conference on Language in the Judicial Process, Georgetown University, Washington, D.C. (July).

———. 1987. The intersection of testimony styles in interpreted judicial proceedings: Pragmatic alterations in Spanish testimony. *Linguistics* 25:1087–1125.

———. 1988a. The impact of politeness in witness testimony: The influence of the court interpreter. *Multilingua* 7(4):411–39.

———. 1988b. The importance of linguistics in court interpreting. *La Raza Law Journal* 2(1):201–35.

———. 1989. The role of register in the bilingual courtroom: Evaluative reactions to interpreted testimony. In *U.S. Spanish: The Language of Latinos.* Irene Wherritt and Ofelia García, eds. Special issue (no. 5) of the *International Journal of the Sociology of Language* 79:79–91.

———. forthcoming. Bilingual court proceedings: The role of the court interpreter. In *Language in the Judicial Process.* Judith N. Levi and Ann Graffam Walker, eds. New York: Plenum Publishing Corporation.

Bills, G. 1987. The U.S. Census of 1980 and Spanish in the Southwest. Paper presented at the eighth Conference on Spanish in the United States, University of Iowa, Iowa City (October).

Bolinger, D. 1975. *Aspects of Language.* New York: Harcourt, Brace, and Jovanovich.

Bourhis, R. Y., and H. Giles. 1976. The language of cooperation in Wales: A field study. *Language Sciences* 42:13–16.

Bourhis, R. Y., H. Giles, and W. E. Lambert. 1975. Some consequences of accommodating one's style of speech: A cross-national investigation. *International Journal of the Sociology of Language* 6:55–72.

Bresnahan, M. I. (1979). Linguistic limbo: The case of the non-native English-speaking defendant in the American courtroom. Paper presented at the Ninth Annual Colloquium on New Ways of Analyzing English, Montreal.

Brown, B. 1969. The social psychology of variations in French Canadian speech. Doctoral dissertation, McGill University.

Brown, B., W. J. Strong, and A. C. Rencher. 1973. Perceptions of personality from speech: Effects of manipulations of acoustical parameters. *Journal of the Acoustical Society of America* 54:29–35.

Brown, B., W. J. Strong, and A. C. Rencher. 1974. Fifty-four voices from two: The effects of simultaneous manipulations rate, mean fundamental frequency, and variance of fundamental frequency of ratings of personality from speech. *Journal of the Acoustical Society of America* 55:313–18.

Brown, P., and S. Levinson. 1978. Universals in language usage: Politeness phenomena. In E. Goody, ed., *Questions and Politeness.* Cambridge: Cambridge University Press.

Carranza, M. A., and E. B. Ryan. 1975. Evaluative reactions of bilingual Anglo and Mexican American adolescents toward speakers of English and Spanish. *International Journal of the Sociology of Language* 6:83–104.

Charrow, R. P., and V. R. Charrow. 1979a. Making legal language understandable: A psycholinguistic study of jury instructions. *Columbia Law Review* 79:1306–74.

———. 1979b. Characteristics of the language of jury instructions. In J. E. Alatis and G. R. Tucker, eds., *Language in Public Life.* Georgetown University Roundtable on Language and Linguistics 1979. Washington, D.C.: Georgetown University Press.

Charrow, V. R., and J. A. Crandall. 1978. Legal language: What is it and what can we do about it? Arlington, Va.: American Institutes for Research and Center for Applied Linguistics.

Christian, C., and J. M. Christian. 1966. Spanish language and culture in the Southwest. In J. A. Fishman, ed., *Language Loyalty in the United States: By American Ethnic and Religious Groups*. The Hague: Mouton.

Churchill, L. 1978. *Questioning Strategies in Sociolinguistics.* Rowley, Mass.: Newbury House.

Conley, J. M., W. M. O'Barr, and E. A. Lind. 1978. The power of language: Presentational style in the courtroom. *Duke Law Journal* 78:1375–99.

Cooper, R. L. 1975. Introduction. In *Language Attitudes II*. R. L. Cooper, ed. Special issue of the *International Journal of the Sociology of Language* 6:5–10.

Costa, R. 1975. Functional solution for illogical reflexives in Italian. In R. E. Grossman, L. J. San, and T. J. Vance, eds., *Papers from the Parasession on Functionalism.* Chicago Linguistic Society.

Crystal, D., and D. Davy. 1969. *Investigating English Style.* Bloomington: Indiana University Press.

Danet, B. 1976. Speaking of Watergate: Language and moral accountability. *Centrum 135 (Working Papers of the Minnesota Center for Advanced Studies in Language, Style, and Literary Theory)* 4.

———. 1980a. Language in the legal process. *Law and Society Review* 14:445–564.

———. 1980b. 'Baby' or 'fetus'? Language and the construction of reality in a manslaughter trial. *Semiotica* 32:187–219.

Danet, B., and B. Bogoch. 1980. Fixed fight or free-for-all? An empirical study of combativeness in the adversary system of justice. *British Journal of Law and Society* 7(1):36–60.

Danet, B., K. B. Hoffman, and N. C. Kermish. 1980. Accountability for verbal offenses. *International Journal of the Sociology of Law* 9.

Danet, B., K. B. Hoffman, N. C. Kermish, H. J. Rafn, and D. G. Stayman. 1980. An ethnography of questioning. In R. Shuy and A. Shnukal, eds., *Language Use and the Uses of Languages: Papers from the Fifth Annual Colloquium on New Ways of Analyzing Variation in English.* Washington, D.C.: Georgetown University Press.

Danet, B., and N. Kermish. 1978. Courtroom questioning: A sociolinguistic perspective. In L. N. Massery II, ed., *Psychology and Persuasion in Advocacy.* Washington, D.C.: Association of Trial Lawyers of America, National College of Advocacy.

Danet, B., and H. J. Rafn. 1977. Strategies of control in courtroom questioning. Paper presented at the Annual Meeting of the American Sociological Association, Chicago (August).

D'Anglejan, A., and G. R. Tucker. 1973. Sociolinguistic correlates of speech style in Quebec. In R. Shuy and R. Fasold, eds., *Language Attitudes: Trends and Prospects.* Washington, D.C.: Georgetown University Press.

de la Zerda, N., and R. Hopper. 1979. Employment interviewers' reactions to Mexican American speech. *Communication Monographs* 46, 126–34.

Dixon, R. M. W. 1979. Ergativity. *Language* 55:59–138.

Elwork, A., B. D. Sales, and J. J. Alfini. 1977. Juridic decisions: In ignorance of the law or in light of it? *Law and Human Behavior* 1:163–89.

Erickson, B., E. A. Lind, B. C. Johnson, and W. M. O'Barr. 1978. Speech style and impression formation in a court setting: the effects of "powerful" and "powerless" speech. *Journal of Experimental Social Psychology* 14, 266–79.

Fagan, T. 1983. Lecture, Institute for Court Interpretation, Tucson, Arizona (June).

Farmer, M. 1983. Outcome of case may depend on court interpreter's language skills. *Christian Science Monitor* June 27, p. 14.

Ferrara, P. 1987. Talk given at the Colloquium on Issues in Court Interpretation, Montclair State College. Montclair, New Jersey (July 24–25).

Fishman, J. A. 1966. *Language Loyalty in the United States.* The Hague: Mouton.

Flores, N., and R. Hopper. 1975. Mexican Americans' evaluations of spoken Spanish and English. *Speech Monographs* 42:91–98.

Frankenthaler, M. R. 1980. Spanish translation in the courtroom. *Social Action and the Law* 6(4):51–62.

Frankenthaler, M. R., and H. L. McCarter. 1978. A call for legislative action: The case for a New Jersey court interpreters act. *Seton Hall Legislative Journal* 3(2):125–65.

Giles, H. 1970. Evaluative reactions to accents. *Educational Review* 22:211–27.

———. 1971. Ethnocentrism and the evaluation of accented speech. *British Journal of Social and Clinical Psychology* 10:187–88.

Giles, H., and R. Y. Bourhis. 1975. Language assimilation among West Indian immigrants in a British city. *Language Sciences* 38:9–12.

Giles, H., and R. Y. Bourhis. 1976. Black speakers and white speech: A real problem. In G. Nickel, ed., *Proceedings of the 4th AILA Congress.* Stuttgart: Hochschul Verlag.

Gleason, H. A. 1965. *Linguistics and English Grammar.* New York: Holt, Rinehart and Winston.

Goldin, M. 1968. *Spanish Case and Function.* Washington, D.C.: Georgetown University Press.

Goody, E. N. 1978. Towards a theory of questions. In E. N. Goody ed., *Questions and Politeness.* Cambridge: Cambridge University Press.

Green, J. N. 1975. On the frequency of passive constructions in modern Spanish. *Bulletin of Hispanic Studies* 2(1):345–62.

Grice, H. P. 1975. Logic and conversation. In L. P. Cole and J. L. Morgan, eds., *Syntax and Semantics 3: Speech Acts.* New York: Academic Press.

Hadlich, R. 1971. *A Transformational Grammar of Spanish.* Englewood Cliffs, N.J.: Prentice-Hall.

Hager, J. 1959. Let's simplify legal language. *Rocky Mountain Law Review* 32:74–86.

Haverkate, H. 1985. La desfocalización referencial en el español moderno. *Hispanic Linguistics* 2(1):1–22.

Hippchen, L. H. 1977. Development of a plan for bilingual interpreters in the criminal courts of New Jersey. *The Justice System Journal* 213:258–69.

Hopper, P. G., and S. A. Thompson. 1980. Transitivity in grammar and discourse. *Language* 56(2):251–99.

Hopper, R., and F. Williams. 1973. Speech characteristics and employability. *Communication Monographs* 44:346–51.

Hymes, D. H. 1962. The ethnography of speaking. In T. Gladwin and W. C. Sturtevant, eds., *Anthropology and Human Behavior.* Washington, D.C.: Anthropological Society of America.

———. 1972. On communicative competence. In J. B. Pride and J. Holmes, eds., *Sociolinguistics: Selected Readings.* Harmondsworth, England: Penguin Books.

Joos, M. 1967. *The Five Clocks.* New York: Harcourt, Brace, Jovanovich.

Kaspryzk, D., D. E. Montano, and E. Loftus. 1975. Effects of leading questions on jurors' verdicts. *Jurimetrics Journal* 16:48.

Kirsner, R. S. 1976. On the subjectless "pseudo-passive" in Standard Dutch and the semantics of background agents. In C. N. Li, ed., *Subject and Topic.* New York: Academic Press.

Labov, W. 1966. *The Social Stratification of English in New York City.* Washington, D.C.: Center for Applied Linguistics.

———. 1969. Contraction, deletion, and inherent variability of the English copula. *Language* 45(4):715–63.

———. 1972. *Sociolinguistic Patterns.* Philadelphia: University of Pennsylvania Press.

Lado, R., and E. Blansitt. 1967. *Contemporary Spanish.* New York: McGraw-Hill.

Lakoff, R. 1970. Questionable answers and answerable questions. In B. B. Kachru et al., eds., *Issues in Linguistics: Paper in Honor of Henry and Renée Kahane.* Urbana: University of Illinois Press.

———. 1973. Language and woman's place. *Language in Society* 2:45–160.

———. 1975. Language and Woman's Place. New York: Harper and Row.

Lambert, W. E., R. C. Hodgson, and S. Fillenbaum. 1960. Evaluational reactions to spoken language. *Journal of Abnormal and Social Psychology* 60:44–51.

Langacker, R. W. 1970. Review of Goldin, M., *Spanish Case and Function. Language* 46(1):167–85.

Leeth, J. 1986. Talk given at the meeting of the Pittsburgh chapter of the American Translators Association.

———. no date. The court interpreter examination. Paper published by the National Resource Center for Translation and Interpretation, Georgetown University, Washington, D.C., and the State University of New York, Binghamton, N.Y.

Lind, E. A., and W. M. O'Barr. 1979. The social significance of speech in the courtroom. In H. Giles and R. St. Clair, eds., *Language and Social Psychology.* College Park, Md.: University Press.

Lind, E. A., B. Erickson, J. M. Conley, and W. M. O'Barr. 1978. Social attributions and conversational style in trial testimony. *Journal of Personality and Social Psychology* 36:1558–67.

Llorente Maldonado de Guevara, A. 1977. Las construcciones de carácter impersonal en español. In *Estudios ofrecidos a Emilio Alarcos Llorach.* M. V. Conde et al. eds., 1:107–27.

Loftus, E., and J. Palmer. 1974. Reconstruction of automobile destruction: An example of the interaction between language and memory. *Journal of Verbal Learning and Verbal Behavior* 13:585–89.

Loftus, E., and G. Zanni. 1975. Eyewitness testimony: Influence of the wording of a question. *Bulletin of the Psychonomic Society* 5:86–88.

London, H. 1973. *Psychology of the Persuader.* Morristown, N.J.: General Learning Press.

Lopez, J. E. 1984. Letter to the Editor of the *Los Angeles Times,* reprinted in *The Polyglot* (May):3.

Lown, L. 1979. *An Overview of the Plain English Movement.* Jerusalem: Communications Institute, Hebrew University (working paper).

Lyons, J. 1969. *Introduction to Theoretical Linguistics.* Cambridge: Cambridge University Press.

Malinowski, B. 1923. The problem of meaning in primitive languages. In C. K. Ogden and I. A. Richards, *The Meaning of Meaning.* London: Routledge & Kegan Paul.

Martinet, H. 1985. Why do we know how to translate what? *Semiotica* 55:19–42.

McCroskey, J. C., and R. S. Mehrley. 1969. The effects of disorganization and non-fluency on attitude change and source credibility. *Speech Monographs* 36:13–21.

McEwan, A. 1986. Spanish interpreters take to the airwaves. *Polyglot* 16(7):5.

McMorinne, A. 1987. Talk given at the Colloquium on Issues in Court Interpretation, Montclair State College. Montclair, New Jersey (July 24–25).

Melinkoff, D. 1963. *The Language of the Law.* Boston: Little, Brown.

Mikkelson, H. 1989. Interpreter Survey. *Polyglot* 19(2):11.

Miller, G. R., and M. A. Hewgill. 1964. The effects of variations in nonfluency on audience rates of source credibility. *Quarterly Journal of Speech* 50:36–44.

Morrill, A. E. 1971. *Trial Diplomacy.* Chicago: Court Practice Institute.

Morris, B. G. 1967. The Sixth Amendment's right of confrontation and the non-English speaking accused. *Florida Bar Journal* 41(7):475–82.

Mujica, B. 1982. *Entrevista.* New York: Holt, Rinehart and Winston.

National Center for Law and the Deaf. 1984. Compilation of state interpreter laws. Unpublished.

New Jersey Consortium of Educators in Legal Interpretation and Translation. 1988. Curricular guidelines for the development of legal interpreter education. Upper Montclair, N.J.: Montclair State College.

New Jersey Supreme Court Task Force on Interpreter and Translation Services. 1986. *Equal Access to the Courts for Linguistic Minorities.* New Jersey: Supreme Court of New Jersey.

Niyekawa-Howard, A. M. 1968. A psycholinguistic study of the Whorfian hypothesis based on the Japanese passive. Paper presented at the Thirteenth Annual National Conference on Linguistics, New York.

O'Barr, W. M. 1981. The language of the law. In C. A. Ferguson and S. B. Heath, eds., *Language in the U.S.A.* New York: Cambridge University Press.

———. 1982. *Linguistic Evidence: Language, Power, and Strategy in the Courtroom.* New York: Academic Press.

O'Barr, W. M., and B. K. Atkins. 1980. "Women's language" or "powerless language"? In S. McConnell-Ginet, R. Borker, and N. Furman, eds., *Women and Language in Literature and Society*. New York: Praeger.

O'Barr, W. M., and J. M. Conley. 1976. When a juror watches a lawyer. *Barrister* 3:8–11 and 33.

O'Barr, W. M., and E. A. Lind. 1977. Ethnography and experimentation—partners in legal research. In B. D. Sales, ed., *Perspectives in Law and Psychology*, vol. 1: *The Criminal Justice System*. New York: Plenum.

O'Barr, W. M., L. W. Walker, J. M. Conley, B. Erickson, and B. Johnson. 1976. Political aspects of speech styles in American trial courtrooms. In *Working Papers in Culture and Communication*. Philadelphia: Temple University Department of Anthropology, 1:27–40.

Otero, C. 1972. Acceptable ungrammatical sentences in Spanish. *Linguistic Inquiry* 3(2):233–42.

Owen, Marion. 1983. *Apologies and Remedial Interchanges*. The Hague: Mouton.

Parkinson, M. 1979. Language behavior and courtroom success. Paper presented at the International Conference on Language and Social Psychology, University of Bristol (July).

Pearce, W. B. 1971. The effect of vocal cues on credibility and attitude change. *Western Speech* 35:176–84.

Pearce, W. B., and B. J. Brommel. 1972. Vocal communication in persuasion. *Quarterly Journal of Speech* 58:298–306.

Pearce, W. B., and F. Conklin. 1971. Nonverbal vocalic communication and perceptions of a speaker. *Speech Monographs* 38:235–41.

Perlmutter, D. M. 1970. Surface structure constraints in syntax. *Linguistic Inquiry* 1(2):187–255.

Philips, S. U. 1979. Syntactic variation in judges' use of language in the courtroom. Paper presented at the International Conference on Language and Social Psychology, University of Bristol (July 16–20).

———. 1984. Contextual variation in courtroom language use: Noun phrases referring to crimes. *International Journal of the Sociology of Language* 49:29–50.

Politzer, R. L., and A. G. Ramirez. 1973a. Judging personality from speech: A pilot study of the attitudes toward ethnic groups of students in monolingual schools. *R & D Memorandum* no. 107. Stanford: Stanford Center for Research and Development in Teaching, Stanford University.

Politzer, R. L., and A. G. Ramirez. 1973b. Judging personality from speech: A pilot study of the effects of bilingual education on attitudes toward ethnic groups. *R & D Memorandum* no. 106. Stanford: Stanford Center for Research and Development in Teaching, Stanford University.

Pomerantz, A. 1975. Second Assessments: A Study of Some Features of Agreements/Disagreements. Irvine: University of California doctoral dissertation.

———. 1978. Attributions of responsibility: Blaming. *Sociology* 12:115–21.

Pousada, A. 1979. Interpreting for language minorities in the courts. In J. E. Alatis and G. R. Tucker, eds., *Language in Public Life*. Georgetown University Round Table on Language and Linguistics 1979. Washington, D.C.: Georgetown University Press.

Pressman, R. 1979. *Legislative and Regulatory Progress on the Readability of Insurance Policies*. Washington, D.C.: Document Design Center.

Ramirez, A. G., E. Arce-Torres, and R. L. Politzer. 1978. Language attitudes and achievement of bilingual pupils in English language arts. *The Bilingual Review/La Revista Bilingüe* 5:169–206.

Ramsey, M. M. 1957. *A Textbook of Modern Spanish*. New York: Holt, Rinehart and Winston, Inc.

Reese, B. P., and A. J. Reese. 1984. Case comment. *The Polyglot* (June/July):1 & 5.

Rey, A. 1977. Accent and employability: Language attitudes. *Language Sciences* 47:7–12.

Ryan, E. B., and M. Carranza. 1975. Evaluative reactions of adolescents toward speakers of standard English and Mexican American accented English. *Journal of Personality and Social Psychology* 31:855–63.

Ryan, E. B., and M. A. Carranza. 1977. Ingroup and outgroup reactions toward Mexican American language and varieties. In H. Giles, ed., *Language, Ethnicity and Intergroup Relations*. London: Academic Press.

Ryan, E. B., M. Carranza, and R. W. Moffie. 1975. Mexican American reactions to accented English. In J. W. Berry and W. J. Lonner, eds., *Applied Cross-Cultural Psychology*. Amsterdam: Swets & Zeitlinger B.V., 174–78.

Ryan, E. B., M. Carranza, and R. W. Moffie. 1977. Reactions toward varying degrees of accentedness in the speech of Spanish-English bilinguals. *Language and Speech* 20:267–73.

Ryan, E. B., and R. Sebastian. 1980. The effects of speech style and social class background on social judgements of speakers. *British Journal of Social and Clinical Psychology* 19:229–33.

Sacks, H., E. A. Schegloff, and G. Jefferson. 1974. A simplest systematic for the organization of turn-taking in conversation. *Language* 50:696–735.

Sales, B. D., A. Elwork, and J. Alfini. 1977. Improving jury instructions. In B. D. Sales, ed., *Perspectives in Law and Psychology*, vol. 1: *The Criminal Justice System*. New York: Plenum.

Schegloff, E. 1972. Sequencing in conversational openings. In J. J. Gumperz and D. Hymes, eds., *Directions in Sociolinguistics*. New York: Holt, Rinehart and Winston.

Scherer, K. R. 1972. Judging personality from voice: A cross-cultural approach to an old issue in interpersonal perception. *Journal of Personality* 40:191–210.

———. 1979. Voice and speech correlates of perceived social influence in simulated juries. In H. Giles and R. St. Clair, eds., *Language and Social Psychology*. Oxford: Basil Blackwell.

Schiffrin, Deborah. 1985. "Conversational Coherence: The Role of 'Well,'" *Language* 61:640–67.

Schweizer, D. A. 1970. The effect of presentation on source evaluation. *Quarterly Journal of Speech* 56:33–39.

Searle, J. R. 1969. *Speech Acts*. Cambridge: Cambridge University Press.

Semegan, P. 1980. Plain language legislation. *Case and Comment* 42 (January-February).

Sereno, K. K., and G. J. Hawkins. 1967. The effects of variations in speakers' non-fluency upon audience of attitudes toward the speech topic and speakers' credibility. *Speech Monographs* 34:58–64.

Shuy, R. 1969. Subjective judgments in sociolinguistic analysis. In J. E. Alatis, ed., *Linguistics and the Teaching of Standard English to Speakers of other Languages and Dialects.* Arlington, Va.: The Center for Applied Linguistics.

Shuy, R., and D. K. Larkin. 1978. Linguistic considerations in the simplification/clarification of insurance policy language. Washington, D.C.: Georgetown University and The Center for Applied Linguistics.

Siegel, A. 1981. The Plain English revolution. In L. Bergman, ed., *Across the Board.* New York: The Conferences Board.

Solé, Y. R., and C. A. Solé. 1977. *Modern Spanish Syntax: A Study in Contrast.* Lexington, Mass.: D. C. Heath and Company.

Soto, O. N. 1969. *Repaso de gramática.* New York: Harcourt, Brace and World.

Timney, B., and H. London. 1973. Body language concomitants of persuasiveness and persuasibility in dyadic interaction. *International Journal of Group Tensions* 3:48–67.

Tucker, G. R., and W. E. Lambert. 1969. White and Negro listeners' reactions to various American English dialects. *Social Forces* 47:463–68.

Valdés, G., T. Dvorak, and T. Pagán Hannum. 1984. *Composición: Proceso y síntesis.* New York: Random House.

Valdés, G., and P. Wilcox (no date, circa 1986). The use of court interpreters in New Mexico: A handbook for judges, attorneys, and interpreters. Administrative Office of the New Mexico Courts (unpublished MS.).

Vázquez-Ayora, G. 1977. *Introducción a la traductología.* Washington, D.C.: Georgetown University Press.

Vidal, M. 1988. Personal communication (July).

Walker, A. G. 1985. Transcription of legal proceedings: Theoretical issues and application to the appellate process. Paper presented at the Conference on Language in the Judicial Process, Georgetown University, Washington, D.C. (July).

———. 1987. Linguistic manipulation, power and the legal setting. In L. Kedar, ed., *Power through Discourse.* Norwood, N.J.: Ablex Publishing Corporation.

Williams, F., N. Hewitt, L. M. Miller, R. C. Naremore, and J. L. Whitehead. 1976. *Explorations of the Linguistic Attitudes of Teachers.* Rowley, Mass.: Newbury House.

Woehr, R., J. Barson, and G. Valadez. 1974. *Español esencial: Un repaso.* Corte Madera, Calif.: Holt, Rinehart, and Winston.

Wölck, W. 1973. Attitudes toward Spanish and Quechua in bilingual Peru. In R. W. Shuy and R. W. Fasold, eds., *Language Attitudes: Current Trends and Prospects.* Washington, D.C.: Georgetown University Press.

Woodbury, H. 1984. The strategic use of questions in court. *Semiotica* 48:197–228.

Wootton, A. 1981. The Management of Grantings and Rejections by Parents in Request Sequences. *Semiotic* 37:59–89.

Zahler, S. 1985. Simultaneous . . . ? Preferences vary. *Polyglot* 15(7):5.

Cases

Gardiana v. Small Claims Court In and For San Leandro-Haya
59 Cal. App. 3d 412, 130 Cal. Rptr. 675 (1976).

Jara v. Municipal Court
21 Cal. 3d 181, 578 P.2d 94, 145 Cal. Rptr. 847 (1978).

Mercure v. A. G. Saskatchewan
(1988).

People v. Annett
251 Cal. App. 2d 858, 59 Cal. Rptr. 888 (1967).

People v. Bragg
68 Ill. App. 3d 622, 25 Ill. Dec. 214, 386 N.E.2d 485 (1979).

People v. DeLarco
190 Cal. Rptr. 757 (App. 1983).

People v. Díaz
140 Cal. App. 3d 812 (1983).

People v. Medrano
N.Y.S. 2d 375 (Co. Ct. 1986).

People v. Mendes
219 P.2d 1 (1950).

People v. Molina
418 N.E.2d 831 (Ill. App. 1981).

People v. Ramos
26 N.Y. 2d 272, 258 N.E.2d 906 (1970).

People v. Rivera
13 Ill. App. 3d 264, 267, 300 N.E.2d 869 (1st Dist. 1973).

People v. Salas
2 Cal. App. 537, 539, 84 P. 285.

People v. Shok
12 Ill. 2d 93, 95, 145 N.E.2d 86 (1957).

People v. Soldat
32 Ill. 2d 478, 207 N.E.2d 449 (1965).

People v. Starling
315 N.E.2d 163 (1974).

People v. Valencia
27 Cal. App. 407, 408, 150 P. 68.

State v. Casipe
686 P. 2d (Hawaii App. 1984).

State v. Mitjans
394 N.W.2d 221 (Minn. App. 1986).

Tapia-Corona v. United States
369 F.2d 366, 9th Cir. (1966).

United States v. Aleman
417 F. Supp. 117 (1976).

United States v. Anguloa
598 F.2d 1182 (1979).

United States v. Desist
384 F.2d 888, 891–92, 2d Cir. (1967).

United States v. Guerra
334 F.2d 138 (1964).
United States ex rel Negrón v. N.Y.
310 F. Supp. (E.D. N.Y. 1970), *aff'd* 434 F.2d 386 (2d Cir. 1970).
United States v. Perez
658 F.2d 654 (1981).
United States v. Torres
793 F.2d 436 (1st Cir. 1986).

Name Index

Subject Index